Communications in Computer and Information Science 2885

Series Editors

Rationale

The CCIS series is devoted to the publication of proceedings of computer science conferences. Its aim is to efficiently disseminate original research results in informatics in printed and electronic form. While the focus is on publication of peer-reviewed full papers presenting mature work, inclusion of reviewed short papers reporting on work in progress is welcome, too. Besides globally relevant meetings with internationally representative program committees guaranteeing a strict peer-reviewing and paper selection process, conferences run by societies or of high regional or national relevance are also considered for publication.

Topics

The topical scope of CCIS spans the entire spectrum of informatics ranging from foundational topics in the theory of computing to information and communications science and technology and a broad variety of interdisciplinary application fields.

Information for Volume Editors and Authors

Publication in CCIS is free of charge. No royalties are paid, however, we offer registered conference participants temporary free access to the online version of the conference proceedings on SpringerLink (http://link.springer.com) by means of an http referrer from the conference website and/or a number of complimentary printed copies, as specified in the official acceptance email of the event.

CCIS proceedings can be published in time for distribution at conferences or as post-proceedings, and delivered in the form of printed books and/or electronically as USBs and/or e-content licenses for accessing proceedings at SpringerLink. Furthermore, CCIS proceedings are included in the CCIS electronic book series hosted in the SpringerLink digital library at http://link.springer.com/bookseries/7899. Conferences publishing in CCIS are allowed to use our online conference service (Meteor) for managing the whole proceedings lifecycle (from submission and reviewing to preparing for publication) free of charge.

Publication process

The language of publication is exclusively English. Authors publishing in CCIS have to sign the Springer CCIS copyright transfer form, however, they are free to use their material published in CCIS for substantially changed, more elaborate subsequent publications elsewhere. For the preparation of the camera-ready papers/files, authors have to strictly adhere to the Springer CCIS Authors' Instructions and are strongly encouraged to use the CCIS LaTeX style files or templates.

Abstracting/Indexing

CCIS is abstracted/indexed in DBLP, Google Scholar, EI-Compendex, Mathematical Reviews, SCImago, Scopus. CCIS volumes are also submitted for the inclusion in ISI Proceedings.

How to start

To start the evaluation of your proposal for inclusion in the CCIS series, please send an e-mail to ccis@springer.com

Zengguang Hou · Huimin Lu · Qinghua Hu ·
Wenqiang Zhang · Junying Chen · Changhe Tu ·
Shan An
Editors

Intelligent Robotics

6th China Intelligent Robotics Academic Conference, CIRAC 2025
Nantong, China, September 20–22, 2025
Proceedings

Editors
Zengguang Hou
Institute of Automation, Chinese Academy of Sciences
Beijing, China

Qinghua Hu
Tianjin University
Tianjin, China

Junying Chen
South China University of Technology
Guangzhou, China

Shan An
Tianjin University
Tianjin, China

Huimin Lu
Southeast University
Nanjing, China

Wenqiang Zhang
Fudan University
Shanghai, China

Changhe Tu
Shandong University
Jinan, China

ISSN 1865-0929 ISSN 1865-0937 (electronic)
Communications in Computer and Information Science
ISBN 978-981-92-0044-3 ISBN 978-981-92-0045-0 (eBook)
https://doi.org/10.1007/978-981-92-0045-0

This Springer imprint is published by the registered company Springer Nature Singapore Pte Ltd.
The registered company address is: 152 Beach Road, #21-01/04 Gateway East, Singapore 189721, Singapore

Preface

As the Program Chairs of the 6th China Intelligent Robotics Academic Conference (CIRAC 2025), it is our great pleasure to present the proceedings of this prestigious event. Held in Nantong, China, from September 20 to 22, 2025, CIRAC 2025 was organized by the China Computer Federation (CCF) and co-hosted by various esteemed universities and professional bodies. Building on the success of previous iterations, this conference served as a dynamic international platform for researchers, engineers, and practitioners to converge, exchange cutting-edge insights, and advance the frontiers of intelligent robotics.

The theme of CIRAC 2025 centered on five core thematic pillars that reflect the most innovative and impactful directions in contemporary robotics research: UAV Technology; Robot Mechanism & Control; SLAM & Visual Navigation; Medical Robotics & Perception; and Robotic Radar Perception.

A total of 26 papers were submitted to CIRAC 2025, each undergoing a rigorous single-blind peer-review process to ensure the highest scientific standards. Every submission was assigned to an average of three qualified reviewers, all of whom were distinguished members of the conference's international Program Committee. Reviewers evaluated papers based on four key criteria: novelty of research concepts, methods, or findings; technical soundness of methodologies and experimental validation; relevance to the conference's thematic focus; and clarity of presentation. Following this meticulous review process, 12 full papers (12–15+ pages each) and 3 short papers (6–11 pages each) were accepted for publication, representing an overall acceptance rate of 58%. Notably, all accepted works underwent the same stringent evaluation, as no invited papers were included in these proceedings.

We extend our deepest gratitude to the entire Program Committee and reviewers for their dedication and expertise. Their rigorous assessments and constructive feedback not only ensured the quality of the published proceedings but also helped authors refine their research and gain deeper insights into their respective fields. We also wish to thank the Organizing Committee for their meticulous planning and execution, which laid the foundation for the conference's success.

Our sincere appreciation goes to the team at Springer for their professional support throughout the proceedings' production process. Their expertise in academic publishing has been invaluable in bringing this volume to fruition. Finally, we would like to express our heartfelt thanks to all authors for their valuable submissions and to the 488 participants from diverse geographical backgrounds—your contributions and engagement made CIRAC 2025 a vibrant and intellectually stimulating event.

We hope this proceedings volume will serve as a valuable resource for the global robotics research community, inspiring further innovation, collaboration, and advancements in this rapidly evolving field.

December 2025

Zengguang Hou
Huimin Lu
Qinghua Hu
Wenqiang Zhang
Junying Chen
Changhe Tu
Shan An

Organization

Advisory Committee

Han Ding	Huazhong University of Science and Technology, China
Liyun Ding	Huazhong University of Science and Technology, China
Lizhong Yu	Nantong Municipal People's Government, China
Haibin Yu	Shenyang Institute of Automation, Chinese Academy of Sciences, China
Yaonan Wang	Hunan University, China
Hong Qiao	Institute of Automation, Chinese Academy of Sciences, China
Hong Liu	Harbin Institute of Technology, China
Yu Sun	Dalian University of Technology, China
Hui Li	Harbin Institute of Technology, China
You He	Tsinghua University, China
Xuemin Shen	University of Waterloo, Canada
Jianwei Zhang	University of Hamburg, Germany
Jie Chen	Harbin Institute of Technology, China
Nanning Zheng	Xi'an Jiaotong University, China
Wenqi Zhong	Southeast University, China
Wen Gao	Peking University, China

General Chairs

Zengguang Hou	Institute of Automation, Chinese Academy of Sciences, China
Lianqing Liu	Shenyang Institute of Automation, Chinese Academy of Sciences, China
Aiguo Song	Southeast University, China

Program Committee Chairs

Qinghua Hu	Tianjin University, China
Wenqiang Zhang	Fudan University, China

Shihua Li	Southeast University, China
Zhigang Zeng	Huazhong University of Science and Technology, China

Organizing Chairs

Hongde Qin	Harbin Engineering University, China
Hongbin Zha	Peking University, China
Hui Huang	Shenzhen University, China
Huimin Lu	Southeast University, China

Publication Chairs

Changhe Tu	Shandong University, China
Junying Chen	South China University of Technology, China
Xianping Fu	Dalian Maritime University, China
Duanling Li	Beijing University of Posts and Telecommunications, China

Publicity Chairs

Xiaofeng Liu	Hohai University, China
Dong Wang	Dalian University of Technology, China
Bin Fang	Beijing University of Posts and Telecommunications, China
Tao Kong	ByteDance, China

Exhibition Chairs

Xinhong Hei	Xi'an University of Technology, China
Jun Wang	China University of Mining and Technology (Xuzhou), China
Quan Zhou	Nanjing University of Posts and Telecommunications, China
Tao Zhang	Southeast University, China

Poster Chairs

Fei Gao	Zhejiang University, China
Zhiqiang Liao	Hunan University, China
Rushu Lan	Guilin University of Electronic Technology, China
Li Chen	Unitree Robotics, China

Sponsorship Chairs

Shan An	Tianjin University, China
Yixing Gao	Jilin University, China
Lei Huang	Southeast University, China

Competition Chairs

Fumin Zhang	Hong Kong University of Science and Technology, China
Riying Wang	Shanghai University, China
Hang Xu	University of Electronic Science and Technology of China, China
Feng Chen	Robot Era (Beijing) Technology Co., Ltd., China

Finance Chairs

Yuping Wang	Beijing Institute of Technology, China
Runmin Cong	Shandong University, China
Hui Zhang	Southeast University, China

Program Committee Members

Shan An	Tianjin University, China
Junying Chen	South China University of Technology, China
Shihai Chen	China University of Mining and Technology, China
Houde Dai	Fujian Institute, Chinese Academy of Sciences, China
Zhen Deng	Fuzhou University, China

Zengguang Hou	Institute of Automation, Chinese Academy of Sciences, China
Qinghua Hu	Tianjin University, China
Duanling Li	Tianjin University, China
Jun Li	Beijing University of Posts and Telecommunications, China
Manyi Li	Fujian Institute, Chinese Academy of Sciences, China
Yingtian Li	Shandong University, China
Xu Liang	Academy of Sciences, China
Anan Liu	Beijing Jiaotong University, China
Huimin Lu	Tianjin University, China
Xin Ma	Southeast University, China
Xinglu Ma	Shandong University, China
Yunkai Ma	Qingdao University of Science and Technology, China
Zhiqiang Miu	Institute of Automation, Chinese Academy of Sciences, China
Hongde Qin	Hunan University, China
Liyong Shen	Harbin Engineering University, China
Xuesong Shi	University of Chinese Academy of Sciences, China
Huyuan Sun	Intel Labs, China
Shengjing Tian	Institute of Automation, Chinese Academy of Sciences, China
Changhe Tu	China University of Mining and Technology, China
Jun Wang	Shandong University, ChinaLin WangChina University of Mining and Technology, China
Zhu Wang	Shenzhen Institutes of Advanced Technology, Chinese Academy of Sciences, China
Jing Xin	North China Electric Power University, China
Yifan Xue	Xi'an University of Technology, China
Tong Yang	Harbin Engineering University, China
Junfeng Yao	Nankai University, China
Lanyong Zhang	Xiamen University, China
Ping Zhang	Harbin Engineering University, China
Wenqiang Zhang	Fudan University, China
Yimin Zhang	Intel China Research Institute, China
Yong Zhang	Liaoning Normal University, China
Yujia Zhang	Institute of Automation, Chinese Academy of Sciences, China
Fengda Zhao	Yanshan University, China

Xingwen Zheng	Zhejiang University, China
Yong Zhong	South China University of Technology, China
Yining Zhu	Northwestern Polytechnical University, China
Qin Zou	Wuhan University, China

Contents

Medical Robotics & Perception

Robotic Radar Perception

UAV Technology

Learning Attitude and Airspeed Control for Minimum-Time Flight of Fixed-Wing UAVs

Guanzheng Wang[1,2], Ruiqi Feng[1,2], Xiangke Wang[1,2], and Zhihong Liu[1,2](✉)

[1] College of Intelligence Science and Technology, National University of Defense Technology, Changsha 410073, China
zhliu@nudt.edu.cn

[2] National Key Laboratory of Equipment State Sensing and Smart Support, National University of Defense Technology, Changsha 410073, China

Abstract. To address the minimum-time flight control problem of fixed-wing UAVs in three-dimensional space, we propose a reinforcement learning-based method for attitude and airspeed control. Unlike conventional attitude control methods, our approach focuses on optimizing flight time through end-to-end learning, effectively preventing the error accumulation associated with cascade architectures. Given the underactuated and highly coupled nature of fixed-wing UAVs, we employ a high-fidelity six-degrees-of-freedom dynamics model, allowing the UAV to learn the optimal policy through interaction with the environment. Compared to the traditional control method, our learning-based approach, trained using the Proximal Policy Optimization (PPO) algorithm, reduces the average flight time by 24.6% while maintaining strong generalization and stability. The code is available as open-source at https://github.com/running-mars/OpenFlight.

Keywords: fixed-wing UAV · reinforcement learning (RL) · minimum-time flight · high-fidelity dynamics · attitude control

1 Introduction

Fixed-wing UAVs, renowned for their long endurance and extensive operational range, are widely employed in applications such as aerial surveillance, target detection, and communication relay [1,2]. As UAV missions often require traveling between points, minimizing flight time for this fundamental task is crucial to enhancing overall mission efficiency.

Traditional control methods for fixed-wing UAVs include proportional-integral-derivative (PID) controllers, linear quadratic regulators (LQR), robust control, model predictive control (MPC), and adaptive control [3]. These approaches often rely on cascade control architectures, which can lead to issues such as error accumulation and limited real-time responsiveness, restricting the UAV's ability to fully leverage its performance capabilities [4,5]. Additionally,

Z. Hou et al. (Eds.): CIRAC 2025, CCIS 2885, pp. 3–15, 2026.
https://doi.org/10.1007/978-981-92-0045-0_1

many of these methods struggle to manage complex nonlinear dynamics and uncertain external disturbances effectively, limiting their robustness and adaptability under practical flight conditions [6].

In recent years, the rapid advancement of deep learning technologies has led to significant breakthroughs in reinforcement learning-based UAV control methods, particularly in areas such as racing [4,5,7], autonomous landing [8,9], and obstacle avoidance [10,11]. Research on reinforcement learning-based flight control for fixed-wing UAVs generally focuses on two main categories: attitude control and navigation control [3]. Specifically, attitude control refers to the inner-loop control of roll and pitch angles [12–15], while navigation control involves guiding the UAV from one point to another or regulating the yaw angle [16–19]. These methods primarily aim to maintain stable attitude or direction, with little consideration for task execution efficiency, such as minimizing flight time.

In this paper, we address the point-to-point flight problem of fixed-wing UAVs in three-dimensional space. With the objective of minimizing flight time, we propose a reinforcement learning-based inner-loop control method for attitude and airspeed. This approach eliminates the error accumulation typically associated with cascading architectures. When trained using the Proximal Policy Optimization (PPO) algorithm, the resulting policy achieves a 24.6% reduction in flight time compared to traditional methods, while maintaining robust stability.

2 Methodology

In this section, we present a comprehensive introduction to the proposed method in the paper, which consists of four main parts: problem description, dynamics modeling, the learning method for inner-loop attitude and airspeed control, and training details.

2.1 Problem Formulation

In this work, we address the flight control problem of fixed-wing UAVs in three-dimensional space, aiming to minimize the time required for point-to-point flight while adhering to dynamic constraints. Since the UAV can only access partial state information through sensors during flight, we model this problem as a Partially Observable Markov Decision Process (POMDP). A POMDP is typically represented by the tuple $\langle S, A, T, R, \Omega, O, \gamma \rangle$ [20], where S denotes the state space, A is the action space, T is the state transition function, and R represents the reward function. Ω refers to the observation space, while O defines the observation probability function, which models the likelihood of observing a particular outcome given the current state and action. Lastly, γ is the discount factor, which determines the relative importance of future rewards compared to immediate ones. In this process, the UAV continuously interacts with the environment to learn the optimal policy (denoted as π^*) in order to maximize the reward.

2.2 6-DOF Dynamics Model

To characterize the flight behavior of a fixed-wing UAV, we use a six-degree-of-freedom (6-DOF) rigid body dynamics model. The translational motion in three-dimensional space is governed by Newton's second law, while the rotational motion is described by Euler's equations of motion, as expressed in Eq. 1:

$$\begin{aligned} m\dot{\mathbf{v}} + \omega \times m\mathbf{v} &= \mathbf{F}, \\ \mathbf{I}\dot{\omega} + \omega \times \mathbf{I}\omega &= \mathbf{M}. \end{aligned} \tag{1}$$

In this model, m represents the UAV's mass, v is the linear velocity, ω denotes the angular velocity, $\mathbf{I}$ is the inertia matrix, and $\mathbf{F}$ and $\mathbf{M}$ represent the total applied force and moment, respectively.

The total force $\mathbf{F}$ primarily consists of the aerodynamic force $\mathbf{F}_a$, the thrust force $\mathbf{F}_t$, and the gravitational force $\mathbf{F}_g$. The total moment $\mathbf{M}$ is mainly composed of the moments generated by the aerodynamic force $\mathbf{M}_a$, and the thrust force $\mathbf{M}_t$, as shown in Eq. 2. For simplicity, we assume that the UAV's rotation occurs about its center of gravity, meaning the moment generated by gravity is negligible.

$$\begin{aligned} \mathbf{F} &= \mathbf{F}_a + \mathbf{F}_t + \mathbf{F}_g, \\ \mathbf{M} &= \mathbf{M}_a + \mathbf{M}_t. \end{aligned} \tag{2}$$

For our experiments, we use the Skywalker X8 UAV model, with aerodynamic parameters derived from wind tunnel tests and Computational Fluid Dynamics (CFD) simulations [21]. This UAV is equipped with left and right elevon control surfaces but lacks a dedicated tail or rudder. To enable independent control of roll and pitch, we introduce the concept of virtual aileron and elevator [12], as shown in Eq. 3. Here, δ_a and δ_e denote the deflections of the virtual aileron and elevator, while $\delta_{e,r}$ and $\delta_{e,l}$ represent the deflections of the right and left elevon control surfaces, respectively.

$$\begin{bmatrix} \delta_a \\ \delta_e \end{bmatrix} = \begin{bmatrix} -0.5 & 0.5 \\ 0.5 & 0.5 \end{bmatrix} \begin{bmatrix} \delta_{e,r} \\ \delta_{e,l} \end{bmatrix} \tag{3}$$

2.3 Learning Method for Inner-Loop Attitude and Airspeed Control

Within the framework of a POMDP, we utilize deep reinforcement learning methods to train the UAV, enabling it to learn the optimal policy through interaction with the environment. The policy π maps from the observation space Ω to the action space A and is approximated using a neural network. The design of the learning method is outlined below.

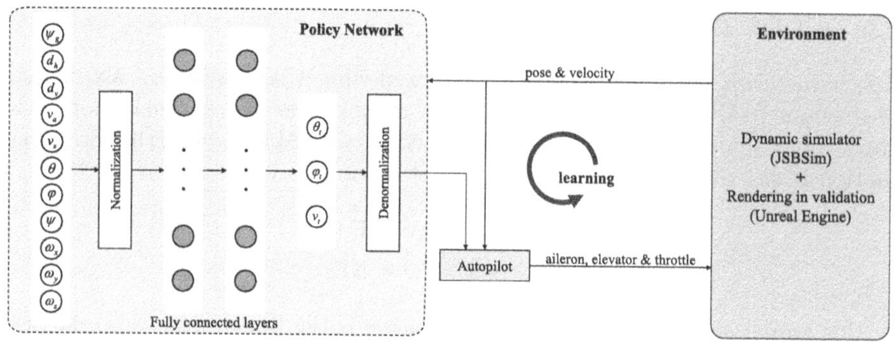

Fig. 1. The learning procedure and network architecture. The rendering engine (Unreal Engine) can be disabled during training to accelerate the process.

Observation and Action. The design of the observation space should include all relevant information necessary for neural network inference while remaining compact to avoid excessive sampling complexity. Since the UAV needs to achieve minimum-time flight to the target, the observation space is designed to encompass the following four categories of information:

- Target: heading angle deviation ψ_g, horizontal distance d_h, vertical distance d_v;
- Speed: airspeed v_a and vertical speed v_z in the North-East-Down (NED) frame;
- Attitude angles: roll θ, pitch ϕ, yaw ψ;
- Angular velocities: ω_x, ω_y and ω_z in the body frame.

Thus, the observation $\mathbf{o}$ of the UAV is defined as:

$$\mathbf{o} = [\psi_g, d_h, d_v, v_a, v_z, \theta, \phi, \psi, \omega_x, \omega_y, \omega_z]. \tag{4}$$

The UAV's actions are designed to control the inner-loop attitude and airspeed. Since the UAV's heading is primarily controlled through roll, the actions consist of the desired inner-loop attitude angles θ_t and ϕ_t, as well as the target airspeed v_t, as shown in Eq. 5:

$$\mathbf{a} = [\theta_t, \phi_t, v_t]. \tag{5}$$

These actions are then translated into control inputs for the virtual ailerons, elevators, and throttle by the lower-level autopilot, as detailed by the transformation in Eq. 3.

Network Architecture. In the reinforcement learning framework, the UAV learns control policies through interactions with the environment to achieve its objectives, as shown in Fig. 1. At each time step, the UAV receives observations from the environment (simulator) and takes an action. This action is then converted into control inputs for the ailerons, elevators, and throttle by the lower-level controller (autopilot) to manage flight control.

The policy is represented by a neural network consisting of two fully connected layers, each containing 64 neurons. The ReLU activation function is applied after each layer. Observations are normalized before being input into the neural network, and the network's output is denormalized before being passed to the lower-level controller for UAV flight management. The details of the normalization and denormalization processes are explained below.

Reward Shaping and Termination. The primary goals of the task are to minimize the time required to reach the destination and to ensure safe flight (i.e., avoid crashes). To achieve these goals, we define a reward function to guide the UAV toward minimal flight time while employing episode termination conditions to encourage safe flight.

To address the challenges associated with sparse rewards, we design a dense reward function that includes terms for horizontal distance, vertical distance, and heading angle deviation. This approach encourages the UAV to reduce the distance to the target as quickly as possible, while the heading angle deviation term helps guide the UAV to align its flight direction toward the target point. The reward at time t is defined as follows:

$$r_t = k_1 \Delta d_h + k_2 \Delta d_v + k_3 \Delta \psi_g, \tag{6}$$

where Δd_h, Δd_v, and $\Delta \psi_g$ represent the deviation of d_h, d_v, and ψ_g at each step, respectively, and k_1 to k_3 are weight coefficients set to 0.25, 1, and 20, respectively.

During the learning process, the episode termination conditions primarily include the following four criteria: exceeding the flight altitude limit, the distance to the target being smaller than a set threshold, exceeding the maximum flight time, and exceeding the angular velocity limit. The UAV's flight altitude is restricted to a range of 10 m to 190 m, the threshold for determining if the target is reached is set at 30 m, the maximum flight time is limited to 40 s, and the maximum allowable value for any component of the angular velocity is 10 rad/s.

2.4 Training Details

Deep reinforcement learning (DRL) often faces challenges such as high sample complexity and low learning efficiency during training [22]. To address these challenges, we employ two strategies: normalization and denormalization techniques, along with multi-threaded parallel training, to enhance the overall efficiency of the learning process.

Normalization and Denormalization. In the point-to-point flight navigation problem for UAVs, the observations include various types of information, such

Fig. 2. Parallel training of multiple UAVs (rendered using Unreal Engine 5, with the option to disable during training).

as distance, velocity, and attitude angles, as shown in Eq. 4. These components span a wide range of values, which can negatively impact the policy learning process. To mitigate this, normalizing each observation component is essential. Additionally, we constrain the neural network's output to lie within the range of $[-1, 1]$, followed by denormalization to map the output back to its actual range. To avoid ambiguity, we use $\mathbf{o}_n$ to denote the normalized observation, which serves as the input to the neural network. The normalization of the observations is performed as follows:

$$\begin{cases} \mathbf{o}_n[1] = \psi_g/2\pi \\ \mathbf{o}_n[2] = \tanh(\alpha_1 d_h) \\ \mathbf{o}_n[3] = \tanh(\alpha_2 d_v) \\ \mathbf{o}_n[4] = \tanh(\alpha_3(v_a - \beta_1)) \\ \mathbf{o}_n[5] = \tanh(\alpha_4 v_z) \\ \mathbf{o}_n[i] = \mathbf{o}[i]/2\pi, i = 6, 7, 8 \\ \mathbf{o}_n[j] = \mathbf{o}[j]/4\pi, j = 9, 10, 11 \end{cases}, \tag{7}$$

where α_1 to α_4 are scaling factors, with values of 0.01, 0.02, 0.05, and 0.1, respectively. β_1 is the intermediate value of the feasible speed, which is $20\,\text{m/s}$.

Similarly, we use $\mathbf{a}_d$ to represent the denormalized action, which is used to control the UAV. The denormalization operation is as follows:

$$\begin{cases} \mathbf{a}_d[1] = \alpha_5 \mathbf{a}[1] \\ \mathbf{a}_d[2] = \alpha_6 \mathbf{a}[2] \\ \mathbf{a}_d[3] = \alpha_7 \mathbf{a}[3] + \beta_1 \end{cases}, \tag{8}$$

where α_5 to α_7 are scaling factors, with values of π, 0.5π and 6, respectively.

Training Algorithms and Parallel Acceleration. We employ four state-of-the-art (SOTA) algorithms for policy learning, provided by the open-source project Stable-Baselines3 (SB3) [23]: A2C [24], TD3 [25], SAC [26], and PPO [27], all of which are designed for continuous action spaces. To reduce training time, we adopt the centralized training and distributed execution (CTDE) paradigm [22] to accelerate the experience collection process. Specifically, we use a vectorized environment to simultaneously drive multiple UAVs interacting with the environment, as shown in Fig. 2, thereby improving training efficiency.

3 Results

In this section, we evaluate the convergence and training efficiency of the proposed method alongside various reinforcement learning algorithms, as well as the generalization of the learned control policies, their time efficiency, and control stability.

3.1 Training

The UAV is initialized 100 m directly above the origin in the North-East-Down (NED) coordinate system. The target points are defined using spherical coordinates, with the origin as the reference point. These coordinates are represented by (r, θ, ϕ), where r is the radial distance, θ is the elevation angle, and ϕ is the azimuth angle. The target point coordinates are generated randomly based on continuous uniform distributions: $r \sim \mathcal{U}(di - 50, di + 50)$, $\theta \sim \mathcal{U}(1.41, 1.73)$, and $\phi \sim \mathcal{U}(-\pi, \pi)$. Here, d_i denotes the predefined goal distance. Using these values, the target point coordinates in the NED coordinate system can be calculated. The points are distributed between two spheres, with the height restricted to a specific range.

The training was conducted on a desktop computer equipped with an AMD 5950X CPU, an Nvidia RTX 3090 GPU, and 128 GB of RAM. All reinforcement learning algorithms used in this study were configured with the same default parameters. Furthermore, 16 threads were employed to control the UAVs, enabling parallel interaction with the environment and efficient experience collection. For each algorithm, five independent training sessions were conducted, and the results are presented in Fig. 3, where T0 to T4 represent these five separate training sessions.

Regarding convergence, the proposed method, when combined with the PPO algorithm, achieves the highest reward value within the same number of time steps (2×10^6). In contrast, the A2C algorithm performs the poorest in this task, showing no noticeable improvement in the reward value throughout the training process. Moreover, the combination of the proposed method with the PPO algorithm exhibits the fastest convergence speed.

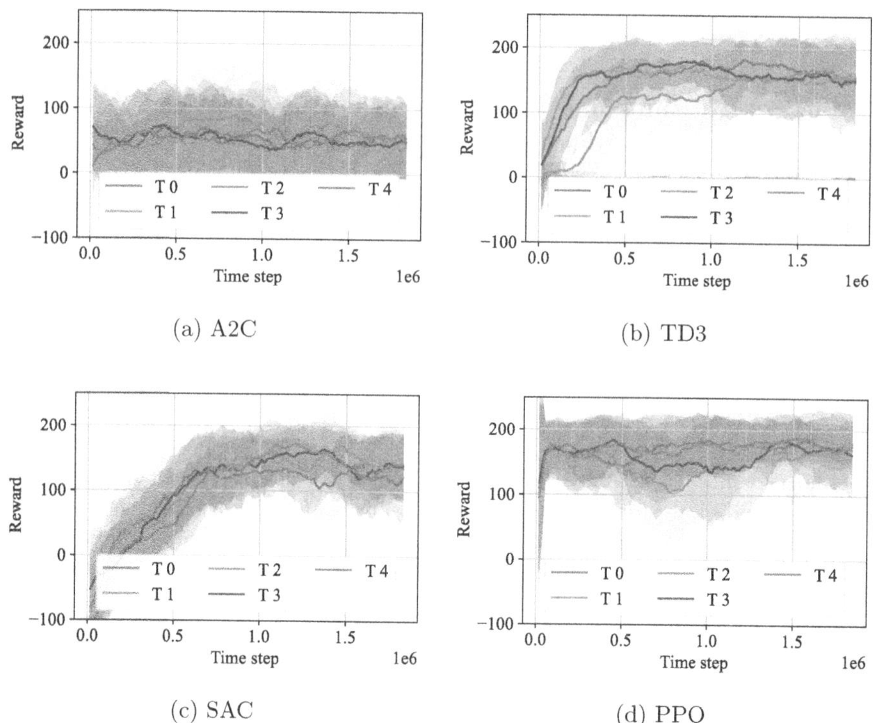

(a) A2C

(b) TD3

(c) SAC

(d) PPO

Fig. 3. Smoothed reward during training with A2C, TD3, SAC, and PPO algorithms. T 0 refers to the first training, with subsequent values following a similar pattern.

3.2 Generalization and Efficiency

To comprehensively evaluate the generalization ability and time efficiency of the control policies trained using the proposed method, we defined 64 target points in various directions, with their heights uniformly distributed between ±80 m. The initial horizontal distance to the target points is 500 m. For comparison, the Dubins curve and PID control methods were used, with target airspeeds set at a minimum of 14 m/s, an intermediate speed of 20 m/s, and a maximum speed of 26 m/s. The average flight time and standard deviation are presented in Table 1. Since the policies trained with A2C and SAC encountered crashes during flight, their average flight times are excluded, indicating poor generalization. The primary constraint in minimizing flight time is avoiding crashes.

When using the Dubins curve method, some target points cannot be reached under both the minimum and maximum speed conditions, exceeding the time limit of 50 s, as shown in Fig. 4 (a–c). This occurs because when the UAV's airspeed is too low, the lift is insufficient to climb to a sufficient altitude within the limited distance. Similarly, when the airspeed is too high, the UAV generates more lift, leading to a very small descent rate. This highlights the coupled

Table 1. Average flight time (in seconds) and standard deviation. The Dubins curve with cruising speeds of 14 m/s and 26 m/s results in some flights being unable to reach the target point within the specified time (50 s). The policies trained with A2C and SAC lead to crashes, so the average time is not included in the table.

Method	Dubins Curve			Attitude Control			
	14 m/s*	20 m/s	26 m/s*	A2C*	TD3	SAC*	PPO
Average Time (s)	35.36	27.94	32.32	-	26.44	-	**21.08**
Standard Deviation	4.08	4.19	13.73	-	1.78	-	**1.66**

relationship between the UAV's airspeed and climb rate, which is one of the key challenges in controlling fixed-wing UAVs.

The method proposed in this paper leverages reinforcement learning to directly control the fixed-wing UAV's airspeed, roll angle, and pitch angle, allowing the UAV to learn the coupling relationships through interaction with the environment. In terms of average flight time, the approach using the PPO-trained policy significantly outperforms the Dubins curve-based method, reducing flight time by 24.6%. Compared to the TD3-trained policy, the time is reduced by 20.1%. As shown in Fig. 4 (d, e), the flight trajectories generated using reinforcement learning are more aggressive. Notably, the flight trajectories generated using the TD3-trained method are less smooth, which will be further analyzed later.

3.3 Stability

To compare the stability of various methods, we analyze the flight trajectory to the target point $(-300, -400, -180)$ in the NED frame. This setup encompasses key aspects such as turns, climbs, and straight-line flight, as shown in Fig. 5. It is evident that the Dubins curve method exhibits stable linear and angular velocities, but it fails to fully utilize the UAV's flight performance.

In contrast, the reinforcement learning-based method proposed in this paper, trained using both the TD3 and PPO algorithms, demonstrates stronger maneuverability, especially during turns. However, the policy trained with the TD3 algorithm exhibits poor control stability, with oscillations in both linear and angular velocities, which is undesirable for actual flight. In contrast, the PPO-trained policy offers excellent control stability, with no oscillations in the velocities.

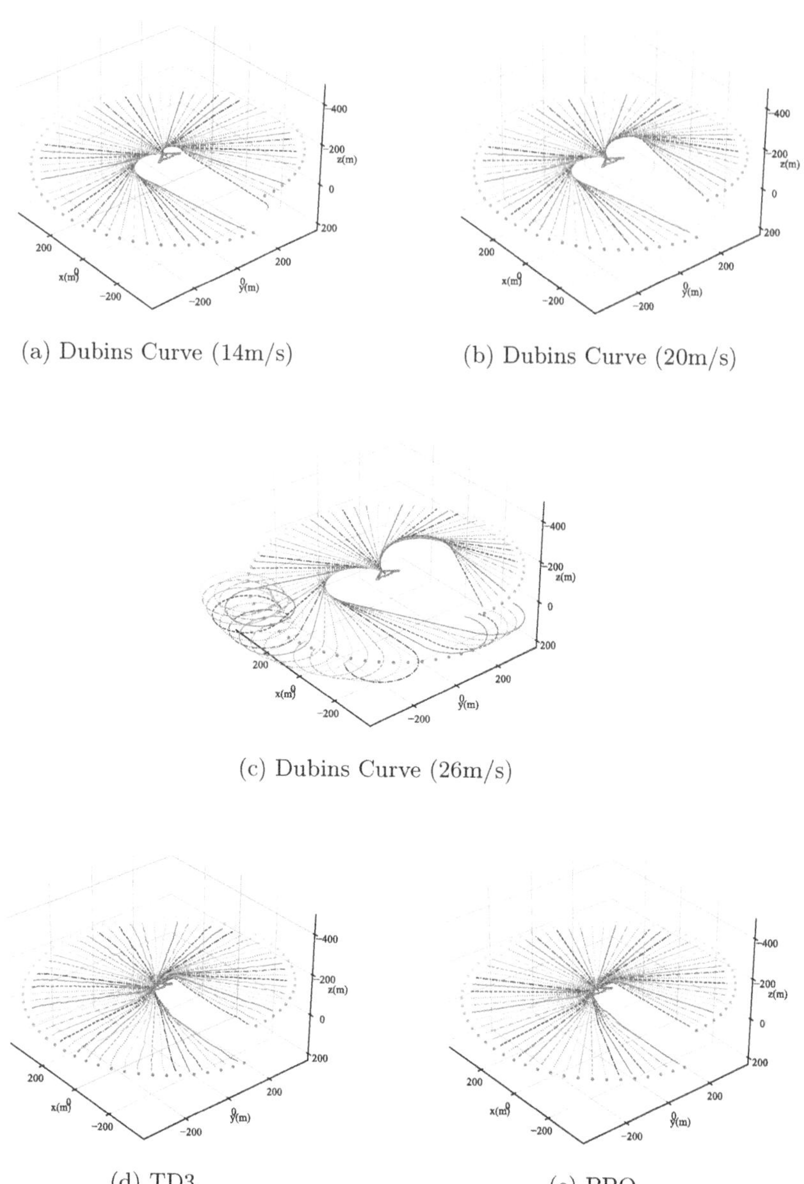

(a) Dubins Curve (14m/s)

(b) Dubins Curve (20m/s)

(c) Dubins Curve (26m/s)

(d) TD3

(e) PPO

Fig. 4. UAV trajectories for target points at varying altitudes and directions, driven by Dubins curves with different cruise speeds. The UAV's initial position is at (0, 0, −100) m, and the blue dots indicate the target points.

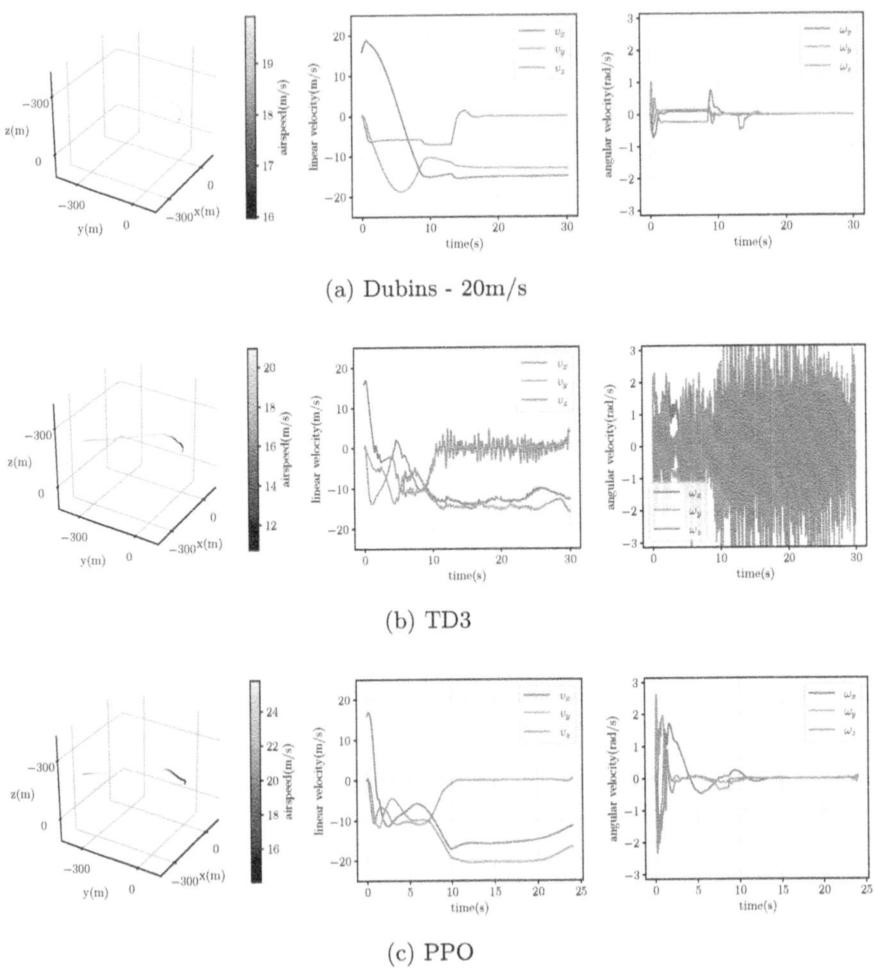

(a) Dubins - 20m/s

(b) TD3

(c) PPO

Fig. 5. Trajectories and velocities for the target point at (−300, −400, −180) m, driven by policies trained using PPO. The color of the trajectores indicate the airspeed at that moment, as shown in the legend on the right. (Color figure online)

4 Conclusions

In this paper, we presented a reinforcement learning-based approach using the PPO algorithm to optimize attitude and airspeed control of fixed-wing UAVs, reducing flight time by 24.6% compared to traditional methods. Our approach focuses on minimizing flight time while ensuring safety, leveraging a high-fidelity six-degree-of-freedom dynamics model and a dense reward function that encourages efficient navigation. The learned policies demonstrate strong generalization, making them suitable for applications. Future work will explore incorporating environmental factors and multi-UAV cooperation for further optimization.

Acknowledgements. This work was supported by National Natural Science Foundation of China (Grant Nos. U23B2032, U2241214, and 62576355) and the Postgraduate Scientific Research Innovation Project of Hunan Province (Grant No. CX20220055).

References

1. Liu, Z., et al.: Mission-oriented miniature fixed-wing UAV swarms: a multilayered and distributed architecture. IEEE Trans. Syst. Man Cybern. Syst. **52**(3), 1588–1602 (2020)
2. Hu, S., Yuan, X., Ni, W., Wang, X., Jamalipour, A.: Visual-based moving target tracking with solar-powered fixed-wing UAV: a new learning-based approach. IEEE Trans. Intell. Transp. Syst. **25**(8), 9115–9129 (2024)
3. Richter, D.J., Calix, R.A., Kim, K.: A review of reinforcement learning for fixed-wing aircraft control tasks. IEEE Access **12**, 103,026–103,048 (2024)
4. Kaufmann, E., Bauersfeld, L., Loquercio, A., Müller, M., Koltun, V., Scaramuzza, D.: Champion-level drone racing using deep reinforcement learning. Nature **620**(7976), 982–987 (2023)
5. Song, Y., Romero, A., Müller, M., Koltun, V., Scaramuzza, D.: Reaching the limit in autonomous racing: optimal control versus reinforcement learning. Sci. Robot. **8**(82), eadg1462 (2023)
6. Yan, C., et al.: Collision-avoiding flocking with multiple fixed-wing UAVs in obstacle-cluttered environments: a task-specific curriculum- based Madrl approach. IEEE Trans. Neural Netw. Learn. Syst. **35**(8), 10894–10908 (2024)
7. Song, Y., Steinweg, M., Kaufmann, E., Scaramuzza, D.: Autonomous drone racing with deep reinforcement learning. In: IEEE/RSJ International Conference on Intelligent Robots and Systems (IROS), pp. 1205–1212. IEEE (2021)
8. Backman, K., Kulić, D., Chung, H.: Learning to assist drone landings. IEEE Robot. Autom. Lett. **6**(2), 3192–3199 (2021)
9. Bartolomei, L., Kompis, Y., Teixeira, L., Chli, M.: Autonomous emergency landing for multicopters using deep reinforcement learning. In: 2022 IEEE/RSJ International Conference on Intelligent Robots and Systems (IROS), pp. 3392–3399. IEEE (2022)
10. Song, Y., Shi, K., Penicka, R., Scaramuzza, D.: Learning perception-aware agile flight in cluttered environments. In: IEEE International Conference on Robotics and Automation (ICRA), pp. 1989–1995. IEEE (2023)
11. Kulkarni, M., Alexis, K.: Reinforcement learning for collision-free flight exploiting deep collision encoding. In: IEEE International Conference on Robotics and Automation (ICRA), pp. 15,781–15,788. IEEE (2024)
12. Bøhn, E., Coates, E.M., Moe, S., Johansen, T.A.: Deep reinforcement learning attitude control of fixed-wing UAVs using proximal policy optimization. In: International Conference on Unmanned Aircraft Systems (ICUAS), pp. 523–533 (2019)
13. Richter, D.J., Calix, R.A.: Using double deep q-learning to learn attitude control of fixed-wing aircraft. In: International Conference on Signal-Image Technology and Internet-Based Systems (SITIS), pp. 646–651. IEEE (2022)
14. Bøhn, E., Coates, E.M., Reinhardt, D., Johansen, T.A.: Data-efficient deep reinforcement learning for attitude control of fixed-wing UAVs: field experiments. IEEE Trans. Neural Netw. Learn. Syst. **35**(3), 3168–3180 (2023)

15. Chowdhury, M., Keshmiri, S.: Interchangeable reinforcement-learning flight controller for fixed-wing UASs. IEEE Trans. Aerosp. Electron. Syst. **60**(2), 2305–2318 (2024)
16. Rennie, G.: Autonomous control of simulated fixed wing aircraft using deep reinforcement learning. Master's thesis, The University of Bath, Bath, United Kingdom (2018)
17. Eckstein, F.: Learning to fly – building an autopilot system based on neural networks and reinforcement learning. Master's thesis, FernUniversität Hagen, Hagen (2020)
18. Zhang, S., Du, X., Xiao, J., Huang, J., He, K.: Reinforcement learning control for 6 dof flight of fixed-wing aircraft. In: Chinese Control and Decision Conference (CCDC), pp. 5454–5460 (2021)
19. Zhou, Y., Shu, J., Hao, H., Song, H., Lai, X.: UAV 3D online track planning based on improved SAC algorithm. J. Braz. Soc. Mech. Sci. Eng. **46**(1), 12 (2024)
20. Wang, X., et al.: Deep reinforcement learning: a survey. IEEE Trans. Neural Netw. Learn. Syst. **35**(4), 5064–5078 (2024). https://doi.org/10.1109/TNNLS.2022.3207346
21. Gryte, K., Hann, R., Alam, M., Roháč, J., Johansen, T.A., Fossen, T.I.: Aerodynamic modeling of the skywalker x8 fixed-wing unmanned aerial vehicle. In: International Conference on Unmanned Aircraft Systems (ICUAS), pp. 826–835. IEEE (2018)
22. Liu, Z., Xu, X., Qiao, P., Li, D.: Acceleration for deep reinforcement learning using parallel and distributed computing: a survey. ACM Comput. Surv. **57**(4), 1–35 (2024)
23. Raffin, A., Hill, A., Gleave, A., Kanervisto, A., Ernestus, M., Dormann, N.: Stable-baselines3: reliable reinforcement learning implementations. J. Mach. Learn. Res. **22**(268), 1–8 (2021)
24. Mnih, V., et al.: Asynchronous methods for deep reinforcement learning. In: International Conference on Machine Learning, pp. 1928–1937 (2016)
25. Fujimoto, S., Hoof, H., Meger, D.: Addressing function approximation error in actor-critic methods. In: International Conference on Machine Learning, pp. 1587–1596 (2018)
26. Haarnoja, T., Zhou, A., Abbeel, P., Levine, S.: Soft actor-critic: off-policy maximum entropy deep reinforcement learning with a stochastic actor. In: International Conference on Machine Learning, pp. 1861–1870 (2018)
27. Schulman, J., Wolski, F., Dhariwal, P., Radford, A., Klimov, O.: Proximal policy optimization algorithms. arXiv preprint arXiv:1707.06347 (2017)

Robust UAV Multi-object Tracking via Enhanced BoT-SORT with Altitude-Modulated Association and Occlusion Recovery

Jibing Wu, Shikun Yang, Junqing Wang, and Xianqiang Yang(✉)

School of Astronautics, Harbin Institute of Technology, Harbin 150001, Heilongjiang, China
xianqiangyang@hit.edu.cn

Abstract. In order to solve the common occlusion and complex nonlinear motion interference problems in drone target tracking, this paper proposes an improved algorithm based on YOLOv12 and BoT-SORT. This paper systematically improves the target tracking algorithm, introduces altitude state information as a potential clue, and introduces the target's motion information into the correlation matrix for motion modeling, significantly optimizing the prediction of the target's motion trend. To address the challenge of trajectory interruption caused by target occlusion, virtual observation interpolation is used to effectively restore trajectory continuity during occlusion, and for short-term occlusion, historical observations are used to reduce the risk of target identity switching (ID Switch). The performance of this method is verified on the MOT20, Dance Track and Visdrone2019 datasets. Experimental results demonstrate that the proposed method outperforms the original BoT-SORT across all three datasets, with particularly significant gains on Dance Track. Without ReID integration, HOTA and IDF1 improve by 1.1 and 0.9 percentage points, respectively. Integrating the ReID module further increases these gains to 2.6 and 2.2 percentage points.

Keywords: UAV · Computer Vision · BoT-SORT · Target Tracking

1 Introduction

The rapid development of Unmanned Aerial Vehicle (UAV) technology has led to its widespread application in agricultural monitoring, border security, disaster relief, and intelligent transportation. UAVs have the advantages of high maneuverability, flexible viewing angles, and low-cost data collection capabilities, providing a new way to solve the problem of dynamic target tracking in complex environments. At the same time, breakthroughs in the field of computer vision, especially representative algorithms for target detection and tracking based on deep learning (such as YOLO, BoT-SORT, OC-SORT, etc.) [1–3], have significantly improved the recognition accuracy and real-time tracking performance of UAVs for moving targets. The coordinated evolution of the two is driving the development of autonomous environmental perception and intelligent decision-making capabilities into a key technical direction for the new generation of UAVs.

Z. Hou et al. (Eds.): CIRAC 2025, CCIS 2885, pp. 16–29, 2026.
https://doi.org/10.1007/978-981-92-0045-0_2

However, the proportion of small objects in drone aerial images is much higher than in images of natural scenes. While their viewing angles and wide image widths provide rich information, they also introduce significant background noise due to the lack of prominent objects. Furthermore, the low flight altitude and complex airspace environment lead to frequent occlusions, making target observations often discontinuous and incomplete [4]. In addition, existing tracking algorithms have difficulty modeling complex nonlinear motions and lack robust and efficient solutions to short-term occlusion and trajectory recovery problems, which often leads to frequent switching of target identities (IDs) and the generation of a large number of redundant new IDs.

Currently, Tracking-by-Detection is still the mainstream paradigm for multi-target tracking. To address the above problems, this paper proposes a new solution, using YOLOv12 as the detector and BoT-SORT as the tracking module [5]. YOLOv12 is chosen as the detector because it has higher accuracy in handling small objects and occluded objects, providing a strong foundation for the system. This combination demonstrates superior performance over alternatives employing YOLOv8 with DeepSORT or other model-tracker pairs [6, 7]. We also optimized the architecture of BoT-SORT, significantly improving the accuracy and robustness of target tracking. In particular, the main contributions of our work can be summarized as follows:

- Introducing target height and speed information as supplementary weak cues and modeling them can effectively compensate for the degradation of spatial and appearance strong cues caused by target occlusion or aggregation, thereby enhancing tracking robustness in complex scenes.
- To address occlusion recovery, we integrated the Observation Re-update (ORU) and Observation Centered Reasoning (OCR) mechanisms. ORU smoothes state updates during occlusion periods through virtual observation interpolation, while OCR leverages historical observation information for robust reassociation, significantly reducing ID switching.
- To solve the data association problem in multi-target tracking, this study integrates multi-source information clues in the cost matrix construction of the association matching stage, and designs different weighting strategies according to different association stages to improve the robustness and accuracy of the tracking algorithm.

2 Related Work

2.1 Object Detection

YOLOv12 redefines the architectural paradigm of real-time target detection [8]: for the first time, it uses the regional attention mechanism (A2) as the core to replace the traditional CNN-based design, and compresses the computational complexity to 1/4 of the traditional method through feature map segmentation and reshaping strategies; it innovatively introduces the residual enhancement R-ELAN module, combined with gradient scaling technology to overcome the stability problem of deep network training; and reconstructs the position perception method - using 7×7 separable convolution to implicitly encode spatial information, replacing explicit position encoding. Its structure diagram is shown in Fig. 1.

These innovations make the model significantly more robust in small target detection (such as medical imaging lesion localization) and dynamic scenes (such as autonomous driving dense target tracking). Compared with the incremental improvements of YOLOv11 [9], YOLOv12 has made significant progress, especially in scenarios with extremely high real-time and precision requirements such as industrial detection and security monitoring. The deep integration of YOLOv12 with the attention mechanism makes it the first general detection framework that strikes a balance between edge device deployment efficiency and cloud platform high precision.

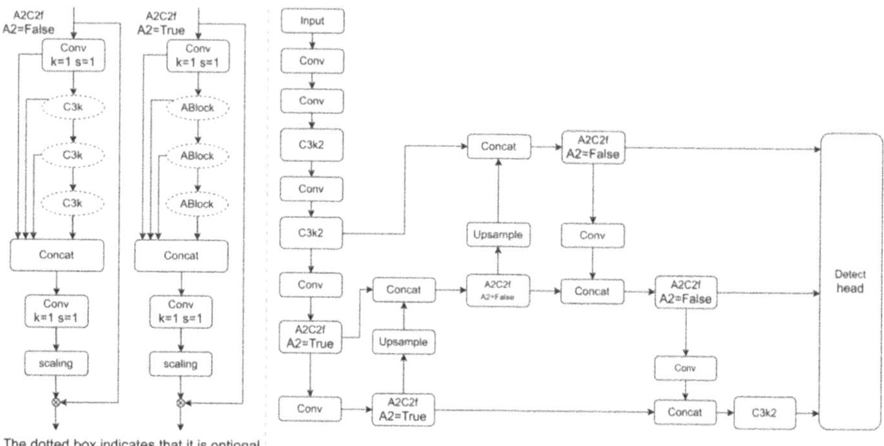

Fig. 1. The network structure diagram of YOLOv12. A2 is the name of its core attention mechanism, which is embedded in C2f in practical applications.

2.2 Object Tracking

Multi-object tracking (MOT) is one of the fundamental research topics in the current computer vision field. Its purpose is to simultaneously detect and continuously track the position, size and motion trajectory of multiple target objects of interest (such as pedestrians, vehicles, animals, etc.) in a video sequence, and maintain a unique and consistent identifier for each target in the entire video. Its kernel task can be divided into three parts: detection, association and prediction [6, 10]. At present, Tracking-by-detection has become the most effective paradigm in the MOT task [11], that is, detection and tracking are divided into two modules. SORT is a milestone in the history of MOT [10]. It realizes real-time multi-target tracking for the first time through an extremely concise and efficient framework (detection + Kalman filter prediction + IoU (Intersection over Union) matching association + Hungarian algorithm), and sets the gold standard of "detection-based tracking". It proves the power of simple component combination.

BoT-SORT is a derivative version of SORT [2]. It inherits ByteTracker's phased matching in matching strategy [12], and introduces motion camera compensation

(CMC), as shown in Fig. 2, to rectify prediction bias caused by Kalman filter in complex scenes. The synergistic integration of the camera motion compensation (CMC) and global motion compensation (GMC) modules is shown to achieve stable trajectory generation. The key process includes the derivation of the affine transformation matrix through OpenCV key points [13] and the random sampled simultaneous adversarial algorithm (RANSAC), where CMC performs Kalman filter state correction through inter-frame coordinate transformation.

3 Methods

In this article, we retain the main part of BoT-SORT. At the same time, based on our task requirements, we make the following changes to some of BoT-SORT's processes:

- Improving association robustness by highly modulating IoUs [14].
- Motion Direction Matching with Robust OCM [14].
- Multi-cue matching optimization integrating motion information and confidence.
- Observation Reverse Re-update (ORU) mechanism during trajectory loss [3, 15].
- OCR association mechanism and calculation method based on observation consistency in multi-target tracking [3, 15].

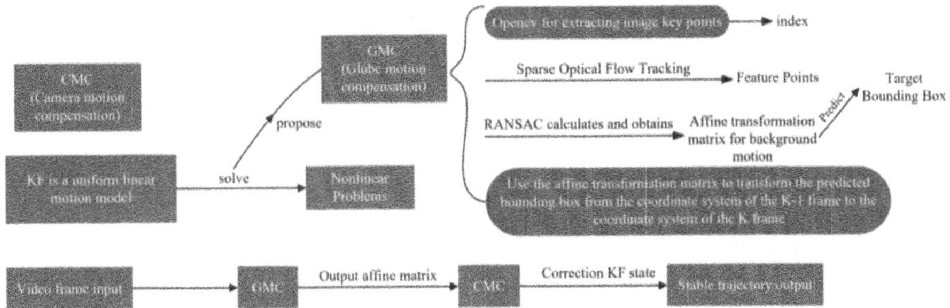

Fig. 2. Schematic diagram of the motion-compensated target tracking framework.

3.1 Height Modulated IoU

In multi-object tracking (MOT), height state, as a weak cue with temporal stability, significantly improves the robustness of object association by compensating for the limitations of strong cues (such as spatial position and appearance features). By compensating the height information of the target, not only can the depth information of the target be introduced, thereby distinguishing overlapping targets to a certain extent, but also the stability of the lifting state estimation can be improved [14].

Therefore, this paper introduces the height IoU, as shown in formula (1). Here, we denote the detection box as d and the trajectory prediction box as p, $d = ({x_1}^d, {y_1}^d, {x_2}^d, {y_2}^d)$, $p = ({x_1}^p, {y_1}^p, {x_2}^p, {y_2}^p)$. (x_1, y_1) represent the upper left corner and (x_2, y_2) lower right corner respectively. Similarly, we define the area of the detection box as D and the area of the trajectory prediction box as P, so the traditional IoU calculation formula is shown in formula (2).

$$HIoU = \frac{\min\left(y_2{}^d, y_2{}^p\right) - \max\left(y_1{}^d, y_1{}^p\right)}{\max\left(y_2{}^d, y_2{}^p\right) - \min\left(y_1{}^d, y_1{}^p\right)} \tag{1}$$

$$IoU = \frac{|D \cap P|}{|D \cup P|} \tag{2}$$

In order to better utilize the height information, this paper adopts the height modulated IoU (HMIoU), which is defined by the element-wise multiplication of the height IoU (HIoU) and the regular IoU (Formula 3).

$$HMIoU = HIoU \cdot IoU \tag{3}$$

3.2 The Robust OCM

Most MOT methods generally only consider appearance information and motion features when calculating the cost matrix. In observation-centered SORT, the target's motion trend (i.e., observation-centered momentum calculation, abbreviated as OCM) is also included in the final cost matrix calculation [3]. Denote θ_d as the speed direction of the detection, θ_t as the speed direction of the trajectory segment, and the final speed direction calculation is shown in Formula 4, 5.

$$\theta_{\Delta t} = \arctan\frac{\Delta y}{\Delta x} \tag{4}$$

$$\Delta\theta = |\theta_d - \theta_t| \tag{5}$$

Similarly, in Hybrid-SORT, it is confirmed that the original OCM modeling is limited to fixed time intervals and sparse point data with the object center as the only information source, so the OCM calculation is further improved, and the speed direction calculation of fixed frames is extended to the average speed direction of 1 to 3 frames [14]. The calculation formulas are shown in 6.

$$\theta_{Vel} = \sum\nolimits_{\Delta t=1}^{i} \frac{\theta_{\Delta t}^{lt} + \theta_{\Delta t}^{rt} + \theta_{\Delta t}^{lb} + \theta_{\Delta t}^{rb}}{4}, i = 2, 3, 4, \cdots \tag{6}$$

Among them, lt, rt, lb, and rb represent the upper left, lower left, upper right, and lower right points of the box respectively. The final cost matrix C_{Vel} is the result of normalization of θ_{Vel}.

3.3 Multi-cue Fusion Matching

BoT-SORT continues ByteTracker's two-stage matching strategy and adopts different association strategies according to different confidence scores [2]. Our pipeline still follows the two-stage matching strategy, and in order to further improve the matching accuracy when the boxes overlap, this method integrates the motion trend of the detection box into the motion information, and introduces additional weak clues on the high information association. At the same time, considering that the appearance information may become unreliable at low confidence situation, the fusion of appearance information is only introduced at the first association. The final two-stage cost matrix calculation formula is as follows:

$$C_{first} = \lambda_1 C_{fuse\_iou} + \lambda_2 C_{Vel} + \lambda_3 C_{Appr} \tag{7}$$

$$C_{second} = \lambda_{hmiou} C_{hmiou} + \lambda_2 C_{Vel} \tag{8}$$

Where C_{fuse_iou} represents the fusion information of confidence and HMIoU, C_{Vel} represents the average speed direction information of the box corners, C_{Appr} represents the appearance information and C_{hmiou} represents the HMIoU information. The value of the weight coefficient λ_2 follows the setting of OC-SORT [3] and is kept at 0.2. When the ReID module is not enabled in the system, the value of λ_1 is defined as the sum of λ_1 and λ_3.In order to suppress random fluctuations in detection results and reduce the risk of tracking errors caused by fluctuations in single-frame detection quality, in the process of calculating C_{fuse_iou}, we refer to the strategy of smoothing feature similarity in the BoT-SORT paper [2]. This paper also introduces the exponential moving average (EMA) mechanism to smooth the detection confidence score, as shown in Formula 9.

$$e_i^k = \beta e_i^{k-1} + (1 - \beta) s_i^k \tag{9}$$

Where s_i^k represents the confidence score of the detected target in the current frame, β controls the coefficient of smoothness, and e_i^k is the confidence value after exponential moving average (EMA) processing.

3.4 Observation Re-update

Observation Re-Update (ORU) is a trajectory recovery strategy for multi-target tracking systems [3]. It was first proposed in the OC-SORT paper and proved that this method can effectively improve the state estimation accuracy during trajectory recovery. The core idea is that when the target trajectory is temporarily lost due to occlusion, detection failure, etc., it is not simply replaced or reset with new observations when it is re-associated with the detection result, but virtual observations during the loss period are generated by interpolation, and these observations are gradually incorporated into the state estimation process.

Specifically, the ORU mechanism uses the spatial information of the previous and next observations to smoothly complete the target state of the lost interval by linearly interpolating between the two moments of trajectory loss and reassociation [3]. These virtual observations are then used in the prediction and update steps of the filter to achieve continuous correction of the trajectory state. The calculation formula for this process is as follows:

$$\hat{z}_t = z_{t_1} + \frac{(t-t_1)}{t_2-t_1}\left(z_{t_2} - z_{t_1}\right), \quad t \in [t_1, t_2] \tag{10}$$

Where $\hat{z}_t$ is the estimated observation value of the trajectory during the period when the trajectory is lost, z_{t_1} is the last observation value of the trajectory, and z_{t_2} is the observation value when the trajectory is recovered. During the period of time when the trajectory is lost, the estimated value $\hat{z}_t$ is then used to update the state, and the formula is as follows:

$$\begin{cases} K_t = P_{t|t-1}H_t^T\left(H_tP_{t|t-1}H_t^T + R_t\right)^{-1} \\ \hat{x}_{t|t} = \hat{x}_{t|t-1} + K_t\left(\hat{z}_t - H_t\hat{x}_{t|t-1}\right) \\ P_{t|t} = (I - K_tH_t)P_{t|t-1} \end{cases} \tag{11}$$

The main purpose of using the ORU mechanism is to improve the spatiotemporal continuity and ID stability of the trajectory, and reduce the error and ID switching caused by trajectory breakage or jump [3]. By smoothly transitioning the trajectory state of the lost interval, ORU effectively enhances the robustness and overall performance of the multi-target tracking system in complex scenarios.

3.5 Observation-Centric Reasoning

In order to improve the association robustness of the multi-target tracking system in complex scenarios, this paper introduces the observation-centered reasoning (OCR) association mechanism proposed in the OC-SORT paper. The core idea of this mechanism is to make full use of observation information [3]. After the low-confidence detection box is associated and matched, for all unmatched trajectories, denoted as $T_{unmatched}^{remain}$, the last successful association observation value of the trajectory is extracted instead of the prediction result of the Kalman filter, denoted as D_{last}. When the detection target reappears after the trajectory is lost, it is represented by $D_{unmatched}$. The detection value when the trajectory is lost and the detection value that reappears are directly associated, and the similarity measure of their spatial positions is calculated to restore the trajectory. IoU is selected as the metric, and the calculation formula is as follows:

$$C_{ocr} \leftarrow C_{iou}(D_{unmatched}, D_{last}) \tag{12}$$

Based on the above cost matrix, the Hungarian algorithm is used to pair trajectories and detections globally. To ensure matching reliability, association is established only when the cost matrix is less than 0.3, and the OCR mechanism is only used for trajectories within 2 frames that are lost. This mechanism can still achieve accurate target association and continuous tracking in extreme cases such as occlusion and target loss, significantly improving the overall performance and robustness of multi-target tracking.

4 Experimental Results and Discussion

This paper uses two videos to evaluate the performance of the proposed tracking algorithm: one video was captured by a camera fixed to the overpass, and the other was captured by a low-altitude drone at the overpass. Both videos have a resolution of 1920 × 1080. Both selected videos contain dense traffic and cover different lighting conditions during the day and at night, which can fully evaluate the adaptability and robustness of the tracking algorithm in this paper in multiple scenarios.

In addition, to evaluate the performance of the algorithm, this paper tested it on multiple public datasets, including MOT20 [16], DanceTrack [17], and Visdrone2019 [18]. Among them, the Visdrone2019 dataset is collected from the aerial perspective. To ensure the fairness of the algorithm comparison, this paper directly uses the public detection model and re-identification (ReID) model for benchmarking. The detection part uses the yolov12 small model, and the yolov12 small model is trained for 200 epochs using the corresponding datasets; the re-identification task uses the OSNet model [19]. All experiments were completed on a hardware platform equipped with the Windows 11 operating system and an NVIDIA GeForce RTX 3050 GPU (4 GB video memory). During the experimental testing phase, when the ReID module was introduced, the GPU utilization remained at around 40%, the video memory usage was approximately 1.5 GB, and the system frame rate was between 7 and 8 FPS; after disabling the module, the computational complexity dropped significantly, the GPU utilization remained at around 13%, the video memory usage was approximately 1 GB, and the frame rate increased to approximately 10 FPS.

4.1 Tracking Results under Occlusion

In the video tracking results, representative frame images with obvious benchmarks are selected for comparative analysis, and the comparison results are presented in Figs. 3 and 4 respectively.

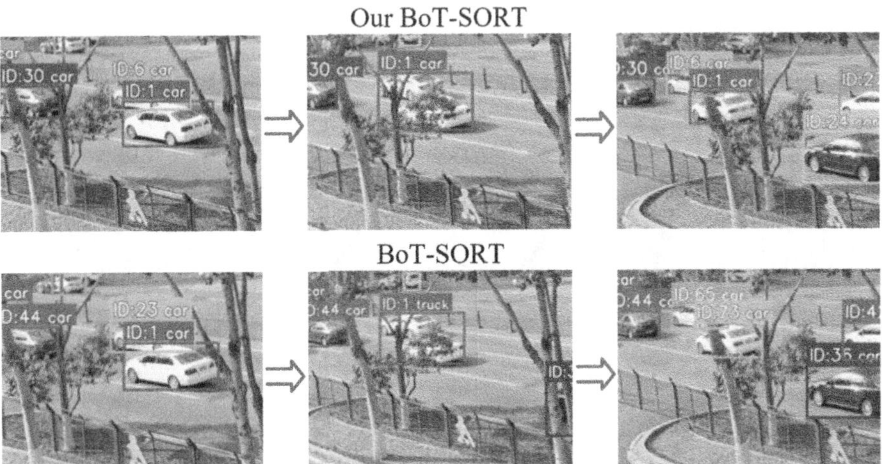

Fig. 3. Visualization of highly similar objects being tracked after occlusion.

The improved version of BoT-SORT effectively solves the ID switching problem when the target is occluded. As shown in Fig. 3, even if two highly similar vehicles pass through the occluded area at the same time, although the two vehicles are identified as one target in the middle, our algorithm can maintain its ID continuity after the target reappears. Fig. 4 further verifies that the algorithm does not have ID switching after occlusion when tracking multiple targets and under severe occlusion. As can be seen from the above figure, our BoT-SORT does not change the ID number. In contrast, after occlusion, the ID number of the white car in the above figure changes from 351 to 451 (pointed by the white arrow), and in the figure below, the ID numbers of all three cars change, and even change more than once. In addition, when three vehicles are driving in parallel, the vehicles are too densely spaced and the original BoT-SORT generates an incorrect tracking box (indicated by the green arrow).

The comparison of experimental results shows that compared with the traditional method, the improved scheme in this paper not only effectively reduces the ID switching frequency during the tracking process, but also achieves higher target tracking accuracy. Its comprehensive performance significantly exceeds the traditional scheme.

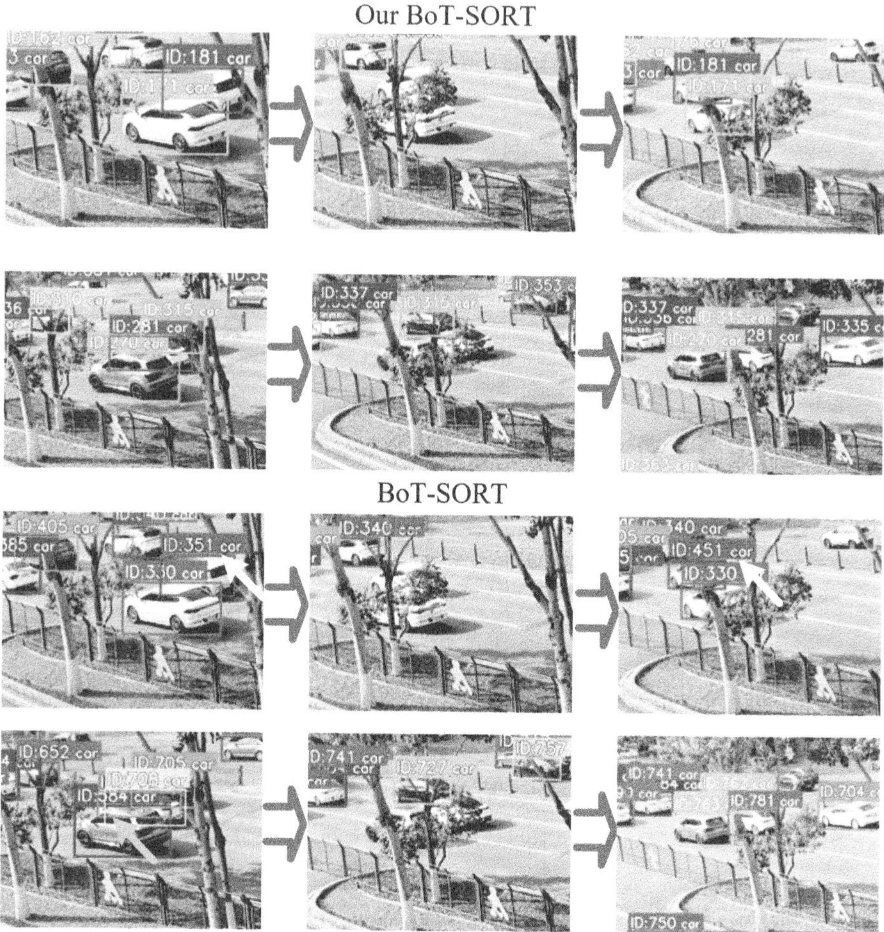

Fig. 4. Visualization of occlusions while tracking multiple vehicles simultaneously.

4.2 Aerial View Tracking Results

The test data includes a sequence of nighttime aerial images of vehicles captured by a drone in an overpass environment. To intuitively demonstrate the contrast effect, we selected several frames of images with sharp contrast in visual information in the sequence for analysis. The tracking results in the fig. 5 show that the target vehicles with IDs 1, 6, 9, 17, and 35 are continuously tracked, while the remaining ID targets are lost because they leave the sensor's field of view. In addition to the tracking test in simple scenarios, we also added an experiment to verify the identity preservation capability in occlusion scenarios. As shown in Fig. 6, in the strong occlusion scenario where the vehicle crosses the overpass, our tracker successfully maintains the identity consistency of all targets (no ID switching occurs). However, the original BoT-SORT algorithm shows significant ID switching under the same conditions: after crossing the overpass, the IDs of two vehicles traveling in opposite directions switch from 36 to 64 and 33 to 55 respectively.

Fig. 5. Visualization of tracking results from an aerial perspective.

The above results show that the improved tracking algorithm in this paper successfully adapts to the unique observation perspective and multimodal working conditions of the UAV platform, and shows excellent robustness in the target tracking task.

4.3 Test Results on Other Datasets

To rigorously validate the proposed framework, we conduct comprehensive evaluations across multiple public benchmarks. For pedestrian tracking scenarios, we choose MOT20 and DanceTrack datasets for testing. The Dance Track dataset is an important benchmark for evaluating the robustness of multi-target tracking algorithms, with a special focus on two key challenges that are common in real-world scenarios: highly dynamic nonlinear motion patterns and severe occlusion problems between targets [17]. To further evaluate

Fig. 6. Visualization of tracking results after the aerial vehicle crosses the overpass.

the applicability of the target tracking algorithm in complex aerial scenes, this paper uses the Visdrone2019 dataset for verification. This dataset is a large-scale drone aerial vehicle dataset built by Tianjin University, covering multiple time periods from day to night, focusing on the unique challenges of low-altitude drone perspectives [4]. We selected HOTA, MOTA and IDF1 as indicators: HOTA and MOTA evaluate detection and positioning accuracy, while IDF1 evaluates the robustness of cross-frame associations. The results are shown in Tables 1, 2, and 3.

The comparison of experimental results shows that compared with the unmodified BoT-SORT, the improved scheme in this paper has advantages in overall performance, especially after the introduction of the ReID module. In the evaluation of three benchmark datasets, the key indicators of HOTA, MOTA and IDF1 all show considerable improvement.

Table 1. Results on MOT20-test with the private detections. Our BoT-SORT and the unmodified BoT-SORT share the same detectors

Tracker	HOTA↑	MOTA↑	IDF1↑
DeepSORT	57.4	63.3	66.1
ByteTrack	58.7	65.1	66.3
BoT-SORT	59.8	65.5	67.4
Our BoT-SORT	59.6	64.9	68.3
Our BoT-SORT-ReID	**60.7**	**65.7**	**69.5**

Table 2. Results on DanceTrack-test with the private detections. Our BoT-SORT and the unmodified BoT-SORT share the same detectors

Tracker	HOTA↑	MOTA↑	IDF1↑
DeepSORT	40.2	73.6	41.3
ByteTrack	42.3	74.1	44.2
BoT-SORT	53.7	75.2	54.9
Our BoT-SORT	54.8	75.6	55.8
Our BoT-SORT-ReID	**56.3**	**77.3**	**56.7**

Table 3. Results on Visdrone2019-test with the private detections. Our BoT-SORT and the unmodified BoT-SORT share the same detectors

Tracker	HOTA↑	MOTA↑	IDF1↑
DeepSORT	39.7	38.9	52.3
ByteTrack	40.4	39.5	53.8
BoT-SORT	41.8	40.9	54.1
Our BoT-SORT	42.3	40.7	54.6
Our BoT-SORT-ReID	**43.1**	**41.4**	**55.9**

4.4 Computational Cost Analysis

While the improved methods proposed in this paper achieve significant tracking performance improvements on multiple benchmark datasets, we also conducted preliminary experimental evaluation and analysis of their computational complexity. Specifically, HMIOU only introduces a height calculation module, and the OCR and ORU mechanisms are only activated when a track is lost. Therefore, the additional computational burden imposed by these improvements is negligible. However, ablation experiments revealed that the module for calculating the four-corner velocity information introduces a relatively high computational overhead, resulting in a frame rate reduction of approximately 2 frames per second compared to the unmodified BoT-SORT. We then tested the frame rates of all algorithms before and after improvements on the NVIDIA RTX 3050 platform. The original BoT-SORT had an average frame rate of 12.5 frames per second, and the improved version had an average frame rate of 10.4 frames per second.

Fig. 7. Visualization of tracking after the vehicle is occluded.

5 Conclusion and Future Work

Our improved BoT-SORT tracking algorithm effectively reduces ID switching and false detection by fusing the target's height information and speed information, and improves the robustness of multi-target tracking. Experimental results show that both pedestrian tracking and target tracking from the perspective of drones have superior performance over traditional BoT-SORT. However, it is worth noting that in some scenarios, our tracking algorithm still has abnormal ID switching and false detection, as shown in Fig. 7. In the picture above, the ID number of the red vehicle was 13 before being blocked, and became 30 after being blocked; in the picture below, the ID number of the white vehicle was 36 before being blocked, and became 70 after being blocked. Next, we plan to make changes to the detection model and try to fuse the target's infrared information and visible light information to further improve the accuracy of detection and achieve accurate tracking of multiple targets.

Acknowledgments. This work was supported by the Aviation Science Foundation of China (Grant No. 2024Z071077007).

Disclosure of Interests The authors have no competing interests to declare that are relevant to the content of this article.

References

1. Redmon, J., Divvala, S., Girshick, R., et al.: You only look once: unified, real-time object detection. In: Proceedings of the IEEE Conference on Computer Vision and Pattern Recognition, pp. 779–788 (2016)
2. Aharon, N., Orfaig, R., Bobrovsky, B.Z.: BoT-SORT: Robust associations multi-pedestrian tracking. arXiv preprint https://arxiv.org/abs/2206.14651 (2022).
3. Cao, J., Pang, J., Weng, X., et al.: Observation-centric sort: rethinking sort for robust multi-object tracking. In: Proceedings of the IEEE/CVF Conference on Computer Vision and Pattern Recognition, pp. 9686–9696 (2023)
4. Luo, X., Wu, Y., Zhao, L.: YOLOD: a target detection method for UAV aerial imagery. Remote Sens. **14**(14), 3240 (2022)
5. Chen, Y.H.: Strong baseline: multi-UAV tracking via YOLOv12 with BoT-SORT-ReID. In: Proceedings of the Computer Vision and Pattern Recognition Conference, pp. 6573–6582 (2025)
6. Wojke, N., Bewley, A., Paulus, D.: Simple online and realtime tracking with a deep association metric. In: 2017 IEEE International Conference on Image Processing (ICIP), pp. 3645–3649. IEEE (2017)
7. Zhao, J., Chen, J.: Yolov8 detection and improved bot-sort tracking algorithm for iron ladles. In: Proceedings of the 2024 7th International Conference on Image and Graphics Processing, pp. 409–415 (2024)
8. Tian, Y., Ye, Q, Doermann, D.: Yolov12: Attention-centric real-time object detectors. arXiv preprint https://arxiv.org/abs/2502.12524 (2025)
9. Khanam, R., Hussain, M.: Yolov11: An overview of the key architectural enhancements. arXiv preprint https://arxiv.org/abs/2410.17725 (2024).
10. Bewley, A., Ge, Z., Ott, L., et al.: Simple online and realtime tracking. In: 2016 IEEE International Conference on Image Processing (ICIP), pp. 3464–3468. IEEE (2016)
11. Pereira, R., Carvalho, G., Garrote, L., et al.: Sort and deep-sort based multi-object tracking for mobile robotics: evaluation with new data association metrics. Appl. Sci. **12**(3), 1319 (2022)
12. Zhang, Y., Sun, P., Jiang, Y., et al.: Bytetrack: multi-object tracking by associating every detection box. In: European Conference on Computer Vision, pp. 1–21. Springer Nature Switzerland, Cham (2022)
13. Bradski, G.: The opencv library. Dr. Dobb's J. Softw. Tools Prof. Programmer. **25**(11), 120–123 (2000)
14. Yang, M., Han, G., Yan, B., et al.: Hybrid-sort: weak cues matter for online multi-object tracking. Proceedings of the AAAI conference on artificial intelligence. **38**(7), 6504–6512 (2024)
15. Maggiolino, G., Ahmad, A., Cao, J., et al.: Deep oc-sort: multi-pedestrian tracking by adaptive re-identification. In: 2023 IEEE International Conference on Image Processing (ICIP), pp. 3025–3029. IEEE (2023)
16. Dendorfer, P., Rezatofighi, H., Milan, A., et al.: Mot20: A benchmark for multi object tracking in crowded scenes. arXiv preprint https://arxiv.org/abs/2003.09003 (2020).
17. Sun, P., Cao, J., Jiang, Y., et al.: Dancetrack: multi-object tracking in uniform appearance and diverse motion. In: Proceedings of the IEEE/CVF Conference on Computer Vision and Pattern Recognition, pp. 20993–21002 (2022)
18. Du, D., Zhu, P., Wen, L., et al.: VisDrone-DET2019: the vision meets drone object detection in image challenge results. In: Proceedings of the IEEE/CVF International Conference on Computer Vision Workshops, 0-0 (2019).
19. Zhou, K., Yang, Y., Cavallaro, A., et al.: Omni-scale feature learning for person re-identification. In: Proceedings of the IEEE/CVF International Conference on Computer Vision, pp. 3702–3712 (2019)

Robot Mechanism & Control

Bioinspired Design and Analysis of a Spherical Parallel Mechanism

Zhouyi Ren[1,2,3], Kaijie Dong[1,2,3](✉), Ziqi Li[1,3], Xiang Huai[1,3], Jingyao Li[1,3], and Duanling Li[4,5]

[1] School of Mechanical Engineering, University of Science and Technology Beijing, Beijing 100083, China
dongkaijie@ustb.edu.cn

[2] National KeyLaboratory of Aerospace Mechanism, Shanghai 201108, China

[3] Innovation School, University of Science and Technology Beijing, Foshan 528300, China

[4] School of Automation, Beijing University of Posts and Telecommunications, Beijing 100086, China

[5] College of Mechanical and Electrical Engineering, Shaanxi University of Science and Technology, Xi'an 710021, China

Abstract. With the rapid development of bionic robotics technology, spherical parallel mechanisms have attracted significant attention due to their structural compactness and kinematic decoupling. However, conventional mechanisms face the bottleneck of balancing high load-bearing capacity with precision, which urgently requires configurational innovations to enhance comprehensive performance. This paper proposes a novel coaxial-input 3-RRR/S spherical parallel mechanism to address the limited workspace and insufficient load stiffness of existing configurations through structural optimization. Firstly, based on shoulder-joint biomimetic principles, a redundant configuration was constructed using spherical hinge constraint branches and spatial compactness was improved through coaxial shaft design. Secondly, the Jacobian matrix of the 3-RRR/S mechanism was derived through static analysis, with mechanical performance comparisons between coaxial-input 3-RRR and 3-RRR/S configurations conducted via finite element simulations. Finally, rigid-flexible coupled dynamic simulations validated motion accuracy improvements by comparing simulation results of both configurations. Experimental results demonstrate that the 3-RRR/S mechanism exhibits superior stress distribution characteristics and deformation resistance under load conditions, along with significant reduction in motion errors. This study provides a novel approach for resolving the dynamic stiffness-accuracy contradiction in spherical parallel mechanisms, offering valuable references for bionic joint development.

Keywords: Coaxial Input · Redundant Branch · Kinematic Analysis Model

1 Introduction

The rapid advancement of bionic robotics is revolutionizing medical rehabilitation and elderly care systems, necessitating bionic joints with superior dynamic performance and high spatial integration [1, 2]. Drawing biological inspiration from the human shoulder

Z. Hou et al. (Eds.): CIRAC 2025, CCIS 2885, pp. 33–42, 2026.
https://doi.org/10.1007/978-981-92-0045-0_3

joint—where the ball-and-socket structure and ligament constraint system enable large-range motions within a confined space [3]—current bionic joint designs face inherent trade-offs. Serial architectures achieve biomimetic motion ranges but suffer from inadequate stiffness and spatial redundancy, while tendon-driven designs improve flexibility via antagonistic actuation principles yet grapple with control stability limitations [4–6]. By contrast, spherical parallel mechanisms (SPMs) inherently achieve motion decoupling, precision, and structural compactness through concurrent kinematic-pair axes, positioning them as promising candidates for high-performance joints. However, balancing high load-bearing capacity with motion accuracy remains a critical challenge.

As a typical three-degree-of-freedom spatial mechanism, the spherical parallel mechanism realizes the pure rotational output of the moving platform around a fixed point through a closed-loop kinematic chain with an annular distribution. Since GOSSELIN [7] proposed the classic 3-RRR configuration and successfully applied it to the bionic eye drive system, many researchers have been engaged in the research of spherical parallel mechanisms. WU and others [8] designed an asymmetric three-link mechanism that achieved infinite torsional decoupling motion through the central axis. The 3-RRRRR metamorphic mechanism developed by KONG et al. [9] achieved the switching of different configurations through the kinematic pair locking strategy. HUANG et al. [10] adopted a 3-PRS configuration with crossed roller bearings to increase the rotational stiffness by 27%. GUO et al. [11] revealed the advantages of the 3-RRP configuration in singularity avoidance based on screw theory, and the condition number of its Jacobian matrix was reduced by 42% compared with the traditional 3-RRR. However, the existing spherical parallel mechanisms face the contradiction between high load-bearing capacity and high precision. Therefore, this paper proposes a 3-RRR/S spherical parallel mechanism with coaxial input, which further improves the performance of the spherical parallel mechanism by reducing the structural complexity and redundant link design through coaxial input, enabling the mechanism to have high structural compactness, high precision, and high load-bearing capacity at the same time.

This paper firstly presents the analysis of a coaxial-input 3-RRR spherical parallel mechanism. Secondly, inspired by the biomechanical principles of shoulder joints, a novel 3-RRR/S mechanism is proposed. Subsequently, the static characteristics of the 3-RRR/S spherical parallel mechanism are investigated through mechanical modeling. Finally, a comparative study on the positioning accuracy between the 3-RRR/S and conventional 3-RRR configurations is conducted based on rigid-flexible coupled dynamic simulations.

2 Design of 3-RRR/S Mechanism Based on Shoulder Joint

As shown in Fig. 1a, conventional spherical parallel mechanisms typically adopt a 3-RRR configuration, which can only provide limited rotational motion within a confined workspace. Notably, rotation about the Z-axis is severely restricted, while the kinematic performance is complicated by structural constraints. By concentrically aligning all three rotational input axes on a single shaft (Fig. 1b), this coaxial-input design enables unlimited Z-axis rotation of the moving platform relative to the base platform. This innovative configuration significantly enhances the mechanism's flexibility compared to conventional distributed-input designs. The coaxial arrangement of three drive shafts not only expands the operational workspace but also achieves higher integration density in the input system. Consequently, it requires less design space and better facilitates miniaturization and modular design. However, under heavy-load conditions, the inherent compliance of links in this configuration induces undesirable elastic deformations, ultimately degrading motion accuracy. This limitation prevents the mechanism from meeting high-precision requirements in demanding load-bearing applications.

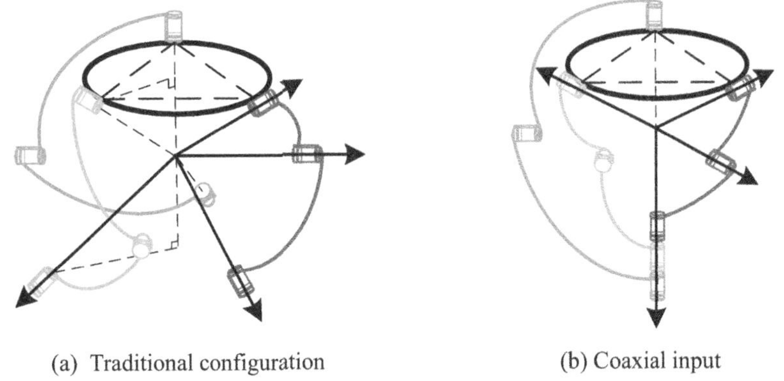

(a) Traditional configuration (b) Coaxial input

Fig. 1. Spherical parallel mechanism of 3-RRR

The human shoulder joint can likewise be conceptualized as a three-degree-of-freedom spherical kinematic pair. As shown in Fig. 2, this biological system features a hybrid constraint mechanism comprising the glenoid labrum, capsular ligaments, and shoulder blade. This sophisticated architecture achieves remarkable dynamic load-bearing capacity while preserving abduction range of motion.

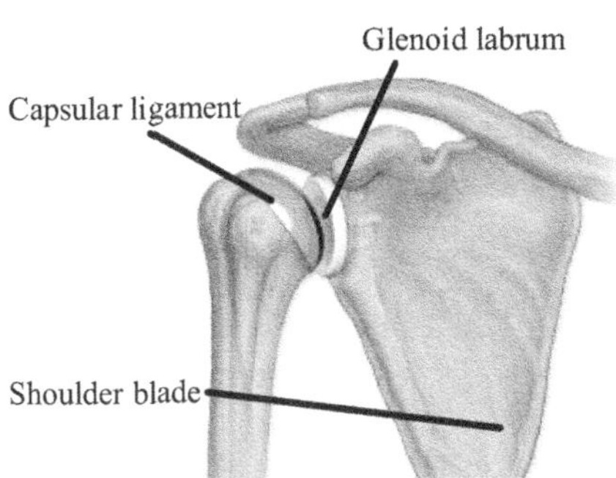

Fig. 2. Shoulder joint

Therefore, by introducing a fourth branch method to add a redundant structure, namely the 3-RRR/S coaxial input configuration, the load-bearing capacity of the structure can be improved to meet the high-precision requirements under high-load conditions, as shown in Fig. 3a. According to the theoretical prototype, it can be obtained that the spherical parallel mechanism with coaxial input consists of a moving platform capable of three-degree-of-freedom rotational motion and three equally spaced legs connected to the base, as shown in Fig. 3b and Fig. 3c. Each leg is composed of two curved connecting rods, namely the proximal connecting rod and the distal connecting rod. The angles and define the curvatures of these connecting rods, that is, the angles between the axes of the two rotational joints at both ends of the connecting rod. The axes of all motion joints intersect at a point, which is the rotational center of the mechanism. The axes of the base center joint (the first-level rotational joint), the connecting rod intermediate joint (the second-level rotational joint), and the rotating platform joint (the third-level rotational joint) intersect at the rotational center. And to not affect the degrees of freedom of the parallel mechanism, the spherical pair rotational center should also be located at the rotational center. The distal connecting rod is circular arc-shaped, and the proximal connecting rod is polygonal line-shaped, and they are connected by means of rotational joints. The ball hinge shaft adopts a segmented structure to ensure its structural strength. The transmission part adopts a gear transmission scheme, and through the sleeve shaft design method, the three gear shafts and a ball hinge shaft are sleeved layer by layer, making the overall structure have high stiffness and stability.

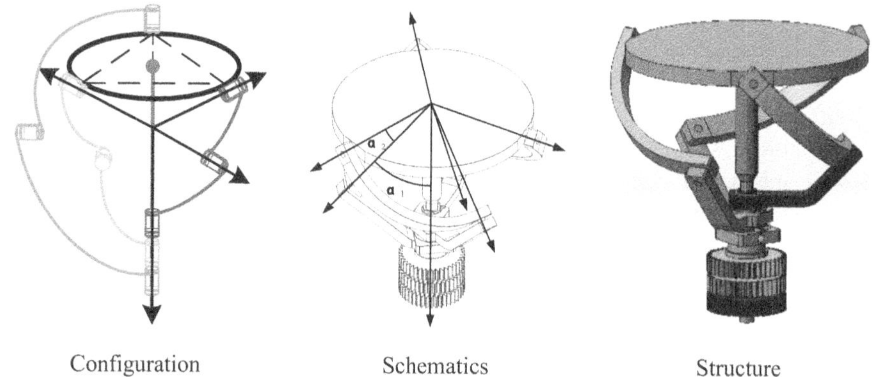

Configuration Schematics Structure

Fig. 3. Spherical parallel mechanism with 3-RRR/S coaxial input

3 Static Analysis of 3-RRR/S

3.1 Theoretical Analysis

The inverse kinematics model is established based on the coordinate system. The central joint of the base (the first-stage rotating joint), the intermediate joint of the connecting rod (the second-stage rotating joint), the rotating platform joint (the third-stage rotating joint), and the axes of the spherical axis intersect the rotating center and are represented by the unit vectors $\mathbf{u}_i$, $\mathbf{w}_i$, $\mathbf{v}_i$ and $\mathbf{z}$ respectively ($i = 1,2,3$) (In this article, "i" refers to the three side chains of the three rotating joints in the order from bottom to top), as shown in Fig. 4.

During the motion, all the proximal connecting rods always rotate around the same axis, which is the unit vector pointing from the rotating center to the base point. Therefore, $\mathbf{u}_1 = \mathbf{u}_2 = \mathbf{u}_3 = \mathbf{z} = [0, 0, -1]^T$. In the initial pose state, the rotating platform remains horizontal, and the three proximal connecting rods are evenly distributed around the central axis. Let the input rotating angle on the central gear shaft be equal to $\boldsymbol{\theta} = [\theta_1, \theta_2, \theta_3]^T$, and the counterclockwise direction be the positive rotating direction. In the initial pose state, the input rotating angles are all 0. When the mechanism starts to move, the central gear shaft first drives the proximal connecting rod to rotate around the **Z**-axis. When it rotates counterclockwise by θ_i, the vector $\mathbf{w}_i$ also changes accordingly:

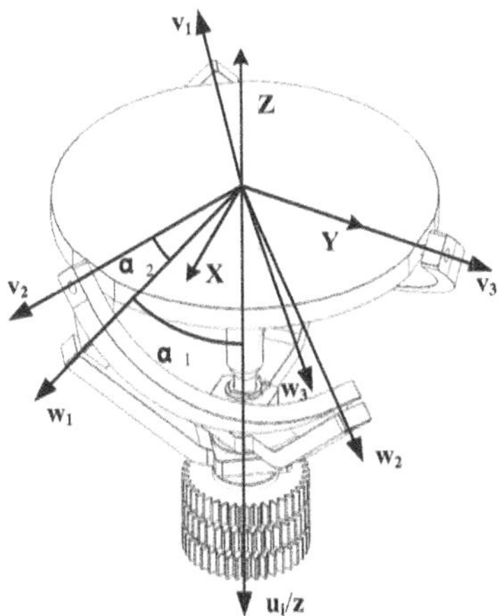

Fig. 4. Inverse kinematics model Settings

$$\mathbf{w}_i = \begin{bmatrix} \cos(\eta_i + \theta_i)\sin\alpha_1 \\ \sin(\eta_i + \theta_i)\sin\alpha_1 \\ -\cos\alpha_1 \end{bmatrix} \tag{1}$$

where, $\eta_i = 2*(i\text{-}1)*\pi/3$, $i = 1,2,3$, indicates that the three side chains are uniformly distributed around the Z-axis.

When the rotating platform is in the initial pose, let the Angle between the projection of $\mathbf{w}_i$ on the plane of the rotating platform and $\mathbf{v}_i$ be β (as shown in Fig. 5). The coordinates of the $\mathbf{v}_i$ vector at the initial moment can be obtained as:

$$\mathbf{v}_i^* = \begin{bmatrix} \cos(\beta + \eta_i) \\ \sin(\beta + \eta_i) \\ 0 \end{bmatrix} \tag{2}$$

In the 3-RRR/S parallel mechanism, the rotating platform can only perform three-degree-of-freedom rotating motion around the rotating center. Its position can be described by the pose Angle: $\boldsymbol{\varphi} = (\varphi_1, \varphi_2, \varphi_3)$. Where, φ_1, φ_2 and φ_3 respectively represent the angles at which the rotating platform rotates around the ***X***-axis, ***Y***-axis,

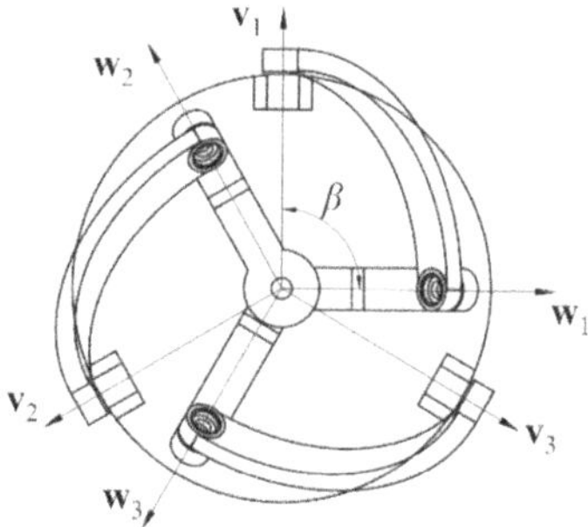

Fig. 5. Top view of the mechanism

and **Z**-axis. At this point, the coordinates of $\mathbf{v}_i$ in the fixed coordinate system are:

$$\mathbf{v}_i = \mathbf{R}_Z(\varphi_3)\mathbf{R}_Y(\varphi_2)\mathbf{R}_X(\varphi_1)\begin{bmatrix} \cos(\delta + \eta_i) \\ \sin(\delta + \eta_i) \\ 0 \end{bmatrix} \tag{3}$$

where, $\mathbf{R}_\mathrm{Z}$, $\mathbf{R}_\mathrm{Y}$ and $\mathbf{R}_\mathrm{X}$ represent the coordinate transformation matrices around the *Z*-axis, *Y*-axis and *X*-axis respectively.

The Angle between $\mathbf{w}_\mathrm{i}$ and $\mathbf{v}_\mathrm{i}$ is α_2, so the constraint equation is:

$$\mathbf{w}_i \cdot \mathbf{v}_i = \cos\alpha_2 \tag{4}$$

Combined Eq. (1), (3) and (4) can be simplified to obtain the inverse kinematics equation:

$$A_i T_i^2 + B_i T_i + C_i = 0 \tag{5}$$

where:

$$T_i = \tan\left(\frac{\theta_i}{2}\right) \tag{6}$$

$$\begin{aligned} A_i &= \left(\sin\eta_i \sin\alpha_1 \mathbf{v}_{ix} - \cos\eta_i \sin\alpha_1 \mathbf{v}_{iy} - \cos\alpha_1 \mathbf{v}_{iz} - \cos\alpha_2\right) \\ B_i &= \left(-2\cos\eta_i \sin\alpha_1 \mathbf{v}_{ix} - 2\sin\eta_i \sin\alpha_1 \mathbf{v}_{iy}\right) \\ C_i &= \left(\cos\eta_i \sin\alpha_1 \mathbf{v}_{iy} - \sin\eta_i \sin\alpha_1 \mathbf{v}_{ix} - \cos\alpha_1 \mathbf{v}_{iz} - \cos\alpha_2\right) \end{aligned} \tag{7}$$

The Jacobi matrix can be obtained by differentiating Eq. (4):

$$\mathbf{J}_i = \frac{\mathbf{w}_i \times \mathbf{v}_i}{(\mathbf{u}_i \times \mathbf{w}_i) \cdot \mathbf{v}_i} \tag{8}$$

3.2 Finite Element Analysis

As a high-precision spatial positioning mechanism, the motion accuracy of spherical parallel mechanism is very important for practical application. However, the ex ternal load will lead to the elastic deformation of the connecting rod, which will affect the overall accuracy of the mechanism. Therefore, in this study, the static analysis of 3-RRR / S and 3-RRR spherical parallel mechanisms is carried out. By establishing an accurate mechanical model, the stress and strain distribution of the connecting rod under load-bearing state is mainly studied, and the influence of spherical hinge constraint on the mechanical properties of the mechanism is discussed.

Based on WORKBENCH software, the finite element analysis of the two configurations is carried out. The material of the rod and the moving platform is aluminum alloy 2A12, and the material of the gear shaft is stainless steel. The vertical downward load of 1000 N is applied to the moving platform, and the stress and strain distribution

cloud diagram is obtained (as shown in Fig. 6). The analysis results show that the maximum strain of the 3-RRR mechanism is 0.008 m / m, the maximum stress is 447.5 MPa, and the stress concentration area is located near the corner hole. In contrast, the maximum strain of the 3-RRR / S mechanism is 0.0006 m / m, and the maximum stress is 34.5 MPa. It can be seen that after the introduction of the ball hinge constraint, the stress and strain level of the mechanism is reduced by an order of magnitude, and the bearing performance of the mechanism is significantly improved.

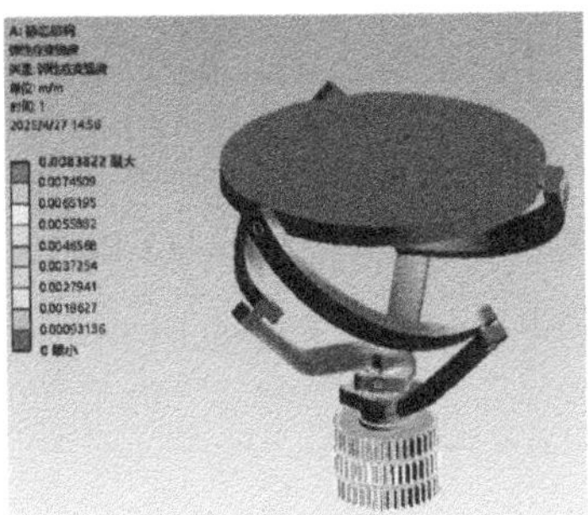

(a) Strain cloud diagram of 3-RRR

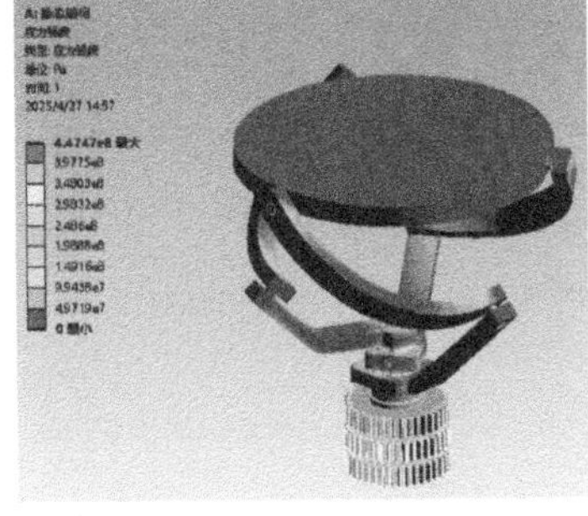

(b) The stress cloud diagram of 3-RRR

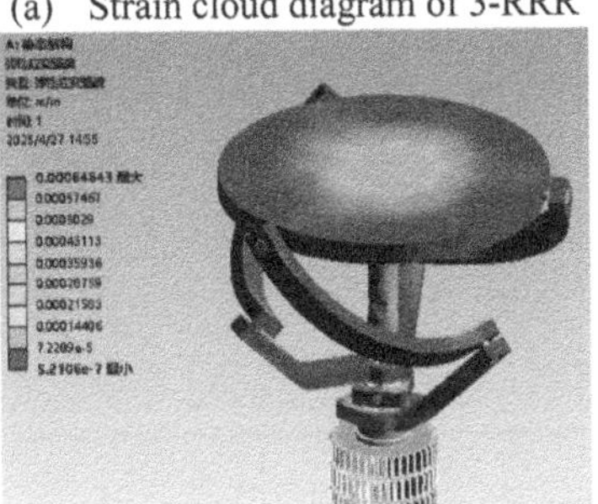

(c) Strain cloud diagram of 3-RRR/S

(d) The stress cloud diagram of 3-RRR/S

Fig. 6. finite element analysis results

4 Rigid-Flexible Coupling Dynamics Simulation Analysis

Under the bearing state of the spherical parallel mechanism with coaxial output, the stiffness of the rod will affect the motion accuracy of the end of the mechanism. Therefore, the rigid-flexible coupling dynamics simulation of the 3-RRR mechanism and the 3-RRR / S mechanism is carried out, and the simulation results are compared to verify the effectiveness of the spherical hinge to improve the performance of the mechanism.

Based on Adams and Ansys, 3-RRR rigid model, 3-RRR rigid-flexible coupling model and 3-RRR / S rigid-flexible coupling model are established, and 1000 N vertical downward force is added to the moving platform, as shown in Fig. 7. By applying a drive to the moving platform of the 3-RRR rigid model, the motion parameters of the three gear shafts are obtained, as shown in Fig. 8.

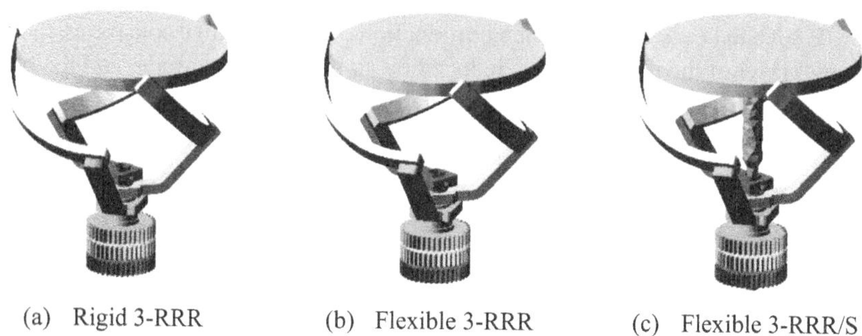

(a) Rigid 3-RRR (b) Flexible 3-RRR (c) Flexible 3-RRR/S

Fig. 7. Rigid and rigid-flexible coupling model of 3-RRR and 3-RRR / S parallel mechanism

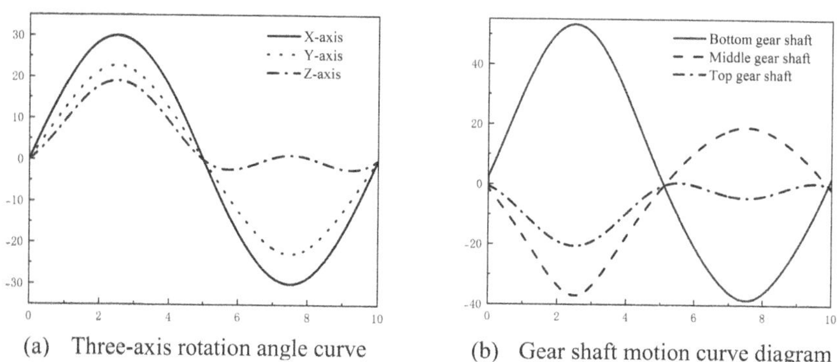

(a) Three-axis rotation angle curve (b) Gear shaft motion curve diagram

Fig. 8. 3-RRR rigid model moving platform and gear shaft motion curve

The obtained three gear shaft motion parameters are substituted into the other two models, and finally the motion comparison curves of the moving platform in the three models are obtained, as shown in Fig. 9. It can be seen that the maximum absolute error of the 3-RRR mechanism is 3.74°, while the maximum absolute error of the 3-RRR/S mechanism is 0.56 °, which is much lower than the error of the 3-RRR mechanism. Therefore, it can be proved that the spherical hinge can significantly improve the motion accuracy of the spherical parallel mechanism.

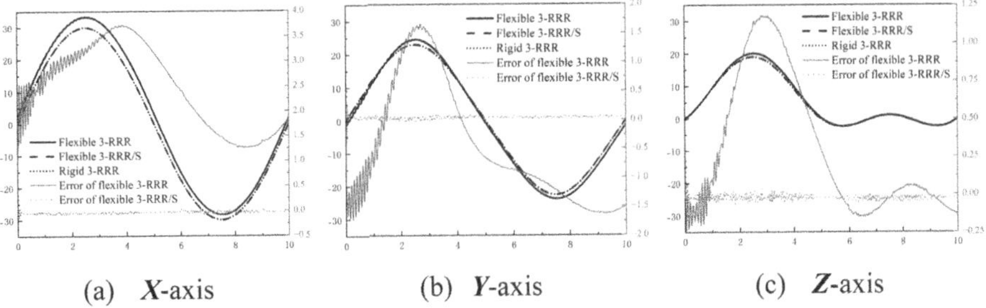

(a) *X*-axis (b) *Y*-axis (c) *Z*-axis

Fig. 9. The three mechanisms and the error diagram of the flexible mechanism

5 Conclusions

(1) Inspired by the human shoulder joint's biomechanics, the 3-RRR/S mechanismachieves infinite Z-axis rotation via coaxial input and reduces space occupancy with a sleeve-type design, mirroring the shoulder's compact ligament-bone system for modular bionic joint miniaturization.

(2) The introduction of redundant limb (spherical hinge constraint) significantly improves the structural stiffness. The static simulation shows that the stress and strain of the 3-RRR / S mechanism are 92.3% (447.5 MPa → 34.5 MPa) and 92.5% (0.008 m/m → 0.0006 m/m) lower than those of the 3-RRR parallel mechanism with coaxial input under the load of 1000 N, which effectively solves the problem of elastic deformation under high load conditions.

(3) The rigid-flexible coupling dynamics simulation results show that the maximum absolute error of the moving platform of the 3-RRR / S mechanism is 0.567 °, which is 84.8% lower than that of the 3-RRR mechanism (3.74 °) with coaxial input. The ball hinge constraint suppresses the influence of the flexible deformation of the branch on the end accuracy by optimizing the load distribution path.

Funding. The Joint Funds of the National Natural Science Foundation of China (No. U23A20338), the National Natural Science Foundation of China (Nos. 52175019 and 52405007), the Natural Science Foundations of Beijing (Nos. 3212009 and L222038), the Guangdong Basic and Applied Basic Research Foundation (No. 2023A1515110150), the Space Drive and Manipulation Mechanism Laboratory of BICE (No. SDMM-2024-04), and the Open Project of National Key Laboratory of Aerospace Mechanism (2024ASM-KFZY02)

References

1. He, Z., Iyo, Y., Saito, S., et al.: Development of a cable-driven bionic spherical joint for a robot wrist. Biomimetics. **10**, 52 (2025)

2. Gao, Z., Qing, S., Toshio, F., et al.: An overview of biomimetic robots with animal behaviors. Neurocomputing. **332**, 339–350 (2019)
3. Yang, H, Wei, G, Ren, L:. Development and Characteristics of a Highly Biomimetic Robotic Shoulder Through Bionics-Inspired Optimization. arxiv preprint arxiv (2023). 2310. 18283.
4. Shah, M.F., Hussain, S., Goecke, R., et al.: Mechanism design and control of shoulder rehabilitation robots: a review. IEEE Trans. Med. Robot. Bionics. **5**(4), 780–792 (2023)
5. Hou, Y., Hu, X., Zeng, D., et al.: Biomimetic shoulder complex based on 3-PSS/S spherical parallel mechanism. Chin. J. Mech. Eng. **28**(1), 29–37 (2015)
6. taunyazov, T., Rubagotti, M., Shintemirov, A.: Constrained orientation control of a spherical parallel manipulator via online convex optimization. IEEE/ASME Trans. Mechatron. **23**(1), 252–261 (2018)
7. Li, X., Qu, H., Li, G., et al.: Optimal design of a kinematically redundant planar parallel mechanism based on error sensitivity and workspace. J. Mech. Des. **145**(2), 023305 (2025)
8. Wu, G., Caro, S., Bai, S., et al.: Dynamic modeling and design optimization of a 3-DOF spherical parallel manipulator. Robot. Auton. Syst. **62**(10), 1377–1386 (2014)
9. Shen, H., Zhao, Y., Li, J., et al.: A novel partially-decoupled translational parallel manipulator with symbolic kinematics, singularity identification and workspace determination. Mech. Mach. Theory. **164**, 104388 (2021)
10. Dong, Z., Jiang, F., Tan, Y., et al.: Review of the modeling methods of bucket tooth wear for construction machinery. Lubricants. **11**(6), 253 (2023)
11. Guo, D, Xu, J, Zhang, S, et al.: Data-driven mode shape selection and model-based vibration suppression of 3-rrr parallel manipulator with flexible actuation links. arxiv preprint arxiv. 2310. 06542 (2023).
12. Han, B., Jiang, Y., Yang, W., et al.: Kinematics characteristics analysis of a 3-UPS/S parallel airborne stabilized platform. Aerosp. Sci. Technol. **134**, 108163 (2023)

Design and Flexibility Analysis of Puncture Guide Mechanism Based on Flexible Hinge

Hongyu Ma, Duanling Li(✉), Junwei Zhang, Jiahui Cai, and Junfeng Huang

Beijing University of Posts and Telecommunications, 10 Xi Tu Cheng Road, Haidian District, Beijing 100876, China
lduanling_bupt@163.com

Abstract. In order to meet the needs of high precision and high stability of puncture robot in modern neuromedicine, a puncture guide mechanism based on flexible hinge is proposed. The flexible mechanism is based on a hybrid flexible hinge unit composed of hyperbola and parabola, and then a three-layer flexible hinge composed of the hybrid flexible hinge unit constructs a unilateral flexible structure, and then symmetrically arranged to form a bilateral flexible guiding mechanism. In order to ensure the flexibility and accuracy of the puncture guide mechanism and reduce the risk of injury when contacting with human tissues, the flexibility model of hybrid flexible hinge unit is obtained by superposition principle, and the flexibility matrix of parallel flexible hinges on both sides is established according to the flexibility matrix of one side of each layer, and the flexibility model of parallel mechanism is obtained. According to the flexibility value of functional direction, the parameters are optimized and determined by MATLAB software. Finally, the flexibility value of the guiding mechanism in the functional direction is analyzed and verified by Ansys software. The analysis results show that it is basically consistent with the theoretical flexibility model, which ensures the accuracy of the three-dimensional model and theoretical model of the guiding mechanism. Therefore, this guidance mechanism can provide theoretical basis and design basis for the research on auxiliary guidance in the field of medical integration.

Keywords: Puncture Guidance · Flexible Mechanism · Flexibility Model · Flexibility Analysis

1 Introduction

With the development and integration of modern medical technology and robot technology, the puncture robot is an important medical equipment for nerve rehabilitation, in which the accuracy of the guiding mechanism for assisting puncture into the tissue is increasingly demanding. In order to accurately guide electrodes or other medical equipment into the human body, such as skin and brain tissue, to perform tasks such as treatment, diagnosis or recording EEG signals, a guiding mechanism is needed to assist in guiding the puncture needle into the human body. Usually, a metal catheter is used for guiding the puncture needle, but when the puncture site is located in the head, it

Z. Hou et al. (Eds.): CIRAC 2025, CCIS 2885, pp. 43–56, 2026.
https://doi.org/10.1007/978-981-92-0045-0_4

requires high puncture accuracy and stability. Because the experiments of human tissue puncture at home and abroad tend to focus on the trunk and limbs below the head, the precision requirements of the guiding mechanism are lower than those of brain tissue puncture, and the common catheter mechanism forms can not meet the requirements of high precision and high stability.

Therefore, this paper proposes to use flexible mechanism for auxiliary guidance. Among them, flexible hinge, as the core component of puncture guide mechanism, is a new type of motion mechanism, which has the advantages of no gap, no friction and high precision, and is widely used in occasions where precise positioning is needed.[7] Since the 1960s, flexible hinges have been designed and applied, and a variety of flexible mechanisms have been derived.[8] According to the different shapes of flexible hinge notches, a variety of flexible hinges with different shapes of notches are proposed, such as Wei Huaxian.[9] The flexible hinge with elliptical cross section is designed, and the flexible model is established according to the bending theory to realize the analysis of flexibility and stress concentration characteristics. Zhang Zhijie et al[10] hyperbolic flexible hinge based on closed-loop flexibility analytical formula is designed, and the rotation ability and accuracy of hyperbolic flexible hinge are verified. Jiao Chenlei and others,[11]the stiffness model of parabolic flexible hinge and WEI H[12] are established and analyzed a flexible hinge with circular notch is proposed.[13] According to whether it is symmetrical about the sensitive axis, a symmetrical shape is proposed. And asymmetric hybrid flexible hinge.[14] And according to the connection mode, flexible mechanisms can be divided into series flexible mechanisms.[15]And parallel flexible mechanism.[16] Most of the application scenarios of these flexible hinges and flexible mechanisms are used in industrial micromanipulation field, and there is a lack of research on auxiliary guidance in medical field, and the accuracy and stability of general research results can not meet the needs of this application scenario, such as Muhammad.[17] A kind of guide mechanism composed of inclined rods is developed, but because of its structural limitation, it can not meet the high-precision application scene. In order to meet the requirements of high precision and high stability in auxiliary guidance of human tissue puncture, this paper proposes a flexible mechanism as a guiding mechanism, which is based on three-layer flexible hinges to construct a unilateral flexible structure, and then symmetrically arranged to form a bilateral flexible guiding mechanism. Because its design and flexibility analysis are very important to ensure the safety and accuracy of the puncture process, stiffness analysis is needed after the design of the flexible hinge to ensure the flexibility and accuracy of the puncture guide mechanism and reduce the risk of injury when it comes into contact with human tissues.

In this paper, firstly, we will focus on the research of human tissue puncture guidance, put forward a puncture guidance mechanism based on flexible hinge, and explain the principle of the guidance mechanism

and the structural design of the flexible parallel system. Secondly, aiming at the flexible hinge design of the guidance mechanism in this paper, we will establish the flexible hinge unit and the flexibility model of the variable cross-section beam, and construct the flexibility model of the flexible mechanism. Finally, the parameters are determined and analyzed and verified by MATLAB and Ansys software.

2 Systematic Analysis of Guiding Mechanism

2.1 Principle of Puncture Guidance

The working content of the puncture guide mechanism is to guide the implantation device with puncture electrode to be inserted into the tissue accurately, and its working principle is shown in Fig. 1. As the main body of the puncture electrode, the electrode needle is fixed at the end of the implant device. With the advancement of the implantation device in the puncture direction, under the guidance of the puncture guide mechanism composed of flexible hinges, the electrode needle passes through each layer of flexible hinges of the guide mechanism in turn until the electrode needle is implanted into the tissue target area.

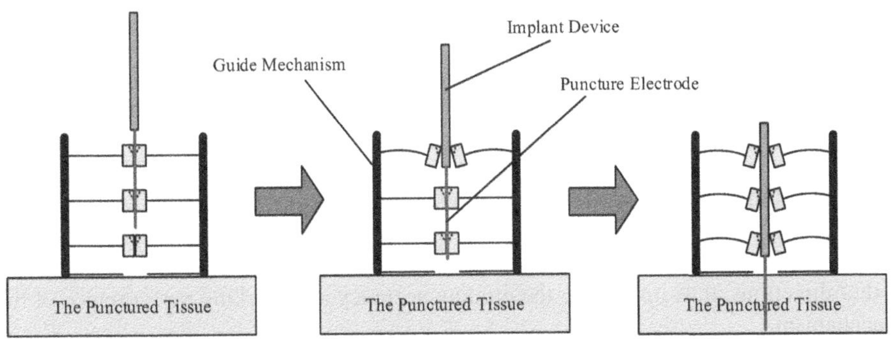

Fig. 1. Working principle of guide mechanism.

In the process of puncture, it is necessary to ensure that the flexibility of the guide mechanism is high enough in the puncture direction to ensure that the strength of the implant device will not be destroyed when it passes through each flexible hinge, and to meet the requirement of nano-level positioning accuracy during electrode puncture and to adapt to the small cross-section and flexibility of the electrode needle inserted into the tissue, so the guide mechanism needs to maintain high accuracy and flexibility in the functional direction.

2.2 Structure Design of Flexible Parallel Mechanism

In this paper, a guide mechanism composed of a hybrid flexible hinge is proposed. Its basic unit is composed of a parabolic flexible hinge, a straight beam and a hyperbolic flexible hinge in series. As shown in Fig. 2, the structural parameters of the hybrid flexible hinge are the maximum thickness d_1, the minimum thickness d_2, the width k, the length l of the straight beam and the total length L of the hybrid flexible hinge respectively. The projection lengths of the parabola and the hyperbola in the x direction are l_{pa} and l_{h} respectively, and there is the following relationship: $L = 2l_{\mathrm{pa}} = 2l_{\mathrm{h}}$.

The flexible parallel mechanism is composed of two flexible hinges connected in parallel, as shown in Fig. 3, in which the electrode of the implant device passes through

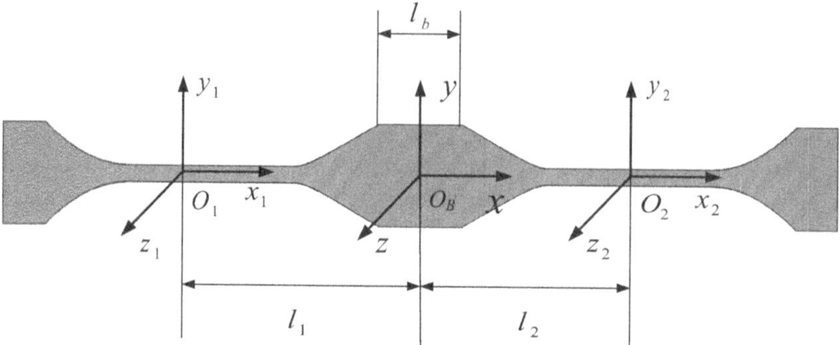

Fig. 2. Hybrid flexible hinge.

the electrode guide hole of the guide mechanism for tissue puncture, and the fixing groove is used to fix the guide device on the puncture robot. One-sided flexible hinges are arranged by flexible hinge unit arrays, which not only ensures the movement accuracy and flexibility in functional direction, but also ensures that the flexible mechanism can quickly recover its original structure after the electrode needle passes through each layer of flexible hinges, that is, it increases the restoring force of the structure. Moreover, the parallel structure of flexible hinges on both sides can ensure that the flexible structure has a high degree of freedom only in the movement direction, which limits the movement in other directions, thus improving the guiding accuracy and working performance of the mechanism.

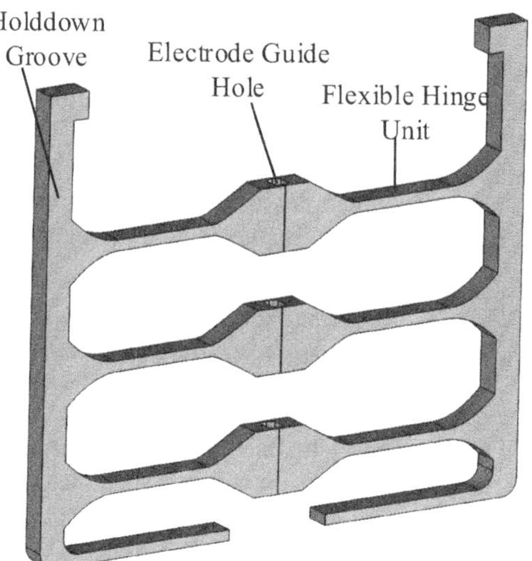

Fig. 3. Model of Flexible Parallel System.

3 Flexible Hinge Design of Guiding Mechanism

3.1 Flexible Element Model Principle

The flexible mechanism is composed of flexible elements as basic units, and any flexible element is actually a flexible beam, so a general mechanical model of the flexible beam can be established based on the assumption of small elastic deformation.[18] As shown in Fig. 4, taking a homogeneous cantilever beam as an example, a local coordinate system $O_P X_P Y_P Z_P$ is established at the end **P** of the flexible beam, and a global coordinate system *OXYZ* is established at the fixed end O. Assuming that the cantilever beam is deformed within the elastic limit of linear elastic materials, the linear relationship between the generalized spatial force $\boldsymbol{F_P} = [F_x, F_y, F_z, M_x, M_y, M_z]^T$ acting at point p and the deformation vector $\boldsymbol{T_P} = [u_x, u_y, u_z, \theta_x, \theta_y, \theta_z]^T$ at the reference point can be expressed by the flexibility matrix $\boldsymbol{C_P}$:

$$\mathbf{T_P} = \mathbf{C_P F_P} \tag{1}$$

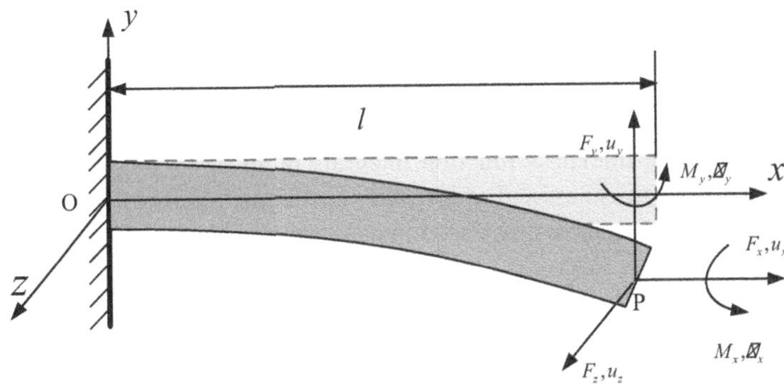

Fig. 4. Load and Deformation at the End of Flexible Hinge.

According to Castigliano's second theorem and the strain equation of material mechanics under tension, compression, torsion and bending,[19] the relationship between the deformation $\boldsymbol{T_P}$ at the end **P** of the flexible beam and the flexibility matrix $\boldsymbol{C_P}$ can be obtained, namely:

$$\mathbf{T_P} = \begin{bmatrix} \frac{F_z l}{EA} \\ \frac{F_y l^3}{3EI_x} + \frac{M_z l^2}{2EI_z} \\ \frac{F_z l^3}{3EI_y} - \frac{M_y l^2}{2EI_y} \\ \frac{M_z l}{GJ} \\ \frac{M_y l}{EI_y} - \frac{F_z l^2}{2EI_y} \\ \frac{F_y l^2}{2EI_z} + \frac{M_z l}{EI_z} \end{bmatrix} = \begin{bmatrix} \frac{l}{EA} & 0 & 0 & 0 & 0 & 0 \\ 0 & \frac{l^3}{3EI_z} & 0 & 0 & 0 & -\frac{l^2}{2EI_z} \\ 0 & 0 & \frac{l^3}{3EI_y} & 0 & -\frac{l^2}{2EI_y} & 0 \\ 0 & 0 & 0 & \frac{l}{GJ} & 0 & 0 \\ 0 & 0 & -\frac{l^2}{2EI_y} & 0 & \frac{l}{EI_y} & 0 \\ 0 & \frac{l^2}{2EI_z} & 0 & 0 & 0 & \frac{l}{EI_z} \end{bmatrix} \bullet \begin{bmatrix} F_x \\ F_y \\ F_z \\ M_x \\ M_y \\ M_z \end{bmatrix} = \mathbf{C_P W_P} \tag{2}$$

In the formula,

I_x ——Moment of inertia of section in X direction;

I_y ——Moment of inertia of section in Y direction;

J ——Polar moment of inertia, $J = I_x + I_y$;

E ——Young's modulus of elasticity;

G——Shear modulus;

A ——Cross-sectional area of homogeneous flexible beam.

When the flexible beam is a variable cross-section beam, all non-zero elements in the flexibility matrix $\boldsymbol{C}_\mathbf{P}$ are as follows:

$$\begin{cases} C_{P,11} = \frac{I_1}{2kE} \\ C_{P,22} = \frac{3l_P{}^2 I_4 - 6l_P{}^2 I_5 + 3I_6}{2kE} + \frac{J_k I_1}{2kG} \\ C_{P,33} = \frac{6l_P{}^2 I_1 - 12 l_P I_2 + 6I_3}{kE} + \frac{J_k I_1}{2kG} \\ C_{P,44} = \frac{c(v)}{2kG}\left(\frac{3I_4}{2k} + 6\frac{I_1}{k^3}\right) \\ C_{P,55} = 6\frac{I_1}{k^3 E} \\ C_{P,66} = \frac{3I_4}{2kE} \\ C_{P,26} = -C_{P,26} = \frac{3l_P}{2Ek}(I_4 - I_5) \\ C_{P,35} = -C_{P,53} = \frac{6}{k^3 E}(I_2 - l_P I_1) \end{cases} \tag{3}$$

In the formula,

J_K —— Shear coefficient of rectangular section.

Since I_1 to I_6 are thickness function integrals in all directions of variable cross-section, the minimum thickness and width ratio v are defined, and the formula of accuracy compensation $c(v)$ for variable cross-section can be established as follows:

$$\begin{cases} J_K = \frac{12+11\mu}{10(1+\mu)} \\ v = \frac{h_0}{k} \\ c(v) = \frac{7(v^2+2.609v+1)}{24(1.17v^2+2.191v+1.17)} \end{cases} \tag{4}$$

Combining eqs. (1) to (4), the flexibility matrix $\boldsymbol{C}_\mathbf{P}$ of flexible beam with variable cross-section can be obtained.

3.2 Flexibility Model of Parallel Mechanism

In order to establish an accurate flexibility model of the guide mechanism, the flexible hinge unit in this paper is composed of different thickness functions in series, and a flexibility matrix corresponding to different function models is needed.[20] As can be seen from fig. 5, the thickness function $d(x)$ of this flexible hinge can be expressed as:

$$\begin{cases} d_{pa}(x) = d_2 + \frac{4(x-0.5l)^2(d_1-d_2)}{l^2} & 0 \le x \le l_{pa} \\ d_s(x) = d_2 & l_{pa} \le x \le l + l_{pa} \\ d_h(x) = \left[\frac{d_2^2\left(1+4(x-1.5l)^2(d_1^2-d_2^2)\right)}{d_2^2 l^2}\right]^{1/2} & l + l_{pa} \le x \le L \end{cases} \tag{5}$$

In the formula,
h —— Hyperbolic thickness function type;
s —— Type of linear thickness function;
pa—— Parabolic thickness function type.
Therefore, the variables of hyperbolic thickness function in this flexible hinge element in the flexibility matrix can be obtained:

$$\begin{cases} I_{h,1} = \frac{\alpha l_h \ln(\sec\beta_m + \tan\beta_m)}{(1+2\alpha)^{\frac{1}{2}} h_h} \\ I_{h,2} = \frac{\alpha^2 l_h^2 (\sec\beta_m - 1)}{1+2\alpha} \\ I_{h,3} = \frac{\alpha^3 l_h^3 (\sin\beta_m \cos^{-2}\beta_m - \ln\tan(\pi/4+\beta_m/2))}{2h_h} \\ I_{h,4} = \frac{\alpha l_h \sin\beta_m}{h_h^3 (1+2\alpha)^{\frac{1}{2}}} \\ I_{h,5} = \frac{\alpha^2 l_h{}^2 (1-\cos\beta_m)}{h_h^3 (1+2\alpha)} \\ I_{h,6} = \frac{\alpha^3 l_h^3 [\ln\tan(\pi/4+\beta_m/2) - \sin\beta_m]}{h_h^3 (1+2\alpha)^{\frac{3}{2}}} \end{cases} \tag{6}$$

Among them:

$$\begin{cases} \rho = \frac{h_h}{j_h} \\ x = \frac{\rho l_h \tan\beta}{(1+2\beta)^{\frac{1}{2}}} \\ \beta = \arctan\left[(1+2\alpha)^{\frac{1}{2}} \beta^{-1}\right] \end{cases} \tag{7}$$

Therefore, the variables of parabolic thickness function in the flexibility matrix in this flexible hinge element can be obtained:

$$\begin{cases} I_{pa,1} = \frac{l_{pa} \rho^{\frac{1}{2}} \alpha_m}{h_{pa}} \\ I_{pa,2} = \frac{l_{pa} \rho \ln \frac{1}{\cos\alpha_m}}{h_{pa}} \\ I_{pa,3} = \frac{l_{pa}^3 \rho^{\frac{3}{2}} (\tan\alpha_m - \alpha_m)}{h_{pa}} \\ I_{pa,4} = \frac{l_{pa} \rho^{\frac{1}{2}} [8\sin 2\alpha_m + \sin 4\alpha_m + 12\alpha_m]}{32 h_{pa}^3} \\ I_{pa,5} = \frac{l_{pa} \rho (1-\cos^4\alpha_m)}{4 h_{pa}^3} \\ I_{pa,6} = \frac{l_{pa}^3 \rho^{\frac{2}{3}} (4\alpha_m - \sin 4\alpha_m)}{32 h_{pa}^3} \end{cases} \tag{8}$$

Among them:

$$\begin{cases} \rho = \frac{h_{pa}}{j_{pa}} \\ x = l_{pa} \rho \tan\alpha \\ \alpha = \arctan\left(\frac{1}{\rho}\right) \end{cases} \tag{9}$$

Flexibility matrices of hyperbolic and parabolic flexible hinges can be obtained by bringing Eqs. (6) and (7) into Eq. (8), and the flexibility matrix of straight beam can be obtained by Eq. (2), that is, the flexibility matrices of different thickness functions in this flexible hinge unit have been obtained. According to the small deformation theory, if y_2 is regarded as an independent flexible unit, the total flexibility matrix of this flexible unit can be equivalent to connecting flexible hinges with different thicknesses in series, as shown in Fig. 5.

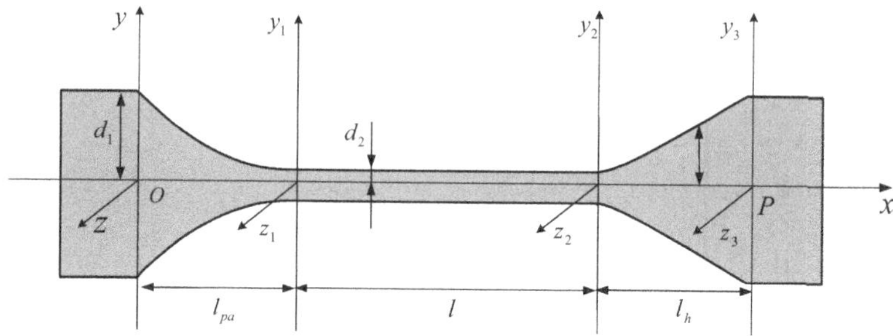

Fig. 5. Series Connection of Hybrid Flexible Hinges and Establishment of its coordinate system.

Based on the principle of static balance and superposition deformation, the thickness of adjacent joints and the slope of thickness function should be equal.[19] It can be obtained that the flexibility matrix $\boldsymbol{C}_{\mathrm{P}}$, c of the multi-segment flexible hinge at the end P is:

$$\mathbf{C_{P,C}} = J_{pa}C_{pa}J_{pa}^T + J_sC_sJ_s^T + C_h \tag{10}$$

In the formula, $\boldsymbol{J}_{\mathbf{pa}}$ (6×6) and $\boldsymbol{J}_{\mathrm{s}}$ (6×6) are the pose transformation matrices of hyperbolic beam and linear beam, respectively, which are equivalent to the terminal reference system, namely:

$$\begin{cases} J_{11} = J_{22} = J_{33} = J_{44} = J_{55} = J_{66} = 1 \\ J_{pa,26} = -J_{pa,35} = l + l_h \\ J_{s,26} = -J_{s,35} = l_h \end{cases} \tag{11}$$

Since the flexible mechanism in this guide mechanism is obtained by connecting the left and right flexible hinges in parallel, in this flexible mechanism, the load required for each layer of flexible hinges to generate the same deformation should be the sum of the loads required by each flexible unit of the left and right flexible hinges, so the global flexibility matrix of the parallel flexible mechanism should be the sum of the stiffness matrices of each flexible unit in the reference coordinate system O_BXYZ. In order to facilitate calculation, electrode guide holes are filled and used as parallel platforms. Assuming that the outer sides of the two flexible hinge units are fixed on an infinite rigid body, local coordinate systems $O_1X_1Y_1Z_1$ and $O_2X_2Y_2Z_2$ are established at the center of the left and right flexible hinges, and lb. is the parallel platform length of the parallel reference coordinate system O_BXYZ, satisfying the condition of $l_1 = l_2 = l + l_b/2$, as shown in Fig. 6.

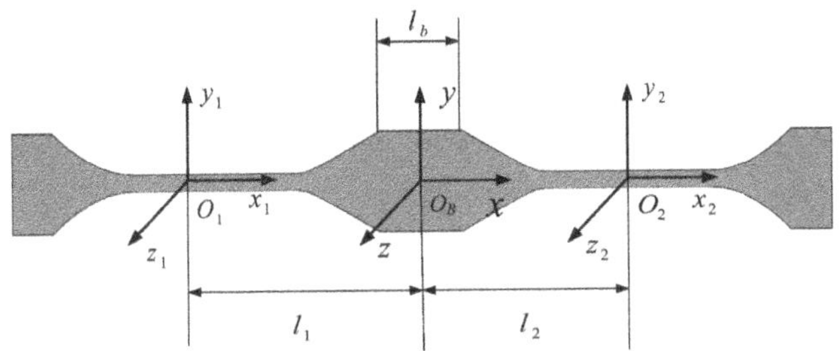

Fig. 6. Single-layer parallel flexible hinge and establishment of its coordinate system

The expression of coordinate transformation operation $\boldsymbol{Ad_i}$ from flexible unit in parallel flexible mechanism to reference coordinate system O_BXYZ is:

$$\mathbf{Ad_i} = \begin{bmatrix} R_i & 0 \\ T_iR_i & R_i \end{bmatrix}$$
$$\mathbf{T_i} = \begin{bmatrix} 0 & -z & y \\ z & 0 & -x \\ -y & x & 0 \end{bmatrix} \tag{12}$$

In the formula,

$\boldsymbol{R}$ ——Rotation matrix of coordinate transformation, $\boldsymbol{R_1} = \boldsymbol{R_2} = \boldsymbol{R}(\pi)$;

$\boldsymbol{T}$ ——The translation matrix of coordinate transformation, which consists of $\boldsymbol{t} = (x,y,z)^T$, $\boldsymbol{t_1} = (l_1,0,0)^T$, $\boldsymbol{t_l} = (-l_2,0,0)^T$.

The flexibility matrices $C_{P,B1}$ and $C_{P,B2}$ of the left and right flexible elements are symmetrical with respect to the coordinate system O_BXYZ, that is, the two flexibility matrices can have the relation:

$$C_{P,B1} = T_yC_{P,B2}{T_y}^T \tag{13}$$

Where $\boldsymbol{T_y}$ (6 × 6) is the mapping matrix of two flexible units, and its non-zero elements are respectively:

$$\begin{cases} T_{11} = T_{44} = T_{55} = T_{66} = 1 \\ T_{22} = T_{33} = -1 \;\; T_{26} = -T_{35} = L \end{cases} \tag{14}$$

Therefore, the single-layer flexibility matrix $\boldsymbol{C_{P,B}}$ of the parallel flexible mechanism with left and right flexible units can be obtained as follows:

$$\mathbf{C_P} = \left[\left(Ad_1C_{P,B1}Ad_1^T\right)^{-1} + \left(Ad_2C_{P,B2}Ad_2^T\right)^{-1}\right]^{-1} \tag{15}$$

By introducing Formula (12–14) into Formula (15), the flexibility matrix of single-layer parallel flexible hinge of flexible parallel mechanism can be obtained.

4 Verification and Optimization of Finite Element Analysis

At this time, the main parameters of the flexible hinge unit of the flexible parallel mechanism are set as shown in Table 1, and the material selection is Nylon 101, with a material density of 1150 kg/m^3, Young's modulus of 1GPa and Poisson's ratio of 0.3. At the same time, a control group with a guide mechanism composed of diagonal bars is set up. Its structure is shown in Fig. 6, with width $k_d = k$, thickness $d_1 = d_2$, diagonal bar length $L_d = L$ and the angle between diagonal bars and the horizontal plane is 45.

Table 1. Main structural parameters

Physical dimension	Value /mm
Maximum thickness d_1	6
Minimum thickness d_2	1
Width k	5
Projection of parabolic flexible hinge in X direction l_{pa}	10
Projection of hyperbolic flexible hinge in X direction l_h	10
Total length of hybrid flexible hinge L	40
Parallel platform length l_b	10

Through MATLAB calculation, the flexibility values of single-layer flexible hinge unit and control unit of the flexible parallel mechanism designed in this paper in all directions can be obtained, as shown in Table 2.

Table 2. Flexibility values of flexible hinge unit and control group

Flexibility direction	Flexible hinge unit /(m/N)	Control group unit /(m/N)
X direction	1.466×10^{-6}	4.000×10^{-6}
Y direction	2.921×10^{-3}	1.484×10^{-3}
Z direction	3.088×10^{-6}	2.682×10^{-3}

As can be seen from Table 2, the flexibility value of the flexible hinge unit is lower than that of the control group in the X and Z directions, and higher in the Y direction. In the practical application scene of the flexible mechanism, the main movement direction is called the functional direction of the flexible mechanism. Because the flexibility and stiffness are reciprocal, the smaller the stiffness in the functional direction, the greater the flexibility and the less the force required to drive it to generate displacement. The non-functional direction refers to the direction that produces parasitic motion, which reduces the motion accuracy of the flexible mechanism, so it is often necessary to be as flexible as possible in the functional direction and as rigid as possible in the parasitic motion direction in the flexible mechanism. Therefore, it can be concluded that the flexible hinge unit designed in this paper is more suitable as a guide mechanism unit than the diagonal bar in the control group.

It can be seen from Fig. 1 that the functional direction of this flexible mechanism is Y direction. Since this flexible hinge unit is composed of conic curve and straight line, this paper focuses on the influence of conic curve parameters. By changing the maximum thickness d_1 and the minimum thickness d_2 in the main structural parameters, the hyperbolic and parabolic function images are changed, and the change law of flexibility in Y direction is obtained, as shown in Fig. 7.

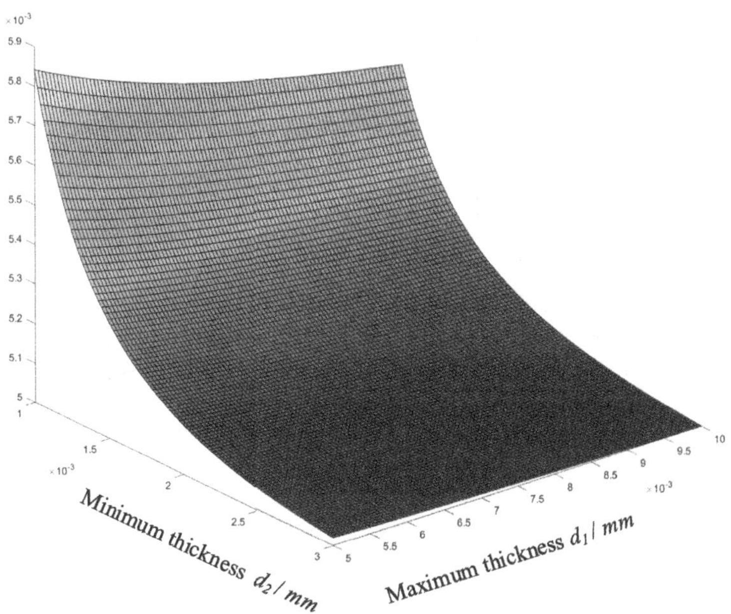

Fig. 7. Relationship Between Functional Direction Flexibility and Maximum Thickness and Minimum Thickness

As can be seen from Fig. 7, in the definition domain provided by this experimental scene, the flexibility of functional direction increases with the decrease of the maximum thickness and the minimum thickness, so we finally choose the maximum thickness d_1 = 5 mm and d_2 = 1 mm as the final structural parameters.

In the parallel flexible mechanism of this guiding mechanism, its guiding accuracy, stability and bearing capacity correspond to its flexibility matrix model. In order to verify the accuracy of the flexibility model, the structure is statically analyzed and verified by Ansys Workbench.

In Ansys Workbench environment, the three-dimensional model of guiding mechanism designed by Solid Works is imported. The fixed groove of the guide mechanism is fixed. In theoretical analysis, the electrode guide hole is filled and used as a parallel platform. Therefore, in order to facilitate analysis and verification, the parallel platform is continued to be used, and the unit force and unit moment are set at the center of the parallel coordinate system, so the corresponding structural displacement of each floor can be obtained, and the corresponding flexibility value can be obtained through conversion. Since the unilateral flexible hinge is obtained from the array of flexible hinge units, the flexibility test is only carried out on the second floor and the third time.

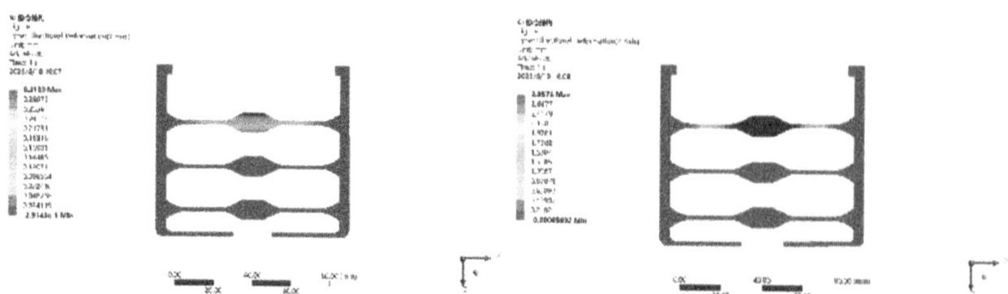

(a) X-direction flexibility of the first layer (b) Z-direction flexibility of the first layer

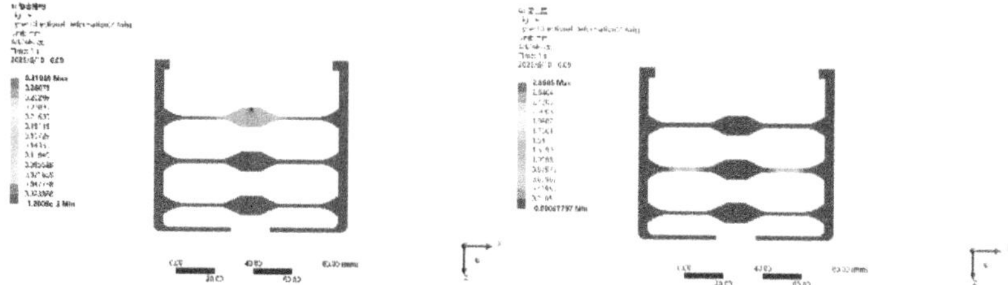

(c) Y-axis flexibility of the first layer (d) Y-direction flexibility of the second layer.

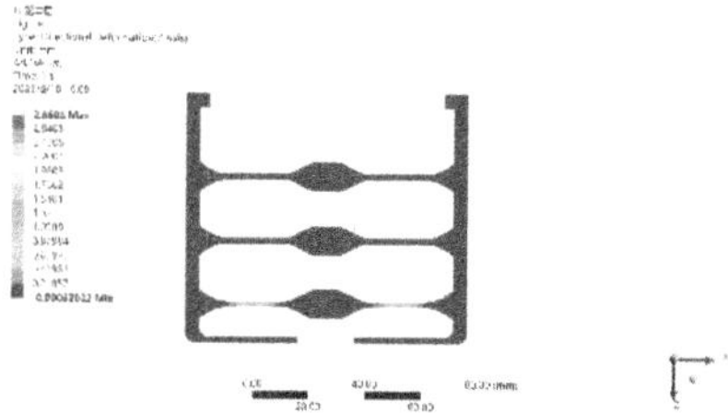

(e) Y-direction flexibility of the third layer

Fig. 8. Finite Element Flexibility Analysis of Parallel Flexible System

Through the displacement in the corresponding direction obtained in Fig. 8, the corresponding flexibility value can be obtained through parameter operation, and then compared with the results of MATLAB operation, as shown in Table 3, the numerical error is within 5.543%, which proves that the parallel flexible mechanism of the guiding mechanism designed in this paper has high solving accuracy. The design and flexibility analysis of flexible guiding mechanism in this paper is the basis of kinematics and dynamics of the mechanism, and provides theoretical basis and design basis for the overall design and flexibility analysis of puncture robot in neuromedicine.

Table 3. Flexibility analysis results of parallel flexible systems

Compliance	Theoretical Model /(m/N)	Finite Element Model/(m/N)	Relative Error /(%)
X-direction flexibility of the first layer	2.982 × 10–3	2.858 × 10–3	2.191
Z-direction flexibility of the first layer	3.313 × 10–3	3.139 × 10–3	5.543
Y-axis flexibility of the first layer	2.981 × 10–4	3.107 × 10–4	4.055
Y-direction flexibility of the second layer	2.982 × 10–3	2.861 × 10–3	4.229
Y-direction flexibility of the third layer	2.982 × 10–3	2.861 × 10–3	4.229

5 Conclusion

The main results are as follows:

(1) A kind of flexible parallel mechanism with symmetrical sides and flexible hinges on one side made of flexible hinge unit array is proposed. Compared with the foreign diagonal guide mechanism, its flexibility in the functional direction is 1.97 times, and it not only meets the requirements of high accuracy and flexibility in the functional direction, but also improves the structural resilience and working motion stroke.

(2) For this flexible element and the whole parallel mechanism, which are mixed by functional hinges with different thicknesses, the flexibility model of parallel flexible hinges of each layer is established by using the small deformation theory and matrix displacement method.

(3) Using MATLAB and Ansys Workbench, the important parameters in the thickness function are determined, and the finite element analysis of each layer of parallel flexible hinges is verified. The results show that the established three-dimensional model is basically consistent with the theoretical flexibility model.

Acknowledgments. This work is supported by the National Natural Science Foundation of China (Grant No. 52575005,52175019), Beijing Municipal Natural Science Foundation (Grant No. L222038 and No. 20240484699), Joint Funds of Industry-university-research of Shanghai Academy of Spaceflight Technology (Grant No. SAST2022-017), Beijing Municipal Key Laboratory of Space-ground Interconnection and Convergence of China and Key Laboratory of IoT Monitoring and Early Warning, Ministry of Emergency Management, Project 'Vice President of Science and Technology' of Changping District, Beijing.

References

1. Ruitian, X., Shurui, L., Jing, J.: Research status and prospect of brain-computer interface technology in motor function rehabilitation after stroke. Shanghai Med. Coll. **47**(04), 220–223 (2024)
2. Shui-lan, J., Xin-zhi, C., Ming, L., et al.: Application of simple and accurate neuro-director in directional puncture for brain stem hemorrhage. Zhejiang Med. Coll. **42**(22), 2456–2459 (2020)
3. Rong, L., Jie, F.: Design of an intracranial hematoma puncture location device and hematoma location method. J. Snake. **32**(01), 125–127+130 (2020)
4. Pengfei, Z., Yong, Z., Peng, Z., et al.: Design and application of an automatic venipuncture device. China Med. Equipment. **16**(2), 12–14 (2019)
5. Abiei, M., Konh, B.: A portable robot to perform prostate brachytherapy with active needle steering and robot-assisted ultrasound tracking. In: 2022 Design of Medical Devices Conference, pp. 106–132. Am. Soc. Mech. Eng. Digit. Collect. (2022)
6. Jingjun, Y., Guangbo, H., Guimin, C., et al.: Research progress of flexible mechanism and its application. J. Mech. Eng. **51**(13), 53–68 (2015)
7. Ping, G.: Zhang Jianfeng, Development and Prospect of flexible mechanism. China Plant Eng. (05), 249–251 (2021)
8. Huaxian, W., Yongjie, Z., Nan, Y., et al.: Design and analysis of a new biaxial flexible hinge with elliptical cross section. China Mech. Eng. **35**(08), 1348–1357 (2024)
9. Zhijie, Z., Yuan, Y.: Research on hyperbolic flexible hinge based on closed-loop flexibility analytic formula. Chinese J. Sci. Instrum. (6), 1055–1059 (2007)
10. Chenlei, J., Guilian, W., Haibo, Z., et al.: Influence of structural parameters on the stiffness of parabolic flexible hinges. Mech. Des. **34**(11), 63–67 (2017)
11. Wei, H., Shirinzadeh, B., Tang, H., et al.: Closed-form compliance equations for elliptic-revolute notch type multiple-axis flexure hinges. Mech. Mach. Theory. **156**, 104–154 (2021)
12. Lijian, L., Jiantao, Y., Fei, G., et al.: Configuration design and flexibility modeling of hybrid flexible hinge. J. Mech. Eng. **58**(21), 78–91 (2022)
13. Cheng, L., Chuanli, W., Tao, H., et al.: Study on mechanical properties of irregular asymmetric flexible hinges. Mech. Transm. **44**(09), 34–39 (2020)
14. Ming, C., Zhenghong, D., Shanshan, R., et al.: Multi-stage damping stabilization control of series flexible capture mechanism on board. Vib. Impact. **37**(05), 42–49 (2018)
15. Haiyang, L., Guangbo, H., Jingjun, Y., et al.: Research on system design method of spatial translational flexible parallel mechanism. J. Mech. Eng. **54**(13), 57–65 (2018)
16. Arafat, M.A., Rubin, L.N., Jefferys, J.G.R., et al.: A method of flexible micro-wire electrode insertion in rodent for chronic neural recording and a device for electrode insertion. IEEE Trans. Neural Syst. Rehabil. Eng. **27**(9), 1724–1731 (2019)
17. Schoeftner, J.: Extension of Castigliano's method for isotropic beams. Acta Mech. **231**(11), 1–20 (2020)
18. Yuanzhao, C., Jiancheng, Z., Wenjun, W., et al.: Deformation gradient element of large deformation flexible beam in floating coordinate system. Acta Mech. **57**(01), 249–260 (2025)
19. Li, L., Zhang, D., Guo, S., et al.: Design, modeling, and analysis of hybrid flexure hinges. Mech. Mach. Theory. **131**, 300–316 (2019)
20. Jibin, C., Dai, N., Pei, G., et al.: Design technology of flexible manipulator based on mechanical metamaterials. China Mech. Eng. **34**(16), 1900–1906 (2023)

A Screw Theory Based Analytical Approach for Elastodynamics Modeling of a 2-Limb 4-DOF High-Speed Parallel Robot

Dun Peng[1,2], Yue Ma[1,2(✉)], Bin Li[1,2], Qi Liu[1,2], Honggui Peng[1,2], and Long Chen[1,2]

[1] Tianjin Key Laboratory for Advanced Mechatronic System Design and Intelligent Control, School of Mechanical Engineering, Tianjin University of Technology, Tianjin 300384, China
mayue002@126.com

[2] National Demonstration Center for Experimental Mechanical and Electrical Engineering Education, Tianjin University of Technology, Tianjin 300384, China

Abstract. An analytical approach for elastodynamic modeling of a 2-limb 4-DOF (3T1R) high-speed parallel robot is proposed. Based on screw theory combined with structural dynamics, the kinetic energy and potential energy of the robot are derived, and the expressions for the first 6 natural frequencies of the mechanism are obtained. A full finite element analysis of the robot is carried out using finite element software, and the results show that the low-order natural frequencies are in good agreement with those from the analytical method. This indicates that the analytical elastodynamic model can estimate the low-order dynamic behaviors over the entire workspace in a very effective and accurate manner.

Keywords: Elastodynamics · Screw Theory · High-Speed Parallel Robot

1 Introduction

As a core component of modern high-end equipment, high-speed parallel robots have been widely applied in high-end manufacturing fields such as precision assembly, high-speed sorting, and laser processing. Their dynamic performance directly determines production efficiency and operational accuracy [1, 2]. With the continuous increase in industrial demands for higher speed and precision, the problem of elastic deformation of robots under high-speed motion conditions has become increasingly prominent. For instance, the flexible vibration of components not only causes trajectory deviation of the end effector but also may lead to resonance risks, which severely restrict the dynamic performance and service life of the system [3–5]. Therefore, establishing an accurate and efficient elastodynamic model has become a key scientific issue to break through the bottleneck in the dynamic performance of high-speed parallel robots.

Currently, the elastodynamic modeling of parallel robots mainly faces two major challenges. Firstly, due to the topological characteristics of parallel robots, such as

Z. Hou et al. (Eds.): CIRAC 2025, CCIS 2885, pp. 57–70, 2026.
https://doi.org/10.1007/978-981-92-0045-0_5

multi-limb collaborative driving and multi-degree-of-freedom coupling, the transmission mechanism of elastic deformation exhibits extremely strong nonlinearity and coupling [6]. Meanwhile, the collaborative motion with multiple degrees of freedom can also lead to modal coupling, making the assumption of "absolute rigidity of components" in traditional rigid-body dynamics models no longer valid. This makes it impossible to accurately depict the mapping relationship between the elastic vibration of flexible components and the dynamic response of the end effector. Especially under high-speed working conditions, such model errors may result in millimeter-level deviations in the end positioning accuracy, seriously restricting its application scenarios [7, 8]. Secondly, although full finite element analysis can capture the fine deformation characteristics of components through discretized modeling and achieve dynamic performance prediction with micron-level accuracy [9, 10], the full finite element model needs to process massive amounts of element and node information. A single dynamic analysis often takes several hours or even days. For online dynamic control scenarios, the high computational delay of the finite element model makes it impossible to achieve real-time dynamic compensation, which greatly limits its promotion value in engineering practice [11]. Therefore, developing an analytical or semi-analytical modeling approach with both accuracy and efficiency has become a common goal of the academic and industrial communities [12, 13]. In this context, screw theory, as an efficient mathematical tool for describing rigid-body motion and force transmission, has shown unique advantages in multi-body system dynamics modeling. It uniformly characterizes complex spatial motions and deformations through screw parameters, which can provide new ideas for simplifying the coupling relationship between elastic deformations and motion parameters and is expected to break through the inherent limitations between accuracy and efficiency in traditional modeling methods [14, 15].

In this paper, aiming at a 2-limb 4-DOF (3T1R) high-speed parallel robot, an analytical elastodynamic modeling approach integrating screw theory and structural dynamics is proposed. By establishing the mapping relationship between the deformation screw of the end component and elastic deformation, the quadratic expressions of the system's kinetic energy and potential energy are derived. Combined with the Lagrangian energy method, the dynamic equations are established, and finally the low-order natural frequencies and modal characteristics are obtained. The accuracy of the model is verified through finite element analysis. This research breaks through the trade-off dilemma between accuracy and efficiency in traditional modeling approaches, and is of great significance for promoting the development of dynamic design theory of high-end equipment and its engineering applications.

2 System Description and Modeling Framework

Figure 1 shows the CAD model of the new 2-limb single-platform 4-DOF high-speed parallel robot under study. This robot is mainly composed of a lead screw, a spline shaft, a moving platform, and two limbs connecting the base and the moving platform. Each limb includes components such as a driving rod set, a passive rod set, a active plate, and a connecting plate. In one of the limb, two parallelogram mechanisms connected by a toggle frame are added to constrain the rotation of the moving platform around the direction perpendicular to the plane formed by the two limbs. To define the joint and link parameters required for modeling, the limb with the parallelogram closed-loop mechanism is defined as limb 1, and the other limb as limb 2.

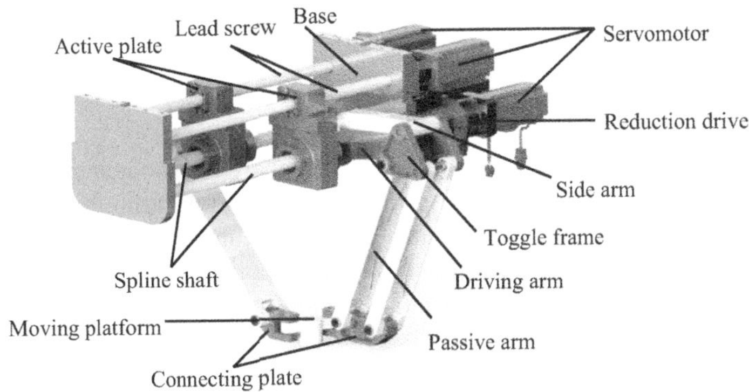

Fig. 1. 2-limb 4-DOF high-speed parallel robot mechanism

Figure 2 presents the schematic diagram of the robot's CAD model, showing the main nodes relevant to the modeling and analysis. The lead screw intersects the active plate at point A_i ($i = 1, 2$); the Spline shaft intersects the driving arm at point B_i ($i = 1, 2$); the side arm intersects the active plate at point B'_1; the driving arm intersects the passive arm at point C_i ($i = 1, 2$); the passive arm intersects the connecting plate at point D_i ($i = 1, 2$); the limb chain intersects the moving platform at point P_i ($i = 1, 2$); and the center point of the end of the moving platform is denoted as point P.

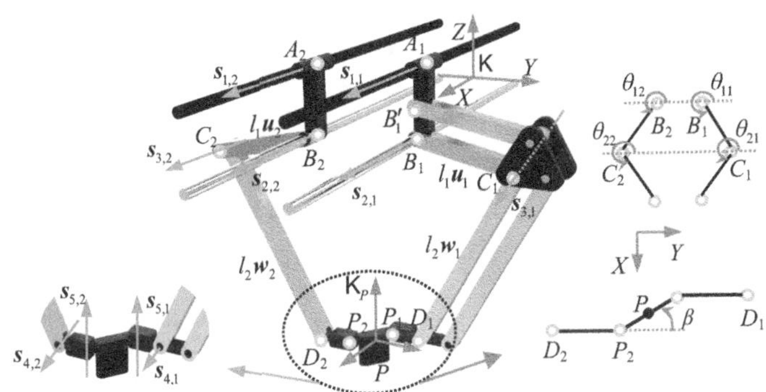

Fig. 2. Schematic diagram of a 2-limb 4-DOF high-speed parallel robot

Furthermore, let $\mathbf{s}_{j,i}$ represent the direction vector of the axis of the jth single-DOF joint in limb i. Moreover, for limb 1, the side arm and the driving arm of the frame, as well as the outer passive arm and the inner passive arm, always maintain a parallel relationship, that is, their direction vectors remain consistent. Therefore, when considering the direction vector, the two arms in the parallelogram mechanism can be simplified and merged into one. The specific expression is shown in Fig. 2.A fixed frame $\mathcal{K}$ is established with the center of the two rotating shafts of the spline shaft as the origin, and a follower reference frame $\mathcal{K}_P$ is established with a point O instantaneously coinciding with the end point P of the high-speed parallel robot as the origin, whose axis orientations are the same as those of the fixed frame.

3 Elastodynamic Modeling

This section presents a theoretical approach for the analytical modeling and analysis of the elastodynamics of this high-speed parallel robot. Starting from the analysis of the quasi-static deformation field of the limbs in the robot mechanism, an elastodynamic model with the deformation screw of the end reference point as the generalized coordinate is established based on screw theory combined with structural dynamics. The modeling process is shown in Fig. 3.

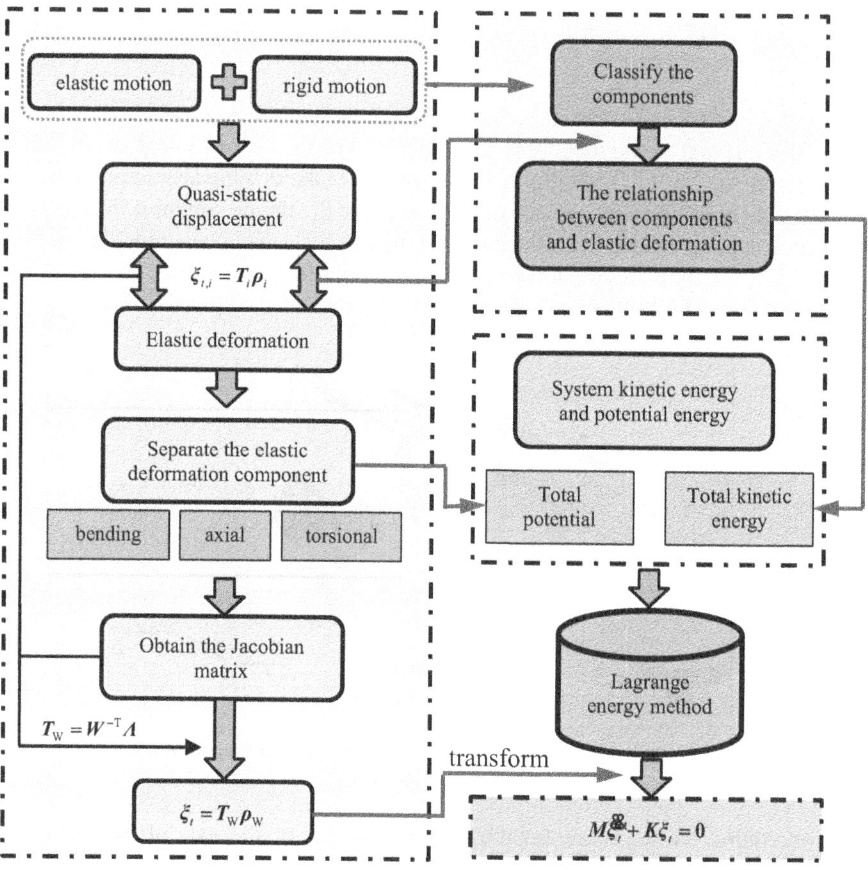

Fig. 3. Elastodynamic theory modeling flowchart

3.1 The relationship between the rotational quantity of the twist at the end component and the elastic deformation

Make the system become the instantaneous structure near its equilibrium position. Based on the servo reference frame $\mathcal{K}_P$, establish the relationship between the deformation rotation quantity of this component about point O and the deformations of each elastic link in the system. According to the theory of spinors, in the ith limb, the twist $\xi_{t,i}$ of the moving platform with respect to point O can be expressed as

$$\xi_{t,i} = \sum_{k=1}^{3} \rho_{e,k,i}\hat{\xi}_{e,k,i} + \sum_{k=1}^{3} \rho_{d,k,i}\hat{\xi}_{d,k,i} = \mathbf{T}_i\boldsymbol{\rho}_i, \quad i = 1, 2 \tag{1}$$

Where
$\mathbf{T}_i = \left[\mathbf{T}_{e,i}\ \mathbf{T}_{d,i}\right]$ $\mathbf{T}_{e,i} = \left[\hat{\xi}_{e,1,i}\ \hat{\xi}_{e,2,i}\ \hat{\xi}_{e,3,i}\right]$, $\mathbf{T}_{d,i} = \left[\hat{\xi}_{d,1,i}\ \hat{\xi}_{d,2,i}\ \hat{\xi}_{d,3,i}\right]$

$$\boldsymbol{\rho}_i = \left(\rho_{e,k,i}^{\mathrm{T}}, \rho_{d,j,i}^{\mathrm{T}}\right)^{\mathrm{T}}$$

$\hat{\xi}_{e,1,i} = \begin{pmatrix} \mathbf{s}_{1,i} \\ \mathbf{0} \end{pmatrix}$, $\hat{\xi}_{e,2,i} = \begin{pmatrix} \left(\overrightarrow{PP_i} + \overrightarrow{P_iD_i} - l_2\boldsymbol{w}_i - l_1\boldsymbol{u}_i - \hat{\boldsymbol{x}}b + \hat{\boldsymbol{z}}b'\right) \times \hat{\boldsymbol{y}} \\ \hat{\boldsymbol{y}} \end{pmatrix}$,
$\hat{\xi}_{e,3,i} = \begin{pmatrix} \left(\overrightarrow{PP_i} + \overrightarrow{P_iD_i} - l_2\boldsymbol{w}_i - l_1\boldsymbol{u}_i - \hat{\boldsymbol{x}}b\right) \times s_{2,i} \\ s_{2,i} \end{pmatrix}$, $\hat{\xi}_{d,1,i} = \begin{pmatrix} \left(\overrightarrow{PP_i} + \overrightarrow{P_iD_i} - l_2\boldsymbol{w}_i\right) \times \mathbf{s}_{3,i} \\ \mathbf{s}_{3,i} \end{pmatrix}$, $\hat{\xi}_{d,2,i} = \begin{pmatrix} \left(\overrightarrow{PP_i} + \overrightarrow{P_iD_i}\right) \times \mathbf{s}_{4,i} \\ \mathbf{s}_{4,i} \end{pmatrix}$, $\hat{\xi}_{d,3,i} = \begin{pmatrix} \overrightarrow{PP_i} \times \mathbf{s}_{5,i} \\ \mathbf{s}_{5,i} \end{pmatrix}$

Where, $\rho_{e,1,i}$ denotes the axial elastic deformations of the driving joint (P joints) along $\mathbf{s}_{1,i}$; $\rho_{e,2,i}$ represents the torsional deformation of the limb ith interface around the Y-axis; $\rho_{e,3,i}$ indicates the torsional deformation of the spline shaft around its own axis $\mathbf{s}_{2,i}$; and $\rho_{d,k,i}$, $\hat{\xi}_{d,k,i}$ ($k = 1 \sim 3$) Indicating a small rigid body displacement of the passive joint around its own axis to satisfy the closed-loop constraint and their unit twist of permissions. $\hat{\boldsymbol{y}} = \left(0\ 1\ 0\right)^{\mathrm{T}}$ is the unit vector along the Y-axis; $\hat{\boldsymbol{x}} = \left(1\ 0\ 0\right)^{\mathrm{T}}$ is the unit vector along the X-axis; l_1 is the length of the driving arm; l_2 is the length of the passive arm; b is the distance between the plane formed by the limbs and the plane of the active plate; b' is the distance from the hinge hole of the spline shaft and the active plate to the hinge hole of the lead screw and the active plate. $\overrightarrow{D_iP_i} = -\operatorname{sgn}(i)s_k\hat{\boldsymbol{y}}$; $\overrightarrow{P_iP} = \operatorname{sgn}(i)\frac{P}{2}\boldsymbol{p}$; Among them, $\boldsymbol{p} = \left(\sin\beta\ -\cos\beta\ 0\right)^{\mathrm{T}}$ denotes the unit vector of the active plate in the direction from point P_1 to point P_2; $\boldsymbol{u}_i$ and $\boldsymbol{w}_i$ are the unit vectors of the driving arm and the passive arm of limb ith, respectively, where,

$$\operatorname{sgn}(i) = \begin{cases} 1 & i = 1 \\ -1 & i = 2 \end{cases} \quad \begin{cases} \boldsymbol{u}_i = \left(0\ \cos\theta_{1i}\ \sin\theta_{1i}\right)^{\mathrm{T}} \\ \boldsymbol{w}_i = \left(0\ \cos\theta_{2i}\ \sin\theta_{2i}\right)^{\mathrm{T}} \end{cases}$$

It is noted that the i-th limb provides an actuating force along $\mathbf{s}_{1,i}$ and a torque around $\mathbf{s}_{2,i}$ for the mechanism. Therefore, the branched chain force Jacobian composed of the corresponding unit wrenches of actuations is

$$\mathbf{W}_{1,i}=\hat{\boldsymbol{\xi}}_{wa,1,i},\mathbf{W}_{3,i}=\hat{\boldsymbol{\xi}}_{wa,2,i},i=1,2 \tag{2}$$

Where,

$$\hat{\boldsymbol{\xi}}_{wa,1,i}=\left(\begin{array}{c} s_{1,i} \\ \left(\overrightarrow{PP_i}+\overrightarrow{P_iD_i}-l_2\boldsymbol{w}_i-l_1\boldsymbol{u}_i-\hat{x}b+\hat{z}b'\right)\times s_{1,i}\end{array}\right)$$

$$\hat{\boldsymbol{\xi}}_{wa,3,i}=\left(\begin{array}{c} \boldsymbol{n}_{1,i} \\ \left(\overrightarrow{PP_i}+\overrightarrow{P_iD_i}-l_2\boldsymbol{w}_i\right)\times \boldsymbol{n}_{1,i}\end{array}\right),\boldsymbol{n}_{1,i}=\boldsymbol{u}_i\times s_{3,i}.$$

It should be noted that this robot is a 3T1R 4-DOF high-speed parallel robot. When considering the elastic deformation of the robot, there are two 'virtual joints' at the end, which are rotations around the X-axis and Y-axis. Herein, 'virtual joints' refer to the hypothetical joints introduced to describe the movements that the moving platform is theoretically restricted from but actually occur due to elastic deformation. It is obvious that the constraint restricting the rotation of the moving platform around the X-axis comes from the couple of constraint provided by the two parallelogram mechanisms of limb 1. Therefore, the torsional deformation of the interface of limb 1 around the Y-axis is mainly the work done by the reaction forces along the directions of the driving arm and the connecting frame driven arm. Thus, the limb force Jacobian formed by the 'virtual joints' and their corresponding unit constraint force screws is

$$\mathbf{W}_{2,1}=\hat{\boldsymbol{\xi}}_{wc,2,1},\mathbf{W}_{2,2}=\hat{\boldsymbol{\xi}}_{wc,2,2} \tag{3}$$

Where,

$$\hat{\boldsymbol{\xi}}_{wc,2,1}=\left(\begin{array}{c} \boldsymbol{u}_1 \\ \left(\overrightarrow{PP_i}+\overrightarrow{P_iD_i}-l_2\boldsymbol{w}_i-l_1\boldsymbol{u}_i+\frac{\hat{z}l_b}{2}\right)\times \boldsymbol{u}_1\end{array}\right),\hat{\boldsymbol{\xi}}_{wc,2,2}=\begin{pmatrix}\mathbf{0}\\ \hat{y}\end{pmatrix}.$$

Where, l_b is the vertical distance from the axis line of the spline shaft to the axis line of the connection end of the side arm and the active plate(i.e., $\left|\overrightarrow{B_1'B_1}\right|$).

It is noted that the two limbs share a common moving platform, namely. By left-multiplying Eq. (1) by, and writing the resulting result in matrix form, obtain

$$\mathbf{W}^{\mathrm{T}}\boldsymbol{\xi}_t=\boldsymbol{\Lambda}\boldsymbol{\rho}_{\mathrm{W}} \tag{4}$$

Furthermore, noting that $\boldsymbol{W}$ is a reversible matrix, we denote it as $\mathbf{T}_{\mathrm{W}}=\mathbf{W}^{-\mathrm{T}}\boldsymbol{\Lambda}$. Thus, Eq. (4) can be rewritten as

$$\boldsymbol{\xi}_t=\mathbf{T}_{\mathrm{W}}\boldsymbol{\rho}_{\mathrm{W}} \tag{5}$$

Where, $\mathbf{W}=\left[\boldsymbol{W}_{1,i}\ \boldsymbol{W}_{2,i}\ \boldsymbol{W}_{3,i}\right]$, $\boldsymbol{\rho}_{\mathrm{W}}=\left(\boldsymbol{\rho}_{e,1,i}\ \boldsymbol{\rho}_{e,2,i}\ \boldsymbol{\rho}_{e,3,i}\right)^{\mathrm{T}}$, $\boldsymbol{\Lambda}=\begin{bmatrix}\boldsymbol{\Lambda}_1 & & \\ & \boldsymbol{\Lambda}_2 & \\ & & \boldsymbol{\Lambda}_3\end{bmatrix}$,

$\boldsymbol{\Lambda}_1$ $=$

$\mathbf{1}_{2\times 2}$, $\mathbf{1}_{n\times n}$ indicates an n-order unit matrix, $\boldsymbol{\Lambda}_2 = \begin{bmatrix} \boldsymbol{u}_1\overrightarrow{PA_1} \times \hat{\boldsymbol{y}} + \hat{\boldsymbol{y}}\overrightarrow{PB_1'} \times \boldsymbol{u}_1 & \\ & 1 \end{bmatrix}$

, $\boldsymbol{\Lambda}_3 = \begin{bmatrix} \boldsymbol{n}_{1,1}\overrightarrow{PB_1} \times \boldsymbol{s}_{2,1} + \boldsymbol{s}_{2,1}\overrightarrow{PC_1} \times \boldsymbol{n}_{1,1} & \\ & \boldsymbol{n}_{1,2}\overrightarrow{PB_2} \times \boldsymbol{s}_{2,2} + \boldsymbol{s}_{2,2}\overrightarrow{PC_2} \times \boldsymbol{n}_{1,2} \end{bmatrix}$ 。

At this point, the relationship between the twist ξ_t of the end component of this high-speed parallel robot with respect to point O and the elastic deformation vector $\boldsymbol{\rho}_W$ has been established.

3.2 The relationship between the twist of the moving component and the elastic deformation

In order to construct the motion differential equation with $\boldsymbol{\rho}_W$ as the generalized coordinate, it is necessary to establish the relationship between the twist of the moving components that contribute significantly to the system kinetic energy with respect to point and the deformation of the elastic links in the mechanism. For this purpose, the lead screw is defined as the 'P̲' component; the spline shaft is defined as the 'R̲' component; the active plate and the screw nut are defined as the 'D' component; the side arm, the driving arm 1, the toggle frame are defined as the 'Z1' components, the driving arm 2 is defined as the 'Z2' component; the passive arm is defined as the 'N' component; the connecting plate is defined as the 'L' component; the moving platform is defined as the 'M' component.

According to the above symbol conventions, by using Eq. (1) and (5), the twist $\boldsymbol{\xi}_{t,\underline{P},i}$ of the i-th "P̲" component relative to point O can be expressed as

$$\boldsymbol{\xi}_{t,\underline{P},i} = \rho_{e,1,i}\hat{\boldsymbol{\xi}}_{e,1,i} + \rho_{e,2,i}\hat{\boldsymbol{\xi}}_{e,2,i} \tag{6}$$

It is noted that for the lead screw there is $\rho_{e,\underline{P},i} = \rho_{e,1,i}\frac{2\pi}{p}$, where $\rho_{e,\underline{P},i}$ represents the rotational deformation of the screw. Therefore, eq. (6) can be rewritten as

$$\boldsymbol{\xi}_{t,\underline{P},i} = \rho_{e,\underline{P},i}\hat{\boldsymbol{\xi}}_{e,\underline{P},i} + \rho_{e,2,i}\hat{\boldsymbol{\xi}}_{e,2,i} \tag{7}$$

Where, $\hat{\boldsymbol{\xi}}_{e,\underline{P},i} = \begin{pmatrix} \mathbf{0} \\ s_{1,i} \end{pmatrix}$, Eq. (7) can also be expressed as

$$\boldsymbol{\xi}_{t,\underline{P},i} = \mathbf{T}'_{\underline{P},i}\boldsymbol{\rho}_i = \mathbf{T}'_{\underline{P},i}\mathbf{T}_i^{-1}\boldsymbol{\xi}_t = \mathbf{T}'_{\underline{P},i}\mathbf{T}_i^{-1}\mathbf{T}_W\boldsymbol{\rho}_W = \mathbf{T}_{\underline{P},i}\boldsymbol{\rho}_W \tag{8}$$

Where, $\mathbf{T}'_{\underline{P},i} = \begin{bmatrix} \hat{\boldsymbol{\xi}}_{e,\underline{P},i} & \hat{\boldsymbol{\xi}}_{e,2,i} & \mathbf{0} & \mathbf{0} & \mathbf{0} & \mathbf{0} \end{bmatrix}$.

Similarly, the twist $\xi_{t,\underline{R},i}$ of the "R̲" component relative to point O can be expressed as

$$\boldsymbol{\xi}_{t,\underline{R},i} = \rho_{e,2,i}\hat{\boldsymbol{\xi}}_{e,2,i} + \rho_{e,3,i}\hat{\boldsymbol{\xi}}_{e,3,i} = \mathbf{T}'_{\underline{R},i}\boldsymbol{\rho}_i = \mathbf{T}_{\underline{P},i}\boldsymbol{\rho}_W \tag{9}$$

Where, $\mathbf{T}'_{\underline{R},i} = \begin{bmatrix} \mathbf{0} & \hat{\boldsymbol{\xi}}_{e,2,i} & \hat{\boldsymbol{\xi}}_{e,3,i} & \mathbf{0} & \mathbf{0} & \mathbf{0} \end{bmatrix}$.

The twist $\xi_{t,\mathrm{D},i}$ of the "D" component relative to point O is expressed as

$$\boldsymbol{\xi}_{t,\mathrm{D},i} = \sum_{k=1}^{2} \rho_{e,k,i}\hat{\boldsymbol{\xi}}_{e,k,i} = \mathbf{T}'_{\mathrm{D},i}\boldsymbol{\rho}_i = \mathbf{T}_{\mathrm{D},i}\boldsymbol{\rho}_W \tag{10}$$

Where, $\mathbf{T}'_{\mathrm{D},i} = \left[\hat{\boldsymbol{\xi}}_{e,1,i}\ \hat{\boldsymbol{\xi}}_{e,2,i}\ \mathbf{0}\ \mathbf{0}\ \mathbf{0}\ \mathbf{0}\right]$.
The twist $\xi_{t,\mathrm{Z},i}$ of the "Z" component relative to point O is expressed as

$$\boldsymbol{\xi}_{t,\mathrm{Z},i} = \sum_{k=1}^{3} \rho_{e,k,i}\hat{\boldsymbol{\xi}}_{e,k,i} = \mathbf{T}'_{\mathrm{Z},i}\boldsymbol{\rho}_i = \mathbf{T}_{\mathrm{Z},i}\boldsymbol{\rho}_{\mathrm{W}} \tag{11}$$

Where, $\mathbf{T}'_{\mathrm{Z},i} = \left[\hat{\boldsymbol{\xi}}_{e,1,i}\ \hat{\boldsymbol{\xi}}_{e,2,i}\ \hat{\boldsymbol{\xi}}_{e,3,i}\ \mathbf{0}\ \mathbf{0}\ \mathbf{0}\right]$.
The twist $\xi_{t,\mathrm{N},i}$ of the "N" component relative to point O is expressed as

$$\boldsymbol{\xi}_{t,\mathrm{N},i} = \sum_{k=1}^{3} \rho_{e,k,i}\hat{\boldsymbol{\xi}}_{e,k,i} + \rho_{d,1,i}\hat{\boldsymbol{\xi}}_{d,1,i} = \mathbf{T}'_{\mathrm{N},i}\boldsymbol{\rho}_i = \mathbf{T}_{\mathrm{N},i}\boldsymbol{\rho}_{\mathrm{W}} \tag{12}$$

Where, $\mathbf{T}'_{\mathrm{N},i} = \left[\hat{\boldsymbol{\xi}}_{e,1,i}\ \hat{\boldsymbol{\xi}}_{e,2,i}\ \hat{\boldsymbol{\xi}}_{e,3,i}\ \hat{\boldsymbol{\xi}}_{d,1,i}\ \mathbf{0}\ \mathbf{0}\right]$.
The twist $\xi_{t,\mathrm{L},i}$ of the "L" component relative to point O is expressed as

$$\boldsymbol{\xi}_{t,\mathrm{L},i} = \sum_{k=1}^{3} \rho_{e,k,i}\hat{\boldsymbol{\xi}}_{e,k,i} + \sum_{K=1}^{2} \rho_{d,k,i}\hat{\boldsymbol{\xi}}_{d,k,i} = \mathbf{T}'_{\mathrm{L},i}\boldsymbol{\rho}_i = \mathbf{T}_{\mathrm{L},i}\boldsymbol{\rho}_{\mathrm{W}} \tag{13}$$

And the twist $\xi_{t,\mathrm{M}}$ of the "M" component relative to point O is expressed as

$$\boldsymbol{\xi}_{t,\mathrm{M}} = \boldsymbol{\xi}_t = \mathbf{T}_{\mathrm{W}}\boldsymbol{\rho}_{\mathrm{W}} \tag{14}$$

3.3 The kinetic energy and elastic potential energy of the system

In this section, the deformation amount of the elastic link is taken as the generalized coordinate, and the approach of expressing the system kinetic energy and elastic potential energy as quadratic forms of this set of generalized coordinates is studied. Subsequently, the system elastodynamic model is established through the Lagrangian energy method.

The kinetic energy of the system can be expressed as

$$\begin{aligned} T &= \sum_{i=1}^{2}\left(T_{\underline{\mathrm{P}},i} + T_{\underline{\mathrm{R}},i} + T_{\mathrm{D},i} + T_{\mathrm{Z},i} + T_{\mathrm{N},i} + T_{\mathrm{L},i}\right) + T_{\mathrm{M}} \\ &= \frac{1}{2}\left[\sum_{i=1}^{2}\left(\begin{array}{l} \dot{\boldsymbol{\xi}}_{t,\underline{\mathrm{P}},i}^{\mathrm{T}}\mathbf{M}_{\underline{\mathrm{P}},i}\dot{\boldsymbol{\xi}}_{t,\underline{\mathrm{P}},i} + \dot{\boldsymbol{\xi}}_{t,\underline{\mathrm{R}},i}^{\mathrm{T}}\mathbf{M}_{\underline{\mathrm{R}},i}\dot{\boldsymbol{\xi}}_{t,\underline{\mathrm{R}},i} + \dot{\boldsymbol{\xi}}_{t,\mathrm{D},i}^{\mathrm{T}}\mathbf{M}_{\mathrm{D},i}\dot{\boldsymbol{\xi}}_{t,\mathrm{D},i} \\ + \dot{\boldsymbol{\xi}}_{t,\mathrm{Z},i}^{\mathrm{T}}\mathbf{M}_{\mathrm{Z},i}\dot{\boldsymbol{\xi}}_{t,\mathrm{Z},i} + \dot{\boldsymbol{\xi}}_{t,\mathrm{N},i}^{\mathrm{T}}\mathbf{M}_{\mathrm{N},i}\dot{\boldsymbol{\xi}}_{t,\mathrm{N},i} + \dot{\boldsymbol{\xi}}_{t,\mathrm{L},i}^{\mathrm{T}}\mathbf{M}_{\mathrm{L},i}\dot{\boldsymbol{\xi}}_{t,\mathrm{L},i} \end{array}\right) + \dot{\boldsymbol{\xi}}_{t,\mathrm{M},i}^{\mathrm{T}}\mathbf{M}_{\mathrm{M},i}\dot{\boldsymbol{\xi}}_{t,\mathrm{M},i}\right] \end{aligned} \tag{15}$$

Where, $\mathbf{M}_{\underline{\mathrm{P}},i}$ represents the spatial inertia matrix of the i-th "P" component with respect to the end point P. Specifically,

$$\mathbf{M}_{\underline{\mathrm{P}},i} = \begin{bmatrix} m_{\underline{\mathrm{P}},i}\mathbf{1}_{3\times3} & m_{\underline{\mathrm{P}},i}\left[\mathbf{r}_{PE_{\underline{\mathrm{P}},i}}\times\right] \\ m_{\underline{\mathrm{P}},i}\left[\mathbf{r}_{PE_{\underline{\mathrm{P}},i}}\times\right]^{\mathrm{T}} & \mathbf{I}_{E_{\underline{\mathrm{P}},i}} + m_{\underline{\mathrm{P}},i}\left[\mathbf{r}_{PE_{\underline{\mathrm{P}},i}}\times\right]\left[\mathbf{r}_{PE_{\underline{\mathrm{P}},i}}\times\right]^{\mathrm{T}} \end{bmatrix} \tag{16}$$

Where, $m_{\underline{\mathrm{P}},i}$ and $\mathbf{I}_{E_{\underline{\mathrm{P}},i}}$ respectively represent the mass of the "P" component at the i-th position and the inertia matrix measured in the frame $\mathcal{K}'_{E_{\underline{\mathrm{P}},i}}$. $\mathbf{r}_{PE_{\underline{\mathrm{P}},i}} = \overrightarrow{PE_{\underline{\mathrm{P}},i}}$, It should be noted that $E_{\underline{P},i}$ and $\mathbf{I}_{E_{\underline{P},i}}$ are functions of the mechanism configuration. Here, $\mathcal{K}'_{E_{\underline{P},i}}$ represents a follower reference frame with the center of mass of the i-th "$\underline{P}$" component as the origin, and the coordinate axes are parallel to the corresponding axes of the frame $\mathbf{M}_{\underline{R},i}$, $\mathbf{M}_{D,i}$, $\mathbf{M}_{Z,i}$, $\mathbf{M}_{N,i}$, $\mathbf{M}_{L,i}$ and $\mathbf{M}_{M,i}$ have the same format as $\mathbf{M}_{\underline{P},i}$.

The elastic potential energy of the system can be expressed as

$$V = \frac{1}{2}\boldsymbol{\rho}_{e,1,i}^{T}\boldsymbol{k}_{e,1,i}\boldsymbol{\rho}_{e,1,i} + \frac{1}{2}\boldsymbol{\rho}_{e,2,i}^{T}\boldsymbol{k}_{e,2,i}\boldsymbol{\rho}_{e,2,i} + \frac{1}{2}\boldsymbol{\rho}_{e,3,i}^{T}\boldsymbol{k}_{e,3,i}\boldsymbol{\rho}_{e,3,i} \tag{17}$$

Where, $\boldsymbol{k}_{e,1,i}$ represents the driving stiffness coefficient of the i-th "$\underline{P}$" component, which is a linear function of the position of the nut relative to the lead screw; $\boldsymbol{k}_{e,2,i}$ represents the radial rotational stiffness coefficient of the i-th branch interface, which is the sum of the radial rotational stiffness coefficient of the lead screw and that of the spline shaft; $\boldsymbol{k}_{e,3,i}$ represents the torsional stiffness coefficient of the i-th "$\underline{R}$" component rotating around $s_{2,i}$ (the radial direction of the spline shaft).Where, $\boldsymbol{k}_{e,1,i} = \mathrm{diag}\left(k_{e,1,1}\ k_{e,1,2}\right)$, $\boldsymbol{k}_{e,2,i}$ and $\boldsymbol{k}_{e,3,i}$ have the same format as $\boldsymbol{k}_{e,1,i}$.

According to Eq. (8) to (14), the following equation holds true

$$\begin{gathered}\dot{\boldsymbol{\xi}}_{t,\underline{P},i} = \mathbf{T}_{\underline{P},i}\dot{\boldsymbol{\rho}}_{W},\ \dot{\boldsymbol{\xi}}_{t,Z,i} = \mathbf{T}_{Z,i}\dot{\boldsymbol{\rho}}_{W},\ \dot{\boldsymbol{\xi}}_{t,D,i} = \mathbf{T}_{D,i}\dot{\boldsymbol{\rho}}_{W} \\ \dot{\boldsymbol{\xi}}_{t,N,i} = \mathbf{T}_{N,i}\dot{\boldsymbol{\rho}}_{W},\ \dot{\boldsymbol{\xi}}_{t,L,i} = \mathbf{T}_{L,i}\dot{\boldsymbol{\rho}}_{W},\ \dot{\boldsymbol{\xi}}_{t,M} = \mathbf{T}_{W}\dot{\boldsymbol{\rho}}_{W}\end{gathered} \tag{18}$$

By organizing Eq. (14) and (16), the expressions for the kinetic energy and elastic potential energy of the high-speed parallel robot can be obtained.

$$\begin{gathered}T = \tfrac{1}{2}\dot{\boldsymbol{\rho}}_{W}^{T}\mathbf{M}_{W}\dot{\boldsymbol{\rho}}_{W} \\ V = \tfrac{1}{2}\boldsymbol{\rho}_{W}^{T}\mathbf{K}_{W}\boldsymbol{\rho}_{W}\end{gathered} \tag{19}$$

Where, $\mathbf{M}_{W} = \sum_{i=1}^{2}\begin{pmatrix}\mathbf{T}_{\underline{P},i}^{T}\mathbf{M}_{\underline{P},i}\mathbf{T}_{\underline{P},i} + \mathbf{T}_{\underline{R},i}^{T}\mathbf{M}_{\underline{R},i}\mathbf{T}_{\underline{R},i} + \mathbf{T}_{D,i}^{T}\mathbf{M}_{D,i}\mathbf{T}_{D,i} \\ + \mathbf{T}_{Z,i}^{T}\mathbf{M}_{Z,i}\mathbf{T}_{Z,i} + \mathbf{T}_{N,i}^{T}\mathbf{M}_{N,i}\mathbf{T}_{N,i} + \mathbf{T}_{L,i}^{T}\mathbf{M}_{L,i}\mathbf{T}_{L,i}\end{pmatrix} + \mathbf{T}_{M}^{T}\mathbf{M}_{M}\mathbf{T}_{M}$, $\mathbf{K}_{W} = \mathrm{diag}\left[\boldsymbol{k}_{e,1,i}\ \boldsymbol{k}_{e,2,i}\ \boldsymbol{k}_{e,3,i}\right]$,Where, $\mathbf{M}_{W} \in \mathbb{R}^{6\times 6}$ and $\mathbf{K}_{W} \in \mathbb{R}^{6\times 6}$ respectively represent the mass matrix and stiffness matrix of the lumped parameter model when using as the generalized coordinates.

Furthermore, noting that T is a reversible matrix, then Eq. (13) can be rewritten as

$$\boldsymbol{\rho}_{W} = \mathbf{T}_{W}^{-1}\boldsymbol{\xi}_{t} \tag{20}$$

Furthermore, the kinetic energy and elastic potential energy of this high-speed parallel robot can be expressed as

$$T = \frac{1}{2}\dot{\boldsymbol{\xi}}_{t}^{T}\mathbf{T}_{W}^{-T}\mathbf{M}_{W}\mathbf{T}_{W}^{-1}\dot{\boldsymbol{\xi}}_{t} \tag{21}$$

$V = \frac{1}{2}\boldsymbol{\xi}_{t}{}^{T}\mathbf{T}_{W}^{-T}\boldsymbol{K}_{W}\mathbf{T}_{W}^{-1}\boldsymbol{\xi}_{t}$(22)

From the Lagrange equation, the free vibration equation with $\boldsymbol{\xi}_{t}$ as the generalized coordinate can be obtained.

$$\mathbf{M}\ddot{\boldsymbol{\xi}}_{t} + \mathbf{K}\boldsymbol{\xi}_{t} = \mathbf{0} \tag{23}$$

Where, $\mathbf{M} = \mathbf{T}_{W}^{-T}\mathbf{M}_{W}\mathbf{T}_{W}^{-1}$,$\mathbf{K} = \mathbf{T}_{W}^{-T}\mathbf{K}_{W}\mathbf{T}_{W}^{-1}$.

4 Verification

This section takes the high-speed parallel robot as the research object, and sets a set of scale parameters. Using the finite element software SAMCEF, a full finite element analysis of the robot is conducted to obtain a complete set of natural frequencies and modes. Then, it is compared with the analytical model data calculated in MATLAB to verify the correctness of the analytical model derivation. The geometric dimensions of the robot are shown in Table 1, and the relevant stiffness coefficients and inertia parameters are shown in Tables 2, 3. These data are obtained from the design manual and CAD/CAE software respectively.

Table 1. Dimensional parameters of the high-speed parallel robot

Types	l_1	l_2	s_k	b	b'	l_b	P	p
Parameter (mm)	200	425	30	75	131	60	50	28

Table 2. Inertial parameters

Components	Inertia tensor ($kg \cdot mm^2$)	Mass (kg)
$\underline{P}(i)$	$diag\begin{bmatrix} 122639 & 122639 & 215 \end{bmatrix}$	2.795
$\underline{R}(i)$	$diag\begin{bmatrix} 61948 & 61948 & 156 \end{bmatrix}$	1.393
$D(i)$	$\begin{bmatrix} 18298 & 12 & -21 \\ & 22921 & 1354 \\ sym & & 8089 \end{bmatrix}$	4.2
Z_1	$\begin{bmatrix} 5630 & -997 & -3198 \\ & 20219 & 90 \\ sym & & 18251 \end{bmatrix}$	1.78
Z_2	$\begin{bmatrix} 1855 & 432 & 1924 \\ & 4895 & 245 \\ sym & & 3905 \end{bmatrix}$	1
N_1	$\begin{bmatrix} 29398 & & 10705 \\ & 35590 & \\ sym & & 9854 \end{bmatrix}$	1.69
N_2	$diag\begin{bmatrix} 16090 & 844 & 16743 \end{bmatrix}$	0.845

(continued)

(*continued*)

Components	Inertia tensor ($kg \cdot mm^2$)	Mass (kg)
L_1	$diag\left[314\ 2084\ 2263\right]$	0.677
L_2	$diag\left[163\ 274\ 356\right]$	0.368
M	$diag\left[287\ 312\ 118\right]$	0.291

Table 3. Stiffness coefficients

Part A	Part B	Axial Stiffness (N/mm)	Rotation Axial Stiffness ($N \cdot mm/rad$)	Radial Stiffness (N/mm)	Rotation Radial Stiffness ($N \cdot mm/rad$)
Lead screw	Lead screw nut	1.2×10^5	0	2.1×10^5	1×10^7
Spline shaft	Reducer	1×10^5	2×10^8	1×10^5	1×10^7
	Shaft sleeve	0	1×10^7	1×10^5	1×10^7

Figure 4 shows the complete 6th-order finite element simulation model of the high-speed parallel robot. It can be seen that the first mode and the second mode are caused by the torsional deformation of the spline shaft around its own axis; the third mode and the fourth mode are mainly the deformation of the lead screw along its axis direction; the fifth and sixth modes are more the local mode of the robot. Table 4 shows the natural frequencies obtained from the finite element analysis and the natural frequency values obtained by programming based on the analytical approach. The maximum deviation is no more than 9%, verifying the effectiveness of this approach.

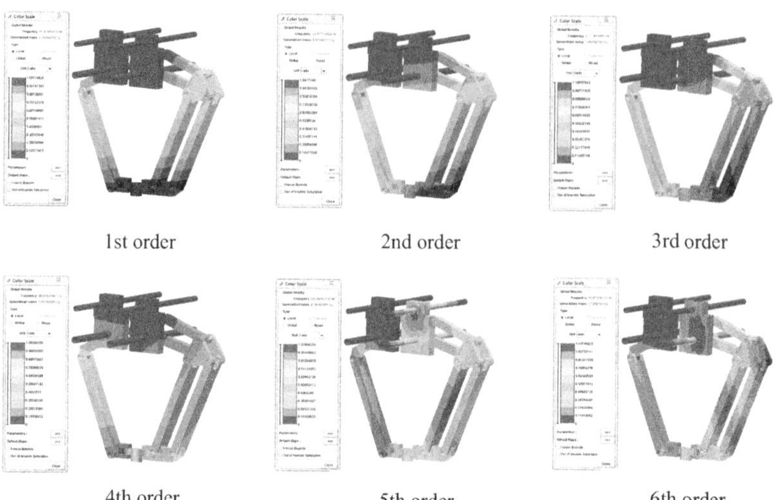

Fig. 4. Mode shapes of the high-speed parallel robot obtained by SAMCEF

Table 4. The natural frequencies obtained by the analytical approach and the finite element analysis

Frequency	1st	2nd	3rd	4th	5th	6th
Analytical (HZ)	17.374	26.913	32.053	40.955	58.654	64.436
FEA (HZ)	15.956	24.977	30.719	40.502	63.208	68.973
Residual (%)	8.88	4.31	4.34	1.12	7.20	6.58

5 Conclusions

This paper proposes an elastodynamics analytical modeling approach based on the screw theory for a two-limb four-DOF (3T1R) high-speed parallel robot. Through the theoretical derivation and verification analysis of the system, the following conclusions are drawn:

1. Based on the screw theory, the mapping relationship between the twist of the end component (moving platform) at the instantaneous coincidence point and the deformation of each elastic link was constructed. By representing the system kinetic energy and elastic potential energy as quadratic forms with elastic deformation as the generalized coordinate, and combining the Lagrangian energy method, the elastic dynamic equation of the entire machine was derived, forming a complete analytical modeling framework from the deformation relationship to the dynamic model, providing a theoretical basis for characterizing the low-order dynamic characteristics under high-speed motion.

2. Given the scale parameters, stiffness coefficients and inertia parameters of the robot, a full finite element analysis was conducted using the finite element software SAMCEF. The results of its low-order natural frequencies and modal shapes were compared with those of the analytical model. The agreement between the two was quite high. This indicates that the analytical model established can accurately capture the low-order dynamic behavior of the mechanism under typical positions, and can be used for the rapid estimation of low-order natural frequencies and modal characteristics within the working space.

In conclusion, the analytical modeling approach based on the screw theory proposed in this paper provides reliable theoretical support for the dynamic characteristic analysis and engineering design of high-speed parallel robots. Moreover, this design method and idea can be widely applied to other parallel robots, which has significant academic significance and application value

Acknowledgements. The authors give many thanks to the editors and the reviewers for their patient work and constructive suggestions.

Disclosure of Interests The authors have no competing interests to declare that are relevant to the content of this article.

Funding This research is partially supported by the National Natural Science Foundation of China (Grant No. 52205030, 52575033), the Special Project for Basic Research Cooperation in Beijing-Tianjin-Hebei Region (24JCZXJC00270).

References

1. Meng, Q., Xie, F., Zhang, S., Liu, X.: Type synthesis and dimensional optimization of a high-speed and high-acceleration parallel robot. J. Mech. Eng. **58**(13), 36–49 (2022). https://doi.org/10.3901/JME.2022.13.036
2. Zhang, J., Xie, F., Ma, Z., et al.: Design of parallel multiple tuned mass dampers for the vibration suppression of a parallel machining robot. Mech. Syst. Signal Process. **200**, 110506 (2023). https://doi.org/10.1016/j.ymssp.2023.110506
3. Law, M., Ihlenfeldt, S., et al.: Position-dependent dynamics and stability of serial-parallel kinematic machines. CIRP Ann. Manuf. Technol. **62**(1), 375–378 (2013). https://doi.org/10.1016/j.cirp.2013.03.134
4. Chen, Q., Zhang, C., et al.: Posture optimization in robotic machining based on comprehensive deformation index considering spindle weight and cutting force. Robot. Comput. Integr. Manuf. **74**, 102290 (2022). https://doi.org/10.1016/j.rcim.2021.102290
5. Lin, Y., Zhao, H., Ding, H.: Spindle configuration analysis and optimization considering the deformation in robotic machining applications. Rob. Comput. Integr. Manuf. **54**, 83–95 (2018). https://doi.org/10.1016/j.rcim.2018.05.005
6. Portman, V.T., Chapsky, V.S., Shneor, Y.: Evaluation and optimization of dynamic stiffness values of the PKMs: CollinearStiffness value approach. Mech. Mach. Theory. **74**(6), 216–244 (2014). https://doi.org/10.1016/j.mechmachtheory.2013.12.009
7. Song, Y., Dong, G., Sun, T., Lian, B.: Elasto-dynamic analysis of a novel 2-DOF rotational parallel mechanism with an articulated travelling platform. Meccanica. **51**(7), 1547–1557 (2016). https://doi.org/10.1007/s11012-014-0099-3

8. Cammarata, A., Condorelli, D., Sinatra, R.: An algorithm to study the Elastodynamics of parallel kinematic machines with lower kinematic pairs. J. Mech. Robot. **5**(1), 1–9 (2013). https://doi.org/10.1115/1.4007705
9. Son, H., Choi, H.J., Park, H.W.: Design and dynamic analysis of an arch-type desktop reconfigurable machine. Int. J. Mach. Tools Manuf. **50**(6), 575–584 (2010). https://doi.org/10.1016/j.ijmachtools.2010.02.006
10. Ma, Y., Niu, W., Luo, Z., Yin, F., Huang, T.: Static and dynamic performance evaluation of a 3-DOF spindle head using CAD-CAE integration methodology. Robot. Comput. Integr. Manuf. **41**, 1–12 (2016). https://doi.org/10.1016/j.rcim.2016.02.006
11. Palmieri, G., Martarelli, M., Palpacelli, M.C., Carbonari, L.: Configuration dependent modal analysis of a Cartesian parallel kinematics manipulator: numerical Modeling and experimental validation. Meccanica. **49**, 961–972 (2014). https://doi.org/10.1007/s11012-013-9842-4
12. Wu, L., Dong, C., Wan, G., Liu, H., Huang, T.: An approach to predict lower-order dynamic behaviors of a 5-DOF hybrid robot using a minimum set of generalized coordinates. Robot. Comput. Integr. Manuf. **67**, 102024 (2021). https://doi.org/10.1016/j.rcim.2020.102024
13. Liu, H., Li, G., Xiao, J.: A C^3 continuous toolpath corner smoothing method for a hybrid machining robot. J. Manuf. Process. **75**, 1072–1088 (2022). https://doi.org/10.1016/j.jmapro.2021.12.057
14. Dong, C., Liu, H., Huang, T., Derek, G.C.: A screw theory-based semi-analytical approach for Elastodynamics of the Tricept robot. J. Mech. Robot. **11**(3), 031005 (2019). https://doi.org/10.1115/1.4043047
15. Dong, L., Yi, M., Yimin, S., Boyan, C., Tao, S.: Complete kinematics/dynamics Modeling and performance analysis of a novel SCARA parallel manipulator based on screw theory. J. Mech. Robot. **16**(10), 101004 (2024). https://doi.org/10.1016/j.mechmachtheory.2009.01.006

Adaptive Asymptotic Tracking Control for Flexible-Joint Robots with Random Noises and Dead-Zone Output

Yixuan Yuan[1,2,3] and Liping Xie[1,2,3](✉)

[1] School of Automation, Southeast University, Nanjing, Jiangsu, China
[2] China Key Laboratory of Measurement and Control of Complex Systems of Engineering, Ministry of Education, Nanjing, Jiangsu, China
[3] Advanced Ocean Institute of Southeast University, Nantong 226334, China
{yuanyixuan,lpxie}@seu.edu.cn

Abstract. The present paper is concerned with the control challenges posed by output dead-zones and stochastic noise in flexible-joint robot systems. A novel tracking control strategy, grounded in the principles of adaptive control theory, is hereby proposed. The Nussbaum function is employed to address the unknown output dead-zone, thereby ensuring effective control input despite this nonlinearity. Furthermore, the incorporation of fuzzy techniques facilitates the circumvention of the intricate analytical computations necessitated by the virtual controller derivative, thereby enabling the accurate approximation of nonlinear functions. Concurrently, given that unmodeled dynamics are an inevitable component of numerous practical control problems, this paper employs adaptive techniques to address unmodeled dynamics without necessitating additional conditions. These innovations contribute to enhanced system robustness and tracking precision. The efficacy of the strategy is validated by simulation results, which demonstrate significant improvements in control performance under stochastic disturbances.

Keywords: Flexible-joint robots · Random noises · Dead-zone output · Unmodeled dynamics

1 Introduction

The mobile robot manipulator serves as an integrated robotic system that combines the flexibility of a mobile platform with the high precision of a manipulator. It is capable of adapting to a wide range of application scenarios and offers innovative solutions to meet the complex demands in fields such as industry, manufacturing, and medical services [1–4]. However, the traditional rigid manipulators, which are essential components of mobile manipulators, may pose significant risks if they malfunction and lose control. Fortunately, the advent of flexible-joint manipulator (FJM) technology provides an effective solution to this issue. The flexibility and adaptability of FJM enable it to effectively absorb

Z. Hou et al. (Eds.): CIRAC 2025, CCIS 2885, pp. 71–83, 2026.
https://doi.org/10.1007/978-981-92-0045-0_6

and mitigate impact forces when facing potential risks, thereby significantly reducing potential damage [5,6]. Despite these advantages of FJM technology, it is inevitably subject to stochastic noise during operation, which can significantly degrade tracking performance and potentially destabilize the system. Recent theoretical research has revealed that many engineering systems, such as guided-missile systems and aerospace systems, are subject to stochastic factors. The control performance and stability of the overall closed-loop system cannot be ensured without considering these stochastic factors [7–11].

Moreover, the process of modeling real-world systems often involves intrinsic uncertainties that are difficult to precisely represent using mathematical techniques. The application of system simplification methods may lead to the loss of certain dynamic characteristics. As evidenced in [12–16], unmodeled dynamics are an inevitable part of many practical control problems. Zhao et al. employed a three-layer neural network identifier to reconstruct the completely unknown functions and investigated the optimal control problem of interconnected nonlinear systems with unmodeled dynamics [17]. Hua et al. employed the dynamic gain technique and the idea of changing supply functions to deal with the time-delay terms and unmodeled dynamics in the system [18]. Yuan et al. employed neural network technology to address the unmodeled dynamics and stochastic disturbances while ensuring that the system states do not violate the constraints [19]. Therefore, how to solve the problem of unmodeled dynamics is one of the main contributions of this paper.

For control systems that are in operation, the impact of dead-zone is equally significant and should not be ignored. Zong et al. adopted an unknown dead-zone input elimination parameter boundary [20]. Liu et al. addressed the unknown dead-zone input problem in continuous stirred tank reactors by employing reinforcement learning algorithms [21]. Zhan et al. regarded the asymmetric input dead-zone as a time-varying uncertain system in the context of large-scale nonstrict feedback systems [22]. In practical applications, the output of the factory is affected by dead-zone nonlinearity, also referred to as dead-zone output. In comparison to the intricacies and challenges posed by dead-zone input issues, those arising from dead-zone output present a more complex landscape. The dead-zone input primarily affects the input signal, whereas dead zone output directly affects the feedback signal. This makes accurately grasping the system's dynamic characteristics difficult, which increases the difficulty of designing a control strategy. The dead-zone input primarily affects the input signal, while the dead-zone output directly affects the feedback signal. These effects make grasping the systems dynamic characteristics difficult and increase the difficulty of designing a control strategy [23]. This paper thoroughly investigates the control problem of a flexible manipulator system with output dead-zone and stochastic noise, and proposes a novel tracking control strategy based on adaptive control theory. Firstly, the Nussbaum function is employed to address the unknown output dead-zone issue. In addition, by introducing fuzzy techniques, the analytical calculation of the derivative of the virtual controller is successfully avoided, and the unknown nonlinear functions are effectively approximated with the aid of fuzzy techniques. The main contributions are summarized as follows.

1. In this paper, the control problem of flexible manipulators with stochastic noise is effectively addressed. By employing a novel tracking control strategy based on adaptive control theory, the system's performance is significantly enhanced. Specifically, the introduction of fuzzy techniques not only avoids the complex analytical calculation of the derivative of the virtual controller but also effectively approximates the unknown nonlinear functions, thereby improving the system's robustness against stochastic noise. This approach ensures that the flexible manipulator can maintain accurate tracking performance even in the presence of stochastic disturbances, thus contributing to the development of more reliable and efficient control solutions for flexible robotic systems.
2. The presence of output dead-zones in flexible manipulators can significantly degrade control performance and complicate the control design. In this paper, a novel control strategy is proposed to effectively address this issue. By employing the Nussbaum function, the problem of unknown output dead-zones is successfully resolved. This approach ensures that the control input can effectively overcome the dead-zone effects, thereby maintaining the desired system performance.

2 Preliminaries and Problem Formulation

The dynamic model of an n-link flexible-joint robot can be expressed as

$$\begin{cases} I(x_1)\dot{x}_2 = \dfrac{\dot{x}_1}{2}\dfrac{dI(x_1)}{dx_1}x_2 - \dfrac{d\mathcal{G}(x_1)}{dx_1} + F_1(x_1, x_2) \\ \qquad - K(x_1 - x_3) + D_1(x_1, x_2)d, \\ J\dot{x}_4 - K(x_1 - x_3) = u + Mx_4 + D_2(x_3, x_4)d, \end{cases} \tag{1}$$

where E represent the kinetic energy, P represent the potential energy, q, $\dot{q}$, q_m, $\dot{q}_m \in R^n$ represent the link position, link velocity, rotor angular position and velocity, respectively. $I(q)$ is the inertia matrix, J is the actuator inertia, $\mathcal{G}(q)$ is the motor potential energy, M is the natural damping term, D is the random excitation forces, and K is the joint flexibility. In real-world systems, stochastic disturbances and unmodeled dynamics are inevitable phenomena. It is imperative to take these factors into consideration when constructing the model and designing the control strategy. Specifically, this study incorporates stochastic disturbances that satisfy the condition $g^T d\omega$ and also incorporates unmodeled dynamics within the system. The unmodeled dynamics may stem from the system's inherent complexity or from uncertainties in the external environment. By defining the state variables $x_1 = q$, $x_2 = \dot{q}$, $x_3 = q_m$, and $x_4 = \dot{q}_m$, then (1) can be rewritten as

$$\begin{cases} d\hbar = \sigma(\hbar, x)dt, \\ dx_1 = x_2 dt, \\ dx_2 = (K_I x_3 + f_2(\bar{x}_2) + d_2(\hbar, x))dt + g_2(\bar{x}_2)d\omega, \\ dx_3 = x_4 dt, \\ dx_4 = (J^{-1}u + f_4(x) + d_4(\hbar, x))dt + g_4(x)d\omega, \\ y = \mathcal{S}(x_1), \end{cases} \tag{2}$$

where $\sigma(\hbar, x)$ is smooth function, with $\hbar$ representing unmodeled dynamics. The symbol ω denotes the standard Wiener process and the $\mathcal{S}(x_1)$ represents the dead-zone nonlinearity.

Definition 1. *[23] The unknown dead-zone output model is represented as*

$$\mathcal{S}(x_1) = \begin{cases} p_l(x_1 - h_l), & x_1 \in (-\infty, h_l) \\ 0, & x_i \in [h_l, h_r] \\ p_r(x_1 - h_r), & x_1 \in [h_r, \infty) \end{cases} \tag{3}$$

where h_l and h_r indicate the dead-zone width parameters, which satisfy $h_l < 0 < h_r$. The parameters $p_r, p_l > 0$ denote the slopes of both sides of the dead-zone model. It is further assumed that the parameters p_r, p_l, h_l and h_r in (3) are unknown bounded constants. An adaptive inverse model is presented to approximate the dead-zone model (3)

$$\mathcal{S}_0(y^*) \triangleq \frac{(y + |p_l h_l|)exp\{-ry\}}{(1 + exp\{-ry\})p_l} + \frac{y + p_r h_r}{(1 + exp\{-ry\})p_r}.$$

where the adaptive parameter r satisfies $\dot{r} = k_{r1}\dot{y}_d - k_{r2}(x_1 - y_d) - k_{r3}r$.

Assumption 1. [19] To account for the uncertain disturbances $d_i(\hbar, x)$ $(i = 1, \cdots, n)$, non-negative smooth functions $\bar{d}_{i1}(\|x\|) \geq 0$ and $\bar{d}_{i2}(\|\hbar\|) \geq 0$ are introduced. These functions ensure that the following inequalities hold: $|d_i(\hbar, x)| \leq \bar{d}_{i1}(\|x\|) + \bar{d}_{i2}(\|\hbar\|)$.

Lemma 1. *[9] There exists an FLS $\Psi^T W(x)$ for any $\delta > 0$ and continuous function $\bar{f}(x)$ denoted on a compact set $\beth$ so that*

$$\sup_{x \in \beth} |\bar{f}(x) - \Psi^T W(x)| \leq \delta$$

where $\Psi = [\psi_1, \ldots, \psi_p]^T \in \mathbb{R}^l$, $W(x) = \Big([w_1(x), \ldots, w_l(x)]^T / \sum_{i=1}^{l} w_i(x)\Big)$, $\delta \leq a_3$, and $a_3 > 0$ is positive nonumber.

Lemma 2. [7] Taking into account the defined set $S_e = \{v||v| < 0.2554e\}$ we can deduce that if $v \notin S_e$, it is then implied that

$$1 - 16\tanh^2(\tfrac{v}{e}) \leq 0.$$

3 Main Results

First, based on reference [23], it can be obtained that $\frac{\partial y^*}{\partial x_1} = \mathcal{S}_1(t)$, and there exists a constant $\bar{\mathcal{S}}_1$ such that $\mathcal{S}_1(t) \le \bar{\mathcal{S}}_1$. Define

$$v_1 = y^* - x_d, \quad v_i = x_i - x_{i-1}^*, \quad i = 2, 3, 4, \tag{4}$$

where y_d is reference signal and x_{i-1}^* are virtual controllers.

Step 1: Let

$$V_1 = \frac{1}{4}v_1^4 + \frac{1}{2a_{11}}\tilde{\theta}_{11}^2 + \frac{1}{2a_{12}}\tilde{\theta}_{12}^2 + \frac{n(t)}{a_{13}}, \tag{5}$$

where a_{11}, a_{12}, a_{13} are positive constants and it is further assumed that $\tilde{\theta}_i = \theta_i - \hat{\theta}_i$, where the definition of θ_i will be provided later. According to the Itô formula and (4), (5), we have

$$\mathcal{L}V_1 = \mathcal{S}_1(t)v_1^3 v_2 + \mathcal{S}_1(t)v_1^3 x_1^* - \frac{1}{a_{11}}\tilde{\theta}_{11}\dot{\hat{\theta}}_{11} - \frac{1}{a_{12}}\tilde{\theta}_{12}\dot{\hat{\theta}}_{12} - v_1^3\dot{x}_d + \frac{\dot{n}(t)}{a_{13}}. \tag{6}$$

Application of Assumption 2 leads to

$$\begin{aligned} \frac{\dot{n}(t)}{a_{13}} &= -\frac{a_1 n(t)}{a_{13}} + \frac{\bar{\psi}_5(x_1)}{a_{13}} + \frac{a_2}{a_{13}} \\ &= -\frac{a_1 n(t)}{a_{13}} + v_1^3 \cdot 16\tanh^2\left(\frac{v_1^3}{c_{12}}\right)\frac{\bar{\psi}_5(x_1)}{a_{13}v_1^3} \\ &\quad + \left[1 - 16\tanh^2\left(\frac{v_1^3}{c_{12}}\right)\right]\frac{\bar{\psi}_5(x_1)}{a_{13}} + \frac{a_2}{a_{13}}, \end{aligned} \tag{7}$$

where c_{12} is positive constant. Define

$$\bar{f}_1 = 16\tanh^2\left(\frac{v_1^3}{c_{12}}\right)\frac{\bar{\psi}_5(x_1)}{a_{13}v_1^3} - \dot{x}_d, \tag{8}$$

with the aid of Lemma 1 the approximation ability of FLS, it follows that for any constant $c_{13}, c_{14} > 0$

$$\bar{f}_1 = \mathcal{F}_1^T\mathcal{E}_1(\mathcal{X}_1) + \mathcal{C}_1(\mathcal{X}_1), \qquad \|\mathcal{C}_1(\mathcal{X}_1)\| \le c_{13}, \tag{9}$$

where $\mathcal{X}_1 = [v_1, x_d]^T$. Based on Young's inequality, one has

$$v_1^3\bar{f}_1 \le \frac{1}{2c_{14}^2}v_1^6\tilde{\theta}_{11}\mathcal{E}_1^T\mathcal{E}_1 + \frac{1}{2c_{14}^2}v_1^6\hat{\theta}_{11}\mathcal{E}_1^T\mathcal{E}_1 + \frac{1}{2}v_1^6 + \frac{1}{2}c_{13}^2 + \frac{1}{2}c_{14}^2, \tag{10}$$

$$\mathcal{S}_1(t)v_1^3 v_2 \le \frac{3}{4}\bar{\mathcal{S}}_1^{4/3}v_1^4 + \frac{1}{4}v_2^4 \le \tilde{\theta}_{12}v_1^4 + \hat{\theta}_{12}v_1^4 + \frac{1}{4}v_2^4, \tag{11}$$

where $\theta_{11} = \|\mathcal{F}_1^T\mathcal{F}_1\|$ and $\theta_{12} = \frac{3}{4}\bar{\mathcal{S}}_1^{4/3}$. Let $x_1^* = \mathbb{N}(\mathcal{V})\bar{x}_1^*$

$$x_1^* = \mathbb{N}(\mathcal{V}_1)\bar{x}_1^* = \mathcal{V}_1^2\cos(\mathcal{V}_1), \tag{12}$$

$$\bar{x}_1^* = c_1 v_1 + \hat{\theta}_{12} v_1 + \frac{1}{2c_{14}^2} v_1^3 \hat{\theta}_{11} \mathcal{E}_1^T \mathcal{E}_1 + \frac{1}{2} v_1^3, \tag{13}$$

among which $\dot{\mathcal{V}}_1 = c\bar{x}_1^* v_1^3$, c, c_1, r_{11}, $r_{12} > 0$ are the designed parameters. Substituting (7)-(13) into (6) yields

$$\begin{aligned} \mathcal{L}V_1 \leq & - c_1 v_1^4 + \frac{r_{11}}{a_{11}} \tilde{\theta}_{11}^T \hat{\theta}_{11} + \frac{r_{12}}{a_{12}} \tilde{\theta}_{12}^T \hat{\theta}_{12} + \frac{1}{4} v_2^4 - \frac{a_1 n(t)}{a_{13}} + \frac{a_2}{a_{13}} + \frac{1}{2} c_{13}^2 \\ & + \frac{1}{2} c_{14}^2 + \left[1 - 16 \tanh^2 \left(\frac{v_1^3}{c_{12}}\right)\right] \frac{\bar{\psi}_5(x_1)}{a_{13}} + \frac{1}{c} (\bar{\mathcal{S}}_1 \mathbb{N}(\mathcal{V}_1) + 1) \dot{\mathcal{V}}_1, \end{aligned} \tag{14}$$

where the adaptive laws $\dot{\hat{\theta}}_{11}$ and $\dot{\hat{\theta}}_{12}$ are designed as

$$\dot{\hat{\theta}}_{11} = \frac{a_{11}}{2c_{14}^2} v_1^6 \mathcal{E}_1^T \mathcal{E}_1 - r_{11} \hat{\theta}_{11}, \quad \dot{\hat{\theta}}_{11} = a_{12} v_1^4 - r_{12} \hat{\theta}_{12}. \tag{15}$$

Step 2: Select the Lyapunov function V_2 as

$$V_2 = V_1 + \frac{1}{4} v_2^4 + + \frac{1}{2a_{21}} \tilde{\theta}_{21}^2, \tag{16}$$

where a_{21} is positive constant. According to the Itô formula and (4), (16), we have

$$\mathcal{L}V_2 = \mathcal{L}V_1 + v_2^3 (K_I x_3 + f_2(\bar{x}_2) + d_2(\hbar, x) - \mathcal{L}x_1^*) + \frac{3}{2} v_2^2 \| g_2^T g_2 \| - \frac{1}{a_{21}} \tilde{\theta}_{21} \dot{\hat{\theta}}_{21}. \tag{17}$$

With the help of [19], application of Young's and Assumption 1 leads to

$$v_2^3 d_2(\hbar, x) \leq v_2^3 \bar{d}_2(\hbar, n) + \frac{1}{2} v_2^6 + \frac{1}{2} \bar{d}_{22}^2 (\psi_3^{-1}(C(t))), \tag{18}$$

$$\frac{3}{2} v_2^2 \| g_2^T g_2 \| \leq \frac{3}{4c_{21}^2} v_2^4 \| g_2^T (x) \|^4 + \frac{3}{4} c_{21}^2, \tag{19}$$

$$v_2^3 K_I x_3 \leq \frac{3}{4} K_I^{4/3} v_2^4 + \frac{1}{4} v_3^4 + K_I v_2^3 x_2^*, \tag{20}$$

where $\bar{d}_2(\hbar, n) = \bar{d}_{21}(\|x\|) + \bar{d}_{22}(\psi_3^{-1}(n(t)))$ and c_{21} is positive constant. Define

$$\bar{f}_2 = \frac{1}{4} v_2 + \frac{3}{4} K_I^{4/3} v_2 + f_2(\bar{x}_2) - \mathcal{L}x_1^* + \frac{3}{4c_{21}^2} v_2 \| g_2^T (x) \|^4 + \bar{d}_2(\hbar, n). \tag{21}$$

Similarly to (9), it can be deduce that

$$v_2^3 \bar{f}_2 \leq \frac{1}{2c_{24}^2} v_2^6 \tilde{\theta}_{21} \mathcal{E}_2^T \mathcal{E}_2 + \frac{1}{2c_{24}^2} v_2^6 \hat{\theta}_{21} \mathcal{E}_2^T \mathcal{E}_2 + \frac{1}{2} v_2^6 + \frac{1}{2} c_{23}^2 + \frac{1}{2} c_{24}^2, \tag{22}$$

where $\theta_{21} = \|\mathcal{F}_2^T \mathcal{F}_2\|$, $\mathcal{X}_2 = [x, n, \hat{\theta}_{11}, \hat{\theta}_{12}]^T$, and c_{23}, c_{24} are positive constants. Choose α_i and the adaptive law $\dot{\hat{\theta}}_{21}$ as

$$x_2^* = -\frac{1}{K_I} [c_2 v_2 + v_2^3 + \frac{1}{2c_{24}^2} v_2^3 \hat{\theta}_{21} \mathcal{E}_2^T \mathcal{E}_2], \quad \dot{\hat{\theta}}_{21} = \frac{a_{21}}{2c_{24}^2} v_2^6 \mathcal{E}_2^T \mathcal{E}_2 - r_{21} \hat{\theta}_{21}, \tag{23}$$

where $c_2, r_{21} > 0$ are the designed parameters. Hence, the following result holds

$$\mathcal{L}V_2 \leq \mathcal{L}V_1 - \frac{1}{4}v_2^4 + \frac{1}{4}v_3^4 - c_2 v_2^4 + \frac{r_{21}}{a_{21}}\tilde{\theta}_{21}^T\hat{\theta}_{21} + \frac{1}{2}\bar{d}_{22}^2(\psi_3^{-1}(C(t))) + \frac{3}{4}c_{21}^2 + \frac{1}{2}c_{23}^2 + \frac{1}{2}c_{24}^2. \tag{24}$$

Step 3: Taking $V_3 = V_2 + \frac{1}{4}v_3^4 + \frac{1}{2a_{31}}\tilde{\theta}_{31}^2$. In light of the Itô formula and (4), (23), it holds

$$\mathcal{L}V_3 = \mathcal{L}V_2 + v_3^3(x_4 - \mathcal{L}x_2^*) + \frac{3}{2}v_3^2\|\frac{\partial x_2^*}{\partial v_2}g_2^T\|^2 - \frac{1}{a_{31}}\tilde{\theta}_{31}\dot{\hat{\theta}}_{31}. \tag{25}$$

Similarly to Step 2, the virtual controller and the adaptive update law are designed as

$$x_3^* = -[c_3 v_3 + \frac{1}{2}v_3^3 + \frac{1}{2c_{34}^2}v_3^3\hat{\theta}_{31}\mathcal{E}_3^T\mathcal{E}_3], \quad \dot{\hat{\theta}}_{31} = \frac{a_{31}}{2c_{34}^2}v_3^6\mathcal{E}_3^T\mathcal{E}_3 - r_{31}\hat{\theta}_{31}, \tag{26}$$

where $\theta_{31} = \|\mathcal{F}_3^T\mathcal{F}_3\|$, $\mathcal{X}_3 = [x, n, \hat{\theta}_{11}, \hat{\theta}_{12}, \hat{\theta}_{21}]^T$, and $a_{31}, c_3, c_{34}, r_{31}$ are positive constants. Combining (25) and (26) yields

$$\mathcal{L}V_3 \leq \mathcal{L}V_2 - \frac{1}{4}v_3^4 + \frac{1}{4}v_4^4 - c_3 v_3^4 + \frac{r_{31}}{a_{31}}\tilde{\theta}_{31}^T\hat{\theta}_{31} + \frac{3}{4}c_{31}^2 + \frac{1}{2}c_{33}^2 + \frac{1}{2}c_{34}^2. \tag{27}$$

where c_{31}, c_{33} are the designed positive parameters.

Step 4: The Lyapunov function is defined as follows:

$$V_4 = V_3 + \frac{1}{4}v_4^4 + \frac{1}{2a_{41}}\tilde{\theta}_{41}^2, \tag{28}$$

with the aid of Itô formula and (4), (28), one can further yield

$$\mathcal{L}V_4 = \mathcal{L}V_3 - \frac{1}{a_{41}}\tilde{\theta}_{41}\dot{\hat{\theta}}_{41} + v_4^3(J^{-1}u + f_4(x) + d_4(\hbar, x) - \mathcal{L}x_3^*) + \frac{3}{2}v_4^2\|g_4^T - \frac{\partial x_3^*}{\partial x_2}g_2^T\|. \tag{29}$$

Similarly to (15), one has

$$v_4^3 d_4(\hbar, x) \leq v_4^3\bar{d}_4(\hbar, n) + \frac{1}{2}v_4^6 + \frac{1}{2}\bar{d}_{42}^2(\psi_3^{-1}(C(t))), \tag{30}$$

$$\frac{3}{2}v_4^2\|g_4^T - \frac{\partial x_3^*}{\partial x_2}g_2^T\| \leq \frac{3}{4c_{41}^2}v_4^4\|g_4^T - \frac{\partial x_3^*}{\partial x_2}g_2^T\|^4 + \frac{3}{4}c_{41}^2, \tag{31}$$

where $\bar{d}_4(\hbar, n) = \bar{d}_{41}(\|x\|) + \bar{d}_{42}(\psi_3^{-1}(n(t)))$ and c_{41} is positive constant. With the help of Lemma 1 the approximation ability of FLS, it follows that for any positive constant c_{43}

$$\bar{f}_4 = \mathcal{F}_4^T\mathcal{E}_4(\mathcal{X}_4) + \mathcal{C}_4(\mathcal{X}_4), \quad \|\mathcal{C}_4(\mathcal{X}_4)\| \leq c_{43}, \tag{32}$$

where $\mathcal{X}_4 = [x, n, \hat{\theta}_{11}, \hat{\theta}_{12}, \hat{\theta}_{21}, \hat{\theta}_{31}]^T$ and $\bar{f}_4 = \frac{1}{4}v_4 + \frac{3}{4c_{41}^2}v_4\|g_4^T - \frac{\partial x_3^*}{\partial x_2}g_2^T\|^4 + f_4(x) - \mathcal{L}x_3^* + \bar{d}_4(\hbar, n)$. Then, (29) can be rewritten as follows:

$$\begin{aligned}\mathcal{L}V_4 \leq \mathcal{L}V_3 - \frac{1}{4}v_4^4 - \frac{1}{a_{41}}\tilde{\theta}_{41}\dot{\hat{\theta}}_{41} + v_4^3 J^{-1}u + v_4^6 + \frac{1}{2}\bar{d}_{42}^2(\psi_3^{-1}(C(t))) \\ + \frac{1}{2c_{44}^2}v_4^6\hat{\theta}_{41}\mathcal{E}_4^T\mathcal{E}_4 + \frac{1}{2c_{44}^2}v_4^6\hat{\theta}_{41}\mathcal{E}_4^T\mathcal{E}_4 + \frac{1}{2}v_4^6 + \frac{1}{2}c_{43}^2 + \frac{1}{2}c_{44}^2 + \frac{3}{4}c_{41}^2,\end{aligned} \tag{33}$$

using the above inductive arguments, one can derive that

$$u = -J[c_4v_4 + v_4^3 + \frac{1}{2c_{44}^2}v_4^3\hat{\theta}_{41}\mathcal{E}_4^T\mathcal{E}_4], \quad \dot{\hat{\theta}}_{41} = \frac{a_{41}}{2c_{44}^2}v_4^6\mathcal{E}_4^T\mathcal{E}_4 - r_{41}\hat{\theta}_{41}, \tag{34}$$

where $c_4, c_{42}, c_{44}, r_{41}, a_{41} > 0$ are positive constants.

Theorem 1. *Consider the system described by equation (2) with the dead-zone output model given by equation (3). Under the conditions specified in Assumption 1, the proposed adaptive control laws and the actual control signal ensure that all signals within the closed-loop system remain bounded.*

Proof. It follows from (14), (24), (27) and (33) that

$$\begin{aligned}\mathcal{L}V_4 \leq & -\sum_{i=1}^{4} c_i v_i^4 + \sum_{i=1}^{4}\frac{r_{i1}}{a_{i1}}\tilde{\theta}_{i1}^T\hat{\theta}_{i1} + \frac{r_{12}}{a_{12}}\tilde{\theta}_{12}^T\hat{\theta}_{12} - \frac{a_1 n(t)}{a_{13}} + \frac{a_2}{a_{13}} \\ & + \left[1 - 16\tanh^2\left(\frac{v_1^3}{c_{12}}\right)\right]\frac{\psi_5(x_1)}{a_{13}} + \frac{1}{c}(\bar{\mathcal{S}}_1\mathrm{N}(\mathcal{V}_1) + 1)\dot{\mathcal{V}}_1 \\ & + \sum_{i=2}^{4}\frac{3}{4}c_{i1}^2 + \sum_{i=1}^{4}\frac{1}{2}(c_{i3}^2 + c_{i4}^2) + \sum_{i=2,4}\frac{1}{2}\bar{d}_{i2}^2(\psi_3^{-1}(C(t))).\end{aligned} \tag{35}$$

By Lemma 2, it follows that when $v_1 \in S_{c_{12}}$, that is, $|v_1| < 0.2554c_{12}$, there exists a positive constant $\mathcal{N}$ such that $\left(1 - 16\tanh^2\left(\frac{v_1^3}{c_{12}}\right)\right)\frac{\psi_5(x_1)}{a_{13}} \leq \mathcal{N}$. When $v_1 \notin S_{c_{12}}$, we have $\left(1 - 16\tanh^2\left(\frac{v_1^3}{c_{12}}\right)\right)\frac{\psi_5(x_1)}{a_{13}} \leq 0$. In light of "$\tilde{\theta}^T\hat{\theta} \leq \frac{1}{2}\theta^2 - \frac{1}{2}\tilde{\theta}^2$", there holds

$$\mathcal{L}V_4 \leq -\sum_{i=1}^{4} c_i v_i^4 - \sum_{i=1}^{4}\frac{r_{i1}}{2a_{i1}}\tilde{\theta}_{i1}^2 - \frac{r_{21}}{2a_{21}}\tilde{\theta}_{21}^2 - \frac{a_1 n(t)}{a_{13}} + \frac{1}{c}(\bar{\mathcal{S}}_1\mathrm{N}(\mathcal{V}_1) + 1)\dot{\mathcal{V}}_1 + \mathcal{R}, \tag{36}$$

where

$$\mathcal{R}=\begin{cases}\frac{a_2}{a_{13}}+\sum_{i=2}^{4}\frac{3}{4}c_{i1}^2+\sum_{i=1}^{4}\frac{1}{2}(c_{i3}^2+c_{i4}^2)+\mathcal{N}+\frac{r_{12}}{2a_{12}}\theta_{12}^2\\ \quad+\sum_{i=2,4}\frac{1}{2}\bar{d}_{i2}^2(\psi_3^{-1}(C(t)))+\sum_{i=1}^{4}\frac{r_{i1}}{2a_{i1}}\theta_{i1}^2, & v_1\in S_{c_{12}},\\ \frac{a_2}{a_{13}}+\sum_{i=2}^{4}\frac{3}{4}c_{i1}^2+\sum_{i=1}^{4}\frac{1}{2}(c_{i3}^2+c_{i4}^2)+\frac{r_{12}}{2a_{12}}\theta_{12}^2\\ \quad+\sum_{i=2,4}\frac{1}{2}\bar{d}_{i2}^2(\psi_3^{-1}(C(t)))+\sum_{i=1}^{4}\frac{r_{i1}}{2a_{i1}}\theta_{i1}^2, & v_1\notin S_{c_{12}}.\end{cases} \tag{37}$$

We can further rewrite (36) as

$$\mathcal{L}V_4\leq-\bar{c}V_4+\frac{1}{c}(\bar{\mathcal{S}}_1\mathbb{N}(\mathcal{V}_1)+1)\dot{\mathcal{V}}_1+\mathcal{R}, \tag{38}$$

where $\bar{c}=\min\{4c_i,r_{i1},r_{21},a_1|i=1,2,3,4\}$. Then, it follows

$$EV(t)\leq\frac{exp\{-\bar{c}t\}}{c}\int_0^t(\mathcal{S}_1\mathcal{N}(\mathcal{V}_1)+1)\,\dot{\mathcal{V}}_1exp\{\bar{c}\tau\}d\tau+V(0)+\frac{\Delta}{\bar{c}}. \tag{39}$$

Based on the properties of Nussbaum-type function, we know that all signals within the closed-loop system remain bounded.

4 Simulation Example

In this section, a simulation study on a single-link flexible-joint manipulator system will be carried out to intuitively corroborate the preceding theoretical findings. Consider the flexible-joint manipulator system attitude stochastic nonlinear system

$$\begin{cases} d\hbar=(-0.1\sin(\hbar)-\exp\{0.5\cos(x_1-5)\})dt,\\ dx_1=x_2dt,\\ dx_2=(4x_3-4x_1-cosx_2-9.8\sin x_1+x_2\hbar)dt+g_2(\bar{x}_2)d\omega,\\ dx_3=x_4dt,\\ dx_4=(10u-10x_4-40(x_3-x_1)+0.15x_4\hbar\cos x_1)dt+g_4(x)d\omega,\\ \quad y=\mathcal{S}(x_1),\end{cases} \tag{40}$$

where $g_2(\bar{x}_2)=0$, $g_4(x)=0.25x_4\cos(1+x_1^2)$, $x_d=0.5\sin(0.6t)+0.2\cos(t)$, $\dot{\mathcal{V}}_1=16\bar{x}_1^*v_1^3$. The initial conditions of adaptive update laws are chosen as

$$[x_1(0),x_2(0),x_3(0),x_4(0)]^T=[1,0.1,0.1,0.1]^T. \tag{41}$$

In addition, the design parameters are denoted as $c_1=10$, $c_{14}=1$, $c=0.1$, $a_{11}=a_{12}=0.1$, $r_{11}=r_{12}=1$, $a_{21}=c_{24}=0.1$, $r_{21}=1$, $a_{31}=c_{34}=0.1$, $r_{31}=0.1$, $c3=10$, $a_{41}=0.1$, $c_{44}=2$, $r_{41}=1$, and $c_4=10$. The simulation results are shown in Figs. 1, 2, 3 nd 4.

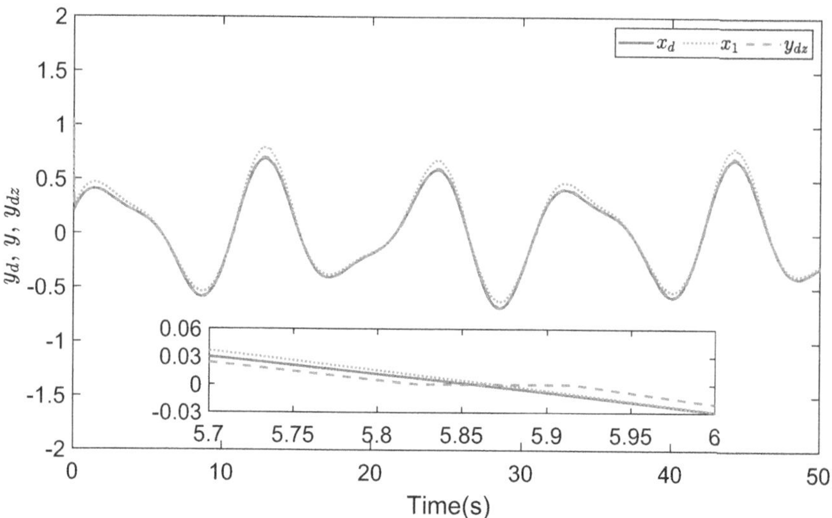

Fig. 1. Output signal y, tracking signal with dead zone y_{dz} and desired trajectory x_d.

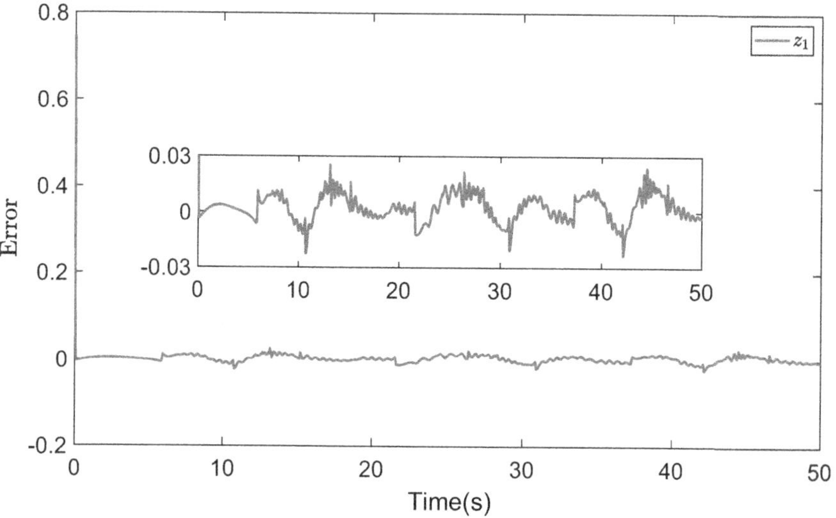

Fig. 2. The trajectories of error.

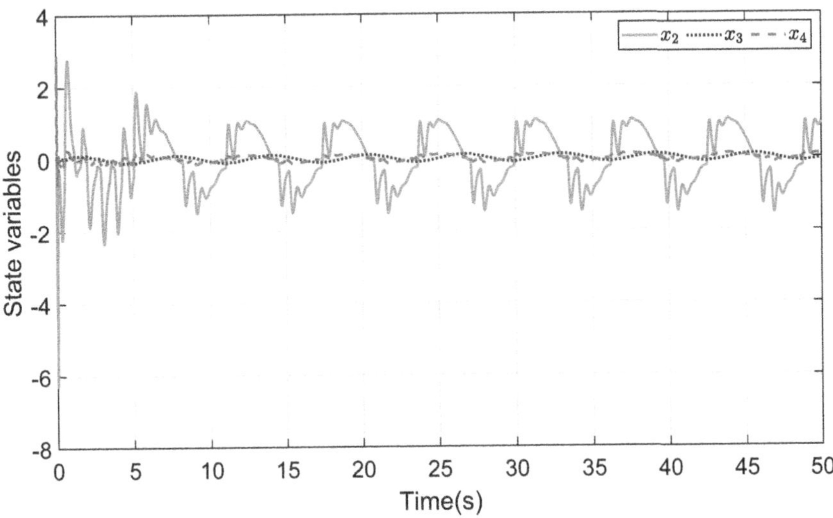

Fig. 3. The trajectories of other states x_2,x_3 and x_4.

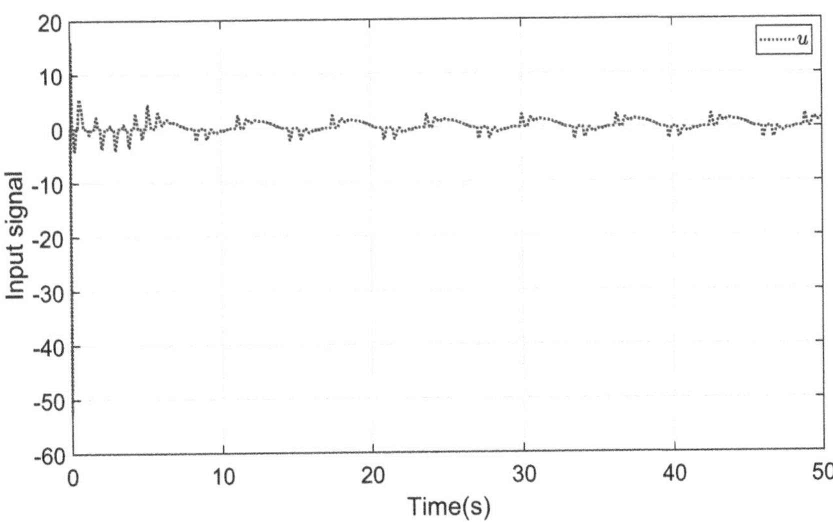

Fig. 4. The trajectories of control input u.

5 Conclusion

This study has addressed the control challenges posed by output dead-zones and stochastic noise in flexible-joint robot systems by proposing a novel tracking control strategy based on adaptive control theory. The Nussbaum function effectively tackled the unknown output dead-zone, ensuring robust control input despite nonlinearity. Fuzzy techniques were integrated to bypass complex analytical computations of the virtual controller's derivative, enabling accurate approximation of nonlinear functions. Adaptive methods were also employed to handle unmodeled dynamics without additional conditions, ensuring the boundedness of all system signals. Despite these advancements, the study has limitations. The approach assumes smooth system dynamics and may not handle severe discontinuities well. Additionally, while simulations demonstrated effectiveness, real-world implementation requires further validation to address hardware imperfections and computational constraints. Future work will focus on overcoming these limitations and extending the methodology to more complex environments.

Acknowledgments. This work was supported in part by the National Natural Science Foundation of China under Grant 62372104, in part by the Research Fund of Key Program for Advanced Ocean Institute of Southeast University under Grant KP202402. Besides, we thank the Taihu Lake Innovation Fund for the School of Future Technology of Southeast University. In addition, we thank the Big Data Computing Center of Southeast University for providing the facility support on the numerical calculations.

References

1. Huang, A., Chen, Y.: Adaptive sliding control for single-link flexible-joint robot with mismatched uncertainties. IEEE Trans. Control Syst. Technol. **12**(5), 770–775 (2004)
2. Su, H., Qi, W., Chen, J., Zhang, D.: Fuzzy approximation-based task space control of robot manipulators with remote center of motion constraint. IEEE Trans. Fuzzy Syst. **30**(6), 1564–1573 (2022)
3. Wang, X., Niu, B., Zhao, X., Zong, G., Cheng, T., Li, B.: Command-filtered adaptive fuzzy finite-time tracking control algorithm for flexible robotic manipulator: a singularity-free approach. IEEE Trans. Fuzzy Syst. **32**(2), 409–419 (2024)
4. Xie, Y., Ma, Q., Gu, J., Zhou, G.: Event-triggered fixed-time practical tracking control for flexible-joint robot. IEEE Trans. Fuzzy Syst. **31**(1), 67–76 (2023)
5. Diao, S., Sun, W., Su, S.: Neural-based adaptive event-triggered tracking control for flexible-joint robots with random noises. Int. J. Robust Nonlinear Control **32**(5), 2722–2740 (2022)
6. Xie, S., Sun, W., Sun, Y., Su, S.-F.: Adaptive prescribed-time optimal control for flexible-joint robots via reinforcement learning. IEEE Trans. Syst. Man Cybern. Syst. **55**(4), 2633–2642 (2025)
7. Zhao, J., Qiu, L., Xie, X., Sun, Z.-Y.: Finite-time stabilization of stochastic nonlinear systems and its applications in ship maneuvering systems. IEEE Trans. Fuzzy Syst. **32**(3), 1023–1035 (2024)
8. Yuan, Y., Zhao, J., Sun, Z.-Y., Xie, X.: Practically fast finite-time stability in the mean square of stochastic nonlinear systems: application to one-link manipulator. IEEE Trans. Syst. Man, Cybern. Syst. **54**(1), 312–323 (2024)
9. Wang, F., Chen, B., Sun, Y., Gao, Y., Lin, C.: Finite-time fuzzy control of stochastic nonlinear systems. IEEE Trans. Cybern. **50**(6), 2617–2626 (2020)
10. Xie, L., Zhang, Y., Zhang, K., Sun, Z.-Y., Xie, X.: Fuzzy adaptive event-driven control strategy and its application in ship maneuvering system with input delay and full-state constraints. IEEE Trans. Syst. Man Cybern. Syst. **55**(10), 7184–7194 (2025)

11. Wang, K., Xie, L., Yuan, Y., Zhang, K.: Fixed-time adaptive tracking event-based control for uncertain stochastic nonlinear systems with output constraints. Int. J. Robust Nonlinear Control **35**(12), 4963–4975 (2025)
12. Wang, H., Ai, Z.: Adaptive fixed-time tracking control of nonlinear systems with unmodeled dynamics. Nonlinear Dyn. **112**(23), 21193–21204 (2024)
13. Zhu, J., Xie, L., Zhang, K.: Distributed adaptive stabilization for stochastic nonlinear systems with unknown boundaries: a novel fixed-time stability in probability. Nonlinear Dyn. (2025)
14. Xie, L., Xu, Y., Fang, S., Ge, J., Zhang, K.: Practical predefined-time consensus control for stochastic nonlinear multiagent systems with time-varying state constraints. J. Frankl. Inst., 108058 (2025)
15. Kharrat, M.: Adaptive fault-tolerant control for a class of nonstrict-feedback nonlinear systems with unmodeled dynamics and dead-zone output using multidimensional taylor networks. Nonlinear Dyn. **112**(15), 13289–13306 (2024)
16. Yang, Y., Tang, L., Zou, W., et al.: A unified fixed-time framework of adaptive fuzzy controller design for unmodeled dynamical systems with intermittent feedback. Inf. Sci. **611**, 628–648 (2022)
17. Zhao, H., Wang, H., Niu, B., Zhao, X., Xu, N.: Adaptive fuzzy decentralized optimal control for interconnected nonlinear systems with unmodeled dynamics via mixed data and event driven method. Fuzzy Sets Syst. **474**, 108735 (2024)
18. Hua, C., Sun, Z., Chen, Z.: Exponential stabilization for time-delay nonlinear interconnected systems with unknown control directions and unmodeled dynamics. IEEE Trans. Syst. Man Cybern. Syst. **53**(7), 3979–3989 (2023)
19. Yuan, Y., Xie, L., Zhao, J., et al.: Fast finite-time stabilizing for pure-feedback stochastic nonlinear systems: a neural network dynamic event-triggered strategy. Nonlinear Dyn. **113**(9), 9915–9929 (2025)
20. Zong, G., Wang, Y., Karimi, H., Shi, K.: Observer-based adaptive neural tracking control for a class of nonlinear systems with prescribed performance and input dead-zone constraints. Neural Netw. **147**, 126–135 (2022)
21. Liu, Y.-J., Gao, Y., Tong, S., Li, Y.: Fuzzy approximation-based adaptive backstepping optimal control for a class of nonlinear discrete-time systems with dead-zone. IEEE Trans. Fuzzy Syst. **24**(1), 16–28 (2016)
22. Zhan, Y., Li, X., Tong, S.: Observer-based decentralized control for non-strict-feedback fractional-order nonlinear large-scale systems with unknown dead zones. IEEE Trans. Neural Netw. Learn. Syst. **34**(10), 7479–7490 (2023)
23. Liu, X., Zhang, H., Sun, J., Guo, X.: Dynamic threshold finite-time prescribed performance control for nonlinear systems with dead-zone output. IEEE Trans. Cybern. **54**(1), 655–664 (2024)

SLAM & Visual Navigation

Visual Navigation of Nonholonomic Mobile Robots Under Low-Light Environments by Novel Integrated YOLightner Architecture

Tenghui Li[1], Peiyong Duan[2], Bin Li[1], and Lixia Liu[1(✉)]

[1] School of Mathematics and Statistics, Qilu University of Technology (Shandong Academy of Sciences), Jinan 250353, China
lixialiu@qlu.edu.cn

[2] Department of Electronics, Electrical and Control, Qilu University of Technology (Shandong Academy of Sciences), Jinan 250353, China

Abstract. In low-light scenarios, the performance of the robot perception system is significantly reduced due to complex environmental factors such as insufficient lighting and noise interference. By constructing a mechanism for enhancing the data fusion environment, the ability to represent environmental features can be effectively improved, thereby optimizing the task execution accuracy of the autonomous decision-making system. In this paper, a novel low-light image enhancement and object detection architecture by integrating EvLight++ and YOLOv11 (renamed as YOLightner) for nonholonomic mobile robot (NMR). First, the multi-scale global fusion strategy of EvLight++ and the signal-to-noise ratio (SNR)-guided regional feature selection method are utilized to extract key information from low-light images. Then, the RGB low-light enhancement technique is employed to optimize brightness distribution and reduce the impact of noise on object recognition. The enhanced images are fed into the YOLOv11 object detection model to improve detection accuracy. Finally, object detection, obstacle avoidance, and tracking tasks are implemented on a ROS-based car. Experimental results demonstrate that the proposed method significantly enhances object detection performance in low-light environments and improves the visual navigation capabilities of robots.

Keywords: low-light image enhancement · nonholonomic wheeled mobile robots · YOLightner architecture · visual navigation

1 Introduction

Wheeled mobile robots exhibit superior performance in complex environments due to their exceptional maneuverability, reliability, and terrain adaptability. Multimodal perception systems integrating visual and LiDAR modalities enable

Z. Hou et al. (Eds.): CIRAC 2025, CCIS 2885, pp. 87–102, 2026.
https://doi.org/10.1007/978-981-92-0045-0_7

precise environmental reconstruction and dynamic object tracking. Contemporary research prioritizes SLAM-based navigation frameworks enhanced by deep learning for real-time path planning optimization in dynamic settings, though requiring higher computational and data requirements compared to vision-centric approaches. Notably, commercially deployed systems like Tesla's Full Self-Driving demonstrate the viability of LiDAR-free solutions through end-to-end deep neural architectures. These systems achieve centimeter-level localization accuracy using multi-camera perception while reducing hardware costs by 90% compared to LiDAR-dependent implementations. This paradigm shift underscores the growing academic and industrial consensus toward lightweight vision-based navigation as a cost-effective and scalable methodology.

In the field of robot visual navigation, especially in complex unstructured and low-light environments [1–4], there are numerous challenges, and the research and application of related technologies are of great significance. In terms of low-light enhancement, existing methods still need to be optimized to meet the visual navigation requirements of wheeled mobile robots. EvLight++ is an advanced approach that performs outstandingly in low-light video enhancement. Based on a large-scale real-world dataset, it achieves efficient enhancement through a designed architecture. In its network structure, convolutional operators are used to perform convolution operations. The convolutional kernel initially extracts the features of images and events in the feature extraction stage, laying the foundation for subsequent processing. It plays a downsampling role in modules such as SNR-guided regional feature selection, which helps integrate information at different scales. This enhances the model's ability to perceive and process complex lighting changes and noise interference in low-light environments, improving the image quality to assist the visual navigation of robots.

The motion control of wheeled mobile robots is complex due to their under-actuated and strongly coupled characteristics. In practical application scenarios, such as logistics warehouses and night-time security patrol environments, robots not only require precise motion control but also need to have good visual perception capabilities under complex lighting conditions. Although some existing control methods have achieved certain results in conventional environments, their adaptability in complex visual environments such as low-light conditions still needs to be improved. This study intends to investigate a multi-modal perception framework for wheeled robots, named YOLightner, which achieves a technological breakthrough by deeply integrating the EvLight low-light enhancement algorithm with the YOLOv11 object detection network. Based on the dual-layer convolution structure of the C3k2 module, the SPPF multi-scale feature pyramid, and the C2PSA spatial attention mechanism of YOLOv11 [5], this framework realizes real-time inference efficiency on embedded platforms and significantly improves the accuracy of object detection in low-light conditions. Experiments show that its adaptive illumination compensation mechanism effectively balances the fidelity of feature representation and computational efficiency, successfully applied to dynamic path planning in autonomous navigation and warehouse logistics at night, solving the problem of perception degradation in traditional vision systems when illumination changes abruptly. In the future, cross-modal data augmentation strategies need to be adopted to further enhance the robustness to extreme working conditions.

Based on the above discussions, a novel visual perception framework named YOLightner is proposed, which integrates the EvLight++ low-light enhancement algorithm and the YOLOv11 object detection network through their collaborative mechanism, to construct a robot perception system for complex dynamic environments [6–12]. This framework employs a multi-scale feature fusion strategy to enhance the quality of low-light images and combines the channel-spatial joint attention mechanism to optimize the robustness of object detection, effectively addressing the feature degradation problem in traditional visual systems under extreme lighting conditions. Experimental verification shows that this technical solution significantly improves the autonomous navigation reliability of wheeled mobile robots in scenarios such as warehouse logistics and night patrols, providing a new technical paradigm for real-time semantic understanding and decision-making control in dynamic environments. This paper aims to successfully implement a visual navigation system based on low-light enhancement and YOLOv11 dynamic object detection through in-depth research and experiments. This will comprehensively improve the autonomous navigation ability of wheeled mobile robots in complex, unstructured, and low-light environments, expand the application scope of robots, and promote the further development of robot technology in the field of complex environments [13–15].

Unlike the existing paradigms where low-light enhancement methods (e.g., URetinex, RUAS) [16] or object detection methods operate independently, the core contribution of this paper lies in proposing an end-to-end integrated architecture (YOLightner). This architecture is not a simple algorithm concatenation, but rather a deep integration of EvLight++ and YOLOv11 through a collaborative mechanism. Its innovations are mainly reflected in three aspects: first, it proposes an SNR-guided regional feature selection (IRFS/ERFS) mechanism to achieve differential processing of halos and noise; second, it designs a holistic-regional fusion (HRF) module to effectively fuse multi-scale information of images and events; third, it jointly optimizes the enhancement module and the detection module, solving the problem of error accumulation in traditional cascaded methods and providing a novel and efficient solution for low-light visual navigation of mobile robots under incomplete constraints.

The rest of this paper is structured as follows. Section 2 introduces the preliminary knowledge related to low-light enhancement algorithms and non-holonomic wheeled mobile robots. In Sect. 3, we elaborate on our main achievements in low-light enhancement, object recognition, and control. Section 4 showcases the simulation and experimental results of the enhancement. Finally, Sect. 5 provides a conclusion.

2 Preliminaries

2.1 Fundamentals of Low-Light Enhancement

This study proposes a low-light image enhancement method that achieves lightweight illumination estimation through a weight-sharing illumination learning mechanism combined with the Retinex theory, and builds a self-calibration module to optimize multi-stage convergence. Based on the unsupervised training, the fidelity loss and smoothness loss respectively constrain the pixel consistency and scene adaptability of the illumination estimation. The optimized illumination is input into the Evlight framework by replacing the traditional Retinexformer brightening algorithm. Firstly, the IRFS module screens the high signal-to-noise ratio regional features, and the ERFS module inversely processes the event features of the low visibility and high noise regions. Then, the multi-head self-attention mechanism and the feedforward network deeply extract the global features, and finally, in the overall-regional fusion (HRF) module, the multi-scale features and event information are collaboratively optimized to generate high-quality enhanced images, significantly improving the low-light enhancement performance.

2.2 Nonholonomic Mobile Robots (NMRs) Dynamical System

A mobile robot is a typical non-holonomic mechanical system. In this paper, taking the mobile robot shown in Fig. 1,

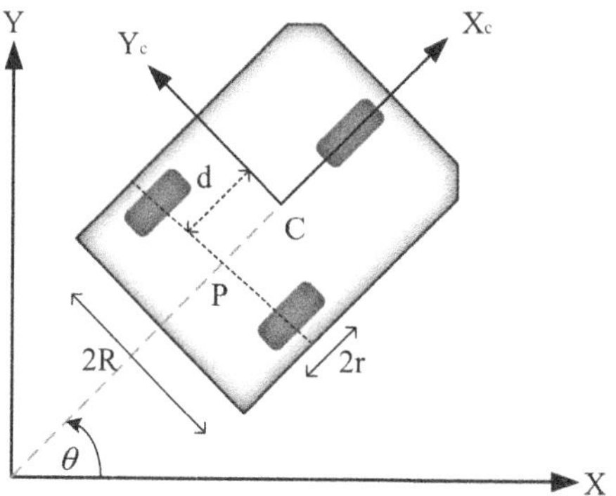

Fig. 1. Mobile robot

which consists of two driving wheels and one front wheel, as an example, its mathematical model is established using the Lagrangian method. The position of the robot in the inertial Cartesian coordinate system is determined by the vector $q = [x_c, y_c, \theta]^T$, where (x_c, y_c) are the coordinates of the reference point C, and θ is the orientation angle of the robot coordinate system relative to the inertial coordinate system. Since the robot's motion is restricted to the horizontal plane, the gravity vector $G(q) = 0$, and the kinetic energy $K = \frac{1}{2}\dot{q}^T M(q)\dot{q}$. Thus, the dynamic equation of the robot is obtained as:

$$M(q)\ddot{q} + V_m(q,\dot{q})\dot{q} + F(\dot{q}) + G(q) + \tau_d = B(q)\tau - A^T(q)\lambda \tag{1}$$

where $M(q)$ is the symmetric positive-definite inertia matrix, $V_m(q,\dot{q})$ is the centripetal and Coriolis matrix, $F(\dot{q})$ represents the surface friction force, τ_d represents the bounded unknown disturbance, $B(q)$ is the input transformation matrix, τ is the input vector, $A(q)$ is the matrix related to the constraints, and λ is the constraint force vector. Moreover,

$$\lambda = -m\left(\dot{x}_c \cos\theta + \dot{y}_c \sin\theta\right)\dot{\theta} \tag{2}$$

The non-holonomic constraint condition is that the robot can only move in the direction perpendicular to the driving wheel axis, that is, it satisfies the conditions of pure rolling and no slipping, and its expression is:

$$\dot{y}_c \cos\theta - \dot{x}_c \sin\theta - d\dot{\theta} = 0 \tag{3}$$

From this, we can obtain:

$$S(q) = \begin{bmatrix} \cos\theta & -d\sin\theta \\ \sin\theta & d\cos\theta \\ 0 & 1 \end{bmatrix} \tag{4}$$

Furthermore, the forward kinematic equation of the mobile platform is derived as:

$$\begin{bmatrix} \dot{x}_c \\ \dot{y}_c \\ \dot{\theta} \end{bmatrix} = \begin{bmatrix} \cos\theta & -d\sin\theta \\ \sin\theta & d\cos\theta \\ 0 & 1 \end{bmatrix} \begin{bmatrix} v_1 \\ v_2 \end{bmatrix} \tag{5}$$

where $|v_1| \le V_{\max}$, $|v_2| \le W_{\max}$, and $V_{\max}$ and $W_{\max}$ are the maximum linear velocity and maximum angular velocity of the mobile robot respectively. This system is also known as the steering system of the vehicle.

Assumption 1. *The positive inertia matrix $\boldsymbol{M}(q_i)$ is bounded, i.e., there exist two constants where $0 < \lambda_1 \le \lambda_2$, such that any eigenvalue $\lambda(\boldsymbol{M})$ of $\boldsymbol{M}(q_i)$, $i = \{0, 1, 2, \cdots, s\}$, satisfy $\lambda_1 \le \lambda(\boldsymbol{M}) \le \lambda_2$.*

3 Main Results

The overall workflow of the YOLightner system proposed in this paper is illustrated in Fig. 2, which mainly consists of three core stages: low-light image enhancement, object detection and recognition, and robot motion control. Firstly, the original low-light image is input into the EvLight++ enhancement module. After SNR map calculation, IRFS/ERFS regional feature selection, and HRF fusion, a high-quality enhanced image is output. Subsequently, this enhanced image is fed into the YOLOv11 detection module. Through the C3k2 backbone network, SPPF pyramid, and detection head, the module outputs object bounding box and category information. Finally, the relative pose between the robot and the target is calculated based on the detection results, and the controller generates motor control commands (linear velocity and angular velocity) to drive the robot to complete navigation and tracking tasks.

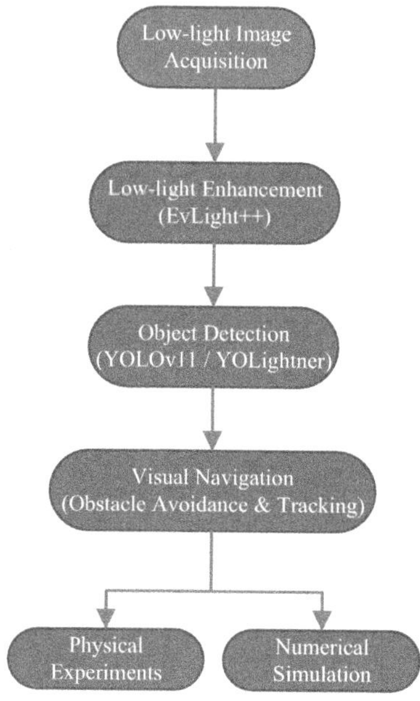

Fig. 2. System framework diagram

3.1 The Enhancement of Low-Light Environments

Based on the Retinex theory, the low-light observation y and the desired clear image z are related by $y = z \otimes x$, where x is the illumination component. We introduce a mapping H_θ with parameter θ to learn the illumination and build a progressive illumination learning process with weight sharing. The basic units are:

$$\mathcal{F}\left(x^t\right) : \begin{cases} u^t = \mathcal{H}_\theta\left(x^t\right), x^0 = y \\ x^{t+1} = x^t + u^t \end{cases} \tag{6}$$

Here, u^t and x^t are the residual term and illumination at the t-th stage ($t = 0, \ldots, T-1$) respectively. With the weight-sharing mechanism, the same H_θ architecture and weights are used in each stage. By learning the residual between illumination and low-light observation, we reduce computational complexity and improve exposure stability.

To make each stage's results converge, we introduce a self-calibration mapping s. This module calculates the difference between the current-stage input x^t and y, and transforms the input as follows:

$$\mathcal{G}\left(x^t\right):\begin{cases} z^t = y \oslash x^t \\ s^t = \mathcal{K}_\vartheta\left(z^t\right) \\ v^t = y + s^t \end{cases} \tag{7}$$

For $t \geq 1$, v^t is the transformed input of each stage, and $\mathcal{K}_\vartheta$ has learnable parameters ϑ. After the self - calibration module's transformation, the basic unit changes to $\mathcal{F}(x^t) \rightarrow \mathcal{F}(\mathcal{G}(x^t))$. This module indirectly corrects the input of each stage, making the results converge. It allows using multiple cascaded blocks in training and a single block in testing to speed up inference.

Due to inaccurate existing paired data, we use unsupervised learning and define the total loss as $L_{total} = \alpha L_f + \beta L_s$. α and β are balancing parameters. L_f is the fidelity loss ensuring pixel - level consistency between the estimated illumination and each - stage input:

$$\mathcal{L}_f = \sum_{t=1}^{T} \left\|x^t - \left(y + s^{t-1}\right)\right\|^2 \tag{8}$$

where T is the total number of stages, and this function constrains x^t with $y + s^{t-1}$.

L_s is the smoothness loss using a spatially variant ℓ_1 norm for illumination smoothness:

$$\mathcal{L}_s = \sum_{i=1}^{N} \sum_{j \in \mathcal{N}(i)} w_{i,j} \left|x_i^t - x_j^t\right| \tag{9}$$

Here, N is the total number of pixels, i is the i-th pixel, $\mathcal{N}(i)$ are its neighboring pixels in a 5×5 window, and $w_{i,j} = \exp\left(-\frac{\sum_c((y_{i,c}+s_{i,c}^{t-1})-(y_{j,c}+s_{j,c}^{t-1}))^2}{2\sigma^2}\right)$ (c is the YUV color - space image channel, $\sigma = 0.1$).

Through the weight-sharing light learning and the self-calibration module, in the testing phase, we use a single light-estimation module to enhance the low-light image, getting an enhanced image I_{lu}^*, which is the input for the subsequent EvLight framework.

We input I_{lu}^*, convert it to a grayscale image I_g, and calculate the SNR map $M_{snr} = \tilde{I}_g / \text{abs}(I_g - \tilde{I}_g)$ ($\tilde{I}_g$ is the denoised I_g obtained by a mean filter).

For the input image feature F_{img}, we extract regional information through two residual blocks (each with two $conv3 \times 3$ layers and one efficient channel-attention layer) to get $\hat{F}_{img}^i$. We expand and normalize the SNR-map M_{snr}^i channel dimension to $[0, 1]$, apply a predefined threshold to get $\hat{M}_{snr}^i$, and then obtain the selected image feature $F_{sel-img}^i = \hat{M}_{snr}^i \odot \hat{F}_{img}^i$ by element-wise multiplication.

We design an ERFS block for edge-rich regions with low SNR due to underexposure in the initially enhanced image and for high-SNR regions with mainly leakage and shot-noise. The ERFS block processes the input event feature F_{ev}^{i} like the IRFS block to get $\hat{F}_{ev}^{i}$, then gets the inverse of the SNR map $\overline{M}_{snr}^{i} = 1 - \hat{M}_{snr}^{i}$, and obtains the selected event-region feature $F_{sel-ev}^{i} = \overline{M}_{snr}^{i} \odot \hat{F}_{ev}^{i}$ by element-wise multiplication.

We construct a holistic-regional fusion branch similar to UNet. It takes the concatenated features of the pre-processed image F_{img} and events F_{ev} as input and outputs the enhanced image I_{en}. In the contracting path, we get different-level holistic features F_{ho}^{i+1} through the holistic-feature extraction (HFE) block (composed of a multi-head self-attention module and a feed-forward network) and $conv4 \times 4$ down-sampling (stride 4). The HFE-block processing for F_{ho}^{i-1} is:

$$\hat{F}_{mid}^{i-1} = Attention\left(F_{ho}^{i-1}\right) + F_{ho}^{i-1} \tag{10}$$

$$\hat{F}_{ho}^{i-1} = FFN\left(LN\left(\hat{F}_{mid}^{i-1}\right)\right) + \hat{F}_{mid}^{i-1} \tag{11}$$

where $\hat{F}_{mid}^{i-1}$ is the intermediate output, LN is layer normalization, FFN is the feed-forward network, and $Attention$ is the channel self-attention. In the expansive path, the upsampled $\hat{F}_{ho}^{i-1}$ is fused with $F_{sel-img}^{i}$ and F_{sel-ev}^{i} in the holistic-regional fusion (HRF) block. The HRF block concatenates these features to get F_{cat}^{i}, generates a spatial-attention map through a $conv3 \times 3$ layer, and finally gets the fused feature $F_{ho}^{i} = \mathcal{F}_3\left(\sigma\left(\mathcal{F}_1\left(F_{cat}^{i}\right)\right) \odot \mathcal{F}_2\left(F_{cat}^{i}\right) + F_{cat}^{i}\right)$ by element-wise multiplication and convolution operations (F_i is the convolution operation, σ is the Sigmoid function), and ultimately obtains the enhanced image I_{en}.

3.2 Moving Target Detection and Recognition

Low-light images are enhanced using techniques like histogram equalization and CLAHE. The enhanced image I_{en} is fed into the YOLOv11 object detection model, which is crucial for efficient object detection and tracking.

YOLOv11 consists of three main parts: the backbone network, the neck, and the head. The backbone extracts multi - scale features from I_{en}. It uses the C3k2 block ($Feature_{C3k2} = Conv_{k1}(I_{en}) + Conv_{k2}(I_{en})$) instead of C2f, along with SPPF and C2PSA blocks. The neck fuses features from the backbone through upsampling and concatenation, and uses the C3k2 block to optimize feature aggregation. The head uses multiple C3k2 blocks for feature processing. When c3k = False, it adopts the standard bottleneck; when c3k = True, it uses the C3 module. The CBS layer ($Feature_{CBS} = Silu(BatchNorm(Conv(Feature_{C3k2}))))$) further optimizes the feature map. Finally, it outputs bounding box coordinates, object existence probabilities, and class scores.

YOLOv11 can accurately identify and locate dynamic obstacle targets in I_{en}. After feature extraction, fusion, and processing, it outputs relevant information. The system calculates the obstacle-avoidance path with $Path_{obstacle-avoidance} = CalculatePath(BoundingBox_{obstacle}, CurrentPosition)$.

For target tracking, YOLOv11 first gets the target's position in the current frame. In video frames, it tracks the target using $NextPosition_{target} = PredictPosition(TargetPosition_{current}, Velocity_{target})$, enabling stable target tracking.

The YOLOv11 model (depth/width = 1.00) uses a backbone with nine C3k2 modules for multi-scale feature extraction from the enhanced image I_{en}, alongside SPPF (kernels [5,9,13]) and a C2PSA attention module in the neck. The architecture processes features through CBS layers and a head with configurable C3k2 blocks. It was trained for 300 epochs at 640 × 640 resolution using SGD (lr = 0.01). The model outputs bounding boxes for obstacle avoidance path planning ($Path_{obstacle-avoidance}$) and enables target tracking via position prediction ($NextPosition_{target}$).

An MPC controller (prediction step = 20, control step = 5, sampling time = 0.1 s) handles motion execution. The deployed system on an embedded platform achieves a processing rate of 11.8 FPS, validating its real-time capability.

3.3 The Visual Navigation Control of NMRs

In this study, the transformation from the camera coordinate system to the world coordinate system is crucial for the realization of robot navigation. Its accuracy directly affects the robot's perception of environmental information and its navigation decision-making. The specific transformation process involves the determination of the camera's internal parameters, external parameter matrices, and the mapping relationships between the coordinate systems. The internal parameters of the camera can be obtained through camera calibration. The resulting internal parameter matrix

$$K_{in} = \begin{bmatrix} f_x & 0 & u_0 \\ 0 & f_y & v_0 \\ 0 & 0 & 1 \end{bmatrix} \tag{12}$$

where f_x and f_y are the normalized focal lengths of the x - axis and y - axis respectively, and u_0 and v_0 are the optical center (principal point coordinates) of the camera. The world coordinate system is set as follows: a perpendicular line is drawn from the camera optical center to the ground, and the intersection point O_s serves as the coordinate origin. The direction of the line connecting point O_H and the camera optical center is the positive direction of Z_w, and the forward direction of the robot is the positive direction of Y_w. The coordinate system follows the right-hand rule. The external parameter matrix of the camera includes the rotation matrix R and the translation matrix T. The rotation matrix R is determined by the rotation angles of the camera around the x_c, Y_c, and z_c axes. Its calculation formula is

$$R = \begin{bmatrix} 1 & 0 & 0 \\ 0 & \cos\theta & \sin\theta \\ 0 & -\sin\theta & \cos\theta \end{bmatrix} \begin{bmatrix} \cos\beta & 0 & -\sin\beta \\ 0 & 1 & 0 \\ \sin\beta & 0 & \cos\beta \end{bmatrix} \times \begin{bmatrix} \cos\delta & \sin\delta & 0 \\ -\sin\delta & \cos\delta & 0 \\ 0 & 0 & 1 \end{bmatrix} \tag{13}$$

where θ, β, and δ are the rotation angles of the camera around the x_c, Y_c, and z_c axes respectively, and the positive direction of the angles follows the right-hand screw rule. The translation matrix T is determined according to the relative position relationship between the camera coordinate system and the world coordinate system, and its expression is

$$T^T = [T_X, T_Y, T_Z] \tag{14}$$

where T_X, T_Y, and T_Z are the moving distances of the camera coordinate system along the X_C, Y_C, and z_c axes. The formula for mapping a target point in the world coordinate system to the camera coordinate system is

$$[X_C, Y_C, Z_C]^T = R\,[X_W, Y_W, Z_W]^T + T = \begin{bmatrix} R_{00} & R_{01} & R_{02} \\ R_{10} & R_{11} & R_{12} \\ R_{20} & R_{21} & R_{22} \end{bmatrix} \begin{bmatrix} X_W \\ Y_W \\ Z_W \end{bmatrix} + \begin{bmatrix} T_X \\ T_Y \\ T_Z \end{bmatrix} \tag{15}$$

where (X_W, Y_W, Z_W) are the coordinates of the point in the world coordinate system, and (X_C, Y_C, Z_C) are the coordinates of the point in the camera coordinate system. In practical applications, by means of the above-obtained camera internal parameter matrix K_{in}, external parameter matrices R and T, the transformation from the camera coordinate system to the world coordinate system can be achieved, providing an accurate coordinate information basis for subsequent navigation line extraction, navigation deviation calculation, as well as the path planning and control of the robot (Fig. 3).

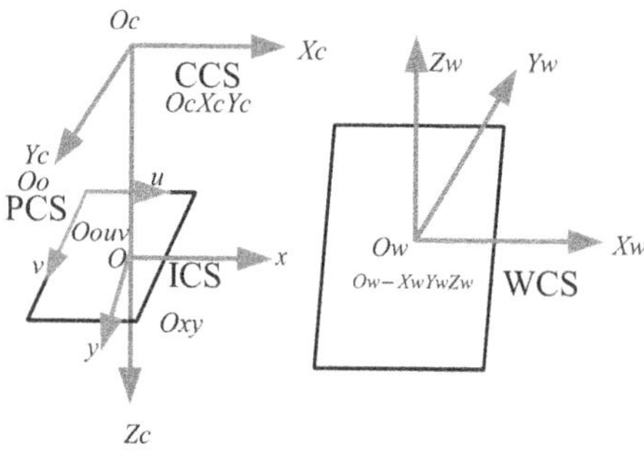

Fig. 3. Coordinate transformation

Design a PID controller to drive the robot to track the target. Define the tracking error. In terms of position, $e_x = X_{target} - x_c$, $e_y = Y_{target} - y_c$; in terms of angle, $e_\theta = \theta_{target} - \theta$, where (X_{target}, Y_{target}) is the position of the target in the inertial coordinate system, and θ_{target} is the desired angle of the target relative to the robot. According to the PID control principle, calculate the control quantities. The calculation formulas for the linear velocity control quantity v and the angular velocity control quantity ω are respectively:

$$v = K_{p_v} e_v + K_{i_v} \int e_v dt + K_{d_v} \frac{de_v}{dt} \tag{16}$$

$$\omega = K_{p_\omega} e_\omega + K_{i_\omega} \int e_\omega dt + K_{d_\omega} \frac{de_\omega}{dt} \tag{17}$$

where K_{p_v}, K_{i_v}, K_{d_v} are the proportional, integral, and derivative coefficients of linear velocity control respectively; K_{p_ω}, K_{i_ω}, K_{d_ω} are the proportional, integral, and derivative coefficients of angular velocity control respectively. $e_v = \sqrt{e_x^2 + e_y^2}$ represents the comprehensive position error, and e_ω is the angular error. By adjusting these coefficients, the robot can dynamically adjust its speed according to the tracking error and stably track the target. Consider the robot's dynamic model and constraint conditions, and construct a model predictive control framework. The prediction model is based on the robot's dynamic equation

$$M(q)\ddot{q} + V_m(q, \dot{q})\dot{q} + F(\dot{q}) + G(q) + \tau_d = B(q)\tau - A^T(q)\lambda \tag{18}$$

to predict the robot's state at multiple future time instants. Set the objective function, for example, to minimize the tracking error and the change of control quantities,

$$J = \sum_{k=1}^{N_p} (e_{x,k}^2 + e_{y,k}^2 + e_{\theta,k}^2) + \sum_{k=0}^{N_c-1} (\Delta v_k^2 + \Delta \omega_k^2) \tag{19}$$

where N_p is the prediction horizon, N_c is the control horizon, and Δv_k, $\Delta \omega_k$ are the changes of control quantities. At the same time, consider the robot's motion constraints, such as the maximum linear velocity $V_{\max}$, the maximum angular velocity $W_{\max}$, etc. At each control cycle, solve the optimization problem to obtain the optimal control quantities v and ω at the current moment, and achieve efficient tracking of the target.

3.4 Robustness Analysis

To comprehensively evaluate the performance of the proposed control system under model uncertainties and practical engineering constraints, an in-depth robustness simulation analysis was conducted. The simulation was constructed in the MATLAB/Simulink environment, with a sampling time T_s set to 0.1 s.

Based on the standard dynamic model (Eq. (1)), uniform random perturbations of ±20% were introduced to key parameters-including robot mass m, moment of inertia I, and damping coefficient B-to simulate practical modelplant mismatch and uncertainties. Under these conditions, by linearizing the system model and applying frequency-domain analysis to the open-loop transfer function, the stability margins of the control system were computed as follows: Gain

Margin (GM) = 8.5 dB, and Phase Margin (PM) = 45.6°. These results indicate that the control system remains stable even under significant variations in model parameters.

4 Numerical Simulation and Physical Experiments

4.1 Numerical Simulation

In the numerical simulation experiment, this study processed the image samples in low-light environments using the low-light enhancement technology based on the EvLight++ algorithm. This algorithm, by virtue of the light-learning mechanism with weight sharing, the self-calibration module, and the carefully defined unsupervised training loss function, effectively optimized the illumination effect of the images, suppressed noise, and highlighted the image edges, significantly improving the image quality.

Subsequently, the enhanced images were input into the YOLOv11 object detection model. Thanks to its unique backbone network, neck, and head structures, especially the innovative components such as C3k2, SPPF, and C2PSA, YOLOv11 demonstrated powerful feature extraction and object recognition capabilities in complex low-light scenarios. Through a comparative analysis of the object detection results of the images before and after enhancement, from multi-dimensional evaluation metrics such as detection accuracy, recall rate, and mean average precision (mAP), it can be seen that the performance of the enhanced images in the object detection task is significantly better than that other enhancement algorithm. If fully verifies that the proposed low-light enhancement method can provide clearer and more distinguishable image data for subsequent object detection tasks, thereby effectively improving the accuracy and reliability of object detection in low-light environments.

In addition to detection performance, computational efficiency was evaluated on an NVIDIA Jetson AGX Orin platform. The proposed YOLightner framework processes a 512×512 image in 85 ms on average, with EvLight++ taking 55 ms and YOLOv11 consuming 30 ms. In contrast, the URetinex+YOLOv11 cascade requires 210 ms per image. These results demonstrate that YOLightner not only achieves higher detection accuracy but also maintains superior real-time performance, making it suitable for online applications on mobile robotic systems. In Fig. 4, (a) shows the original detection image. (b) compares the enhancement effects of the URetinex, RUAS, EvlightenGAN methods and YOLightner. It can be seen that the images enhanced by the former methods have problems such as overexposure and severe information loss. Among them, (c) presents the enlarged image enhanced by YOLightner, and (d) is the detection image of YOLightner.

4.2 Physical Experiments

To verify the effectiveness of the YOLightner method in path planning and obstacle avoidance for wheeled mobile robot, a physical experiment with preset start and end points was conducted to explore the impact of this enhanced technology

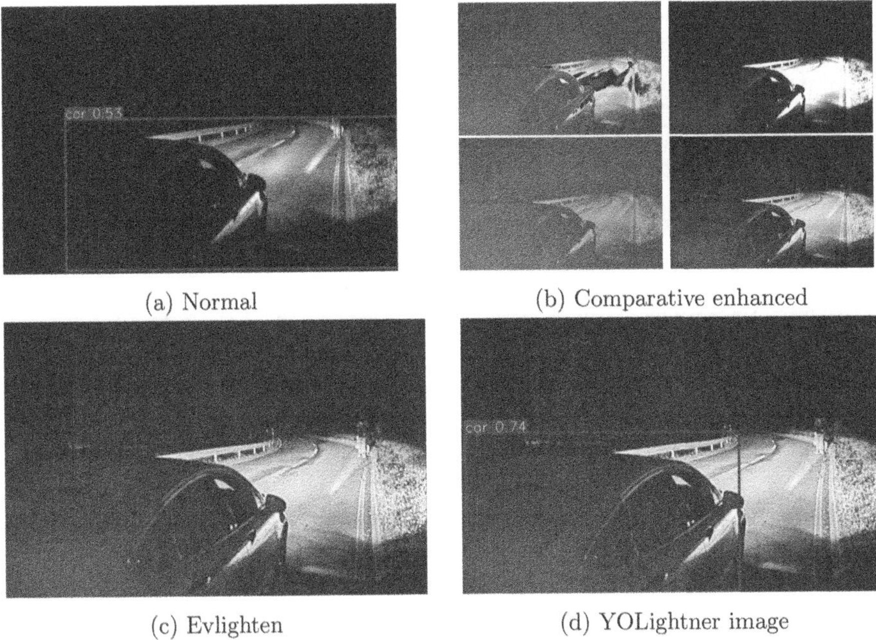

(a) Normal (b) Comparative enhanced

(c) Evlighten (d) YOLightner image

Fig. 4. Image enhancement effect comparison with various methods

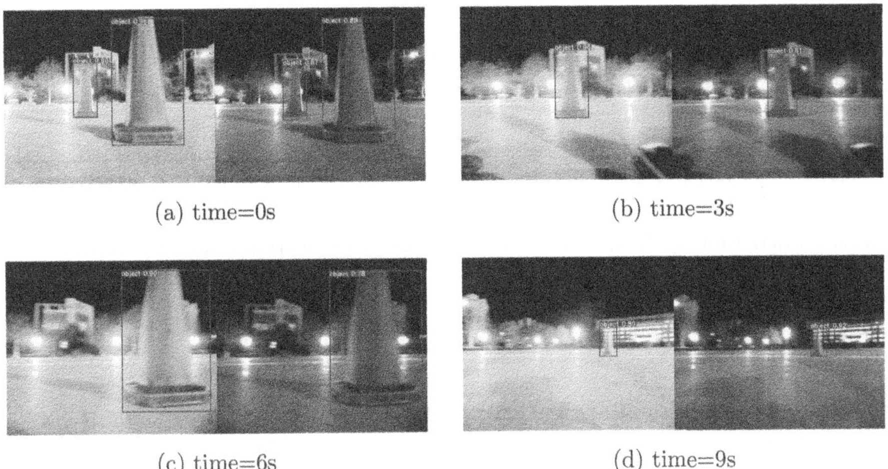

(a) time=0s (b) time=3s

(c) time=6s (d) time=9s

Fig. 5. The effect of YOLightner enhancement for the WMR from the robots perspective

on the robot's obstacle avoidance performance. As can be seen from the robot's perspective images in Fig. 5, The physical experiments demonstrated YOLightner's critical role in enabling robust navigation in low-light conditions. Without

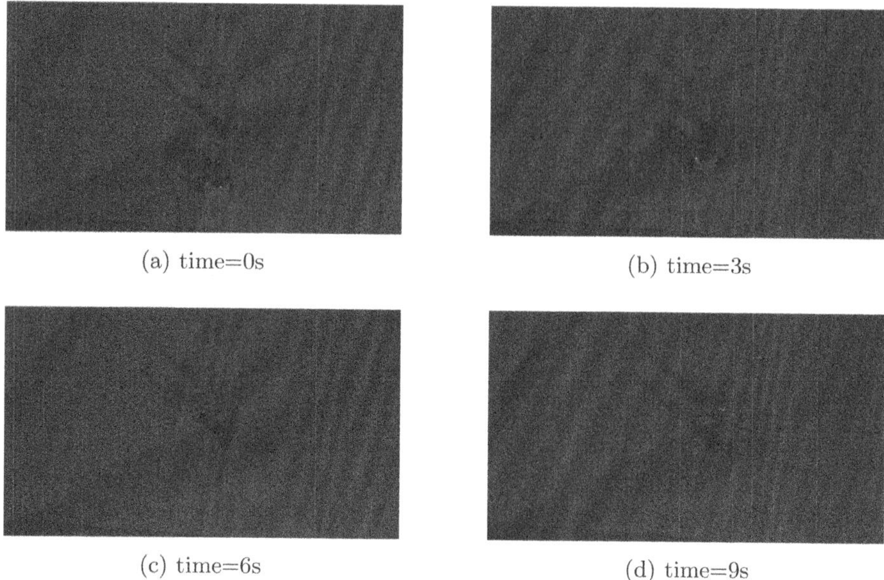

(a) time=0s

(b) time=3s

(c) time=6s

(d) time=9s

Fig. 6. The obstacle avoidance results of YOLightner enhancement for the WMR from the UAV Perspective

it, the robot suffered from poor obstacle recognition, while with enhancement, it successfully identified obstacles and navigated smoothly to its target. A drone's-eye view in Fig. 6 illustrates the robot's efficient, intelligent path planning based on enhanced perception.

Quantitative results from 10 trials confirm high performance, with a 90% mission success rate, an average cross-track error of 0.12 m ± 0.05 m, and an average arrival time of 45.3 s ± 6.8 s. These metrics, along with the representative trials shown in Figs. 5 and 6, verify the system's stability and practicality for real-world applications like warehouse logistics and night patrols.

5 Conclusions

In this paper, the visual navigation problem of non-holonomic mobile robots in low-light environments has studied, and an novel method named YOLightner, which significantly improves the navigation performance of the robots in complex low-light environments, has proposed. In terms of low-light image enhancement, based on the Retinex theory, we have effectively optimized the illumination effect of low-light images by introducing a light-learning mechanism with weight sharing, a self-calibration module, and defining an unsupervised training loss. Subsequently, by using modules including IRFS and ERFS in the EvLight framework, as well as the holistic-regional fusion branch, the image quality has been further enhanced, noise is suppressed, and image edges have been highlighted, providing a clear image basis for subsequent object detection. In object detection, enhanced images were fed into the YOLOv11 model. Its distinct backbone, neck, and head enable accurate identification and localization of dynamic obstacles in low-light environment. The backbone, with innovative modules, boosts efficiency and feature extraction. The neck fuses multi-scale features, and the head outputs detection and classification results. Then, obstacle-avoidance paths and stably tracked the target have been calculated. Next, a typical PID controller based on tracking errors has been applied to steer the motion of the robot. Finally, simulations and physical experiments has performed to verify the effectiveness of the proposed YOLighter method, it greatly improved object detection in low-light and robot visual navigation, showing potential in scenarios like night patrols and warehousing logistics, supporting robot autonomy in complex environments and promoting its development in this field.

References

1. Li, X., Wang, W., Feng, X., Li, M.: Deep parametric Retinex decomposition model for low-light image enhancement. Comput. Vis. Image Underst. **241**, 103948 (2024)
2. Liang, G., Chen, K., Li, H., Lu, Y., Wang, G.: Towards robust event-guided low-light image enhancement: a large-scale real-world event-image dataset and novel approach. In: Proceedings of the IEEE/CVF Conference on Computer Vision and Pattern Recognition (CVPR), pp. 23–33 (2024)
3. Ma, L., Ma, T., Liu, R., Fan, X., Luo, Z.: Toward fast, flexible, and robust low-light image enhancement. In: Proceedings of IEEE/CVF Conference on Computer Vision and Pattern Recognition (CVPR), pp. 5637–5646 (2022)
4. He, B., Wang, Z., Zhou, Y., Chen, J., Fermuller, C., et al.: Microsaccade-inspired event camera for robotics. Sci. Rob. **9**(15) (2024)
5. Varghese, R., Sambath, M.: YOLOv8: a novel object detection algorithm with enhanced performance and robustness. In: Proceedings of 2024 International Conference on Advances in Data Engineering and Intelligent Computing Systems (ADICS), pp. 1–6 (2024)
6. Achirei, S., Mocanu, R., Popovici, A., Dosoftei, C.: Model-predictive control for omnidirectional mobile robots in logistic environments based on object detection using CNNs. Sensors **23**(11), 4992 (2023)
7. Shoeib, M.A., Lewandowski, J., Omara, A.M.: A novel methodology for vision-based path planning and obstacle avoidance in mobile robot applications. Adv. Robot. **38**(12), 802–817 (2024)
8. Adiuku, N., Avdelidis, N.-P., Tang, G., Plastropoulos, A., Diallo, Y.: Mobile robot obstacle detection and avoidance with NAV-YOLO. Int. J. Mech. Eng. Rob. Res. **13**(2), 219–226 (2024)
9. Singh, A., Shakeel, M., Kalaichelvi, V., Karthikeyan, R.: A vision-based bio-inspired reinforcement learning algorithms for manipulator obstacle avoidance. Electronics **11**(21), 3636 (2022)
10. Cherubin, S., Kaczmarek, W., Siwek, M.: YOLO object detection and classification using low-cost mobile robot. Przeglad Elektrotechniczny **100**(9), 29–33 (2024)
11. Mei, M., Zhou, Z., Liu, W., Ye, Z.: GOI-YOLOv8 grouping offset and isolated GiraffeDet low-light target detection. Sensors **24**(17), 5787 (2024)
12. Yi, A., Anantrasirichai, N.: A comprehensive study of object tracking in low-light environments. Int. J. Mech. Eng. Rob. Res. **24**(13), 4359 (2024)

13. Fierro, R., Lewis, F.L.: Control of a nonholonomic mobile robot: backstepping kinematics into dynamics. In: Proceedings of 1995 34th IEEE Conference on Decision and Control, vol. 4, pp. 3805–3810 (1995)
14. Zhang, T., Wang, J., Xu, C., Gao, A., Gao, F.: Continuous implicit SDF based any-shape robot trajectory optimization. In: Proceedings of 2023 IEEE/RSJ International Conference on Intelligent Robots and Systems (IROS), pp. 282–289 (2023)
15. Zhang, R., et al.: Model-based planning and control for terrestrial-aerial bimodal vehicles with passive wheels. In: Proceedings of 2023 IEEE/RSJ International Conference on Intelligent Robots and Systems (IROS), pp. 1070–1077 (2023)
16. Li, C., Guo, C., Loy, C.C.: Learning to enhance low-light image via zero-reference deep curve estimation. In: Proceedings of the IEEE/CVF Conference on Computer Vision and Pattern Recognition (CVPR), pp. 13783–13792 (2021)

FlexiSLAM: Semantic-Geometric Collaborative Filtering for Dynamic Object Rejection

Chenghao Xu[1], Qingxiao Zou[1], Lineng Chen[2], and Wankou Yang[1,3(✉)]

[1] Southeast University, Nanjing, China
wkyang@seu.edu.cn
[2] The Key Laboratory of Education Blockchain and Intelligent Technology, Ministry of Education, Guangxi Normal University, Guilin, China
[3] Advanced Ocean Institute of Southeast University, Nantong, China

Abstract. Accurate localization and environmental mapping are fundamental capabilities for intelligent robots. However, most existing Simultaneous Localization and Mapping (SLAM) systems rely on static environment assumptions, leading to degraded localization accuracy in dynamic scenarios. To address this challenge, this paper proposes a visual SLAM system for dynamic environments based on the ORB-SLAM3 framework. This system innovatively integrates a novel semantic-geometric collaborative architecture for dynamic object rejection through two complementary strategies: (1) combining semantic segmentation with optical flow techniques to effectively filter out feature points in moving regions, thereby improving localization accuracy; (2) employing pixel clustering and outlier feature point detection to further enhance robust dynamic object removal and expand the system's applicability. Experimental results on the TUM RGB-D dataset demonstrate that the proposed system achieves significant performance improvements in dynamic environments.

Keywords: Dynamic Environments · Semantic Segmentation · Optical Flow · Pixel Clustering · Anomalous Feature Point Region Segmentation · SLAM

1 Introduction

Simultaneous Localization and Mapping (SLAM) refers to the technology that enables mobile robots to perform self-localization and environmental mapping simultaneously in unknown environments using perception devices [1]. This technology plays a pivotal role in robotics, autonomous vehicles, unmanned aerial vehicles (UAVs), and augmented reality applications [2,12,15], facilitating not only autonomous navigation but also accurate map generation in dynamic or unfamiliar environments.

Z. Hou et al. (Eds.): CIRAC 2025, CCIS 2885, pp. 103–126, 2026.
https://doi.org/10.1007/978-981-92-0045-0_8

Visual SLAM (VSLAM) is a camera-based SLAM technique that employs computer vision to extract features from captured images for camera pose estimation and 3D environmental reconstruction. Compared to LiDAR or other sensor-based SLAM systems, VSLAM offers distinct advantages: cameras are cost-effective while capturing rich visual information to provide finer environmental features. RGB-D cameras, which acquire both color images and depth data, have gained widespread adoption in mobile robotics due to their high-precision depth sensing capabilities at low cost.

In recent years, VSLAM technology has been extensively researched, with its framework maturing into three core components: feature extraction frontend, state estimation backend, and loop closure detection. The feature extraction frontend identifies key image features to estimate camera pose variations, while the state estimation backend optimizes camera trajectories based on these features to ensure positioning accuracy. Loop closure detection eliminates accumulated errors by recognizing revisited scenes, thereby enhancing map consistency. Advanced algorithms such as ORB-SLAM3 [3], DSO [4], DVO [5] and LSD-SLAM [6] have demonstrated exceptional performance across various applications.

Traditional VSLAM frameworks face significant challenges in complex dynamic scenarios. While geometry-based SLAM systems perform well in static environments, they exhibit limitations when advanced environmental understanding is required. Studies show that VSLAM performance often degrades substantially when applied to novel unknown environments [7], with localization and mapping capabilities severely compromised in highly dynamic scenes [8]. This stems primarily from the static environment assumption inherent in most current VSLAM systems - where all objects are presumed stationary. When moving objects are present, this assumption introduces systemic errors that generate incorrect map points. Such situations are prevalent in real-world applications like urban settings with dense pedestrian/vehicle traffic or indoor spaces with human movement. These dynamic elements disrupt VSLAM systems, causing feature point drift, mismatches, and erroneous map points that not only degrade localization accuracy but also produce substantial faulty data, ultimately hindering subsequent decision-making and navigation tasks.

Therefore, accurate segmentation of dynamic objects has become a core issue that SLAM methods must address in dynamic environments. Unlike traditional moving object segmentation approaches, where either the camera or environmental objects may be in motion simultaneously, methods such as background subtraction or Gaussian Mixture Models [9] struggle to effectively separate dynamic objects. To address this, this paper proposes FlexiSLAM, an improved visual SLAM system based on the ORB-SLAM3 framework, specifically optimized for RGB-D cameras. The system innovatively integrates a dual-verification mechanism combining semantic information and geometric constraints: on one hand, it employs semantic segmentation networks to acquire prior knowledge of potentially dynamic objects; on the other hand, it utilizes multi-view geometric consistency checks to verify dynamic features. These two approaches complement each

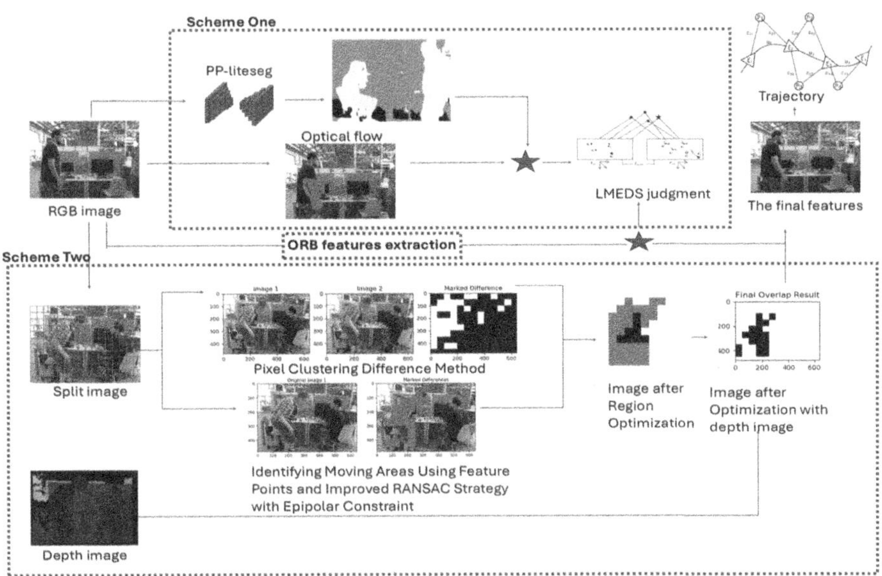

Fig. 1. Overview of the modifications introduced in the FlexiSLAM system compared to the ORB-SLAM3 framework: RGB images are additionally processed through three parallel threads—semantic segmentation, feature point optical flow computation, and image region segmentation. The semantic segmentation and optical flow threads identify the initial moving regions, while the segmentation thread provides input for pixel difference analysis and the improved RANSAC algorithm. After comprehensive optimization, a second moving region is identified. By combining both moving regions, the system performs joint optimization to determine the final moving region, and after filtering, the remaining information is processed to generate the trajectory.

other's advantages - semantic information provides high-level semantic understanding while geometric constraints ensure low-level feature consistency. Their collaborative operation significantly enhances the system's localization robustness in dynamic environments. As shown in Fig. 1, this architecture employs a parallel processing pipeline that enables efficient coordination between semantic analysis, geometric verification modules, and the feature extraction frontend, achieving precise dynamic object identification and filtering without compromising real-time performance.

In Scheme One, FlexiSLAM incorporates a lightweight semantic segmentation network to identify and filter dynamic elements in the scene, such as pedestrians and moving vehicles, preventing them from interfering with feature extraction and map generation. After obtaining feature points from the feature extraction module, the system combines sparse optical flow computation to further filter out feature points in dynamic object regions. Finally, LMedS (Least-Medians of Squares) matrix evaluation [10] is applied to eliminate anomalous feature points, ensuring more accurate pose estimation.

In Scheme Two, FlexiSLAM combines pixel clustering and Scale-Invariant Feature Transform (SIFT) [11] optical flow point detection techniques. Through pixel block clustering analysis and optical flow point region segmentation, the system more accurately identifies regions containing moving objects and filters the feature points in these areas, reducing the impact of dynamic elements. To further improve robustness in dynamic environments, FlexiSLAM adopts pixel block segmentation methods, providing more precise filtering of moving regions.

To evaluate the performance of FlexiSLAM, experiments were conducted using the TUM RGB-D dataset. The results demonstrate that, compared to the original ORB-SLAM3, FlexiSLAM significantly improves both accuracy and robustness in dynamic environments. In addition, when dealing with numerous dynamic objects, FlexiSLAM exhibits better adaptability, effectively mitigating dynamic interference and enhancing the stability of localization and mapping.

The primary contributions of this paper are as follows:

- We introduce a lightweight semantic segmentation network into the ORB-SLAM3 framework to effectively filter dynamic elements in the environment, such as pedestrians and moving vehicles, while incorporating sparse optical flow and LMEDS to further eliminate missed feature points in dynamic object regions.
- We present an effective dynamic object filtering method that utilizes pixel clustering, SIFT optical flow point detection, and pixel block segmentation techniques to achieve more precise identification of moving regions. This approach significantly improves the system's robustness in dynamic environments.
- We innovatively integrate the dual advantages of semantic analysis and geometric verification to construct a collaborative optimization framework. This framework mutually validates high-level object understanding provided by semantic information with feature consistency ensured by geometric constraints. While achieving precise identification of moving regions, it significantly enhances the system's localization robustness in dynamic environments, extends the algorithm's applicability to complex scenarios, and ensures real-time processing performance through a parallel computing architecture.

With these enhancements, FlexiSLAM exhibits substantial performance improvements in dynamic scenes, offering new insights for enhancing the reliability of VSLAM in practical applications.

2 Related Works

2.1 SLAM In Dynamic Environments

The application of SLAM in dynamic environments has long been a significant research topic within the field. With the rapid advancement of robotics and autonomous driving technologies, the operation of SLAM systems in highly dynamic environments, such as those involving pedestrians, vehicles, and other moving objects, has become an inevitable requirement. However, these dynamic elements present considerable challenges to the accuracy and stability of traditional SLAM methods. To address these challenges, various solutions have been proposed, with current mainstream approaches falling into two categories: geometry-based methods and semantic-based methods.

Geometry-based methods primarily rely on the geometric features of the scene, such as optical flow and scene flow [14], to detect and filter dynamic objects by analyzing their motion patterns. The core idea of these methods is to distinguish between static and dynamic objects by examining the consistency or variation in their movement across multiple frames. For instance, Daniela Esparza [22] proposed a method that combines optical flow, SegNet, and depth maps to detect dynamic objects through motion-based segmentation. Similarly, Cheng [23] employed optical flow to detect dynamic feature points and identified dynamic objects by analyzing the motion changes of these points. While these geometry-based methods show some effectiveness in detecting dynamic objects, they also exhibit limitations. Optical flow is mainly used for motion consistency checks, but its accuracy is limited, particularly in dealing with fast-moving objects in complex scenes. Moreover, the computational cost of optical flow is relatively high, especially when processing large-scale data, and the issue of dynamic object removal remains unresolved.

To further enhance the performance of SLAM systems in dynamic environments, researchers have increasingly turned to methods based on semantic information. These approaches typically integrate semantic segmentation or object detection techniques to effectively identify and filter dynamic objects, thereby reducing their interference with localization and map construction. For instance, Berta [24] proposed a method combining Mask R-CNN with geometric approaches to detect both potentially moving and actively moving objects. Although this method achieved notable success in dynamic object detection, the high computational complexity of the Mask R-CNN model limited its ability to achieve real-time processing.

Zhong [25] proposed a method that integrates deep neural network-based object detection algorithms with SLAM to significantly improve the accuracy of both object detection and SLAM performance in dynamic environments. This method uses semantic segmentation techniques based on deep learning to recognize dynamic objects, avoiding the motion consistency issues associated with traditional geometric methods. Additionally, Runz [26] advanced the field by incorporating instance-level semantic information into SLAM systems, embedding semantic labels to generate maps that account for dynamic objects. Similarly, Cheng [13] proposed integrating semantic segmentation into the ORB-SLAM2 system, enhancing the robustness of simultaneous localization and mapping (SLAM) while incorporating semantic information from the map. While this method demonstrated impressive results in complex environments, its computational cost when processing high-resolution images and diverse dynamic scenes remained substantial, limiting its feasibility for real-time applications.

2.2 Semantic Segmentation Models

With the rapid development of deep learning and computer vision technologies, semantic segmentation models have provided new methods for object recognition. High-precision models such as DeepLab [16], HRNet [17], GCN [18], Swin Transformer [19], and K-Net [20] have significantly improved segmentation accuracy through multi-scale feature extraction and global context capturing, demonstrating excellent performance, especially in complex scenes. To reduce the interference of moving objects in dynamic environments on SLAM systems, researchers have gradually integrated these semantic segmentation models into SLAM. For instance, Bescos [24] employed Mask R-CNN, a model specifically designed for high-precision segmentation, to effectively identify dynamic objects. Similarly, Runz [26] utilized the DeepLab v2 model. Although these models demonstrated exceptional performance in terms of segmentation accuracy, their computational cost was significant, making real-time processing particularly challenging, especially on devices with limited computational resources.

To address this issue, Yu [27] introduced the lightweight segmentation model SegNet into the DS-SLAM system. Although the model reduced time consumption to some extent, it still did not meet the minimum real-time requirement of 30 frames per second, and thus failed to fully satisfy the real-time demands of dynamic SLAM systems.

As the demand for real-time processing increased, more lightweight semantic segmentation models emerged, achieving a balance between segmentation accuracy and processing speed.

For example, the ENet model [28], specifically designed for real-time tasks, offers extremely low latency, making it suitable for mobile devices and real-time video processing. The MobileNet series [29] was optimized for efficient CPU usage while maintaining a high level of segmentation accuracy, making it ideal for mobile and embedded systems. ShuffleNet [30] was designed for devices with limited computational resources, ensuring satisfactory segmentation results while reducing computational costs. ESPNet [31] is particularly suited for edge computing devices, enabling real-time image segmentation with limited resources. ICNet [32], designed for urban scene parsing, allows for efficient processing of high-resolution images, making it well-suited for applications such as traffic monitoring and autonomous driving.

In this paper, we integrate an advanced lightweight semantic segmentation network into the SLAM system to significantly enhance its real-time performance.

The lightweight semantic segmentation model PP-LiteSeg [34], provided by PaddlePaddle [33]. According to the data from PaddlePaddle, PP-LiteSeg demonstrates a good balance between real-time performance and accuracy across the same dataset in running and testing, outperforming many other lightweight semantic segmentation models. Moreover, PaddlePaddle offers a wide selection of semantic segmentation models, allowing for convenient replacement with available models in the future.

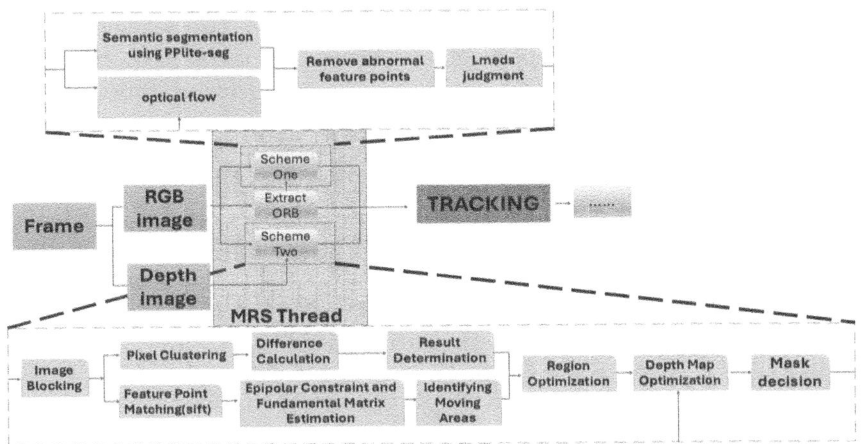

Fig. 2. The framework of the modifications of the FlexiSLAM system compared to the ORB-SLAM3 system. The MRS Thread reprensents moving region segnmentation thread.

3 System Introduction

This section provides a detailed analysis of the FlexiSLAM system, covering four main components. Section III-A presents an overview of the FlexiSLAM framework. Section III-B introduces the method of dynamic region separation using semantic segmentation in FlexiSLAM (Scheme One). Section III-C explores the technique of region filtering using pixel clustering combined with optical flow points (Scheme Two). Section III-D evaluates the advantages and disadvantages of Scheme One and Scheme Two.

3.1 The Framework Of FlexiSLAM

ORB-SLAM3 is widely recognized for its high accuracy, robustness, practicality, and efficiency, making it the system of choice in various real-world applications [3]. Building on this, FlexiSLAM adopts ORB-SLAM3 as its foundational framework, with modifications to detect and exclude dynamic objects.

FlexiSLAM operates five concurrent threads: the dynamic region segmentation thread, tracking thread, local mapping thread, loop closure thread, and map creation thread. As shown in Fig. 2, the main innovation of this system compared to the original ORB-SLAM3 is the addition of the dynamic region segmentation thread. This thread runs before the tracking thread and takes RGB video frames, depth frames from the RGB-D camera, and ORB feature points extracted by the ORB feature extractor as input. After filtering out the dynamic regions, it outputs a feature point cloud corresponding to the static regions.

The moving region segmentation thread is divided into two parts: Scheme One, based on semantic segmentation, and Scheme Two, based on pixel clustering and SIFT optical flow point filtering. These two schemes can run either simultaneously or independently. Scheme One takes RGB frames and ORB feature points as input and significantly improves segmentation accuracy by leveraging prior knowledge of potential dynamic regions in most environments, enabling precise identification of moving regions. However, its accuracy decreases when dealing with unknown dynamic regions. Scheme Two provides a more general approach, taking RGB and depth images as input. Although its accuracy is lower than Scheme One, it is highly generalizable and can effectively filter dynamic regions even without prior information. Both schemes can independently output feature point clouds after filtering dynamic regions, or they can be combined for enhanced filtering effectiveness.

3.2 Scheme One

In Scheme One, the original RGB images obtained from the RGB-D camera are first input into the semantic segmentation module to generate semantic segmentation maps. At the same time, the RGB images are sent to the feature point extraction and optical flow processing modules. The feature point extraction module extracts ORB feature points from the RGB images, while the optical flow processing module calculates the movement distance of target areas using the extracted ORB feature points with optical flow methods. If the movement distance exceeds the normal range, feature points associated with dynamic objects are discarded based on the semantic segmentation maps, and the remaining feature points are filtered based on geometric information.

Semantic Segmentation Model. The FlexiSLAM system creates a separate thread to run in parallel with the ORB feature extraction module in the original ORB-SLAM3 system's tracking thread. It integrates a semantic segmentation module, which performs semantic segmentation on the received image frames, generating segmentation maps with semantic information. Based on this prior information and the module's assumptions—namely, that in practical applications, particularly in indoor environments, FlexiSLAM considers humans as the primary dynamic objects—the system filters out potential moving objects (such as humans) and retains only static elements of the environment for map construction. By utilizing parallel dual-thread processing, the system significantly reduces time consumption and enhances real-time performance.

Identifying Moving Objects with Optical Flow. Given the high processing time requirements of semantic segmentation algorithms (including lightweight models) and the limitations of relying solely on prior information to determine moving regions—such as recognizing pedestrians but failing to detect the shopping carts they are dragging—this approach proposes a method that combines ORB feature points with optical flow computation to identify feature points in regions containing moving objects. To reduce processing time, a parallel processing strategy is adopted, where the semantic segmentation module is executed concurrently with feature point extraction and optical flow selection. This dual-threaded design optimizes the workflow, ensuring the feasibility and efficiency of the algorithm in resource-constrained environments.

Using optical flow to remove moving areas, the main steps are as follows:

- Feature Point Extraction:
  Using the built-in ORB feature extraction function of the ORB-SLAM3 system, key points are extracted from the current frame image. The efficiency and accuracy of the ORB algorithm are critical for real-time processing, providing necessary feature descriptions without sacrificing performance.
- Optical Flow Point Matching:
  The extracted feature points are used as the basis for optical flow calculation. By comparing the feature points and their surrounding environments in the current and previous frames, the most similar matching points are identified. This step is crucial in determining the positions of points in the previous frame that have the highest similarity to those in the current frame.
- Calculation of Optical Flow Values:
  For each pair of matched feature points, their position differences between the two frames are calculated. These differences, represented as vectors $(\boldsymbol{\Delta x}, \boldsymbol{\Delta y})$, are the estimated optical flow vectors, which provide information about the movement between the two frames.
- Elimination of Feature Points in Moving Regions:
  Based on the overall movement caused by the camera, the optical flow values of static targets are typically small and close to zero, whereas the optical flow values of moving targets are relatively large. By setting a threshold, feature points with large optical flow values, i.e., those located in moving regions, can be filtered out.

Although this method reduces time consumption and avoids the high computational cost of semantic segmentation, it is too simplistic and coarse, making it unable to comprehensively identify and remove all moving objects. As shown in Fig. 3, the red areas represent regions identified as moving by the optical flow method. Due to the limited difference information between consecutive frames for fast-moving objects, there may not be significant displacement, or part of a moving object may not actually move within a short time frame, leading to the reception of incorrect information. Therefore, this method should be considered a supplementary approach when using semantic segmentation models.

Removing Anomalous Feature Points. In the process of identifying and correcting anomalous feature points in images processed through semantic segmentation and optical flow, it is acknowledged that semantic segmentation models, particularly lightweight ones, may not perfectly process every frame, resulting in the retention of certain feature points that do not meet the established criteria. Although the number of these residual feature points has been significantly reduced, further processing is required to ensure accuracy.

Fig. 3. The difference of two images with dense optical flow

To address this, a filtering mechanism based on geometric features has been implemented to eliminate anomalous feature points, which is primarily carried out through the following components.

- Feature Point Matching:
  Let there be sets of feature points P and P_i' from two frames, where each feature point $p_i \in P$ and $p_i' \in P'$are matched using descriptors, i is the number of feature points extracted for each image. The choice of descriptor is based on its ability to uniquely represent feature points in an image.
- Anomalous Feature Point Identification:
  By calculating and comparing the Hamming distance between all possible pairs, the best match for each query descriptor is found, that is, by identifying the descriptor in the target image's descriptor set that has the minimum distance to it. If a feature point p_i does not have a matching point p_i' in the other frame, then it is considered an anomalous feature.
- Seek Transformation Matrix:
  Given matched feature points (p_i, p_i'), we seek a transformation matrix M that satisfies:
  $$\min_{M} \text{median}\left(\{||p_i' - M \cdot p_i||\}_{i=1}^{n}\right), \qquad (1)$$
  where M is the transformation matrix from the first frame to the second, $||p_i' - M \cdot p_i||$ means the Euclidean distance between the transformed point and the target point, and median$(\cdot)$ denotes taking the median.
- Consistency Check with the Global Motion Model:

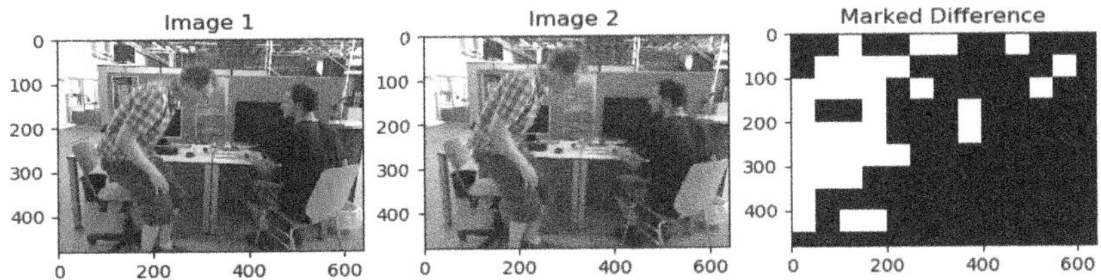

Fig. 4. Illustration of pixel block clustering and frame difference detection

After filtering with the Least Median of Squares (LMedS) method, the retained matched points and their corresponding transformation matrix M should reflect the global motion pattern. Any matched points not conforming to this global motion model are to be eliminated.

- Applicability Conditions:
  It is important to note that the effectiveness of the aforementioned method may be limited if the proportion of moving objects in the image is too high. Therefore, this strategy is primarily applicable in scenarios where the scene has been made static through preprocessing with semantic segmentation.

3.3 Scheme Two

In Scheme Two, the original RGB images and its corresponding depth images are obtained from the RGB-D camera. The RGB and depth images are divided into 40×40 pixel blocks. The segmented RGB images are then sent separately to the pixel clustering module and the SIFT feature Points filtering module. The processed results are further combined with the depth images to determine moving regions, and the feature points are further filtered accordingly.

This scheme primarily identifies moving regions by processing the difference information between image frames. Considering the limited difference information between adjacent frames, as shown in Fig. 5, the scheme selects every third frame for calculation.

This scheme identifies moving regions through two branches. The first branch relies on pixel clustering differences between two frames, effectively detecting moving regions by analyzing color variations. The second branch utilizes epipolar constraints between feature points of the two frames to detect moving regions. While this approach shares similarities with the optical flow method in Scheme One, it includes targeted optimizations. Ultimately, both branches are combined for comprehensive processing, enhancing the accuracy and reliability of the detection.

The main process is as follows:

Branch One-Pixel Clustering Difference Method. This method first divides two consecutive image frames I_t and I_{t+1} into fixed-size pixel blocks,

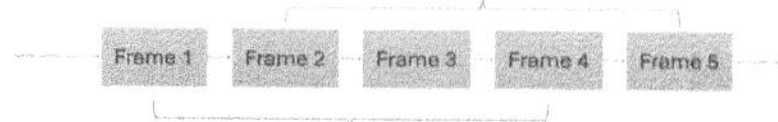

Fig. 5. Frame interval selection for moving region detection

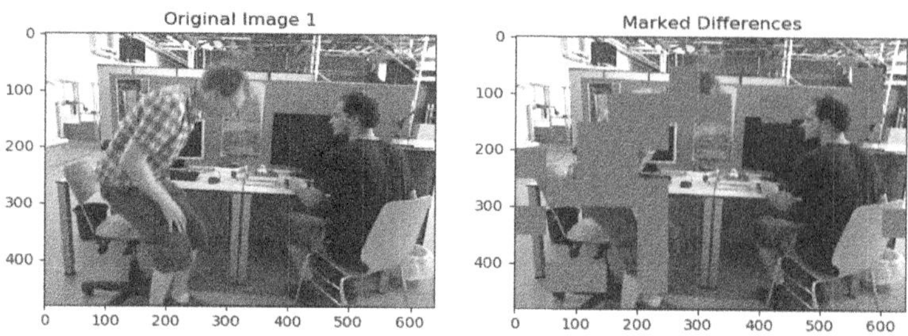

Fig. 6. Moving regions identified in branch two

with a block size of 40×40 pixels in this paper. For each pixel block, a pixel clustering algorithm (such as K-means) is used to cluster based on color or brightness, extracting the main features of each block. By comparing the clustering results of corresponding pixel blocks from the two frames, regions with significant pixel differences are identified. The main process is as follows:

- Image Blocking:
  Assuming the image size is $M \times N$, it is divided into pixel blocks of size $B \times B$. Each pixel block can be represented as:

$$B_{i,j} = \{I(x, y) \mid x \in [iB, (i+1)B), y \in [jB, (j+1)B)\}, \tag{2}$$

  where i, j are the horizontal and vertical indices of the image block, and x, y are the pixel coordinates.
- Pixel Clustering:
  K-means clustering is applied to each pixel block $B_{i,j}$. Assuming k cluster centers are selected, the clustering goal is to minimize the following cost function:

$$J = \sum_{i=1}^{k} \sum_{x \in C_i} ||x - \mu_i||^2, \tag{3}$$

  where C_i is the i-th cluster, μ_i is the cluster center, and $|x - \mu_i|^2$ is the distance between pixel x and the cluster center μ_i.
- Difference Calculation:
  For corresponding pixel blocks in two consecutive frames, the difference between their cluster centers is calculated. Let μ_t and μ_{t+1} represent the cluster centers of the two frames, and the difference is defined as:

$$\Delta \boldsymbol{\mu}_{i,j} = ||\mu_t - \mu_{t+1}||. \tag{4}$$

If $\Delta\mu_{i,j}$ exceeds a preset threshold θ, the region is considered to have significant changes.

- Result Determination:
  Based on the size of $\Delta\mu_{i,j}$, a threshold θ is used to determine the presence of moving objects. The determination rule is as follows:
  If $\Delta\mu_{i,j} > \theta$, the block is marked as a moving region;
  If $\Delta\mu_{i,j} <= \theta$, the block is considered unchanged.
- Advantages and Challenges:
  This method is computationally efficient, especially suitable for low-resolution or scenarios with minimal changes. However, simple methods based on pixel differences are prone to interference from lighting changes or noise, leading to false positives, as shown in the Fig .4, where the segmentation result is not very precise. Therefore, this paper combines an improved feature point-based approach to enhance the robustness of detection.

Branch Two—Identifying Moving Areas Using Feature Points and Improved RANSAC Strategy with Epipolar Constraint. This method combines feature point extraction, the epipolar constraint, and an improved RANSAC strategy for identifying moving regions in dynamic scenes. Image blocking reduces computational complexity, while the epipolar constraint ensures geometric consistency between matching points. Pixel blocks that violate the constraint are marked as moving regions. The method utilizes parallel processing and RANSAC filtering to provide an efficient and robust solution for detecting moving objects. The specific steps are as follows:

- Image Blocking:
  As in Branch one, the image is divided into 50×50 pixel blocks.
- Feature Point Matching:
  For each pixel block $B_{i,j}$, a random pair of feature points is extracted from the two image frames. If no matching feature points are found in a block, that block is skipped. Feature point extraction algorithms such as SIFT are used. Assume that the feature points extracted from the two frames are $p_i \in I_t$ and $p'_i \in I_{t+1}$, and matching is performed based on the similarity of their descriptors.
- Epipolar Constraint and Fundamental Matrix Estimation:
  The epipolar constraint is a key geometric constraint used in stereo vision to describe the relationship between corresponding points in two image frames. The core idea is that for a feature point in the first image, its corresponding point in the second image must lie on a specific epipolar line. This relationship can be expressed using the fundamental matrix F. The fundamental matrix F satisfies the following equation:

$$p_i^T F p_i = 0, \tag{5}$$

where p_i and p'_i are the homogeneous coordinates of the corresponding feature points in the two frames. This constraint indicates that the feature point p_i

in the first image must lie on the epipolar line corresponding to its matched point p_i' in the second image.

- Identifying Moving Areas:
  After solving for the fundamental matrix, the epipolar constraint is used to detect moving areas. The geometric error ϵ_i is calculated as follows:

$$\epsilon_i = \left|p_i^T F p_i\right|. \tag{6}$$

  If the geometric error ϵ_i exceeds a preset threshold θ, it indicates that the feature point does not satisfy the epipolar constraint, and the entire pixel block $B_{i,j}$ containing this feature point is marked as a moving region.
- Result Integration:
  As shown in Fig. 6, all the blocks marked as moving areas are then integrated to form the final global moving object detection result. By processing each block independently, this method supports parallel execution, improving processing efficiency.

Region Optimization and Depth Map Optimization. In the proposed approach, after identifying moving regions using pixel clustering differences and feature point epipolar constraints, the first step is to handle overlapping regions before proceeding with further optimization to improve the accuracy of the results.

Overlapping Region Processing: In the initial stage of region optimization, the overlapping regions from both methods (pixel clustering differences and feature point epipolar constraints) must be processed. Regions identified as moving by both methods are marked as black regions (definite moving regions). If only one method identifies a region as moving, it is marked as a gray region (potential moving region). The remaining areas, not identified as moving by either method, are marked as white regions (stationary regions).

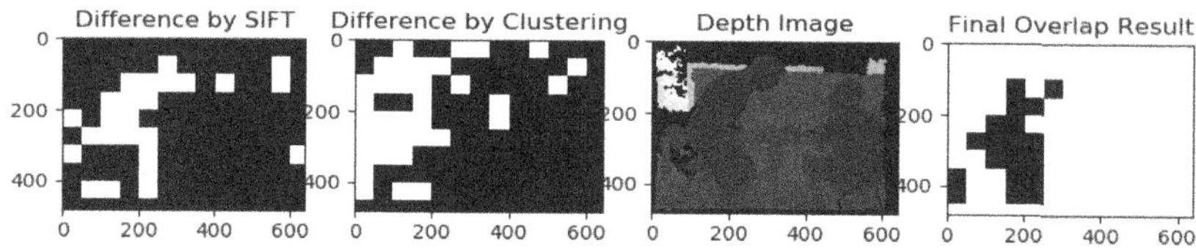

Fig. 7. Final Results Obtained by Combining Two Branches

Region Optimization:

- Black Region (Definite Moving Region) Optimization:
  If a black region has no neighboring regions of the same type, it is considered isolated and downgraded to a gray region.

- Gray Region (Potential Moving Region) Optimization:
  If a gray region has fewer than two neighboring regions of the same type in its adjacent top, bottom, left, or right positions, it is considered isolated and downgraded to a white region.
- Processing of Enclosed White Regions:
  A depth-first search (DFS) algorithm is used to handle small white regions completely surrounded by gray or black regions. These white regions are reclassified as gray, indicating they may be potential moving regions.

Depth Map Optimization:

- Depth Mean Calculation for Black Regions:
  For black-marked definite moving regions, the depth mean of the corresponding areas is calculated.
- Depth Error Matching:
  In both black and gray regions, areas with small depth errors relative to the calculated depth mean are included in the final moving region determination. This step helps to eliminate misidentified areas caused by feature point or pixel differences, improving the accuracy of moving region recognition.

Through the above processing, after depth map and region optimization, the final moving regions are shown in the Fig. 7, ensuring the reliability and accuracy of the identification results. Based on the identified moving regions, feature point filtering can be applied to eliminate the impact of the moving regions.

3.4 Comprehensive Processing of Scheme One and Scheme Two

Scheme One and Scheme Two each have their own strengths and limitations. Scheme One, based on semantic segmentation, enables high-precision detection of moving regions, particularly excelling in complex scenes and detailed feature handling. However, it has high hardware requirements, particularly needing support from high-performance devices such as GPUs. Additionally, it relies on training data, which may lead to incomplete or inaccurate recognition when encountering new or unfamiliar objects.

In contrast, Scheme Two detects moving regions through pixel differences between frames, without relying on prior knowledge, making it suitable for environments with limited hardware resources. It enables fast detection of moving regions, offering high efficiency and flexibility. However, its detection accuracy is relatively lower, especially when dealing with complex backgrounds or subtle movements, where it performs less effectively than Scheme One.

The combination of both schemes can provide complementary advantages, offering a more comprehensive solution for moving region detection. Specifically, Scheme One quickly identifies potential moving regions through semantic segmentation, while Scheme Two further detects all possible moving regions through frame differences, serving as a supplement to Scheme One by expanding the scope of detection and ensuring more complete identification of moving regions. However, in highly complex or rapidly changing environments, the combined

Table 1. Comparison of Absolute Trajectory Error (ATE) across Different SLAM Methods

Test Sequences	ORB-SLAM3			FlexiSLAM			DS-SLAM		
	RMSE	Median	Std	RMSE	Median	Std	RMSE	Median	Std
SITTING_STATIC	0.009893	0.008325	0.004129	**0.006062**	0.005115	**0.003229**	0.0065	**0.0049**	0.0033
WALKING_HALFSPHERE	0.224152	0.189371	0.092743	0.035668	**0.020509**	**0.013157**	**0.0303**	0.0222	0.0159
WALKING_RPY	0.653562	0.521269	0.323767	**0.087753**	**0.026812**	**0.076432**	0.4442	0.2835	0.2350
WALKING_STATIC	0.344838	0.377052	0.111838	**0.007818**	**0.005914**	**0.002603**	0.0081	0.0067	0.0036
WALKING_XYZ	0.463041	0.168476	0.318018	**0.014401**	**0.011011**	**0.007201**	0.0247	0.0151	0.0161

Table 2. Comparison of Relative Pose Error(RPE) across Different SLAM Methods-Translational Error

Test Sequences	ORB-SLAM3			FlexiSLAM			DS-SLAM		
	RMSE	Median	Std	RMSE	Median	Std	RMSE	Median	Std
SITTING_STATIC	0.005147	0.003578	0.002847	**0.005762**	**0.004356**	**0.002945**	0.0078	0.0061	0.0038
WALKING_HALFSPHERE	0.020188	0.011498	0.013294	**0.017236**	**0.008944**	**0.012647**	0.0297	0.0226	0.0152
WALKING_RPY	0.028081	0.016393	0.017522	**0.036305**	**0.010804**	**0.032843**	0.1503	0.0457	0.1168
WALKING_STATIC	0.019586	0.007294	0.016340	**0.007328**	**0.004457**	**0.004717**	0.0102	0.0082	0.0048
WALKING_XYZ	0.021777	0.011845	0.014537	**0.011694**	**0.008850**	**0.006139**	0.0333	0.0181	0.0229

Table 3. Comparison of Relative Pose Error(RPE) across Different SLAM Methods-Rotational Error

Test Sequences	ORB-SLAM3			FlexiSLAM			DS-SLAM		
	RMSE	Median	Std	RMSE	Median	Std	RMSE	Median	Std
SITTING_STATIC	0.160657	0.112902	0.086677	**0.163765**	**0.120518**	**0.085745**	0.2735	0.2351	0.1215
WALKING_HALFSPHERE	0.516113	0.349563	0.306828	**0.446172**	**0.262973**	**0.302213**	0.8142	0.6217	0.4101
WALKING_RPY	0.647762	0.451821	0.367908	**0.743657**	**0.262980**	**0.649428**	3.0042	0.9902	2.3065
WALKING_STATIC	0.380062	0.206221	0.284050	**0.189389**	**0.141093**	**0.103091**	0.2690	0.2259	0.1182
WALKING_XYZ	0.538661	0.298635	0.374091	**0.386328**	**0.228957**	**0.268698**	0.8266	0.4192	0.5826

approach may lead to overfitting, potentially filtering out large portions of the image.

Overall, the integration of both schemes achieves a well-balanced approach between accuracy and efficiency, leveraging both frame differences and semantic segmentation to provide a more comprehensive and precise solution for moving region detection.

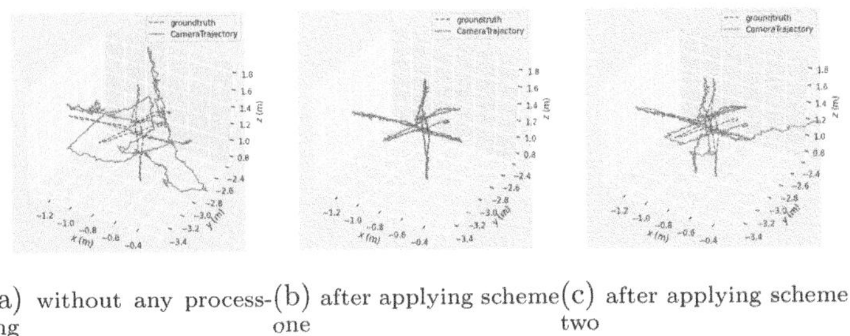

(a) without any processing (b) after applying scheme one (c) after applying scheme two

Fig. 8. The trajectory comparison without any processing, after applying scheme one and after applying scheme two

4 Experiments

This part presents a comprehensive experimental study of the FlexiSLAM system, focusing on four key aspects: performance on the TUM RGB-D dataset compared with other methods, ablation studies, processing time analysis, and result stability testing. All experiments were conducted on a computer equipped with an Intel i7 CPU, 3060ti GPU, and 32 GB of RAM to ensure the reliability and consistency of the results.

4.1 Datasets and Metrics

The TUM RGB-D dataset plays a crucial role in visual SLAM research, widely used to evaluate algorithm performance in both static and dynamic environments. This dataset features a variety of scenes, enabling comprehensive testing of SLAM systems under different conditions. Since visual SLAM systems must handle various scenarios and dynamic changes, the TUM RGB-D dataset provides researchers with an ideal benchmark to effectively assess system robustness and accuracy. TUM RGB-D dataset contains five typical scenes: SITTING_STATIC, WALKING_HALFSPHERE, WALKING_RPY, WALKING_STATIC, WALKING_XYZ. In the SITTING_STATIC scene, the camera remains stationary, making it suitable for testing the system's performance in static environments. The WALKING_HALFSPHERE scene involves the camera moving along a hemispherical path, testing the system's stability under changing perspectives. The WALKING_RPY scene includes complex roll, pitch, and yaw movements, evaluating the system's ability to handle dynamic motion. The WALKING_STATIC scene records the camera's movement in a dynamic background, making it ideal for analyzing the system's adaptability in such conditions. Finally, the WALKING_XYZ scene features the camera moving along the XYZ axes, testing the system's accuracy in multidirectional motion.

The evaluation relies on two key metrics: Absolute Trajectory Error (ATE) and Relative Pose Error (RPE) [35], where ATE assesses the global consistency of the trajectory, and RPE measures the drift in the trajectory.

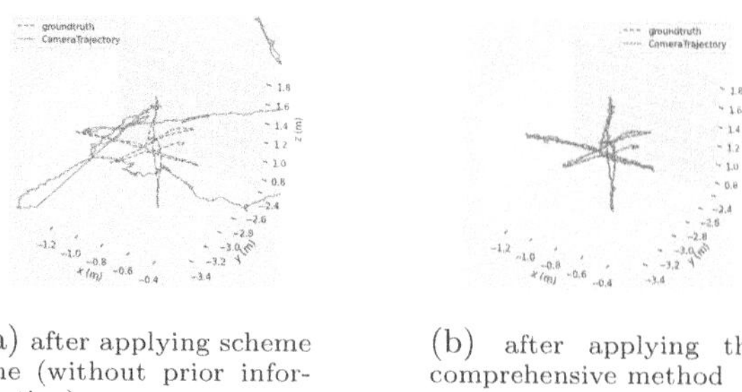

(a) after applying scheme one (without prior information)

(b) after applying the comprehensive method

Fig. 9. The trajectory comparison after applying scheme one (without prior information) and after applying the comprehensive method

4.2 Main Results

In terms of the Absolute Trajectory Error (ATE), as shown in Table 1, FlexiSLAM demonstrates significant performance improvements over ORB-SLAM3 across all selected sequences of the TUM RGBD dataset. Specifically, in the static scene SITTING_STATIC, the ATE of FlexiSLAM is reduced by approximately 38.7% compared to ORB-SLAM3, which is mainly attributed to the effectiveness of its dynamic feature point filtering mechanism. In dynamic scenes, the advantages of FlexiSLAM are even more pronounced. For example, in the WALKING_RPY sequence, the ATE of FlexiSLAM is reduced by approximately 86.6% compared to ORB-SLAM3, and in the WALKING_STATIC and WALKING_XYZ sequences, the ATE is reduced by approximately 97.7% and 96.9% respectively. These results indicate that FlexiSLAM can effectively identify and filter dynamic objects, avoid localization errors caused by dynamic elements, and significantly enhance the trajectory consistency.

Compared with DS-SLAM, this solution shows higher accuracy in datasets that mainly test dynamic capabilities (such as WALKING_RPY, WALKING_STATIC, and WALKING_XYZ). For example, in the WALKING_RPY sequence, the ATE of FlexiSLAM is reduced by approximately 80.3% compared to DS-SLAM, and in the WALKING_STATIC and WALKING_XYZ sequences, the ATE is reduced by approximately 3.5% and 41.7% respectively. However, in the WALKING_HALFSPHERE dataset, which mainly tests perspective changes, the RMSE error of this solution is slightly higher than that of DS-SLAM, which may be due to the increased challenges of feature point matching caused by rapid perspective changes. Nevertheless, FlexiSLAM still has significant advantages in terms of overall accuracy and the ability to handle dynamic environments.

In terms of the Relative Trajectory Error (RPE), Table 2 and Table 3 further demonstrate that FlexiSLAM also outperforms ORB-SLAM3 and DS-SLAM in terms of RPE. Whether it is translational error or rotational error, FlexiSLAM performs excellently in all tested datasets, especially in dynamic environments (such as WALKING_RPY, WALKING_STATIC, WALKING_XYZ,

Table 4. ATEs and RPEs of the Method with Different Settings

Scheme	ATE			RPE (Translational Error)			RPE (Rotational Error)		
	RMSE	Median	Std	RMSE	Median	Std	RMSE	Median	Std
Original scheme	0.712712	0.458267	0.359170	0.025553	0.017330	0.014869	0.608478	0.419907	0.365680
Scheme one	0.017957	0.013515	0.009185	**0.012902**	**0.008717**	0.007977	**0.395710**	0.236204	0.295307
Scheme two	0.193137	0.073380	0.158101	0.017066	0.009586	0.011356	0.446084	0.247449	0.310218
Scheme one (without prior information)	0.927054	0.813747	0.408898	0.049522	0.015538	0.044942	0.886313	0.379777	0.750375
Comprehensive scheme	**0.017231**	**0.013496**	**0.008642**	0.013352	0.008897	**0.007893**	0.407606	**0.232934**	**0.284539**

and WALKING_HALFSPHERE), significantly reducing the trajectory drift error.

In terms of translational error, the RPE of FlexiSLAM in the WALKING_RPY sequence is reduced by approximately 29.3% compared to ORB-SLAM3, and in the WALKING_STATIC and WALKING_XYZ sequences, the RPE is reduced by approximately 62.5% and 46.3% respectively. Compared with DS-SLAM, the RPE of FlexiSLAM in the WALKING_RPY sequence is reduced by approximately 75.8%, and in the WALKING_STATIC and WALKING_XYZ sequences, it is reduced by approximately 28.1% and 64.9% respectively. These results indicate that FlexiSLAM can effectively reduce the interference of dynamic objects on pose estimation, thus significantly reducing the translational error.

In terms of rotational error, FlexiSLAM also performs outstandingly. For example, in the WALKING_RPY sequence, the rotational error of FlexiSLAM is reduced by approximately 14.9% compared to ORB-SLAM3, and in the WALKING_STATIC and WALKING_XYZ sequences, the rotational error is reduced by approximately 50.2% and 28.3% respectively. Compared with DS-SLAM, the rotational error of FlexiSLAM in the WALKING_RPY sequence is reduced by approximately 75.2%, and in the WALKING_STATIC and WALKING_XYZ sequences, it is reduced by approximately 29.6% and 53.3% respectively. These results further verify the robustness and accuracy of FlexiSLAM in dynamic environments.

In addition, FlexiSLAM also achieves high accuracy in the static scene SITTING_STATIC. In terms of translational error, the RPE of FlexiSLAM is reduced by approximately 11.9% compared to ORB-SLAM3, and in terms of rotational error, the RPE of FlexiSLAM is reduced by approximately 1.9% compared to ORB-SLAM3. Compared with DS-SLAM, the translational error and rotational error of FlexiSLAM in the static scene are reduced by approximately 26.2% and 40.1% respectively. This performance improvement benefits from the innovative algorithm design of FlexiSLAM, which can accurately identify and filter dynamic features while focusing on the pose estimation of static regions, thus significantly improving the overall accuracy and robustness of the system.

4.3 Ablation Studies

In this part, we conducted ablation studies to evaluate the effectiveness of our dynamic object filtering methods in FlexiSLAM. We selected the fr3_xyz

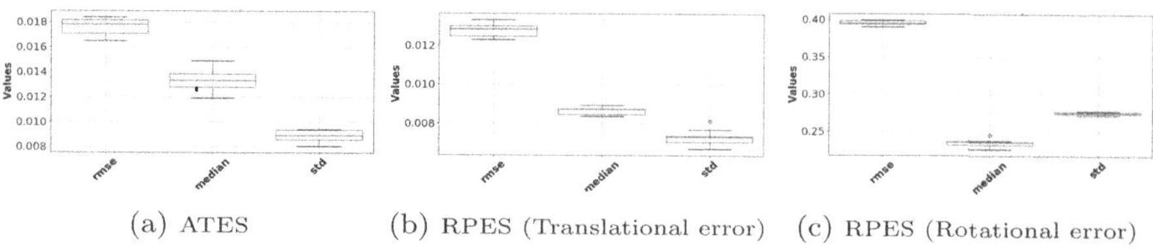

(a) ATES (b) RPES (Translational error) (c) RPES (Rotational error)

Fig. 10. Results of the comprehensive scheme on the TUM RGB-D Walking—XYZ Dataset

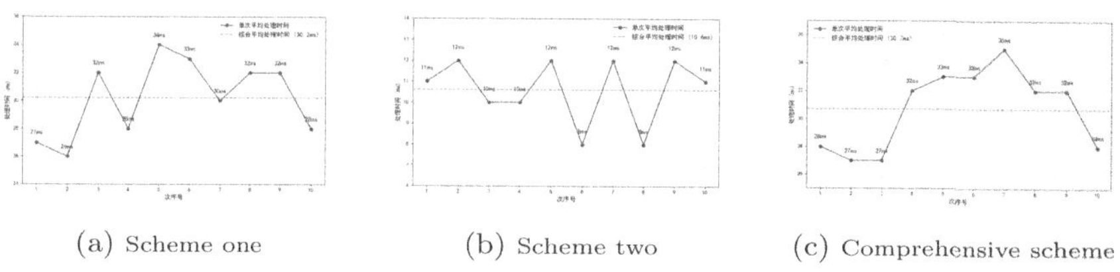

(a) Scheme one (b) Scheme two (c) Comprehensive scheme

Fig. 11. The processing duration of a single frame of image for each scheme

sequence from the TUM-RGBD dataset as the test dataset for its complex roll, pitch, and yaw movements, making it an ideal scenario for comprehensive performance evaluation. Specifically, we test the FlexiSLAM on fr3_xyz sequence with the following different settings: the original method without dynamic region filtering, only Scheme One, only Scheme Two, Scheme One without prior information, and the combined scheme integrating both Scheme One and Scheme Two.

As shown in Fig. 8 and Fig. 9, each image illustrates the differences between the tested trajectory and the ground truth in 3D space. By comparing Fig. 8 (a-c), it is evident that the trajectory processed with dynamic region filtering shows significant improvement over the unprocessed trajectory. Notably, the accuracy of Scheme One is superior to that of Scheme Two, indicating that effective filtering of dynamic regions can greatly enhance trajectory accuracy in dynamic environments.

Further comparison of Fig. 8 (a-b), and Fig. 9 (a) reveals that the performance of Scheme One heavily depends on prior information. Without such information, the improvement provided by Scheme One is minimal, and in some cases, it performs worse than Scheme Two. This indicates that Scheme One has limited applicability in scenarios without prior information. In contrast, Scheme Two, which is not reliant on such information, demonstrates more consistent performance across a wider range of real-world scenarios.

Lastly, comparisons of Fig. 8 (b), Fig. 9 (a-b), along with Tables 4, show that the combined scheme performs similarly to Scheme One, without significant additional improvement. Although there is some improvement in absolute trajectory error, the performance in terms of relative trajectory error even declines in some cases. This is because, in indoor environments with available prior information,

Scheme One has already maximally filtered the dynamic regions, leaving limited room for further enhancement. Over-filtering of dynamic regions can also result in frame loss, negatively affecting overall performance. Even so, the standard deviation shows improvement, indicating that the combined scheme leverages the strengths of both methods, providing greater stability and broader applicability, while being less susceptible to external influences.

4.4 Time Costs

As shown in Fig. 11,In terms of single-frame running time, Scheme 1 takes approximately 30 ms, while Scheme 2 takes around 10 ms. The single-frame running time of the comprehensive scheme is also about 30 ms, similar to that of Scheme 1. This is because the lightweight semantic segmentation model PP-LiteSeg used in Scheme 1 operates at a frame rate close to 70 frames per second in practical applications, and its processing time dominates the running duration of the comprehensive scheme. In addition, the dual-thread processing mechanism ensures that the running time of the comprehensive scheme is based on the longer time of the two schemes.

In the FlexiSLAM system, processing the single-frame semantic segmentation module takes about 15 milliseconds, and the entire tracking part takes approximately 30 milliseconds per frame. The overall frame rate of the system can reach about 33 frames per second, which is sufficient to provide a smooth visual experience, and it can be considered that real-time performance requirements have been achieved.

4.5 Stability Studies

To test the stability, dozens of runs were conducted on the TUM RGB-D walking—xyz dataset to evaluate the results. The results shown in the Fig. 10 indicate that, under the TUM RGB-D walking—xyz dataset, the multiple experiments showed that both the absolute trajectory error and the relative trajectory error remained within a relatively stable range, which sufficiently demonstrates the stability of the scheme.

5 Conclusion

This paper presents a visual SLAM system based on ORB-SLAM3 RGBD, named FlexiSLAM. The system integrates two distinct approaches to effectively mitigate the impact of dynamic objects on pose estimation in SLAM systems operating in dynamic environments. The first approach incorporates a semantic segmentation module, optical flow computation, and outlier feature point removal during tracking to reduce interference from dynamic objects. The second approach handles dynamic objects through pixel clustering, region segmentation, and epipolar constraints. By combining these two methods, FlexiSLAM demonstrates superior performance on the TUM-RGBD dataset. The results from the performance evaluation indicate that FlexiSLAM's pose estimation accuracy significantly surpasses that of ORB-SLAM3, while also exhibiting notable improvements compared to DS-SLAM.

Acknowledgments. This work was supported in part by the National Natural Science Foundation of China under Grant 62276061 and Grant 62436002. It was also supported by the Research Fund of the Advanced Ocean Institute, Southeast University, under Grant MP202404.

References

1. Liu, H., Zhang, G., Bao, H.: A survey of monocular simultaneous localization and mapping. J. Comput.-Aided Des. Comput. Graph. **28**(6), 855–868 (2016)
2. Bresson, G., Alsayed, Z., Yu, L., Glaser, S.: Simultaneous localization and mapping: a survey of current trends in autonomous driving. IEEE Trans. Intell. Veh. **2**(3), 194–220 (2017)
3. Campos, C., Elvira, R., Rodríguez, J.J.G., Montiel, J.M., Tardós, J.D.: Orb-slam3: an accurate open-source library for visual, visual-inertial, and multimap slam. IEEE Trans. Robot. **37**(6), 1874–1890 (2021)
4. Engel, J., Koltun, V., Cremers, D.: Direct sparse odometry. IEEE Trans. Pattern Anal. Mach. Intell. **40**(3), 611–625 (2017)
5. Kim, D.-H., Han, S.-B., Kim, J.-H.: Visual odometry algorithm using an RGB-D sensor and IMU in a highly dynamic environment. Robot Intell. Technol. Appl. **3**, 11–26 (2015)
6. Engel, J., Schöps, T., Cremers, D.: LSD-SLAM: large-scale direct monocular SLAM. In: Proceedings of the European Conference on Computer Vision, Springer, pp. 834–849 (2014)
7. Esparza, D., Flores, G.: The STDyn-SLAM: a stereo vision and semantic segmentation approach for VSLAM in dynamic outdoor environments. IEEE Access **10**, 18201–18209 (2022)
8. Wen, S., Li, P., Zhao, Y., Zhang, H., Sun, F., Wang, Z.: Semantic visual SLAM in dynamic environment. Auton. Robot. **45**(4), 493–504 (2021). https://doi.org/10.1007/s10514-021-09979-4
9. Lee, D.-S.: Effective Gaussian mixture learning for video background subtraction. IEEE Trans. Pattern Anal. Mach. Intell. **27**(5), 827–832 (2005)
10. Rousseeuw, P.J.: Least median of squares regression. J. Am. Stat. Assoc. **79**(388), 871–880 (1984)
11. Otero, I.R: Anatomy of the SIFT method. Ph.D. dissertation, École Normale Supérieure de Cachan, ENS Cachan (2015)
12. Wang, Y., Tian, Y., Chen, J., Xu, K., Ding, X.: A survey of visual SLAM in dynamic environment: the evolution from geometric to semantic approaches. IEEE Trans. Instrum. Meas. (2024)
13. Cheng, S., Sun, C., Zhang, S., Zhang, D.: SG-SLAM: a real-time RGB-D visual SLAM toward dynamic scenes with semantic and geometric information. IEEE Trans. Instrum. Meas. **72**, 1–12 (2022)

14. Wen, S., Tao, S., Liu, X., Babiarz, A., Richard, F.: CD-SLAM: a real-time stereo visual-inertial SLAM for complex dynamic environments with semantic and geometric information. IEEE Trans. Instrum. Meas. (2024)
15. Wen, S., Li, X., Liu, X., Li, J., Tao, S., Long, Y., Qiu, T.: Dynamic SLAM: a visual SLAM in outdoor dynamic scenes. IEEE Trans. Instrum. Meas. (2023)
16. Chen, L.-C., Papandreou, G., Kokkinos, I., Murphy, K., Yuille, A.L.: Deeplab: semantic image segmentation with deep convolutional nets, atrous convolution, and fully connected CRFs. IEEE Trans. Pattern Anal. Mach. Intell. **40**(4), 834–848 (2017)
17. Wang, J., et al.: Deep high-resolution representation learning for visual recognition. IEEE Trans. Pattern Anal. Mach. Intell. **43**(10), 3349–3364 (2020)
18. Peng, C., Zhang, X., Yu, G., Luo, G., Sun, J.: Large kernel matters–improve semantic segmentation by global convolutional network. In: Proceedings of the IEEE Conference on Computer Vision and Pattern Recognition, pp. 4353–4361 (2017)
19. Liu, Z., et al.: Swin transformer: hierarchical vision transformer using shifted windows. In: Proceedings of the IEEE/CVF International Conference on Computer Vision, pp. 10012–10022 (2021)
20. Zhang, W., Pang, J., Chen, K., Loy, C.C.: K-net: towards unified image segmentation. Adv. Neural. Inf. Process. Syst. **34**, 10326–10338 (2021)
21. Sturm, J., Engelhard, N., Endres, F., Burgard, W., Cremers, D.: A benchmark for the evaluation of RGB-D SLAM systems. In: Proceedings of the 2012 IEEE/RSJ International Conference on Intelligent Robots and Systems, pp. 573–580 (2012)
22. Esparza, D., Flores, G.: The STDyn-SLAM: a stereo vision and semantic segmentation approach for VSLAM in dynamic outdoor environments. IEEE Access **10**, 18201–18209 (2022)
23. Cheng, Q.H.: Improving monocular visual SLAM in dynamic environments: an optical-flow-based approach. Adv. Robot. **33**(11–12), 2019–2030 (2019)
24. Bescos, B., Fácil, J.M., Civera, J., Neira, J.: DynaSLAM: tracking, mapping, and inpainting in dynamic scenes. IEEE Robot. Autom. Lett. **3**(4), 4076–4083 (2018)
25. Zhong, F., Wang, S., Zhang, Z., Wang, Y.: Detect-SLAM: making object detection and SLAM mutually beneficial. In: Proceedings of the 2018 IEEE Winter Conference on Applications of Computer Vision (WACV), pp. 1001–1010 (2018)
26. Runz, M., Buffier, M., Agapito, L.: Maskfusion: real-time recognition, tracking and reconstruction of multiple moving objects. In: Proceedings of the 2018 IEEE International Symposium on Mixed and Augmented Reality (ISMAR), pp. 10–20 (2018)
27. Yu, C., et al.: DS-SLAM: a semantic visual SLAM towards dynamic environments. In: Proceedings of the 2018 IIEEE/RSJ International Conference on Intelligent Robots and Systems (IROS), pp. 1168–1174 (2018)
28. Paszke, A., Chaurasia, A., Kim, S., Culurciello, E.: ENet: a deep neural network architecture for real-time semantic segmentation, arXiv preprint arXiv:1606.02147 (2016)
29. Sinha, D., El-Sharkawy, M.: Thin MobileNet: an enhanced MobileNet architecture. In: Proceedings of the 2019 IEEE 10th Annual Ubiquitous Computing, Electronics Mobile Communication Conference (UEMCON), pp. 0280–0285 (2019)
30. Zhang, X., Zhou, X., Lin, M., Sun, J.: ShuffleNet: an extremely efficient convolutional neural network for mobile devices. In: Proceedings of the IEEE Conference on Computer Vision and Pattern Recognition, pp. 6848–6856 (2018)
31. Mehta, S., Rastegari, M., Caspi, A., Shapiro, L., Hajishirzi, H.: ESPNet: efficient spatial pyramid of dilated convolutions for semantic segmentation. In: Proceedings of the European Conference on Computer Vision (ECCV), pp. 552–568 (2018)

32. Zhao, H., Qi, X., Shen, X., Shi, J., Jia, J.: ICNet for real-time semantic segmentation on high-resolution images. In: Proceedings of the European conference on Computer Vision (ECCV), pp. 405–420 (2018)
33. Liu, Y., Chu, L., Chen, G., Wu, Z., Chen, Z., Lai, B., Hao, Y.: Paddleseg: a high-efficient development toolkit for image segmentation, arXiv preprint arXiv:2101.06175 (2021)
34. Peng, J., et al.: Pp-liteseg: a superior real-time semantic segmentation model, arXiv preprint arXiv:2204.02681 (2022)
35. Zhang, Z., Scaramuzza, D.: A tutorial on quantitative trajectory evaluation for visual(-inertial) odometry. In: Proceedings of the IEEE/RSJ International Conference on Intelligent Robots and Systems (IROS), pp. 7244–7251 (2018)

DynaGaussian-SLAM: Lightweight Dynamic Visual SLAM with 3D Gaussian Splatting

Ruiwen Gu[1,2], Lineng Chen[3], Qingxiao Zou[1,2], and Wankou Yang[1,2](✉)

[1] School of Automation, Southeast University, Nanjing 210096, China
{220232042,wkyang}@seu.edu.cn
[2] Advanced Ocean Institute of Southeast University, Nantong 226010, China
[3] Key Lab of Education Blockchain and Intelligent Technology, Ministry of Education, Guangxi Normal University, Guilin 541004, China

Abstract. Robust pose estimation in dynamic environments remains a key challenge for visual SLAM systems. Recent 3D Gaussian Splatting SLAM methods excel in high-fidelity rendering but rely on static scene assumptions, limiting their use in dynamic scenarios and causing performance degradation due to full-map memory storage. We present DynaGaussian-SLAM, the first lightweight visual SLAM framework based on 3D Gaussian Splatting tailored for dynamic environments. Our method introduces Dynamic Subject Removal and Depth-guided Keyframe Selection to reduce uncertainty from moving objects. To further enhance efficiency, we propose Foreground-aware Sub-map Creation, which maintains speed and stability with minimal memory usage. Experiments show that DynaGaussian-SLAM achieves competitive accuracy in pose estimation and map reconstruction, while using only 14% of the memory of state-of-the-art methods.

Keywords: 3D gaussian splatting · lightweight · dynamic environment

1 Introduction

Over the past two decades, Simultaneous Localization and Mapping (SLAM) has been a prominent research area in robotics and computer vision [1]. Visual SLAM algorithms leverage data obtained from sensors, such as monocular, binocular, and RGB-D cameras, to estimate camera poses in previously unknown environments and incrementally build maps of the surrounding scene [2–4]. To be effective in real-world applications, SLAM systems must meet several essential criteria: (1) First, they must operate in real-time, ensuring both rapid and accurate localization; (2) Second, they should demonstrate stable performance in large and complex environments. (3) Lastly, robustness in dynamic environments is crucial.

In recent years, dense visual SLAM has found widespread application in fields such as autonomous driving, indoor robotics, and augmented reality, owing to

Z. Hou et al. (Eds.): CIRAC 2025, CCIS 2885, pp. 127–139, 2026.
https://doi.org/10.1007/978-981-92-0045-0_9

its advantage in intuitive scene representation [5]. Historically, a variety of methods have been proposed for real-time dense visual SLAM systems, particularly for RGB-D cameras. Traditional dense SLAM systems—such as those utilizing feature points, surfaces, and depth maps—have successfully met the demands for real-time performance and stable operation in large-scale environments.

Simultaneously, research on Neural Radiance Fields (NeRFs) has transformed scene representation by offering high-fidelity, view-synthesis models that excel in rendering fine-grained details [6], thus facilitating the development of dense neural SLAM approaches. Recently, Gaussian splatting [7] has marked a breakthrough in scene representation, offering rendering performance comparable to NeRFs while being faster and more efficient. Moreover, Gaussian splatting provides a directly interpretable model, enhancing the applicability of real-time SLAM systems for downstream tasks involving interaction with the environment.

Despite these advancements, the integration of dynamic environments into SLAM remains a significant challenge. Most existing visual SLAM methods, including current Gaussian splatting-based approaches, generally assume static environments. This assumption leads to performance degradation or even catastrophic failure when dynamic objects are present. These objects often disrupt pose estimation by causing incorrect data associations, thereby reducing tracking accuracy. Additionally, dynamic objects distort maps, limiting the long-term effectiveness of the system. To address these challenges, semantic SLAM techniques [8,9] have been proposed, which aim to differentiate dynamic from static elements to improve map consistency.

In this work, we propose DynaGaussian-SLAM, a lightweight and dynamic-environment-oriented dense RGB-D SLAM system based on 3D Gaussians. This system employs semantic segmentation to remove dynamic objects, utilizes 3D Gaussians to construct scene representations, and projects previous visible background onto the current frame to fill in background occlusions caused by dynamic objects. Furthermore, it incorporates an optimized sub-map creation method to ensure the system remains lightweight. The key contributions of this work are as follows:

- We propose a lightweight, dynamic-environment-oriented approach based on 3D Gaussian splatting, capable of removing dynamic objects in real-world environments to ensure robust camera tracking and high-quality mapping.
- We introduce a keyframe selection strategy that leverages effective depth guidance, ensuring the fusion of reliable information, enhancing the accuracy and stability of camera tracking, and substantially reducing drift in SLAM systems when reliable data is scarce.
- We propose a sub-map creation strategy that guarantees adequate foreground, significantly reducing the GPU memory footprint of the SLAM system and preventing slowdowns as more areas are covered, thus supporting large-scale map reconstruction in dynamic environments.

2 Related Work

Dense Visual SLAM. The most common approach in modern visual SLAM, based on the architecture of Klein et al. [10], divides the task into mapping and tracking. Dense visual SLAM methods aim to reconstruct detailed 3D representations of the environment, often optimized through depth maps or pixel-level photometric consistency. ElasticFusion [11] provides an efficient solution for real-time dense SLAM by directly optimizing dense RGB-D maps, bypassing traditional pose graph optimization. Recent advancements in 3D scene representation using radiance fields, particularly Neural Radiance Fields (NeRF) [6], have enabled implicit modeling of both appearance and geometry. Recent works such as NICESLAM [5] and NICER-SLAM [12] introduce neural implicit scene encoding to achieve scalable and memory-efficient dense reconstruction. ESLAM [13] enhances the precision of dense reconstruction by leveraging photometric consistency for optimization. Despite improvements in optimization, NeRF-based methods still suffer from slow rendering speeds due to neural network queries and volume rendering processes.

3D Gaussian Splatting SLAM. Recently, 3D Gaussian Splatting (3DGS) [7] has shown significant promise in 3D reconstruction by overcoming the limitations of the aforementioned NeRF-based representations. Photo-SLAM [14] pioneered the integration of photometric consistency into the SLAM framework, achieving real-time, photorealistic mapping from monocular input. Methods such as SplaTAM [15] and GS-SLAM [16] have expanded on this, utilizing 3DGS for efficient 3D scene representation by incorporating depth and color information. To enable efficient mapping in large-scale scenes, Gaussian-SLAM [17] processes maps as sub-maps and introduces an online Gaussian splatting optimization method with efficient seeding and optimization strategies. These systems support tasks such as object interaction and robot manipulation, further enhancing the application of SLAM in robotics. However, most existing 3DGS SLAM methods are based on the assumption that the environment is static, leading to performance degradation or even catastrophic failure in dynamic environments.

SLAM in Dynamic Scenes. Most existing SLAM methods are based on the assumption of static environments [2,5,13,18–22], which undermines the stability of SLAM systems when dynamic objects are present. The strategy adopted by most researchers to address SLAM issues in dynamic environments is to filter out dynamic regions from the images at the front end of the SLAM system [23–25]. DS-SLAM [8], implemented on ORB-SLAM2 [2], combines a semantic segmentation network (SegNet [26]) with motion consistency checking to reduce the impact of dynamic objects. DynaSLAM [9], also built upon ORB-SLAM2, demonstrates robustness in dynamic scenes across monocular, stereo, and RGB-D datasets by adding dynamic object detection and background inpainting capabilities. DG-SLAM [27], based on SplaTAM [15], incorporates motion and semantic masks, realizing the first dynamic-environment-oriented 3DGS SLAM. However, DG-SLAM requires storing all 3D Gaussians in GPU memory, resulting in a

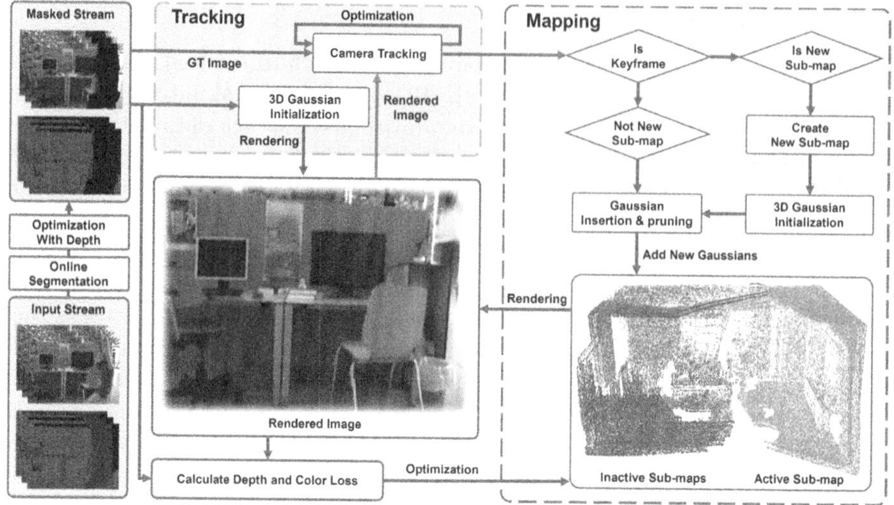

Fig. 1. Framework Overview. Our framework simultaneously estimates camera pose and reconstructs a 3D Gaussian map from RGB-D frame sequences in dynamic environments. DynaGaussian-SLAM consists of three main components: Initialization, Front-end Tracking, and Back-end Mapping. The front-end performs camera pose tracking, while the back-end reconstructs the 3D Gaussian map.

large memory footprint, and the SLAM system experiences deceleration as more areas are covered. In this paper, we propose a lightweight 3DGS SLAM system. We introduce a semantic segmentation network to remove dynamic regions from images, utilize 3D Gaussian Splatting foir high-fidelity environment representation, and incorporate a depth-guided keyframe selection strategy combined with a sub-map creation strategy to ensure sufficient foreground.

3 Methodology

The overview of DynaGaussian-SLAM is illustrated in Fig. 1. As with existing Gaussian-SLAM systems, our framework comprises tracking and mapping modules, which are initialized through a Gaussian map. The state estimation leverages both photometric cues and depth measurements for enhanced accuracy. DynaGaussian-SLAM simultaneously optimizes camera poses and reconstructs 3D Gaussian Splatting sub-maps by removing dynamic elements from the RGB-D input sequence.

3.1 3D Gaussian Splatting

Our dynamic SLAM system incorporates 3D Gaussian splatting [7] as its foundational scene representation framework, a method renowned for its real-time computational efficiency while maintaining photorealistic rendering fidelity. By observing images of the scene from different viewpoints, the Gaussian parameters are optimized using differentiable rendering, enabling real-time rendering and high-fidelity mapping.

A single 3D Gaussian is parameterized by its mean $\mu \in \mathbb{R}^3$, covariance matrix $\Sigma \in \mathbb{R}^{3\times 3}$, opacity $o \in \mathbb{R}$, and RGB color $C \in \mathbb{R}^3$:

$$\mathcal{G} = \{\mathcal{G}_i : (\mu_i \in \mathbb{R}^3, \Sigma_i \in \mathbb{R}^{3\times 3}, o_i \in \mathbb{R}, C_i \in \mathbb{R}^3)\}. \tag{1}$$

The mean of a projected (splatted) 3D Gaussian in the 2D image plane μ^I is computed as

$$\mu^I = \pi(P(T_{wc}\mu_{homogeneous})), \tag{2}$$

where $T_{wc} \in SE(3)$ is the world-to-camera transformation, $P \in \mathbb{R}^{4\times 4}$ is an OpenGL-style projection matrix, and $\pi : \mathbb{R}^4 \rightarrow \mathbb{R}^2$ is a projection to pixel coordinates.

Color C along one channel ch at a pixel i influenced by m ordered Gaussians is rendered as

$$\alpha_j = o_j \cdot \exp(-\frac{1}{2}\Delta_j^T \Sigma_j^{I-1} \Delta_j), \tag{3}$$

$$C_i^{ch} = \sum_{j \leq m} C_j^{ch} \cdot \alpha_j \cdot T_j \quad \text{, with} \quad T_j = \prod_{k<j}(1 - \alpha_k), \tag{4}$$

where $\Delta_j \in \mathbb{R}^2$ is the offset between the pixel coordinates and the 2D mean of a splatted Gaussian. The parameters of the 3D Gaussians are iteratively optimized by minimizing the photometric loss between rendered and training images.

3.2 Dynamic Subject Removal

For dynamic object detection, we employ a semantic segmentation network to obtain pixel-level semantic segmentation of the image. In our experiments, we used PP-LiteSeg [28], a state-of-the-art technique for semantic segmentation. PP-LiteSeg achieves a state-of-the-art balance between accuracy and speed while providing pixel-level segmentation. The input to PP-LiteSeg is the raw RGB image, and its objective is to segment out potentially dynamic or movable classes, producing a binarized dynamic object mask. We fine-tuned the human classification using the Cityscapes dataset to improve segmentation of human bodies.

Although PP-LiteSeg performs well in terms of accuracy and speed, it may still fail to fully capture dynamic objects. Therefore, we incorporate depth information to further optimize the mask. Specifically, we expand the mask's boundary outwards. If the depth value of the outer edge of the mask does not exceed a threshold from the average depth value of the masked area, we consider the outer edge as part of the mask and continue the expansion. In experiments, the expanded mask is able to cover the fine corners of dynamic objects and blurred edges in RGB images caused by the exposure process. This method helps us remove the complete dynamic objects from the SLAM system input, thereby maximally reducing the negative impact of dynamic objects on the system. Figure 2 shows the visualization result after mask expansion based on depth information.

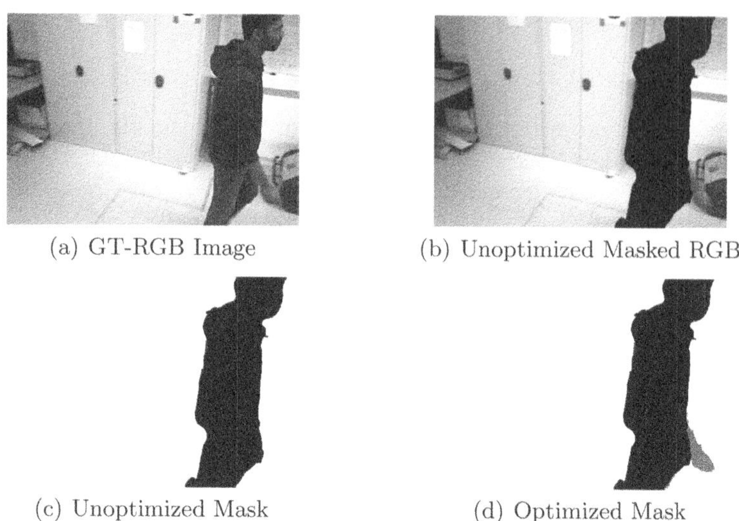

(a) GT-RGB Image (b) Unoptimized Masked RGB (c) Unoptimized Mask (d) Optimized Mask

Fig. 2. Visualization of Depth-guided Keyframe Selection. The black area represents the dynamic object mask generated by semantic segmentation, and the red area shows the additional mask obtained after depth-guided optimization.

3.3 Depth-Guided Keyframe Selection

Since the uncertainty of depth information obtained from depth cameras increases with the distance from the camera, we assume that not all depth data is reliable during the SLAM process. Depth data with significant errors can lead to incorrect data associations, compromising the stability of the SLAM system. In highly dynamic environments, these inaccuracies become more pronounced, increasing the likelihood of camera drift. Therefore, we prioritize frames with a higher proportion of valid depth as keyframes. Specifically, for each input frame k, we extract the maximum and minimum values of the depth data from the masked depth image (excluding 0-value points), denoted as D^k_{min} and D^k_{max}, respectively. We add frame k to the keyframe list K when the median depth value D^k_m satisfies the condition:

$$D^k_m < \frac{D^k_{\min} + D^k_{\max}}{2} \quad \Rightarrow \quad k \in K. \tag{5}$$

After optimizing the camera pose T_k of the input frame k, we optimize the 3D Gaussians $\mathcal{G}$ in the Mapping process. To reduce unnecessary computational overhead from repeatedly inserting and pruning 3D Gaussians from similar viewpoints, we calculate the Intersection over Union (IOU) of visible Gaussians between the current frame k and the previous frame. We only add frame k to the keyframe list K if the IOU is below a predefined threshold ϑ:

$$\mathrm{IOU}(\mathcal{G}k, \mathcal{G}k-1) \leq \vartheta \quad \Rightarrow \quad k \in K. \tag{6}$$

Furthermore, for scenarios where the camera viewpoint continuously stays within a fixed range, we forcibly designate the current frame as a keyframe at a fixed interval to ensure continuous updates of the SLAM system. All the aforementioned keyframe selection strategies are conducted in an online and real-time manner to align with the demands of real-world applications. This method ensures the fusion of more reliable information, enhancing the accuracy and stability of camera tracking. Additionally, the smaller overlap between keyframes allows the keyframe set to capture more diverse scene information.

3.4 Foreground-Aware Sub-map Creation

Most existing 3DGS SLAM systems require storing all 3D Gaussians in GPU memory, resulting in unnecessary performance demands and computational overhead for map optimization. This issue worsens as the SLAM system explores larger areas. Gaussian-SLAM [17] first proposed processing the map as sub-maps, achieving excellent performance in large-scale environments. However, Gaussian-SLAM still assumes a static environment, and its sub-map creation strategy is relatively simplistic, making it challenging to adapt to dynamic environments. To address these limitations, we optimize the sub-map creation strategy, enabling robust operation in dynamic settings. Specifically, we perform block-based (sub-map) processing on the input, with each sub-map covering several keyframes that observe it, represented as a separate 3D Gaussian point cloud. Formally, a sub-map Gaussian point cloud S^i is defined as a set of N 3D Gaussians:

$$S^i = \{\mathcal{G}_i : (\mu_i, \Sigma_i, o_i, C_i) | i = 1, ..., N\}. \tag{7}$$

When determining whether to create each sub-map, the primary consideration is the sub-map's coverage scope. This scope dictates how much environmental information each sub-map should represent, which, from the perspective of camera motion, corresponds to the range of pose variation. We represent a local keyframe sequence used to generate the sub-map Gaussian point cloud S^i as K^S, with K_i^S denoting the i-th frame in K^S. When deciding whether to create a new sub-map, we first evaluate the camera motion within the current sub-map. We compare the camera pose of the current frame K_i^S with that of the first keyframe K_0^S and compute the translation distance ΔT and the attitude difference ΔR. Given that camera tracking is more sensitive to position changes than attitude changes, we assign different weights ω_T and ω_R to ΔT and ΔR. A new sub-map is created only when the weighted sum exceeds a predefined threshold. This approach ensures that each sub-map does not contain an excessive amount of information, thereby preventing undue consumption of computational and storage resources. Furthermore, it guarantees that the Gaussian point cloud within each sub-map is not overly sparse, which could otherwise compromise map construction and optimization.

Merely considering camera motion changes can perform excellently in static environments, but problems arise in dynamic environments. If dynamic objects are very close to the camera or occupy a large area in the camera's field of view, the dynamic object removal method described above will cause large areas of holes in the image. To retain enough keyframes for robust mapping, the depth-guided keyframe selection algorithm described above will not reject some image frames with large areas of holes but a large proportion of valid depth. Not considering sub-map initialization, this is beneficial to mapping stability. However, if the SLAM system uses such an image frame with large areas of holes when initializing a sub-map, the lack of pixels and uneven distribution will lead to defective initialization of the 3D Gaussian map, which in turn affects the joint optimization of camera pose and map, causing catastrophic errors in the SLAM system. Therefore, we set a pixel number threshold ξ. When creating a sub-map, we further determine the proportion of valid pixels in the image frame, preventing unstable initialization of the sub-map. By using sub-maps for scene representation, optimizing the sub-map creation strategy, and only processing active sub-maps when the SLAM system is running, this method limits the computational cost and ensures that optimization remains fast and stable when exploring larger dynamic scenes.

4 Experiments

Datasets. Our method is evaluated using two challenging public datasets: the TUM RGB-D dataset [29] and the BONN RGB-D Dynamic dataset [30]. Both datasets were captured in indoor environments using handheld devices and provide RGB images, depth maps, and ground truth trajectories.

Metrics. To evaluate pose estimation, we use the Root Mean Square Error (RMSE) and Standard Deviation (STD) of the Absolute Trajectory Error (ATE) [31]. Before evaluation, the estimated trajectory is aligned with the ground truth trajectory using Horn's Procrustes method [32] to ensure consistency in the evaluation basis. For map reconstruction quality evaluation, we report several representative photometric metrics: Peak Signal-to-Noise Ratio (PSNR), Structural Similarity Index (SSIM), and Learned Perceptual Image Patch Similarity (LPIPS). To evaluate GPU memory usage, we directly measured the resource consumption for open-source methods on our workstation. For methods without publicly available source code, we adopted the figures reported in their original publications.

Implementation Details. Our DynaGaussian-SLAM experiments were conducted on a workstation equipped with an NVIDIA RTX 4060Ti GPU and an Intel Core i7 13700k CPU, utilizing approximately 1.2GB of memory. On our workstation, DynaGaussian-SLAM achieves an average running speed of 2.36 FPS. For the first keyframe in a sub-map, the number of mapping iterations is set to 100 for both the TUM and BONN datasets. For subsequent keyframes within a sub-map, the iteration count is consistently set to 100 across all datasets. We utilize the FAISS [33] GPU implementation to find nearest neighbors when selecting point candidates for adding new Gaussians, with a search radius of $\rho = 0.01m$ for all datasets. For new sub-map initialization, we set $\Delta T = 0.5m$ and $\Delta R = 50°$.

4.1 Evaluation of Tracking Performance

To evaluate camera tracking performance in dynamic environments, we compared our method with radiance field-based SLAM methods [5,13,21,22,34], and Gaussian Splatting-based SLAM methods [15,17,35], including the latest state-of-the-art (SOTA) 3DGS SLAM method for dynamic environments [27]. As the current state-of-the-art method, DG-SLAM [27], is not publicly available, the relevant comparative data used in this paper are all sourced from its original publication. In Table 1, we present four results on the TUM dataset and three results on the BONN dataset, along with the GPU memory consumption required for SLAM system operation. By incorporating dynamic object removal and other techniques, our proposed DynaGaussian-SLAM achieves superior results compared to traditional radiance field-based SLAM methods and 3DGS SLAM methods. While traditional SLAM methods often struggle in dynamic scenes, our method demonstrates precise camera tracking. Moreover, compared to the state-of-the-art DG-SLAM method, our approach achieves comparable camera tracking accuracy while reducing GPU memory consumption by 87%. This enables our system to operate on compute-constrained edge computing devices.

Table 1. Camera Tracking Results for Several Dynamic Scene Sequences in the *TUM* and *BONN* Datasets. The best result for each sequence is marked in bold, and the second-best result is underlined. The asterisk (∗) indicates the version reproduced by NICE-SLAM, while the dash (-) signifies data that were not provided by the authors. The metric used is the Absolute Trajectory Error (ATE) measured in centimeters (cm), and GPU memory usage is reported in Gigabytes (GB).

Method	GPU Mem.	TUM_f3/w_x	TUM_f3/w_s	TUM_f3/s_x	TUM_f2/d_p	BONN_ps_tk	BONN_ps_tk2	BONN_mv_box2
iMAP* [21]	-	111.5	137.3	23.6	119.0	28.3	52.8	28.3
NICE-SLAM [5]	8.0+	113.8	88.2	7.9	Failed	54.9	45.3	31.9
Vox-Fusion [34]	-	146.6	109.9	3.8	Failed	128.6	162.2	47.5
Co-SLAM [22]	4.0+	51.8	49.5	6.0	7.6	61.0	59.1	70.0
ESLAM [13]	8.0+	45.7	93.6	7.6	Failed	48.0	51.4	17.7
SplaTAM [15]	8.0+	218.3	115.2	1.7	**5.4**	149.7	91.2	19.0
MonoGS [36]	4.0+	73.4	5.5	2.9	6.8	33.4	47.7	24.8
GS-ICP SLAM [35]	-	70.5	98.2	-	-	92.8	44.7	24.8
Gaussian-SLAM [17]	**1.1+**	149.7	49.9	1.4	8.6	106.9	115.0	40.4
DG-SLAM [27]	9.0+	**1.6**	**0.6**	**1.0**	-	**4.5**	**6.9**	**3.5**
DynaGaussian-SLAM (Ours)	1.2+	5.7	2.2	**1.0**	6.7	12.5	14.1	10.3

Table 2. Rendering Performance on the *TUM* Dataset. The best result for each sequence is marked in bold, and the second-best result is underlined.

	TUM_f3/w_x			TUM_f3/w_h			TUM_f3/w_s			Avg.		
	PSNR↑	SSIM↑	LPIPS↓	PSNR↑	SSIM↑	LPIPS↓	PSNR↑	SSIM↑	LPIPS↓	PSNR↑	SSIM↑	LPIPS↓
SplaTAM [15]	14.54	0.539	0.480	13.52	0.507	0.517	<u>17.90</u>	**0.802**	<u>0.270</u>	15.32	0.616	0.422
MonoGS [36]	14.41	0.535	0.391	14.23	0.542	0.457	16.81	0.714	**0.252**	15.15	0.597	0.367
GS-ICP SLAM [17]	**16.92**	<u>0.694</u>	<u>0.356</u>	16.36	0.671	0.392	**18.30**	<u>0.727</u>	0.311	**17.19**	<u>0.697</u>	<u>0.353</u>
Gaussian-SLAM [17]	<u>16.83</u>	0.691	0.409	**18.29**	<u>0.730</u>	<u>0.359</u>	15.89	0.655	0.420	<u>17.00</u>	0.692	0.396
DynaGaussian-SLAM (Ours)	15.77	**0.748**	**0.343**	<u>17.66</u>	**0.820**	**0.243**	17.05	0.689	0.362	16.82	**0.752**	**0.316**

4.2 Evaluation of Mapping Performance

To evaluate the mapping performance of DynaGaussian-SLAM in dynamic environments, we assessed the Gaussian maps it constructs. The rendering quality is evaluated by calculating the difference between rendered and ground truth images for all frames. We compare DynaGaussian-SLAM with the current state-of-the-art open-source Gaussian Splatting-based SLAM method. As shown in Table 2, our method demonstrates competitive mapping performance while ensuring robust camera tracking accuracy in dynamic environments. The reconstructed static maps are rendered with high fidelity, as shown in Fig. 3.

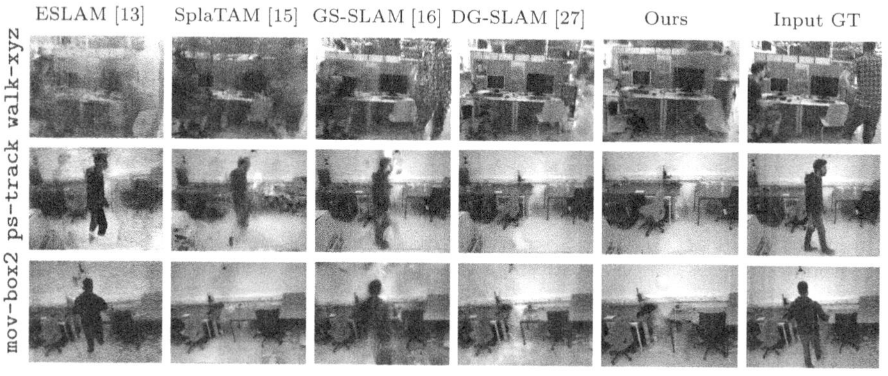

Fig. 3. Visual Comparison of Rendering Image on *TUM* and *BONN* Datasets. Our results are more complete and accurate without the dynamic object floaters.

4.3 Ablation Study

Ablative Analysis. To evaluate the contribution of each component in our framework, we perform an ablation study by removing individual components. Table 3 presents the RMSE ATE and average STD of camera tracking results under the TUM dataset TUM_f3/w_x scene. The results confirm the effectiveness

Table 3. Ablation Study on the *TUM* Dataset.

	ATE[cm]↓	STD[cm]↓
w/o All	149.66	58.94
w/o Depth-guided Keyframe Selection & Foreground-aware Sub-map Creation	18.25	11.33
w/o Foreground-aware Sub-map Creation	14.72	9.66
DynaGaussian-SLAM (Ours)	5.7	2.89

of all proposed methods in improving camera tracking performance. Specifically, the dynamic object removal module eliminates the dynamic components that have the greatest impact on the SLAM system, significantly affecting Gaussian map reconstruction quality, and thus tracking performance. The depth-guided keyframe selection strategy ensures that high-quality input images are selected, reducing camera position drift caused by inaccurate depth data. The foreground visibility-based sub-map creation strategy guarantees stable sub-map initialization, preventing incorrect associations between sub-maps due to issues with initial sub-map quality.

5 Conclusion

In this letter, we introduce DynaGaussian-SLAM, a lightweight and robust SLAM system optimized for dynamic environments based on 3D Gaussian Splatting. By employing dynamic object removal, depth-guided keyframe selection, and foreground-aware sub-map creation techniques, our system significantly enhances the accuracy and robustness of pose estimation in dynamic scenes while maintaining minimal GPU resource usage. The experiments demonstrate the effectiveness of our approach in achieving competitive performance in camera pose estimation and scene reconstruction within dynamic environments.

Acknowledgments. This work was supported in part by the National Natural Science Foundation of China under Grant 62276061 and Grant 62436002. It was also supported by the Research Fund of the Advanced Ocean Institute, Southeast University, under Grant MP202404.

References

1. Kazerouni, I.A., Fitzgerald, L., Dooly, G., Toal, D.: A survey of state-of-the-art on visual slam. Expert Syst. Appl. **205**, 117734 (2022)
2. Mur-Artal, R., Tardós, J.D.: ORB-SLAM2: an open-source slam system for monocular, stereo, and RGB-D cameras. IEEE Trans. Rob. **33**(5), 1255–1262 (2017)
3. Cadena, C., et al.: Past, present, and future of simultaneous localization and mapping: toward the robust-perception age. IEEE Trans. Rob. **32**(6), 1309–1332 (2016)
4. Durrant-Whyte, H., Bailey, T.: Simultaneous localization and mapping: part i. IEEE Robot. Autom. Mag. **13**(2), 99–110 (2006)

5. Zhu, Z., et al.: NICE-SLAM: neural implicit scalable encoding for slam. In: Proceedings of the IEEE/CVF Conference on Computer Vision and Pattern Recognition, pp. 12786–12796 (2022)
6. Mildenhall, B., Srinivasan, P.P., Tancik, M., Barron, J.T., Ramamoorthi, R., Ng, R.: NeRF: representing scenes as neural radiance fields for view synthesis. Commun. ACM **65**(1), 99–106 (2021)
7. Kerbl, B., Kopanas, G., Leimkühler, T., Drettakis, G.: 3D Gaussian splatting for real-time radiance field rendering. ACM Trans. Graph. **42**(4), 139–1 (2023)
8. Yu, C., et al.: DS-SLAM: a semantic visual slam towards dynamic environments. In: 2018 IEEE/RSJ International Conference on Intelligent Robots and Systems (IROS), pp. 1168–1174. IEEE (2018)
9. Bescos, B., Fácil, J.M., Civera, J., Neira, J.: DynaSLAM: tracking, mapping, and inpainting in dynamic scenes. IEEE Roboti. Autom. Lett. **3**(4), 4076–4083 (2018)
10. Klein, G., Murray, D.: Parallel tracking and mapping for small AR workspaces. In: 2007 6th IEEE and ACM International Symposium on Mixed and Augmented Reality, pp. 225–234. IEEE (2007)
11. Whelan, T., Leutenegger, S., Salas-Moreno, R.F., Glocker, B., Davison, A.J.: ElasticFusion: dense slam without a pose graph. In: Robotics: Science and Systems. vol. 11, p. 3. Rome, Italy (2015)
12. Zhu, Z., et al.: NICER-SLAM: neural implicit scene encoding for RGB SLAM. In: 2024 International Conference on 3D Vision (3DV), pp. 42–52. IEEE (2024)
13. Johari, M.M., Carta, C., Fleuret, F.: ESLAM: efficient dense slam system based on hybrid representation of signed distance fields. In: Proceedings of the IEEE International Conference on Computer Vision and Pattern Recognition (CVPR) (2023)
14. Huang, H., Li, L., Cheng, H., Yeung, S.K.: Photo-SLAM: real-time simultaneous localization and photorealistic mapping for monocular stereo and RGB-D cameras. In: Proceedings of the IEEE/CVF Conference on Computer Vision and Pattern Recognition, pp. 21584–21593 (2024)
15. Keetha, N., et al.: SplaTAM: splat track & map 3D Gaussians for dense RGB-D SLAM. In: Proceedings of the IEEE/CVF Conference on Computer Vision and Pattern Recognition, pp. 21357–21366 (2024)
16. Yan, C., et al.: GS-SLAM: dense visual slam with 3D gaussian splatting. In: Proceedings of the IEEE/CVF Conference on Computer Vision and Pattern Recognition, pp. 19595–19604 (2024)
17. Yugay, V., Li, Y., Gevers, T., Oswald, M.R.: Gaussian-SLAM: photo-realistic dense slam with gaussian splatting. arXiv preprint arXiv:2312.10070 (2023)
18. Campos, C., Elvira, R., Rodríguez, J.J.G., Montiel, J.M., Tardós, J.D.: ORB-SLAM3: an accurate open-source library for visual, visual-inertial, and multimap slam. IEEE Trans. Rob. **37**(6), 1874–1890 (2021)
19. Jiang, H., Qian, R., Du, L., Pu, J., Feng, J.: UL-SLAM: a universal monocular line-based slam via unifying structural and non-structural constraints. In: IEEE Transactions on Automation Science and Engineering (2024)
20. Palazzolo, E., Behley, J., Lottes, P., Giguere, P., Stachniss, C.: ReFusion: 3D reconstruction in dynamic environments for RGB-D cameras exploiting residuals. In: 2019 IEEE/RSJ International Conference on Intelligent Robots and Systems (IROS), pp. 7855–7862. IEEE (2019)
21. Sucar, E., Liu, S., Ortiz, J., Davison, A.J.: iMAP: implicit mapping and positioning in real-time. In: Proceedings of the IEEE/CVF International Conference on Computer Vision, pp. 6229–6238 (2021)

22. Wang, H., Wang, J., Agapito, L.: Co-SLAM: joint coordinate and sparse parametric encodings for neural real-time slam. In: Proceedings of the IEEE/CVF Conference on Computer Vision and Pattern Recognition, pp. 13293–13302 (2023)
23. Henein, M., Zhang, J., Mahony, R., Ila, V.: Dynamic SLAM: the need for speed. In: 2020 IEEE International Conference on Robotics and Automation (ICRA), pp. 2123–2129. IEEE (2020)
24. Bescos, B., Campos, C., Tardós, J.D., Neira, J.: DynaSLAM II: tightly-coupled multi-object tracking and SLAM. IEEE Robot. Autom. Lett. **6**(3), 5191–5198 (2021)
25. Li, M., He, J., Jiang, G., Wang, H.: DDN-SLAM: Real-time dense dynamic neural implicit slam with joint semantic encoding. arXiv preprint arXiv:2401.01545 (2024)
26. Badrinarayanan, V., Kendall, A., Cipolla, R.: SegNet: a deep convolutional encoder-decoder architecture for image segmentation. IEEE Trans. Pattern Anal. Mach. Intell. **39**(12), 2481–2495 (2017)
27. Xu, Y., Jiang, H., Xiao, Z., Feng, J., Zhang, L.: DG-SLAM: robust dynamic gaussian splatting SLAM with hybrid pose optimization. In: The Thirty-eighth Annual Conference on Neural Information Processing Systems (2024). https://openreview.net/forum?id=tGozvLTDY3
28. Peng, J., et al.: PP-LiteSeg: A superior real-time semantic segmentation model (2022). https://arxiv.org/abs/2204.02681
29. Sturm, J., Engelhard, N., Endres, F., Burgard, W., Cremers, D.: A benchmark for the evaluation of RGB-D SLAM systems. In: 2012 IEEE/RSJ International Conference on Intelligent Robots and Systems, pp. 573–580. IEEE (2012)
30. Palazzolo, E., Behley, J., Lottes, P., Giguere, P., Stachniss, C.: ReFusion: 3D reconstruction in dynamic environments for RGB-D cameras exploiting residuals. In: 2019 IEEE/RSJ International Conference on Intelligent Robots and Systems (IROS), pp. 7855–7862. IEEE (2019)
31. Sturm, J., Engelhard, N., Endres, F., Burgard, W., Cremers, D.: A benchmark for the evaluation of RGB-D SLAM systems. In: 2012 IEEE/RSJ International Conference on Intelligent Robots and Systems, pp. 573–580. IEEE (2012)
32. Horn, B.K.: Closed-form solution of absolute orientation using unit quaternions. J. Opt. Soc. Am. A **4**(4), 629–642 (1987)
33. Johnson, J., Douze, M., Jégou, H.: Billion-scale similarity search with GPUs. IEEE Trans. Big Data **7**(3), 535–547 (2019)
34. Yang, X., Li, H., Zhai, H., Ming, Y., Liu, Y., Zhang, G.: Vox-fusion: dense tracking and mapping with voxel-based neural implicit representation. In: 2022 IEEE International Symposium on Mixed and Augmented Reality (ISMAR), pp. 499–507. IEEE (2022)
35. Ha, S., Yeon, J., Yu, H.: RGBD GS-ICP SLAM. In: European Conference on Computer Vision, pp. 180–197. Springer (2024)
36. Matsuki, H., Murai, R., Kelly, P.H., Davison, A.J.: Gaussian splatting SLAM. In: Proceedings of the IEEE/CVF Conference on Computer Vision and Pattern Recognition, pp. 18039–18048 (2024)

Medical Robotics & Perception

Video Segmentation of Deformable Instruments in Ultrasound-Guided Interventional Surgeries for Structural Heart Diseases

Haosong Lin[1,2], Shiqi Liu[2(✉)], Xiaoliang Xie[2], Dongxu Zhang[3], Wenbin Ouyang[4], Hong Jiang[4], Xiaohu Zhou[2], Xiyao Ma[1,2], Xiangbin Pan[4], and Zengguang Hou[2(✉)]

[1] School of Artificial Intelligence, University of Chinese Academy of Sciences, Beijing 100049, China

[2] State Key Laboratory of Multimodal Artificial Intelligence Systems, Institute of Automation, Chinese Academy of Sciences, Beijing 100190, China
{shiqi.liu,zengguang.hou}@ia.ac.cn

[3] Xiamen University, Xiamen 361005, China

[4] Structural Heart Disease Center, National Center for Cardiovascular Disease, China and Fuwai Hospital, Chinese Academy of Medical Sciences and Peking Union Medical College, Beijing 100037, China

Abstract. The increasing incidence of structural heart disease has emerged as a significant global health challenge. Recently, ultrasound-guided interventional techniques have demonstrated the potential to replace traditional treatment methods due to their advantages, including the absence of radiation risks and the ability to provide real-time monitoring during surgeries. This study addresses challenges in instrument identification caused by factors such as low imaging resolution, variable instrument morphology in different sections, and the tendency for instruments to disappear or become obstructed. To tackle these issues, we propose a deep learning-based method for Video Instance Segmentation (VIS). The proposed method consists of three key components: 1) A frame-level detector extracts features from each image frame and generates queries for object instances. 2) A model architecture integrates the spatial feature extraction capabilities of convolutional neural networks with the temporal modeling capabilities of transformers, utilizing a windowed attention mechanism to capture inter-frame dependencies. 3) A multi-video segment joint memory learning mechanism is introduced, which stores historical query features in a shared memory bank. This enhances tracking robustness, particularly when instruments disappear or deform. Experimental results show that the model achieves an Average Precision (AP) of 40.640, significantly surpassing the performance of other mainstream VIS models. This method effectively improves the accuracy of instrument recognition and tracking stability in ultrasound images, thereby enhancing the safety and success rate of interventional surgeries. It also contributes to the promotion of this advanced surgical technique.

Keywords: Video instance segmentation · Temporal information association, · Structural heart disease

Z. Hou et al. (Eds.): CIRAC 2025, CCIS 2885, pp. 143–162, 2026.
https://doi.org/10.1007/978-981-92-0045-0_10

1 Introduction

Structural heart disease refers to any condition where the structure of the heart, including the great vessels, is abnormal. It encompasses a broad spectrum of diseases, including congenital heart malformations, valvular heart disease, and cardiomyopathies. According to the China Health Statistics Yearbook 2023 [1], cardiovascular diseases remain the leading cause of death in China, with structural heart disease representing the largest category within this group. Over 30 million people in China suffer from structural heart disease, and it accounts for more than 50% of all cardiovascular disease-related deaths in the country. With global aging and changing lifestyles, the incidence of structural heart disease is increasing annually, making it one of the most significant health challenges worldwide [2].

Historically, the treatment of structural heart disease has primarily relied on surgical procedures and cardiovascular interventions. Vascular interventional therapy involves creating a small incision, just a few millimeters in diameter, on the skin over a vessel, without surgically exposing the lesion site. Under the guidance of imaging equipment, instruments such as guidewires, catheters, and occluders are delivered through the vessel to treat the lesion [3]. Compared to traditional open surgery, this technique offers significant advantages, including minimal trauma, fast recovery, and low risk [4]. In recent years, with advances in interventional techniques, Fuwai Hospital of the Chinese Academy of Medical Sciences has pioneered the replacement of radiation with ultrasound for interventional therapy. This marks the world's first purely ultrasound-guided interventional technique. Ultrasound's green, radiation-free nature, combined with its ability to display cardiac structures in multiple dimensions and monitor the entire procedure in real time, resolves key issues of traditional Digital Subtraction Angiography (DSA), such as radiation hazards, anaphylactic reactions due to contrast agents, and difficulty in locating structures like the interatrial septum and monitoring dynamic cardiac motion changes [5].

Despite these advantages, ultrasound imaging still presents challenges in the context of interventional therapy for structural heart disease. Ultrasound images have relatively low resolution, leading to unclear boundaries of instruments. Additionally, instruments may change shape during the delivery process or disappear from view due to factors like heart movement, making instrument identification difficult [6].

Traditional image processing techniques can no longer meet the requirements for precise identification and localization of instruments under ultrasound guidance [7]. In recent years, deep learning and computer vision technologies have rapidly advanced, making them key research areas in image analysis. Video instance segmentation has the ability to leverage temporal information to accurately identify and analyze dynamic changes of targets in real-time [8]. Traditional static image processing techniques are not suited for the fast-paced and complex nature of surgical environments, while video instance segmentation has shown great potential in tasks like instrument tracking, position recognition, and surgical state judgment in dynamic video streams [9]. However, no video instance segmentation model has been specifically designed for ultrasound-guided interventional therapy of structural heart disease to address issues like instrument blurring, variable morphology, and disappearance in ultrasound images.

To address these challenges, this study proposes a deep learning-based approach using multi-frame processing and temporal reconstruction techniques. This approach tackles issues such as instrument identification, blurring, variable morphology, occlusion, and disappearance in ultrasound images. The proposed solution provides precise technical methods for ultrasound-guided interventional therapy of structural heart disease and contributes to advancing the adoption of ultrasound-guided interventional techniques. The main contributions of this study are summarized as follows:

The study introduces a deep learning-based video instance segmentation (VIS) method, which significantly outperforms existing mainstream VIS models, achieving an Average Precision (AP) of 40.640 in comparative experiments.

The study presents a model architecture that integrates convolutional neural networks for spatial feature extraction with the temporal modeling capabilities of Transformers. It employs a windowed attention mechanism to capture temporal relationships between frames and uses a shared memory bank to store historical query features, balancing spatial and temporal modeling.

In collaboration with relevant hospitals, an ultrasound video dataset for atrial septal occlusion procedures was constructed, covering guidewires, delivery sheaths, and occluders. The dataset is annotated according to strict clinical requirements, providing high-quality benchmark data for related research.

The paper is organized as follows: Chap. 2 reviews related work, Chap. 3 describes the proposed model architecture, Chap. 4 presents the construction of the ultrasound instrument video dataset, Chap. 5 provides experimental results, and Chap. 6 concludes with a summary and outlook.

2 Related Work

2.1 General Video Instance Segmentation

Video instance segmentation has gained significant attention in recent years within the field of computer vision [10]. This task combines both segmentation and multi-object detection, and current methods can be classified into four main categories based on their temporal dependency modeling strategies.

Frame-by-Frame Methods. Frame-by-frame methods process each video frame independently and subsequently perform cross-frame instance association through post-processing. While this approach is simple and efficient, its accuracy in associating instances across frames is compromised when objects are occluded or disappear. Porzi et al. [11] improved instance tracking stability by introducing an optical flow tracking head in Mask R-CNN and combining region features for cross-frame instance association. Similarly, Bolya et al. [12] developed the YOLACT series, which generates mask prototypes and coefficient predictions through a two-branch structure, optimizing real-time performance. However, the absence of explicit temporal modeling limits their effectiveness in handling temporal dependencies in complex scenes.

Wu et al. [13] proposed a Siamese network that achieves cross-frame matching by comparing feature embeddings, delivering high accuracy in static video processing. Furthermore, Li et al. [14] enhanced the Siamese network by incorporating a Transformer-based inter-frame attention mechanism, significantly improving the handling of long-term dependencies in video sequences.

Clip-Based Methods. Clip-based methods model spatiotemporal features within video clips to improve temporal consistency. Voigtlaender et al. [15] introduced TrackR-CNN, which employs 3D convolution to extract spatiotemporal features, significantly improving target tracking accuracy. However, it is unsuitable for real-time processing. On the other hand, Wang et al. [16] proposed VisTR, built on the DETR framework, which performs end-to-end segmentation and tracking. By using the Transformer model to handle long-term dependencies, VisTR faces challenges in memory consumption.

Cheng et al. [17] extended Mask2Former for video processing, introducing mask attention to improve segmentation accuracy across frames. Heo et al. [18] optimized instance tracking in long videos with VISTA by reducing complexity through object token associations, enhancing segmentation efficiency and accuracy.

Memory Feature Propagation Methods. Memory feature propagation methods explicitly store historical features in memory to enhance temporal consistency, excelling in long video sequences. Meinhardt et al. [8] proposed MaskTrack R-CNN, which matches newly detected instances using a memory queue, effectively improving the temporal consistency of targets in videos, although it faces challenges in feature stability. Sun et al. [19] introduced an RNN-based ConvLSTM method that captures sequence dependencies, addressing long-term dependencies effectively.

Building on these techniques, Fu et al. [20] combined Transformers with a memory mechanism to fuse cross-frame features through cross-attention, enhancing robustness in complex scenes.

Memory Object Query Propagation Methods. Memory object query propagation methods dynamically update queries through Transformer object query propagation to achieve efficient target tracking. Meinhardt et al. [21] proposed Trackformer, using an autoregressive approach for query propagation to address occlusion problems, though it incurs high computational costs. Koner et al. [22] introduced Instanceformer, which utilizes a memory queue to store historical instance descriptors and resolves long-term target tracking issues via query propagation.

Heo et al. [23] developed the GenVIS architecture, which balances segmentation accuracy and computational efficiency through clip-level query propagation, excelling in real-time applications. Wu et al. [24] proposed SeqFormer, which enhances long-term tracking through a multi-level attention mechanism.

2.2 Ultrasound Segmentation

Ultrasound Image Segmentation. Ultrasound imaging plays a crucial role in disease detection and treatment planning in medical diagnostics. The application of convolutional neural networks (CNNs) in ultrasound image segmentation has greatly enhanced automation and segmentation accuracy [25].

Early segmentation methods, such as Active Contours and threshold-based segmentation techniques [26], faced challenges with low contrast and irregular tissue boundaries. However, modern deep learning methods, particularly the U-Net architecture with its encoder-decoder structure, have significantly improved performance in learning hierarchical image features and pixel classification tasks.

To address specific challenges posed by ultrasound imaging, several studies have explored strategies for fine-tuning pre-trained U-Net networks. Amiri et al. [27] examined the effects of fine-tuning different layers of U-Net, emphasizing the importance of shallow layers for learning low-level features. Additionally, the incorporation of attention mechanisms and deep supervision strategies in U-Net variants has enhanced the network's focus on critical areas like tissue boundaries, improving segmentation accuracy [28]. Chen et al. [29] proposed DSEU-net, which integrates a deep supervision mechanism with a Squeeze-and-Excitation module to enhance the network's focus on valuable features, demonstrating superior performance in breast tumor and kidney ultrasound segmentation.

Other architectures have also been applied in ultrasound segmentation. Nurmaini et al. [30] used Mask-RCNN for multi-class instance segmentation of fetal heart ultrasound images, achieving high accuracy in segmenting different heart structures, such as the left and right atria. Wang et al. [31] proposed ConvTrans-Net, a model combining Transformer and CNNs, which improved focus on important regions through multi-layer perceptrons and attention mechanisms, surpassing existing models in breast tumor and kidney ultrasound segmentation.

Ultrasound Video Segmentation. Ultrasound video segmentation has found widespread use in medical imaging. A common approach is to integrate spatiotemporal memory modules to enhance the accuracy and stability of video segmentation. Zhao et al. [32] introduced a segmentation method based on adaptive spatiotemporal memory, using a memory network to store previous segmentation results. A skip-gate mechanism adaptively updates the memory bank based on segmentation confidence, retaining high-confidence results to avoid error accumulation and support current frame segmentation. This method addresses segmentation inconsistencies between frames caused by dynamic target changes and noise in ultrasound videos.

Building on this, Ilea et al. [33] proposed a segmentation method based on Cascade R-CNN and adaptive tracking algorithms, which effectively addresses inconsistencies across video frames and mitigates the impact of motion artifacts and image quality fluctuations. Luo et al. [34] further improved this method by incorporating an adaptive normalized correlation algorithm to enhance segmentation consistency and effectiveness in large-scale changes, particularly for the thyroid and surrounding tissues.

Given the rise of large model architectures, recent works have incorporated large models into ultrasound video segmentation. Deng et al. [35] introduced the MemSAM model, which adapts the "Segment Anything Model" for echocardiographic video segmentation. This model uses a memory mechanism to improve segmentation results in noisy conditions, overcoming common ultrasound issues like blurry boundaries and speckle noise. Yang et al. [36] extended this approach with the Vivim framework, which employs a Spatio-Temporal Selective Scan mechanism (ST-Mamba) to efficiently capture long-term dependencies in ultrasound videos, improving segmentation performance while reducing computational resource consumption.

3 Model Design

3.1 Overall Architecture Design

This study proposes a deep learning model aimed at solving the temporal and instance segmentation problems of ultrasound instruments in video files. The model's architecture consists of three main components: the image-level feature extraction and frame-level decoder module, the temporal model with the object encoder-decoder module, and the cross-video learning mechanism through multi-video fragment joint memory. A joint loss function was chosen to effectively train the model. The overall architecture is shown in Fig. 1.

At the initial stage, the processed video clip is input frame by frame. Using the mask attention mechanism and self-attention mechanism within the Transformer framework, these mechanisms interact with high-resolution feature maps to refine features and predict object instances for each frame. This generates independent frame queries for object instances, which are not dependent on other frames. An object encoder-decoder efficiently interacts with instance-level information across different frames within a video clip. A windowed attention mechanism is employed to fuse these features with minimal overhead, and through the cross-attention mechanism, video-level queries interact with encoder features, focusing on the temporal relationships within the video clip. The multi-video segment joint memory learning approach processes multiple video segments by concatenating them, allowing the model to match new segments with past historical queries stored in a shared memory bank.

The model's loss function includes three types: frame-level loss, video-level loss, and similarity loss. During temporal association, the model calculates the similarity between video queries and frame queries to combine spatial and temporal information, ensuring the consistency of objects across frames.

3.2 Frame-Level Detector

In this study, the frame-level detector is responsible for extracting features from each frame image and generating queries for object instances. This approach is inspired by the design concept of Mask2Former [37], particularly in customizing frame queries. The structure is shown in Fig. 2.

In this study, the frame-level detector is responsible for extracting features from each frame image and generating queries for object instances. This approach is inspired by the design concept of Mask2Former [37], particularly in customizing frame queries. The structure is shown in Fig. 2.

The first step in processing involves extracting image data from the input video frames. Each frame is sequentially processed and input into the network. The image data is converted into Tensor format and normalized by subtracting the pixel_mean

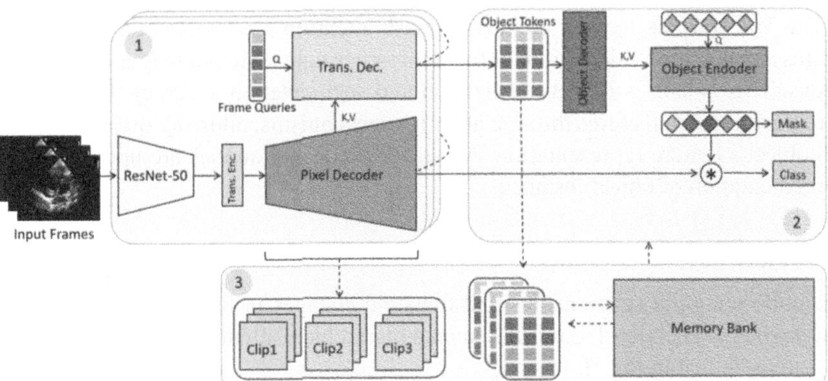

Fig. 1. Overall Architecture Diagram of the Model Design

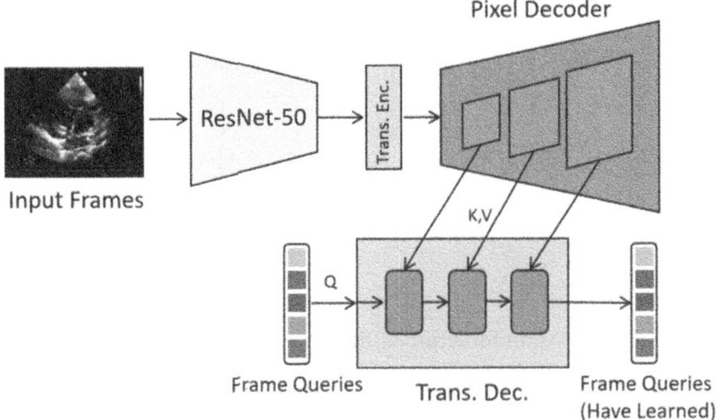

Fig. 2. Main Structure of the Frame-Level Detector

and dividing by pixel_std, ensuring proper pixel value processing during training. The list of images is then converted into a format suitable for network input using ImageList.from_tensors.

The model utilizes ResNet-50 [38], a deep residual network that incorporates residual learning to address vanishing gradients and degradation issues in deep network training. Shortcut connections between network layers allow the model to learn the difference between input and output at each layer, helping to retain essential features from the input image. These features are passed to the semantic segmentation head for further processing.

The semantic segmentation head first processes the extracted features through a pixel decoder and then feeds them into a Transformer decoder to predict object instances. The pixel decoder gradually generates high-resolution image features, which are subsequently passed to a Transformer predictor that uses an attention mechanism to compute frame queries for each frame. Frame queries represent the features of each object instance detected in the image.

The Transformer decoder employs a mask attention mechanism, embedding mask features into attention calculations to focus on foreground regions and ignore background regions. This enhances object localization and segmentation accuracy. Frame queries interact with image features through attention mechanisms, allowing the model to learn each object's feature representation. At each layer, frame queries are updated, refining the segmentation of object instances.

3.3 Object Encoder-Decoder

To capture temporal relationships and dynamic changes in the video, this study proposes an object encoder-decoder based on a hierarchical attention mechanism. Its main structure is shown in Fig. 3.

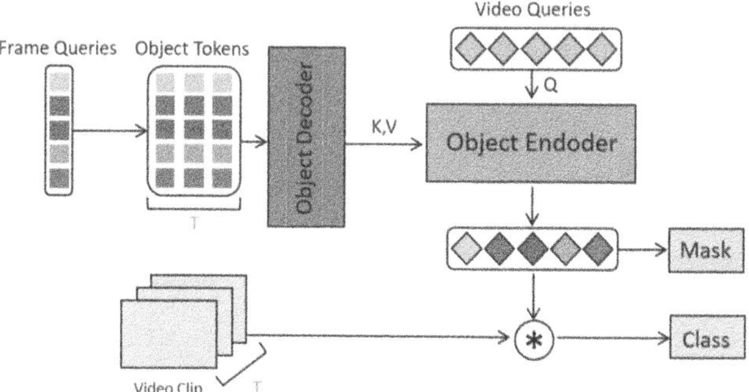

Fig. 3. Main Structure of the Object Encoder-Decoder

The encoder-decoder follows a "encode-decode" two-stage architecture: the encoder fuses features across frames using local window attention, while the decoder generates temporally-aware predictions through spatiotemporal query interaction.

Initial Query. For a given video clip containing T frames, after extracting multi-scale features $F \in R^{H \times W \times C}$ in previous steps, the following processing flow is executed to transform them into object tokens.

Feature Reorganization. Stack the features of each frame along the time dimension to construct a spatiotemporal feature tensor $F \in R^{T \times H \times W \times C}$, Perform spatial down-sampling using deformable convolution to obtain a compact feature representation $\hat{F} \in R^{T \times f_Q \times C}$, where f_Q is the number of feature vectors retained per frame (100).

Query Initialization. Define a learnable positional encoding matrix $\boldsymbol{P} \in \boldsymbol{R}^{T \times f_Q \times C}$. After adding it to the feature vectors, the initial frame-level queries are obtained:

$$Q^{(0)} = LayerNorm\left(\hat{F} + P\right) \in R^{T \times f_Q \times C} \quad (1)$$

Windowed Encoder. The frame-level decoder has obtained single-frame information. By introducing a windowed attention mechanism, the model can efficiently fuse these features with low overhead, obtaining results focused solely on the temporal relationships within a single video clip.

Window Partitioning. Divide the time axis into $N_w = [T/W]$ local windows, each containing W consecutive frames. Use zero-padding to make the total number of frames $T^{'} = Nw \times W$. Construct the reorganized feature $F' \in R^{Nw \times W \times f_Q \times C}$.

Shifted Window Mechanism. Use regular window partitioning in odd-numbered layers. In even-numbered layers, perform a time-axis shift $S = [W/2]$ to construct overlapping windows to enhance temporal continuity. The shift operation is implemented via torch.roll, calculated as:

$$F_{shift} = Roll\left(F^{'}, S, \dim = 1\right) \tag{2}$$

Local Self-attention. Perform multi-head self-attention calculation within each window, formally expressed as:

$$Attention\ (Q, K, V) = Softmax\left(\frac{QK^T}{\sqrt{d_k}} + M\right)V \tag{3}$$

Where $M \in R^{Wf_Q \times Wf_Q}$ is the attention mask generated by the shifted window, used to constrain the effective interaction range.

Feature Aggregation. After L_e layers of alternating window attention, restore the original temporal structure through an inverse transformation. This design reduces the computational complexity from $O\left(T^2 f_Q^2 C\right)$ for global attention to $O\left(N_w W^2 f_Q^2 C\right)$ When $W = 6$, memory consumption is reduced by approximately 64%.

Video-Level Query Decoding. The decoder achieves spatiotemporal feature fusion through progressive query interaction. Object tokens combined with the defined learnable video-level query vectors ($V_q \in R^{N_q \times C}$) for the cross-attention mechanism. Thereby capturing the dynamic changes of objects along the time dimension.

Cross-Attention Stage. The query vectors are spatiotemporally aligned with the encoded features. Positional encoding $P_v \in R^{T \times f_Q \times C}$:

$$V_q^{(l)} = CrossAttn\left(V_q^{\left(l-1\right)}, F_{enc} + P_v\right) \tag{4}$$

Where the attention weights reflect the relevance between the query and each spatiotemporal location, achieving key frame localization.

Self-attention Stage. Semantic relationship modeling is performed among the query vectors. Co-occurrence and mutual exclusion relationships between instances are established through the multi-head attention mechanism:

$$V_q^{(l)} = SelfAttn\left(V_q^{(l)}\right) \tag{5}$$

Feed-Forward Transformation. Non-linear transformation is performed through a two-layer MLP to enhance feature expression capability:

$$V_q^{(l)} = FFN\left(V_q^{(l)}\right) \tag{6}$$

After L_d layers of iterative optimization, the final query vectors $V_q^{(L_d)}$ contain global spatiotemporal context information. This yields results focused solely on the temporal relationships within a single video clip.

3.4 Multi-video Segment Joint Memory

To improve instrument tracking across the entire video, especially when instruments disappear from view, this study introduces a multi-video segment joint memory learning structure, as shown in Fig. 4.

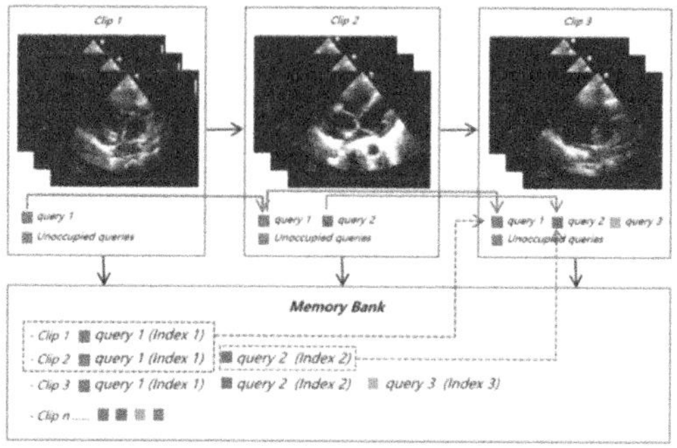

Fig. 4. Main Structure of the Object Encoder-Decoder

Cross-Segment Temporal Modeling. To better track instruments, this chapter splits a long video clip into several smaller video clips, which are then concatenated to form new video clips.

Video Clip Splicing. The *frame_targets, video_targets, fg_indices, frame_queries,* and *mask_features* tensors are split into multiple clips. They are concatenated to facilitate subsequent enhancement of cross-clip object tracking and instance segmentation effects using the memory mechanism.

Memory Reading. Each clip retrieves historical features through an attention matching mechanism.

$$\alpha_{ij} = Softmax\left(\frac{Q_k\ K_j^T}{\sqrt{d}}\right) \tag{7}$$

Where $\boldsymbol{Q_k} \in \boldsymbol{R}^{N_q \times d}$ is the current query vector, $\boldsymbol{K_j} \in \boldsymbol{R}^{N_q \times d}$ is the key vector of the j clip in the memory bank. Among these, cross-clip attention calculation is implemented via torch.einsum, filtering out the most relevant historical features.

Memory Writing. The features of the current clip are projected linearly and stored in the memory bank.

$$K_k = W_k\ H_k, V_k = W_v\ H_k \tag{8}$$

A sliding window mechanism is adopted to retain the features of the most recent M clips, preventing explosive memory growth.

Incremental Propagation. Fuse current features and historical memory through a gating mechanism:

$$\hat{H}_k = \gamma\,(\,1 - \gamma\,)\,\sum_{j=1}^{M} \alpha_{ij}\,V_j \tag{9}$$

Where γ is a learnable parameter.

Unified Video Tag Management. This study adopts a unified video labeling approach. After predicting object labels in each video frame, labels are shared across frames. By sharing object labels across frames, the target labels in different frames are the same, thus avoiding excessive confusion.

Spatial Matching Layer. Calculate the bipartite matching between predictions and ground truth using the Hungarian algorithm. Define a matching cost function, where

$$C_{match} = \lambda_{cls}\,L_{cls} + \lambda_{dice}\,L_{dice} \tag{10}$$

Temporal Matching Layer. Maintain an "occupied/unoccupied" query state matrix $\boldsymbol{S} \in \{\boldsymbol{0}, \boldsymbol{1}\}^{N_q}$ across clips. For a new clip $\boldsymbol{C_k}$:

Prioritize activating historical queries where $\boldsymbol{S_j} = \boldsymbol{1}$, matching them via cosine similarity:

$$\rho_{ij} = \frac{H_i^k \cdot H_j^{k-1}}{\left|\left|H_i^k\right|\right| \left|\left|H_j^{k-1}\right|\right|} \tag{11}$$

For queries where $\boldsymbol{\rho_{ij}}$ **<0.7,** mark them as new instances and assign unused query slots.

ID Continuity Guarantee. During the data preprocessing stage, normalize the instance ID for each video to eliminate absolute numerical differences in IDs across different videos, allowing the model to focus on modeling relative relationships:

$$ID^{'} = ID - \min(ID_{Train}) \tag{12}$$

Memory Enhancement Mechanism. Utilize shared memory to store query records of object instances to solve the problem of object disappearance and reappearance in long and short videos. When the model receives a new video clip, it first updates the query records in memory, searches historical feature records to match objects in the current clip. An algorithm combining the Hungarian matching algorithm with an "queried/unqueried query" query manager is used. When object instances change, the query features are altered to avoid false detections and missed detections.

Memory Projection Layer. Add a new linear transformation in the object encoder-decoder module to project the decoder output into the memory space, keeping the dimension d = 256 unchanged.

Memory Refresh. Maintain a fixed-capacity memory bank using a FIFO algorithm. If $M = 5$, discard the oldest memory unit.

Memory Reading. Achieve fine-grained matching through multi-head attention. This operation has a computational complexity of $\boldsymbol{O}\left(\boldsymbol{K}\boldsymbol{N}_q^2\boldsymbol{d}\right)$ With $\boldsymbol{N}_q = 100$, memory usage only increases by 17%.

Query State Management. Define a binary mask $\boldsymbol{M}_t \in \{\mathbf{0}, \mathbf{1}\}^{N_q}$ to record query activation states. If a query fails to match any instance for $\boldsymbol{M}_t \in \{\mathbf{0}, \mathbf{1}\}^{N_q}$ consecutive clips, reset its state.

Video-Level Query Decoding. The decoder output generates prediction results through dual projection.

Classification Projection. Use a linear layer to calculate instance category probabilities:

$$Y_{cls} = Softmax\left(W_{cls}\, V_q^{(L_d)}\right) \tag{13}$$

Where $\boldsymbol{W}_{cls} \in \boldsymbol{R}^{(K+1)\times C}$, K is the number of semantic categories.

Mask Projection. Generate mask prototype vectors through a 3-layer MLP:

$$Y_{mask} = MLP\left(V_q^{(L_d)}\right) \in R^{Nq\times Dm} \tag{14}$$

Where $\boldsymbol{Dm}$ is the mask embedding dimension. Perform an outer product operation with the encoder features $\boldsymbol{F}_{enc} \in \boldsymbol{R}^{T\times H\times W\times C}$:

$$M_{pred} = Sigmoid\left(Y_{mask} \otimes F_{enc}\right) \tag{15}$$

4 Dataset Construction

4.1 Instrument Selection

Through discussions and collaboration with physicians, this study selected three primary instruments to describe the full process of ultrasound-guided atrial septal defect occlusion: the Ultrasound Guidewire, Delivery Sheath, and Biodegradable Occluder.

Ultrasound Guidewire. The ultrasound positioning guidewire is used to guide other instruments through the blood vessels to the heart to locate the atrial septal defect. Its structure is depicted in Fig. 5(a). The head is a three-dimensional, spindle-shaped mesh, which is approximately rhomboid in two dimensions. It offers excellent flexibility, making it easier to reach the target site through blood vessels. The tail is relatively thin, long, and easy to fix. Under ultrasound, the head appears as a blurry rhombus, and the tail as a thin straight line. Due to the significant shape change between the head and the tail, it is divided into two parts: the echo guidewire head and the echo guidewire tail. This division facilitates easier identification and operation during the procedure.

Delivery SheathUltrasound Guidewire. The delivery sheath is shown in Fig. 5(a). It has a smooth pipe-like structure with a double-track sign inside. After the ultrasound guidewire is positioned at the target, the physician uses it to guide the delivery sheath to the target position. As the primary tool for delivering the occluder, the delivery sheath is highly flexible and strong, ensuring the stable delivery of the occluder to the atrial septal defect site. In ultrasound images, it appears as a distinct double-track sign, which makes it relatively easy to identify.

Biodegradable Occluder. The biodegradable occluder is used to close atrial septal defects. Its structure is shown in Fig. 5(a). Typically, its shape is mesh-like or spherical. In ultrasound images, the occluder may fuse with the atrial septum, appearing as a blurry, mesh-like mass, which can make identification difficult. Over time, the occluder gradually degrades and fuses with the atrial septum, effectively closing the defect in the long term.

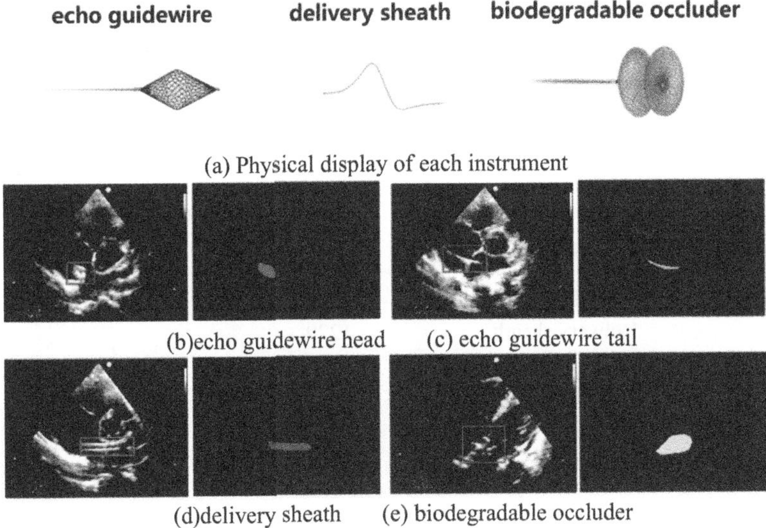

Fig. 5. Schematic diagram of instrument structure and their ultrasound imaging

4.2 Dataset Format

The ultrasound instrument dataset constructed in this study adopts the same data structure as the public YouTube-VIS 2019 dataset. YouTube-VIS 2019 is a large-scale benchmark dataset for video instance segmentation, where the training and validation sets are provided as JSON files containing detailed information about video clips and annotations for each frame [8].

This study extracted frames and annotated instruments as shown in Table 1. Self-written code then reads the frame images from the video segments in the image folders, parses the dimensional information of each frame, and generates JSON files that conform to the YouTube-VIS format requirements. The annotation uses the Run-Length Encoding (RLE) compression algorithm to encode the mask for each instance. The code traverses each pixel of the mask and records the length of consecutive identical pixels.

The *Train.json* and *Valid.json* files include the following sections:

Info. This section records metadata about the dataset, including a brief description, version, contributors, and creation date.

Categories. This section defines the list of all categories in the dataset, including "echo_guidewire_head," "echo_guidewire_tail," "delivery_sheath," and "biodegradable_occluder." Each category is assigned a unique ID for annotation and retrieval.

Videos. This section contains detailed information for each video, including the video's width, height, number of frames, recording date, and the filenames of each frame. Each video is assigned a unique ID, and the filenames of all video frames are listed in order.

Annotations. This section generates detailed annotations for each frame image, including mask information, bounding box, area and other information, for each category. The segmentation part includes counts (RLE) and size.

Table 1. Annotation Counts for Each Instrument

Instrument	Annotation Count
Echo guidewire head	1055
Echo guidewire tail	510
Delivery sheath	1229
Biodegradable occluder	2166
Total	4960

5 Experiment

5.1 Comparative Experiments

The experimental environment was independently set up and executed on an AutoDL cloud server. The hardware configuration included an A40 GPU (48GB) and a 15 vCPU AMD EPYC 7543 32-Core Processor. The base environment consisted of Python 3.8, PyTorch 1.9.0, Torchvision 0.10.0, and CUDA Toolkit 11.1.

Training was conducted using the pre-trained model *vita_r50_coco.pth*, which provided initial learning capabilities. The training parameters were set as follows: PER_BATCH = 2 and ITER = 20000.

Two evaluation metrics were used to assess model performance: Average Precision (AP) and Average Recall (AR). Their calculations are outlined below:

AP: The Intersection over Union (IoU) values ranged from [0.5, 0.95] in steps of 0.05. For each IoU value, detection results were first sorted according to prediction confidence. Precision and Recall were then calculated at different confidence levels, and the average area under the multiple Precision-Recall (P-R) curves was computed. The metrics AP_{50} and AP_{75} refer to the areas calculated under the P-R curve at IoU thresholds of 0.5 and 0.75, respectively.

$$Precison = \frac{TP}{TP + FP}, Recall = \frac{TP}{TP + FN}, IoU = \frac{Area\ of\ Overlap}{Area\ of\ Union} \tag{16}$$

$$AP = \frac{1}{10} \sum_{IoU=0.5,0.55...0.95} \int_0^1 Precision\ (\ Recall\ )\ d\ Recall \tag{17}$$

AR: AR is derived by calculating the model's precision at different recall thresholds, determining the maximum number of targets the model can recognize. AR_1 and AR_{10} represent the average Recall values across all detections, with IoU values in [0.5, 0.95], while considering the top 1/10 detection boxes.

$$AR = \frac{1}{10} \sum_{IoU=0.5,0.55...0.95} Recall\ (\ IoU\ ) \tag{18}$$

The experiment compared several mainstream instance segmentation and object detection models, including Mask2Former for VIS, VITA, MinVIS, and DVIS, all evaluated using the same dataset. The experimental results are summarized in Table 2 and Table 3.

Table 2. Comparative Experimental Results of Each Model

Method	AP	AP_{50}	AP_{75}	AR_1	AR_{10}
Mask2Former for VIS	33.031	70.071	22.118	36.558	37.224
VITA	38.455	81.727	26.713	40.874	41.629
MinVIS	34.476	74.520	28.067	36.537	39.084
DVIS	4.860	23.779	0.000	6.587	6.975
Ours	**40.640**	**82.591**	**29.201**	**42.716**	**44.590**

Based on the results of the comparative experiments, our model outperformed other models across multiple evaluation metrics. The AP score for our model was 40.640, which is significantly higher than those of the compared models. This demonstrates the model's strong performance in handling instrument segmentation tasks. Notably, the model showed significant improvements in performance across different categories of instruments, with the most notable enhancement observed in the Delivery Sheath category.

The segmentation results for the visualization are shown in Fig. 6.

Table 3. Comparative Experimental Results of AP for Each Instrument by Model

Method	Echo guidewire head	Echo guidewire tail	Delivery sheath	Biodegradable occluder
Mask2Former for VIS	11.337	24.057	57.068	39.663
VITA	22.323	27.220	60.843	43.436
MinVIS	17.220	19.288	57.220	44.179
DVIS	0.594	2.113	16.028	0.706
Ours	**23.196**	**28.649**	**65.196**	**47.380**

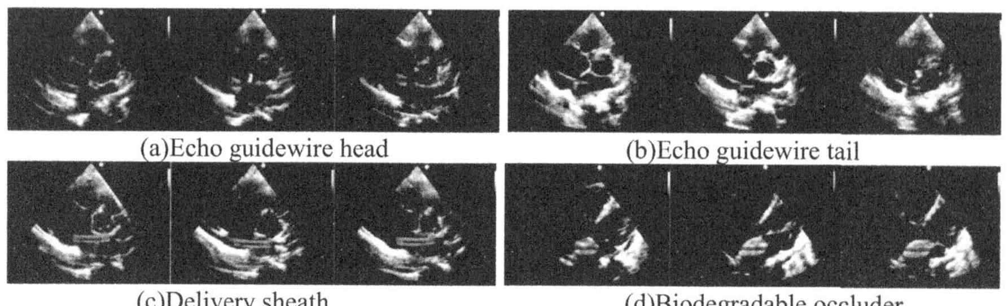

(a)Echo guidewire head (b)Echo guidewire tail

(c)Delivery sheath (d)Biodegradable occluder

Fig. 6. Visualization Results Display for Each Instrument

5.2 Controlled Variable Testing Experiments

As part of the model optimization process, we conducted controlled experiments to test the impact of several important hyperparameters on the model's performance:

Segment Window Length (W). This parameter determines the length of the segment window processed by the model during cross-video segment learning. Experimental results are presented in Table 4. The optimal result was achieved when W = 3.

Table 4. Different Values of Segment Window Length (W)

T = 6;FR = 20					
W	AP	AP50	AP75	AR1	AR10
1	38.621	78.205	27.193	39.884	41.441
2	38.255	78.487	**28.228**	40.603	40.897
3	**38.961**	**82.150**	26.523	**40.754**	**42.012**

Frame Sampling Range ± (FR). This parameter defines the dynamic sampling range around each randomly selected frame. Experimental results are presented in Table 5.

The best performance was achieved under T = 6, W = 3, and FR = 3 (smaller sampling range).

Table 5. Different Values of Frame Sampling Range (FR)

T = 6;W = 3					
FR	AP	AP50	AP75	AR1	AR10
3	**40.640**	**82.591**	29.201	**42.716**	**44.590**
5	39.670	80.744	**31.601**	41.539	42.441
20	38.961	82.150	26.523	40.754	42.012

Frame Sampling Number (T). This parameter specifies the number of frames selected per video clip. A higher frame sampling number benefits network and temporal learning but also increases computational load. We compared two types of frame sampling strategies:

Discontinuous Frame Sampling. This strategy samples frames discontinuously within the clip. The experimental results are shown in Table 6.

Table 6. Different Values of Frame Sampling Number (T) (Discontinuous Frame Sampling)

FR = 20;W = 3					
T	AP	AP50	AP75	AR1	AR10
6	38.961	82.150	26.523	40.754	42.012
9	**39.370**	**82.924**	**29.217**	**41.671**	**42.689**
12	38.487	76.305	30.438	40.103	41.044

Continuous Frame Sampling. In this strategy, continuous frames are sampled, with the number of frames T dynamically adjusted alongside FR. The experimental results are shown in Table 7.

The final experimental results indicate that the optimal model performance was achieved under the following parameters:

Frame Sampling Number (T) = 6, Frame Sampling Range (FR) = 3, and Segment Window Length (W) = 3.

5.3 Computational Resource Efficiency Test

The proposed model was tested on an NVIDIA vGPU-48GB, showing efficient resource utilization with only 7.18% GPU utilization and 3529 MB of memory usage out of

Table 7. Different Values of Frame Sampling Number (T) (Continuous Frame Sampling)

W = 3					
T,FR	AP	AP50	AP75	AR1	AR10
6,3	**40.640**	**82.591**	**29.201**	**42.716**	**44.590**
9,4	40.455	81.803	28.978	42.078	42.539
12,6	39.308	83.188	29.775	41.233	42.994

49140 MB available. This demonstrates the model's low computational cost, ensuring efficient performance while leaving ample GPU resources for other tasks, making it suitable for real-time applications with minimal hardware requirements.

6 Conclusion

This study addresses the challenge of limited surgical adoption due to inaccurate instrument identification in ultrasound-guided interventional surgery for structural heart disease. It proposes a deep learning model based on video instance segmentation, which employs temporal model training and cross-segment memory learning to overcome issues such as instrument blurring, variability, occlusion, and disappearance in ultrasound images. By utilizing a real clinical dataset constructed in collaboration with Fuwai Hospital of the Chinese Academy of Medical Sciences, along with an innovative model design, the experimental results demonstrate that the model performs effectively across multiple types of instruments.The key innovations of this study include:1) The proposed video instance segmentation method significantly outperforms existing models.2) A model architecture was designed that integrates the spatial feature extraction capabilities of convolutional neural networks with the temporal modeling capabilities of Transformers, balancing spatial feature extraction with time series modeling.3) An ultrasound video dataset for atrial septal defect closure surgery was constructed through collaboration with relevant hospitals. Looking ahead, the model developed in this study can be extended beyond instrument identification to encompass broader surgical scenarios. For example, it could analyze the surgeon's actions and the intraoperative environment using real-time intraoperative images, thereby providing more comprehensive decision-making support for surgeries.

Acknowledgements. This paper was supported in part by National Key Research and Development Program of China under Grant 2024YFF1206902; in part by the Development Project of National Major Scientific Research Instrument under Grant 82327801; in part by the National Natural Science Foundation of China under Grant 62303463; in part by the Beijing Natural Science Foundation under Grant L246047, L232137, Z241100009024031

Disclosure of Interests. The authors have no competing interests to declare that are relevant to the content of this article.

References

1. National Health Commission of China: China Health Statistics Yearbook 2023, 1st edn. China Union Medical University Press, Beijing (2024)
2. Liu, M., He, X., Yang, X., et al.: Interpretation of "China cardiovascular health and disease report 2023". Chin. J. Cardiovasc. Med. **29**(4), 305–324 (2024)
3. Ge, J., Pan, W.: Progress and prospects of interventional therapy for structural heart disease in China. Chin. J. Cardiol. **47**(9), 689–692 (2019)
4. Liu, M., He, X., Yang, X., et al.: Interpretation of "advantages of vascular interventional surgery". J. Clin. Cardiol. **29**(4), 305–324 (2024)
5. Guo, Y., Zhong, X., Lin, X., et al.: Clinical application value of transesophageal echocardiography in cardiac interventional surgery. J. Clin. Cardiol. **39**(8), 585–590 (2023)
6. Zhao, Y., Yan, Y., Li, Z., et al.: Pure ultrasound-guided percutaneous intervention with fully biodegradable Occluder for atrial septal defect: a case report. Chin. J. Clin. Thorac. Cardiovasc. Surg., 1–4 (2025)
7. Xie, Z., Yi, M., Huang, X.: Application Progress of multi-instance learning in medical image analysis. J. Integr. Technol., 1–10 (2025)
8. Yang, L., Fan, Y., Xu, N.: Video Instance Segmentation. In: IEEE/CVF International Conference on Computer Vision (ICCV), pp. 5187–5196. IEEE, Seoul (2019)
9. Kamtam, D.N., Shrager, J.B., Malla, S.D. et al.: Deep Learning Approaches to Surgical Video Segmentation and Object Detection: A Scoping Review. arXiv preprint (2024).
10. Xu, C., Li, C.T., Hu, Y., et al.: Deep learning techniques for video instance segmentation: a survey. Pattern Recogn. **167**, 111763 (2025)
11. Porzi, L., Hofinger, M., Ruiz, I., et al.: Learning multi-object tracking and segmentation from automatic annotations. In: IEEE/CVF Conference on Computer Vision and Pattern Recognition (CVPR), pp. 6846–6855. IEEE, Seattle (2020)
12. Bolya, D., Zhou, C., Xiao, F., et al.: YOLACT++: better real-time instance segmentation [J/OL]. IEEE Trans. Pattern Anal. Mach. Intell. **44**(2), 1108–1121 (2022)
13. Wu, J., Cao, J., Song, L., et al.: Track to detect and segment: an online multi-object tracker. In: IEEE/CVF Conference on Computer Vision and Pattern Recognition (CVPR), pp. 12352–12361. IEEE, Nashville (2021)
14. Li, X., Wang, J., Li, X. et al.: Hybrid instance-aware temporal fusion for online video instance segmentation. In: AAAI Conference on Artificial Intelligence, vol. 36(2), pp. 1429–1437. AAAI Press (2022).
15. Voigtlaender, P., Krause, M., Osep, A., et al.: MOTS: multi-object tracking and segmentation. In: IEEE/CVF Conference on Computer Vision and Pattern Recognition (CVPR), pp. 7942–7951. IEEE, Long Beach (2019)
16. Wang, Y., Xu, Z., Wang, X., et al.: End-to-end video instance segmentation with transformers. In: IEEE/CVF Conference on Computer Vision and Pattern Recognition (CVPR), pp. 8741–8750. IEEE, Nashville (2021)
17. Cheng, B., Choudhuri, A., Misra, I. et al.: Mask2Former for Video Instance Segmentation. arXiv preprint (2021).
18. Heo, M., Hwang, S., Oh, S.W. et al.: VITA: Video Instance Segmentation via Object Token Association. arXiv preprint (2022).
19. Sun, J., Xie, J., Hu, J.F., et al.: Predicting future instance segmentation with contextual pyramid ConvLSTMs. In: ACM International Conference on Multimedia, pp. 2043–2051. ACM, Nice (2019)
20. Fu, Y., Yang, L., Liu, D., et al.: CompFeat: comprehensive feature aggregation for video instance segmentation. In: AAAI Conference on Artificial Intelligence, vol. 35(2), pp. 1361–1369. AAAI Press (2021)

21. Meinhardt, T., Kirillov, A., Leal-Taixé, L., et al.: TrackFormer: multi-object tracking with transformers. In: IEEE/CVF Conference on Computer Vision and Pattern Recognition (CVPR), pp. 8844–8854. IEEE, New Orleans (2022)
22. Koner, R., Hannan, T., Shit, S. et al.: InstanceFormer: an online video instance segmentation framework. In: AAAI Conference on Artificial Intelligence, vol. 37(1), pp. 1188–1195. AAAI Press (2023).
23. Heo, M., Hwang, S., Hyun, J., et al.: A generalized framework for video instance segmentation. In: IEEE/CVF Conference on Computer Vision and Pattern Recognition (CVPR), pp. 14623–14632. IEEE, Vancouver (2023)
24. Wu, J., Jiang, Y., Bai, S., et al.: SeqFormer: sequential transformer for video instance segmentation. In: European Conference on Computer Vision (ECCV) LNCS, vol. 13684, pp. 553–569. Springer, Tel Aviv (2022)
25. Noble, J.A., Boukerroui, D.: Ultrasound image segmentation: a survey [J]. IEEE Trans. Med. Imaging. **25**(8), 987–1010 (2006)
26. Xu, Y., Wang, Y., Yuan, J., et al.: Medical breast ultrasound image segmentation by machine learning. Ultrasonics. **91**, 1–9 (2019)
27. Amiri, M., Brooks, R., Rivaz, H.: Fine-tuning U-net for ultrasound image segmentation: different layers, different outcomes. IEEE Trans. Ultrason. Ferroelectr. Freq. Control. **67**(12), 2510–2518 (2020)
28. Mishra, D., Chaudhury, S., Sarkar, M., et al.: Ultrasound image segmentation: a deeply supervised network with attention to boundaries. IEEE Trans. Biomed. Eng. **66**(6), 1637–1648 (2019)
29. Chen, G., Liu, Y., Qian, J., et al.: DSEU-net: a novel deep supervision SEU-net for medical ultrasound image segmentation. Expert Syst. Appl. **223**, 119939 (2023)
30. Nurmaini, S., Rachmatullah, M.N., Sapitri, A.I., et al.: Accurate detection of septal defects with Fetal ultrasonography images using deep learning-based multiclass instance segmentation. IEEE Access. **8**, 196160–196174 (2020)
31. Wang, C., Zhang, J., Liu, S.: Medical ultrasound image segmentation with deep learning models. IEEE Access. **11**, 10158–10168 (2023)
32. Zhao, H., Men, Q., Gleed, A., et al.: Ultrasound video segmentation with adaptive temporal memory. In: Kainz, B., Noble, A., Schnabel, J. (eds.) Simplifying Medical Ultrasound, LNCS, vol. 14337, pp. 3–12. Springer, Cham (2023)
33. Ilea, D.E., Duffy, C., Kavanagh, L., et al.: Fully automated segmentation and tracking of the intima media thickness in ultrasound video sequences of the common carotid artery. IEEE Trans. Ultrason. Ferroelectr. Freq. Control. **60**(1), 639–649 (2013)
34. Luo, H., Ma, L., Wu, X., et al.: Deep learning-based ultrasonic dynamic video detection and segmentation of thyroid gland and its surrounding cervical soft tissues. Med. Phys. **49**(1), 382–392 (2022)
35. Deng, X., Wu, H., Zeng, R., et al.: MemSAM: taming segment anything model for echocardiography video segmentation. In: IEEE/CVF Conference on Computer Vision and Pattern Recognition (CVPR), pp. 9622–9631. IEEE, Seattle (2024)
36. Yang, Y., Xing, Z., Yu, L., et al.: Vivim: a video vision mamba for ultrasound video segmentation. IEEE Trans. Circuits Syst. Video Technol. (2025)
37. Cheng, B., Misra, I., Schwing, A.G., et al.: Masked-attention mask transformer for universal image segmentation. In: IEEE/CVF Conference on Computer Vision and Pattern Recognition (CVPR), pp. 1280–1289. IEEE, New Orleans (2022)
38. He, K., Zhang, X., Ren, S., et al.: Deep residual learning for image recognition. In: IEEE Conference on Computer Vision and Pattern Recognition (CVPR), pp. 770–778. IEEE, Las Vegas (2016)

A Structured Representation Learning Framework for Medical Assistant Robotics via Heterogeneous Graph Transformers

Junyang Leng[1], Qun Li[2], Meng Zhang[3], Fang Hu[1(✉)], and Yin Zhang[4]

[1] College of Information Engineering, Hubei University of Chinese Medicine, Wuhan 430065, China
leng11@stmail.hbucm.edu.cn, naomifang@hbucm.edu.cn

[2] Hubei Science and Technology Foreign Exchange Center, Wuhan 430071, China

[3] Endocrinology Department, Hubei Provincial Hospital of TCM, Wuhan 430061, China
zhangmeng@hbhtcm.com

[4] School of Information and Communication Engineering, University of Electronic Science and Technology of China, Chengdu 611731, China
zhangyin123@uestc.edu.cn

Abstract. Recent advances in medical assistant robotics can provide services of personalized medication, treatment planning, clinical decision support, etc., which refer to diverse knowledge entities and their complex relationships, posing significant challenges of effective knowledge representation learning, integration, and reasoning. To address these challenges, this study proposes a structured representation learning framework for medical assistant robotics via heterogeneous graph transformers, termed SRL-HGT, effectively capturing diverse inter-entity relationships to reason medical knowledge. The proposed SRL-HGT consists of three key modules: multi-dimensional joint encoding for feature fusion, similarity-based reconstruction of relational edges, and a transformer-based module to capture both local interactions and global contextual dependencies among heterogeneous data. It adopts a multiple-task learning paradigm to realize the syndrome-based herb combination prediction. Experimental results demonstrate that the proposed SRL-HGT outperforms the baselines, achieving improvements of 8.59% in average precision (AP), 3.00% in precision, 15.28% in recall, and 17.42% in F1-score. The SRL-HGT can effectively empower medical assistant robotics, providing an intelligent and reliable solution for complex clinical decision-making scenarios.

Keywords: Heterogeneous Data Integration · Heterogeneous Graph Transformers · Structured Representation Learning · Medical Assistant Robotics

Z. Hou et al. (Eds.): CIRAC 2025, CCIS 2885, pp. 163–173, 2026.
https://doi.org/10.1007/978-981-92-0045-0_11

1 Introduction

The latest advancements in medical assistive robotics can be applied in various medical scenarios, including personalized treatment plans, intelligent auxiliary decision-making, etc. It requires vast and heterogeneous data from diverse sources, including electronic medical records (EMRs), robotic sensor streams, procedural texts, and task-specific ontologies [1,2]. Traditional representation learning methods often oversimplify or ignore the structural dependencies in these complex data sources, which poses challenges for the effective learning and integration of heterogeneous data in medical assistant robot applications. Emerging transformer-based frameworks have demonstrated superior capability in capturing long-range dependencies and learning expressive representations, especially in natural language processing and vision-language domains. However, their applications to structured, multi-relational medical-robotic data remain limited. Meanwhile, Graph Neural Networks (GNNs) have shown great promise in modeling complex relational structures across healthcare tasks, such as disease prediction, drug discovery, and clinical decision support, thereby enhancing decision-making accuracy and efficiency [3]. For example, in traditional Chinese medicine, graph-based approaches have been used to analyze herb combinations and uncover hierarchical and molecular interaction patterns [4].

Recent studies integrate GNNs with attention and transformer mechanisms to better capture heterogeneous and multi-hop relational dependencies, including the GNN-transformer co-contrastive learning framework GTC [5], the structure-aware transformer SAT [6], etc. Scalability and relational reasoning have been further developed by advanced frameworks, such as HEGformer [7] and HHGT [8], which leverage structure-aware and relation-sensitive attention to extract meaningful representations from large-scale heterogeneous graphs related to medical robotics. Furthermore, semantic and relation-aware frameworks, such as SR-HGN [9], demonstrate the effectiveness of jointly encoding node semantics and relational information. These advanced techniques are critical in medical assistant robotics, which can effectively realize human-robot interaction and device coordination to promote the development of intelligent healthcare.

The increasing requirements in medical assistant robotics have highlighted the importance of integrating and learning heterogeneous data while effectively modeling complex relational dependencies. Wagner et al. [10] proposed a multimodal GNN framework for surgical instrument prediction that fuses visual and non-visual data, whereas Khalid et al. [11] developed SurGNN for surgical skill assessment. Transformer-augmented GNN models have further advanced applications in high-precision robotic automation and clinical decision-making [12,13]. Graph learning applications in robotics have been extensively explored, encompassing object modeling, behavior prediction, and multi-agent coordination [14]. Zhou et al. presented a cooperative sensing approach in multi-robot systems [15], and Ai et al. proposed an effective computing method for eldercare robots [16]. These studies demonstrate that the GNN-based methods for fusing heterogeneous data can effectively improve system performance in robotics. Furthermore, the complicated and domain-specific interactions among patients, medical devices, and robots require expressive graph representation capability for modeling structural dependency relationships. However, existing studies have limitations in modeling complex relations among various medical knowledge and capturing local and global dependencies in heterogeneous data.

To address these challenges, we propose SRL-HGT, a structured representation learning framework for medical assistant robotics. It employs heterogeneous graph transformers to model complex relationships embedded in real-world clinical data. The framework is designed to fuse features from multiple interacting entities, reconstruct relational edges based on a similarity calculation strategy, and encode both local interactions and global contextual dependencies. This design enables effective multiple-task learning for syndrome-based herb combination prediction, enhancing intelligent decision-making for medical assistant robotics. The main contributions of this study are summarized as follows:

- We propose SRL-HGT, a structured representation learning framework for medical assistant robotics. It incorporates multi-dimensional joint encoding for feature fusion, followed by the computation of pairwise similarities to reconstruct the feature matrices. This design facilitates comprehensive structural representation, which can effectively capture complex relationships among various medical knowledge.
- The SRL-HGT enables effective multiple-task learning for syndrome-based herb combination prediction. By integrating graph neural networks with transformer modules, the architecture captures both local interactions and global contextual dependencies among heterogeneous data. This framework can empower medical assistant robotics in real-world scenarios, including personalized medication, treatment planning, adjuvant therapy, clinical decision support, etc.

The subsequent sections of this paper are organized as follows: Sect. 2 introduces the SRL-HGT and its realization steps. In Sect. 3, we present the experiment design, dataset, comparison experiments, parameter sensitivity test, and the result analysis. Finally, we give the conclusions and perspectives in Sect. 4.

2 Methodology

We propose SRL-HGT, a structured representation learning framework for medical assistant robotics via heterogeneous graph transformers, as illustrated in Fig. 1. The framework integrates heterogeneous data from multiple interacting entities, which are preprocessed and normalized based on expert knowledge and standardized guidelines. A multi-dimensional joint encoding mechanism is proposed to fuse diverse features and recompute pairwise similarities, thereby constructing relational edges that reflect the strength of inter-entity associations. Then, a transformer-based graph convolution module is constructed to capture both local structural dependencies and global contextual information within the graph, enabling the joint prediction of syndromes and herbs, respectively. This framework empowers intelligent medical assistant robots to support clinical decision-making, adjuvant therapy, personalized treatment planning, and context-aware humanrobot interaction in complex healthcare environments. By modeling rich relational structures, the SRL-HGT supports medical assistant robotics with more accurate situational understanding and decision-making capabilities.

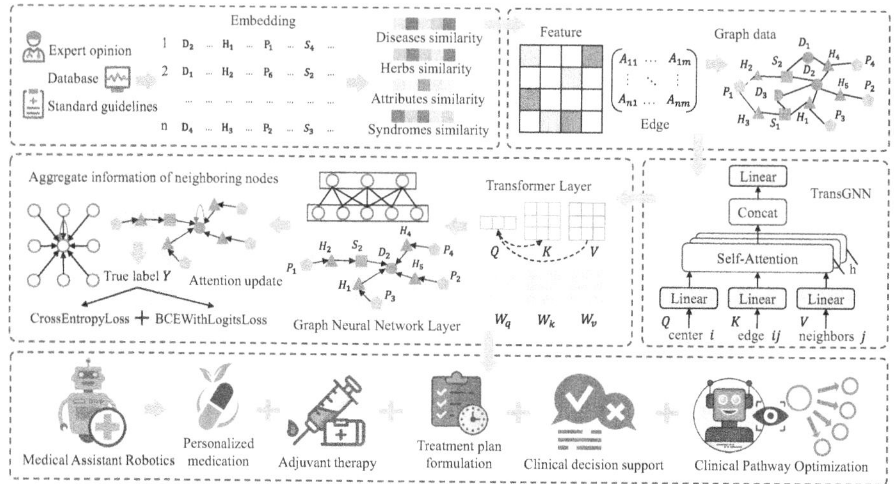

Fig. 1. The architecture of SRL-HGT.

Based on the clinical Electronic Medical Records (EMRs) and external knowledge sources, a heterogeneous information graph is constructed as the designed regularity: nodes represent disease categories, syndromes, herbs, and herbal attributes (e.g., nature, flavor, and meridian association), denoted as $\mathcal{V}_{dis}$, $\mathcal{V}_{syn}$, $\mathcal{V}_{herb}$, and $\mathcal{V}_{att}$, respectively. Multiple edge types were defined to capture inter- and intra-entity associations, forming a multi-relational edge set $\mathcal{E} = \{\mathcal{E}_{11}, \mathcal{E}_{12}, \mathcal{E}_{13}, \ldots, \mathcal{E}_{ij}, \ldots\}$, where each $\mathcal{E}_{ij}$ represents the edge between node types $\mathcal{V}_i$ and $\mathcal{V}_j$.

We propose a multi-dimensional joint encoding mechanism to generate the node representations from multi-source heterogeneous data. For each type of node, a corresponding encoding method has been applied and followed by standardization to ensure consistency across different nodes. Different node embeddings are then concatenated and integrated to form a comprehensive feature matrix. Based on the generated feature matrix, the pairwise similarity matrices, including disease similarity, syndrome similarity, herb similarity, and herbal similarity, are recalculated via the Cosine Similarity method.

$$Sim(i, j) = \frac{A_i \cdot B_j}{||A_i||_2||B_j||_2} \tag{1}$$

where A_i and B_j represent the feature vectors of the ith and j^{th} patients, respectively, $||\cdot||_2$ denotes the Euclidean norm.

Then, as part of the Transformer-based module, a multi-head attention graph convolution layer is applied to perform representation learning over the reconstructed graph. Specifically, this layer enables expressive feature aggregation and relational reasoning among the constructed heterogeneous graph. It updates and generates node representations by integrating their local neighbor information in the graph. For each node i, its feature $\mathbf{x}_i \in \mathbb{R}^F$ is projected into query (q_i), key (k_j), and value (v_j) vectors using learned linear transformations:

$$\mathbf{q}_i^{(h)} = \mathbf{W}_q^{(h)}\mathbf{x}_i, \quad \mathbf{k}_j^{(h)} = \mathbf{W}_k^{(h)}\mathbf{x}_j, \quad \mathbf{v}_j^{(h)} = \mathbf{W}_v^{(h)}\mathbf{x}_j \tag{2}$$

where $h = 1, ..., H$ denotes the attention heads, H is the total number of heads, we set H=4, and $\mathbf{W_q}$, $\mathbf{W_k}$, $\mathbf{W_v}$ are the transformation matrices of Query, Key, and Value. Edge features $\mathbf{e}_{ij}$ are also linearly projected and incorporated into both keys and values:

$$\tilde{\mathbf{k}}_j^{(h)} = \mathbf{k}_j^{(h)} + \mathbf{W}_e^{(h)}\mathbf{e}_{ij}, \quad \tilde{\mathbf{v}}_j^{(h)} = \mathbf{v}_j^{(h)} + \mathbf{W}_e^{(h)}\mathbf{e}_{ij} \tag{3}$$

where $\mathbf{W_e}$ is separate edge transformation matrix.

The attention coefficient α_{ij} between node i and its neighbor j is then computed via scaled dot-product attention:

$$\alpha_{ij}^{(h)} = \text{softmax}_j\left(\frac{(\mathbf{q}_i^{(h)})^\top \tilde{\mathbf{k}}_j^{(h)}}{\sqrt{d}}\right) \tag{4}$$

where d is the output dimensionality of each head. The aggregated message from neighbors is obtained as a weighted sum over value vectors:

$$\mathbf{z}_i^{(h)} = \sum_{j \in \mathcal{N}(i)} \alpha_{ij}^{(h)} \cdot \tilde{\mathbf{v}}_j^{(h)} \tag{5}$$

where $\mathcal{N}(i)$ represents the set of neighbors to node i.

The outputs from all attention heads are concatenated to generate the final representation:

$$\mathbf{z}_i = \operatorname*{\Big\|}_{h=1}^{H} \mathbf{z}_i^{(h)} \tag{6}$$

where $\|$ represents vector concatenation.

In addition, a skip connection is incorporated to retain the original feature information. A learnable gating mechanism $\beta_i \in [0, 1]$ is adopted to balance the original input and the transformed features:

$$\mathbf{h}_i = \beta_i \mathbf{x}_i + (1 - \beta_i)\mathbf{z}_i \tag{7}$$

This attention-driven message-passing mechanism is implemented through multiple layers of multi-head attention graph convolution to capture dependencies among nodes. The generated node embeddings are then employed to predict the probabilities of herb nodes belonging to their syndromes. Based on the purpose of multiple-task learning, different loss functions were employed during the training process: CrossEntropyLoss is used for syndrome prediction, and BCEWithLogitsLoss is utilized for herbal prediction, respectively. These two loss functions are defined as follows:

$$L_{CE} = -\sum_{c=1}^{C} y_c \log(\hat{y}_c) \tag{8}$$

where C is the number of syndrome classes, y_c and $\hat{y}_c$ denote the ground-truth and predicted results for class c.

$$L_{BCE} = -\frac{1}{N}\sum_{i=1}^{N} \left[y_i \log\left(\sigma(\hat{y}_i)\right) + (1 - y_i) \log\left(1 - \sigma(\hat{y}_i)\right)\right] \tag{9}$$

where N is the number of EMRs, $\sigma(\cdot)$ represents the sigmoid function, y_i and $\hat{y}_i$ denote the ground-truth and predicted results of the herbs, respectively. By combining two individual loss terms, the final loss function of the entire framework is obtained as follows:

$$L = L_{CE} + L_{BCE} \tag{10}$$

It enables the simultaneous prediction of both syndromes and herb combinations via a single training process.

3 Experiments

3.1 Experiment Design

To evaluate the effectiveness of the proposed SRL-HGT, we design a series of experiments, including comparison verification and parameter sensitivity tests. All experiments were conducted on a 3.60 GHz Intel(R) Core(TM) i7-9700K CPU and 16 GB RAM.

Framework performance was assessed using four representative evaluation metrics: average precision (AP), precision, recall, and F1-score. AP captures the trade-off between precision and recall across varying thresholds, making it particularly suitable for imbalanced and multi-label classification tasks. Precision reflects the proportion of correctly predicted positive instances among all predicted positives, whereas recall measures the proportion of true positive instances identified out of all actual positives. The F1-score, defined as the harmonic mean of precision and recall, provides a balanced and comprehensive evaluation of the framework's predictive performance.

3.2 Dataset

Based on real-world EMRs of reflux esophagitis with 2,110 patient samples and the Chinese medicine dictionary, the related entities have been extracted, including 53 diseases, 22 TCM syndromes, 178 herbs, and their corresponding 21 herbal attributes of flavor, property, and meridian tropism. Then, these data have been standardized and cleaned using medical terminology from professional dictionaries and TCM terms. We split this dataset with a ratio of 8 : 1 : 1 for training, validation, and test subsets.

3.3 Comparison Experiments

To verify the performance of the proposed SRL-HGT, we compared it with three representative baselines: GraphSAGE [17], GCN [18], and GAT [19]. As shown in Table 1 and Fig. 2, we show the experimental results of the SRL-HGT and the baselines using four representative metrics: average precision (AP), precision, recall, and F1-score.

Table 1. Different framework comparisons on evaluation metrics.

Framework	AP	Precision	Recall	F1-score
SRL-HGT	**0.8209**	**0.8961**	**0.8081**	**0.8391**
GraphSAGE	0.7350	0.8661	0.6553	0.6649
GCN	0.3882	0.6606	0.3973	0.4306
GAT	0.4488	0.7063	0.4696	0.5256

The experimental results demonstrate that the proposed SRL-HGT consistently outperforms the baselines across all four evaluation metrics. Specifically, the SRL-HGT achieves an average precision (AP) of 0.8209, surpassing GraphSAGE (0.7350), GAT (0.4488), and GCN (0.3882). Similarly, it gets a precision of 0.8961, compared to 0.8661 for GraphSAGE, 0.7063 for GAT, and 0.6606 for GCN. The recall of SRL-HGT attains 0.8081, outperforming GraphSAGE (0.6553), GAT (0.4696), and GCN (0.3973). Finally, the F1-score 0.8391 significantly exceeds those of GraphSAGE (0.6649), GAT (0.5256), and GCN (0.4306). Specifically, SRL-HGT shows improvements in AP ranging from 8.59% over GraphSAGE to 43.27% over GCN. Precision improves between 3.00% and 23.55%, recall between 15.28% and 41.08%, and the F1-score between 17.42% and 40.85%. These consistent and substantial improvements across all metrics indicate that the SRL-HGT is more effective at learning meaningful representations and making accurate predictions.

3.4 Parameter Sensitivity Tests

To assess the robustness of the proposed SRL-HGT, we conducted the sensitivity tests on the key hyperparameters: learning rate (lr) and weight decay. As shown in Table 2 and Fig. 3, the framework achieves the best overall performance when `lr` = 0.005 and `weight_decay` = 1e−4, achieving AP of 0.8209, precision of 0.8961, recall of 0.8081, and F1-score of 0.8391. When increasing the weight

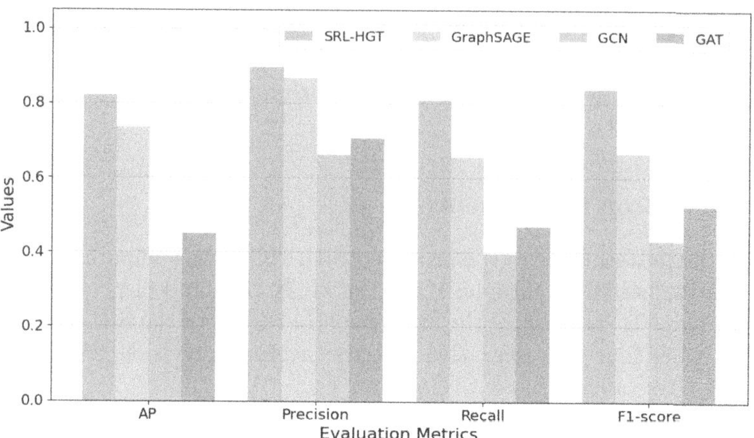

Fig. 2. Performance comparison of SRL-HGT and baselines on the clinical EMR dataset in terms of AP, precision, recall, and F1-score.

Table 2. Performance under different learning rates and weight decay settings.

Learning Rate	Weight Decay	AP	Precision	Recall	F1-score
0.005	1e−1	0.8172	0.8867	0.8042	0.8339
0.005	1e−7	0.8183	**0.9062**	0.7906	0.8272
0.005	1e−4	**0.8209**	0.8961	**0.8081**	**0.8391**
0.001	1e−4	0.6680	0.7781	0.6400	0.6611
0.025	1e−4	0.5003	0.8091	0.4936	0.5021

decay to 1e − 1 or decreasing it to 1e − 7 while keeping the learning rate fixed, the performance slightly declines but remains relatively stable. Specifically, the AP values drop to 0.8172 and 0.8183, respectively, while the F1-score values decrease to 0.8339 and 0.8272, indicating that the framework is moderately robust to changes in weight decay within a reasonable range.

However, when the learning rate is reduced to 0.001, the performance deteriorates significantly, with the AP dropping to 0.6680 and the F1-score to 0.6611, indicating that reducing the learning rate will reduce the convergence speed and the effectiveness of the framework. In contrast, `lr` = 0.025 leads to a decline in performance, with the AP declining to 0.5003 and the F1-score to 0.5021, denoting that increasing the learning rate may have an adverse influence on stable convergence. Specifically, when `lr` = 0.005 and `weight_decay` = 1e−4 emerge as an optimal configuration that can effectively balance convergence speed and regularization strength, yielding the most stable and accurate results.

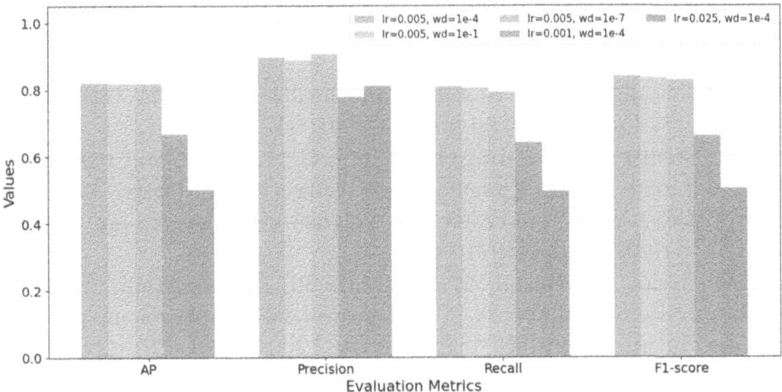

Fig. 3. Sensitivity analysis of weight decay and learning rate (LR) on AP, Precision, Recall, and F1-score.

4 Conclusion

We propose SRL-HGT, a structured representation learning framework for medical assistant robotics, aimed at learning and integration from heterogeneous medical data. The framework adopts a multi-dimensional joint encoding strategy for feature fusion, enabling the integration of diverse medical entities. A similarity computation strategy is presented to reconstruct the feature matrices, facilitating effective modeling of complex inter-entity relationships. The SRL-HGT incorporates a transformer-based module that captures both local interactions and global contextual dependencies among heterogeneous data. Experimental results demonstrate that SRL-HGT outperforms baselines across multiple evaluation metrics, verifying its effectiveness in medical knowledge representation learning and reasoning.

The SRL-HGT shows strong potential for deployment in medical assistant robotics across complex clinical scenarios, including personalized medication, auxiliary therapy, individualized treatment planning, and clinical decision support. In future work, we will extend the application of SRL-HGT to a broader range of clinical settings to validate its effectiveness and adaptability in different healthcare environments. Furthermore, we plan to further optimize the model to handle more complex medical data and reasoning tasks by incorporating temporal information from EMRs and integrating multimodal clinical data, such as medical imaging, to enhance its flexibility and accuracy.

Acknowledgements. We acknowledge the funding support from the Hubei Provincial International Science and Technology Cooperation Project (2025EHA011) and the joint support from the Hubei Provincial Natural Science Foundation and TCM Innovation and Development Foundation of China (2025AFD552).

References

1. Holland, J., et al.: Service robots in the healthcare sector. Robotics **10**(1), 47 (2021). https://doi.org/10.3390/robotics10010047
2. Islam, M., Seenivasan, L., Ming, L.C., Ren, H.: Learning and reasoning with the graph structure representation in robotic surgery. In: Martel, A.L., et al. (eds.) MICCAI 2020. LNCS, vol. 12263, pp. 627–636. Springer, Cham (2020). https://doi.org/10.1007/978-3-030-59716-0_60
3. Paul, S.G., Saha, A., Hasan, M.Z., Noori, S.R.H., Moustafa, A.: A systematic review of graph neural network in healthcare-based applications: recent advances, trends, and future directions. IEEE Access **12**, 15145–15170 (2024). https://doi.org/10.1109/ACCESS.2024.3354809
4. Wang, N., et al.: Network patterns of herb combinations in traditional Chinese clinical prescriptions. Front. Pharmacol. **11** (2020).https://doi.org/10.3389/fphar.2020.590824
5. Sun, Y., Zhu, D., Wang, Y., Fu, Y., Tian, Z.: GTC: GNN-transformer co-contrastive learning for self-supervised heterogeneous graph representation. Neural Netw. **181**, 106645 (2025)
6. Chen, D., O'Bray, L., Borgwardt, K.: Structure-aware transformer for graph representation learning. In: Proceedings of the International Conference on Machine Learning (ICML), vol. 2022, pp. 3469–3489 (2022)
7. Qin, T., Su, J., Wu, C.:HEGformer: representation learning on heterogeneous graph neural network with efficient transformer. In: Proceedings of the 2024 IEEE International Conference on Knowledge Graph (ICKG), vol. 2024, pp. 266–273 (2024)
8. Zhu, Q., Zhang, L., Xu, Q., Liu, K., Long, C., Wang, X.: HHGT: hierarchical heterogeneous graph transformer for heterogeneous graph representation learning. In: Proceedings of the Eighteenth ACM International Conference on Web Search and Data Mining (WSDM), vol. 18, pp. 318–326 (2025)
9. Wang, Z., Yu, D., Li, Q., Shen, S., Yao, S.:SR-HGN: semantic-and relation-aware heterogeneous graph neural network. Expert Syst. Appl. **224**, 119982 (2023)
10. Wagner, L., et al.: Towards multimodal graph neural networks for surgical instrument anticipation. Int. J. Comput. Assist. Radiol. Surg. **19**(10), 1929–1937 (2024)
11. Khalid, S., Rudzicz, F.: SurGNN: explainable visual scene understanding and assessment of surgical skill using graph neural networks. arXiv preprint arXiv:2308.13073 (2023)
12. Petrescu, R.V.: Medical service of robots. J. Mech. Robot. **3**, 60–81 (2019)
13. Jadon, R., Srinivasan, K., Chauhan, G.S., Budda, R., Awotunde, J.B.: Advanced robotic automation with transformer-guided GNNs, hybrid neural architectures, and fuzzy decision frameworks for accurate and scalable breast cancer prediction. Int. J. Autom. Smart Technol. **15**(1), 23–45 (2025). https://doi.org/10.1234/ijast.2025.00123
14. Pistilli, F., Averta, G.: Graph learning in robotics: a survey. IEEE Access **11**, 112664–112681 (2023)
15. Zhou, Y., Xiao, J., Zhou, Y., Loianno, G.: Multi-robot collaborative perception with graph neural networks. IEEE Robot. Autom. Lett. **7**(2), 2289–2296 (2022)
16. Ai, Y., Zhang, Y., Wang, J., Xu, N.: Optimizing the interaction of service robots in elderly care institutions using multi-modal emotion recognition system based on transfer learning. Discov. Artif. Intell. **5**(1), 1–24 (2025). https://doi.org/10.1007/s44163-025-00280-2

17. Wu, Z., Pan, S., Chen, F., Long, G., Zhang, C., Yu, P.: A comprehensive survey on graph neural networks. IEEE Trans. Neural Netw. Learn. Syst. **32**(1), 4–24 (2021). https://doi.org/10.1109/TNNLS.2020.2978386
18. Zhou, J., et al.: Graph neural networks: a review of methods and applications. AI Open **1**, 57–81 (2020). https://doi.org/10.1016/j.aiopen.2021.01.001
19. Ying, R., Bourgeois, D., You, J., Zitnik, M., Leskovec, J.: Graph neural networks: a review of methods and applications. IEEE Trans. Pattern Anal. Mach. Intell. (2021). https://doi.org/10.1109/TPAMI.2021.3057446

Diffusion-Aware Multi-view Hypergraph Representation Learning Model for Intelligent Medical Robotics

Juanzi Zhou[1], Xiong Zhang[2], Hongci Chen[2], Fang Hu[1(✉)], and Yin Zhang[3]

[1] College of Information Engineering, Hubei University of Chinese Medicine, Wuhan 430065, People's Republic of China
zjz678@stmail.hbucm.edu.cn, naomifang@hbucm.edu.cn

[2] Geriatric Department, Hubei Provincial Hospital of TCM, Wuhan 430061, People's Republic of China
{zhangxiong,chenhongci}@hbhtcm.com

[3] School of Information and Communication Engineering, University of Electronic Science and Technology of China, Chengdu 611731, People's Republic of China
zhangyin123@uestc.edu.cn

Abstract. Intelligent medical robotics in Traditional Chinese Medicine (TCM) focuses on clinical decision support, personalized health management, intelligent question-answering systems, etc. Effective and accurate syndrome-based prescription recommendation is the most significant application scenario. The learning and extraction of multi-dimensional knowledge embedded in herbal prescriptions—including herb properties, co-occurrence structures, and dosage dependencies—pose challenges for the development of TCM. This study proposes a diffusion-aware multi-view hypergraph representation learning model for intelligent medical robotics (DMVH-RL) to enhance the performance of intelligent medical robotics in accurate syndrome-based prescription recommendation. The model proposes a similarity-driven hypergraph reconstruction strategy with a Top-K strategy to capture intricate relational patterns across prescriptions, herbs, properties, and dosages. A hypergraph diffusion fusion network is presented to enable joint representation learning and extract high-order relationships. To address the challenge of data sparsity, a hypergraph diffusion path sampling augmentation strategy is designed, combined with an integrated loss function. Comprehensive experimental results demonstrate that the proposed DMVH-RL outperforms other baselines in the syndrome-based prescription recommendation model, thereby offering a paradigm for advancing intelligent medical robotics in TCM applications.

Keywords: Hypergraph Diffusion · Feature Fusion · Data Augmentation · Syndrome-based prescription recommendation

Z. Hou et al. (Eds.): CIRAC 2025, CCIS 2885, pp. 174–187, 2026.
https://doi.org/10.1007/978-981-92-0045-0_12

1 Introduction

Intelligent medical robotics has rapidly advanced in recent years, leading to increasingly mature applications in areas such as surgical assistance [1], diagnostic imaging [2], and rehabilitation [3], a fact that has demonstrated significant clinical benefits [4]. Currently, intelligent medical robotics has begun to expand into the field of Traditional Chinese Medicine (TCM), where tasks such as recommending prescriptions and predicting syndromes exhibit promising application prospects [5]. Driven by the growing demands for personalized and contactless healthcare services [6], the development and deployment of intelligent medical robotics has attracted increasing attention. They aim to enhance diagnostic accuracy, reduce subjective bias, and facilitate the standardization and automation of therapeutic decision-making processes [7]. Recent progress in artificial intelligence, particularly in graph-based learning models and knowledge-driven frameworks, has further strengthened the analytical and predictive capabilities of TCM prescription systems [8].

By leveraging multi-dimensional knowledge-driven models, the reliability and utility of human-robot interaction can be significantly enhanced. The application framework for intelligent medical robotics includes intelligent herbal dispensing [9], prescription verification [10], clinical decision support [11], educational training [12], personalized health management [13], and intelligent question-answering systems [14] (see Fig. 1). Under this framework, the syndrome-based prescription recommendation models serve as a key component, enabling enhanced decision-making and interaction capabilities across various clinical scenarios. This framework demonstrates the potential of the syndrome-based prescription recommendation model to enhance the intelligence of robotic systems and support complex clinical applications.

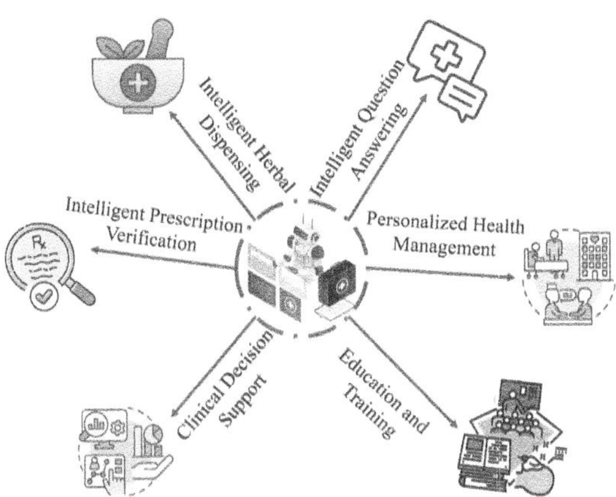

Fig. 1. Application Framework for Intelligent Medical Robotics.

To support the development of intelligent medical robotics, researchers have proposed a variety of computational models that enhance prescription analysis by leveraging advanced learning paradigms. Yang et al. proposed a graph convolutional model that incorporates herbal properties via a knowledge graph to enhance the representation learning of symptoms and herbs [15]. Dong et al. developed PresRecST, a prescription recommendation framework that integrates TCM clinical workflows, knowledge graphs, and multi-stage prediction mechanisms [16]. Zhou et al. introduced TCM-FTP, a fine-tuned language model trained on the DigestDS dataset, enabling accurate prediction of both prescriptions and dosages [17]. Zheng et al. proposed FMCHS, a graph-based framework that captures multiscale herb-symptom correlations by integrating chemical and clinical features [18]. Liu et al. designed TCM-KDIF, a knowledge-data interaction framework that integrates TCM knowledge graphs with training data to improve generalization and interpretability under limited data conditions [19]. However, current TCM prescription analysis models mainly rely on single-view representations, which fail to capture the complex dosage relationships and higher-order interactions among herbal components. These limitations restrict the development and application of autonomous intelligent medical robotics in clinical TCM practice.

To address these challenges, we integrate and analyze TCM knowledge and propose a diffusion-aware multi-view hypergraph representation learning model for intelligent medical robotics (DMVH-RL). Similarity matrices for the property-based herb, co-occurrence-based herb, and dosage-based prescription views are derived from feature matrices using tailored similarity measures. Hyperedges are then reconstructed via a Top-K strategy to capture high-order relationships. It proposes a hypergraph diffusion-aware strategy for deep feature extraction and fuses herb and prescription representations. Hypergraph diffusion path sampling augmentation is presented to enrich training samples and boost the generalization of the proposed model. The DMVH-RL model represents an innovative paradigm that drives the integration of intelligent medical robotics into TCM practices. Overall, the contributions of the DMVH-RL model are summarized as follows:

- This study investigates a diffusion-aware multi-view hypergraph modeling with feature representation learning, termed DMVH-RL. A similarity-based hypergraph reconstruction strategy is proposed to capture intricate patterns in prescriptions through the TOK-K strategy.
- The proposed DMVH-RL presents a hypergraph diffusion-based fusion network to model multi-view high-order relationships and generate embeddings for prescriptions and herbs. Furthermore, it incorporates a dosage-aware embedding fusion strategy to integrate herb dosage information, enabling a comprehensive joint representation of herbs and prescriptions.
- The DMVH-RL presents a hypergraph diffusion path sampling augmentation strategy to improve the diversity of the training set and mitigate data sparsity. An integrated loss function is investigated, considering classification and augmentation losses, to optimize the model's performance.

The remainder of this paper is structured as follows. Section 2 introduces the DMVH-RL framework, including its architecture and the model steps. Subsequently, in Sect. 3, we present the experimental design, the evaluation metrics, and the experimental results. Finally, Sect. 4 presents the conclusions and future perspectives.

2 Methodology

We propose a diffusion-aware multi-view hypergraph representation learning model for intelligent medical robotics, termed DMVH-RL. As shown in Fig. 2, DMVH-RL consists of three components, including (A) Similarity-Driven Hypergraph Reconstruction Module, (B) Hypergraph Diffusion Fusion Network, and (C) Hypergraph Diffusion Path Sampling Augmentation Module. First, the Similarity-Driven Hypergraph Reconstruction Module constructs multi-view hypergraphs, which are then fused by the Hypergraph Diffusion Fusion Network to capture cross-view relations. Finally, the Hypergraph Diffusion Path Sampling Augmentation Module generates augmented samples from the learned embeddings. These modules operate sequentially, with each stage providing inputs to the next.

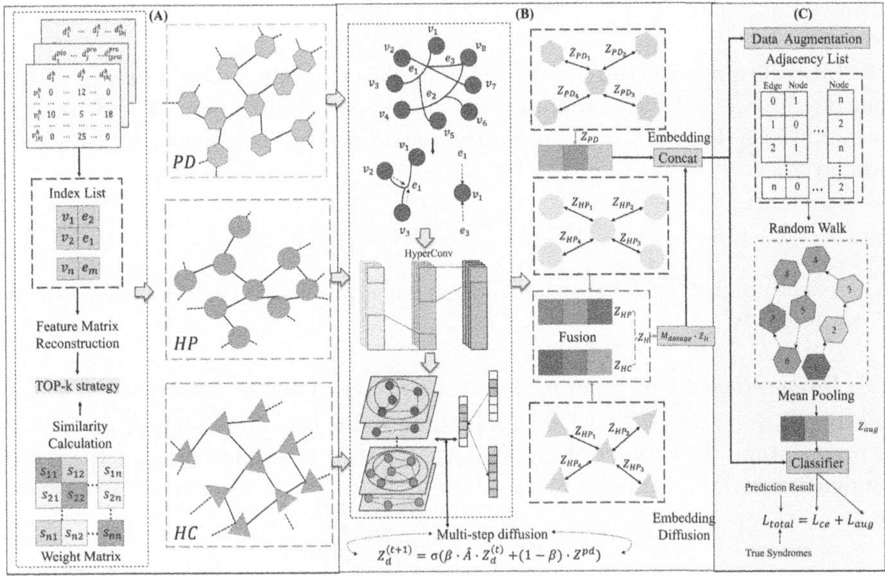

Fig. 2. The architecture of the DMVH-RL model

2.1 Similarity-Driven Hypergraph Reconstruction

We reconstruct three similarity-driven views: a property-based herb view, a co-occurrence-based herb view, and a dosage-based prescription view. The first two views are defined on the sets of herb nodes $V_H = \{v_1^H, v_2^H, \ldots, v_{|H|}^H\}$, while the third one is defined on the set of prescription nodes $V_P = \{v_1^P, v_2^P, \ldots, v_{|P|}^P\}$, where $|H|$ and $|P|$ denote the numbers of herbs and prescriptions, respectively.

For each view, we propose a two-step process: computing similarity matrices from input feature matrices with a flexible selection strategy and reconstructing hyperedges using a Top-K strategy.

(1) Property-Based Herb View (HP): We define a feature matrix $X_{HP} \in \mathbb{R}^{|H|\times|Prop|}$, where $|Prop|$ denotes the number of properties, and each value is set as 1 if the corresponding herb contains the specific property and 0 otherwise. Then, the herb-property similarity matrix $S_{HP}(i,j)$ is recomputed using the Jaccard similarity:

$$S_{HP}(i,j) = \frac{\left|x_i^{HP} \cap x_j^{HP}\right|}{\left|x_i^{HP} \cup x_j^{HP}\right|} \tag{1}$$

where x_i^{HP} and x_j^{HP} denote the property feature vectors of herbs i and j, respectively.

(2) Co-occurrence-Based Herb View (HC): We construct a co-occurrence feature matrix $X_{HC} \in \mathbb{R}^{|H|\times|H|}$, representing the co-occurrence frequency of herbs in prescriptions. The herb-herb similarity matrix is then recomputed by the cosine similarity:

$$S_{HC}(i,j) = \frac{x_i^{HC} \cdot x_j^{HC}}{||x_i^{HC}||_2 \cdot ||x_j^{HC}||_2} \tag{2}$$

where x_i^{HC} and x_j^{HC} denote the co-occurrence frequency vectors of herbs i and j, respectively.

(3) Dosage-Based Prescription View (PD): We define a dosage-based feature matrix $X_{PD} \in \mathbb{R}_{\geq 0}^{|P|\times|H|}$, where each entry indicates the dosage of an herb in a prescription. The prescription similarity is then recomputed using the cosine similarity:

$$S_{PD}(i,j) = \frac{x_i^{PD} \cdot x_j^{PD}}{||x_i^{PD}||_2 \cdot ||x_j^{PD}||_2} \tag{3}$$

where x_i^{PD} and x_j^{PD} denote the normalized herb dosage feature vectors of prescriptions i and j, respectively.

(4) Hyperedge Generation via Top-K Strategy: For each node in each view, we reconstruct hyperedges by selecting its top K most similar nodes according to the corresponding similarity matrix:

$$E_i^{view} = \text{Top-K}(S_i^{view}, k), \quad view \in HP, HC, PD \tag{4}$$

Specifically, each hyperedge connects a node with its k nearest neighbors in the corresponding similarity space. We obtain three hypergraphs: $\mathcal{G}_{HP} = (V_H, \mathcal{I}_{HP}, \mathbf{\Phi}_{HP})$, $\mathcal{G}_{HC} = (V_H, \mathcal{I}_{HC}, \mathbf{\Phi}_{HC})$, and $\mathcal{G}_{PD} = (V_P, \mathcal{I}_{PD}, \mathbf{\Phi}_{PD})$. For each hypergraph, we generate the hyperedge index list $\mathcal{I}_{view}$ and compute the edge weight set $\mathbf{\Phi}_{view}$.

2.2 Hypergraph Diffusion Fusion Network

The previous three hypergraphs are processed using a proposed diffusion-aware strategy. In this process, each hypergraph is represented by its node feature matrix, the corresponding hyperedge index lists ($\mathcal{I}_{HP}$, $\mathcal{I}_{HC}$, $\mathcal{I}_{PD}$), and the edge weight matrices ($\mathbf{\Phi}_{HP}^{(l)}$, $\mathbf{\Phi}_{HC}^{(l)}$, $\mathbf{\Phi}_{PD}^{(l)}$), a fact that incorporates the diffusion information at each layer l. In each hypergraph, the node embeddings at layer l, represented as $\mathbf{Z}_{HP}^{(l)}$, $\mathbf{Z}_{HC}^{(l)}$, and $\mathbf{Z}_{PD}^{(l)}$, are iteratively generated using hypergraph convolutional operations. An activation function σ, such as ReLU, is applied after each convolutional transformation. The hypergraph convolutional operation is defined as follows:

$$\mathbf{Z}_{view}^{(l+1)} = \sigma\left(\mathcal{F}_{hypergraph}(\mathbf{Z}_{view}^{(l)}, \mathcal{I}_{view}, \mathbf{\Phi}_{view}^{(l)})\right) \tag{5}$$

where $view \in \{HP, HC, PD\}$, $\mathcal{F}_{\text{hypergraph}}$ denotes the hypergraph convolution function, and $\mathcal{I}_{view}$ represents the hyperedge index list for the corresponding view.

We perform a multi-step diffusion process on each hypergraph $view \in \{HP, HC, PD\}$. First, the embedding obtained from multi-layer hypergraph convolution, denoted as $\mathbf{Z}_{view}^{\text{conv}}$, is combined with the initial feature matrix $\mathbf{X}_{view}^{(0)}$ through a 1D convolution operation to form the initial state for diffusion:

$$\mathbf{Z}_{view}^{(0)} = \mathbf{Z}_{view}^{\text{conv}} + \text{Conv1D}(\mathbf{X}_{view}^{(0)}). \tag{6}$$

The embeddings are iteratively generated in T steps by aggregating neighboring information via the normalized adjacency matrix $\hat{\mathbf{A}}_{view}$:

$$\mathbf{Z}_{view}^{(t+1)} = \sigma(\beta \hat{\mathbf{A}}_{view} \mathbf{Z}_{view}^{(t)} + (1-\beta)\mathbf{Z}_{view}^{(0)}), \quad t = 0, \ldots, T-1, \tag{7}$$

where σ is an activation function, such as ReLU, and $\beta \in [0, 1]$ is a balance coefficient. The normalized adjacency matrix $\hat{\mathbf{A}}_{view}$ is constructed from the hypergraph incidence matrix $\mathbf{H}_{view}$:

$$(\mathbf{H}_{view})_{ij} = \begin{cases} w_j, & \text{if node } i \in \text{ hyperedge } j, \\ 0, & \text{otherwise,} \end{cases} \qquad \hat{\mathbf{A}}_{view} = \mathbf{D}_{view}^{-\frac{1}{2}} \mathbf{A}_{view} \mathbf{D}_{view}^{-\frac{1}{2}} \tag{8}$$

where w_j denotes the weight of the hyperedge j, and $\mathbf{D}_{view}$ is the diagonal degree matrix derived from $\mathbf{A}_{view} = \mathbf{H}_{view}^{\top}$.

After T diffusion steps, $\mathbf{Z}_{view}^{(T)}$ is regularized using dropout and then passed through a fully connected layer to generate the final embedding.

$$\mathbf{Z}'_{view} = \mathrm{FC}(\mathrm{Dropout}(\mathbf{Z}_{view}^{(T)})). \tag{9}$$

The final embeddings are denoted as $\mathbf{Z}'_{\mathrm{HP}}$, $\mathbf{Z}'_{\mathrm{HC}}$, and $\mathbf{Z}'_{\mathrm{PD}}$, respectively. We propose a dosage-aware embedding fusion strategy to jointly encode herb and prescription embeddings. Specifically, we fuse $\mathbf{Z}'_{\mathrm{HP}}$ and $\mathbf{Z}'_{\mathrm{HC}}$ using a weighted coefficient $\alpha \in [0, 1]$, and then integrate dosage information, formulated as:

$$\mathbf{Z}_{\mathrm{fused}} = \mathbf{Z}'_{\mathrm{PD}} \oplus (\mathbf{M}_{\mathrm{dosage}} \odot [\alpha \cdot \mathbf{Z}'_{\mathrm{HC}} + (1 - \alpha) \cdot \mathbf{Z}'_{\mathrm{HP}}]) \tag{10}$$

where $\mathbf{M}_{\mathrm{dosage}}$ is the dosage weight matrix, $\oplus$ denotes concatenation, and $\odot$ represents element-wise multiplication.

2.3 Hypergraph Diffusion Path Sampling Augmentation

To alleviate data sparsity and enhance the diversity of the training set, we propose a diffusion path sampling strategy on hypergraphs to perform embedding-level data augmentation. Starting from randomly selected seed nodes, paths are generated with the walk lengths $L \sim \mathcal{U}[3, 7]$ through hyperedge connections. The augmented data is generated as follows:

$$\mathbf{Z}_{\mathrm{aug}} = \frac{1}{|\mathcal{P}|} \sum_{j \in \mathcal{P}} \mathbf{Z}_j \tag{11}$$

where $\mathcal{P}$ denotes the node set in the valid path, $|\mathcal{P}|$ represents the path length, and $\mathbf{Z}_j$ represents the embedding of node j along the path.

The overall loss function combines classification loss with data augmentation loss, as shown in Eqs. (12, 13).

$$y_{\mathrm{smooth}}[n] = \begin{cases} 1 - \epsilon, & \text{if } n = \text{true\_class} \\ \frac{\epsilon}{C-1}, & \text{otherwise} \end{cases} \tag{12}$$

$$\mathcal{L}_{\mathrm{total}} = \mathcal{L}_{\mathrm{ce}}(y_{\mathrm{smooth}}, \hat{y}) + \mathcal{L}_{\mathrm{aug}} \tag{13}$$

where y_{smooth} denotes the smoothed label distribution, ϵ is the smoothing coefficient, C represents the number of classes, and n is the class index. $\mathcal{L}_{\mathrm{CE}}$ is the cross-entropy loss as defined in Eq. (14), and $\mathcal{L}_{\mathrm{aug}}$ is the augmentation loss according to Eq. (15).

$$\mathcal{L}_{\mathrm{ce}}(y, \hat{y}) = -\frac{1}{B} \sum_{i=1}^{B} \sum_{c=1}^{C} y_{i,c} \log(\hat{y}_{i,c}) \tag{14}$$

where B represents the batch size, $y_{i,c}$ represents the target label distribution, and $\hat{y}_{i,c}$ is the softmax probability output from the classifier.

$$\mathcal{L}_{\text{aug}} = \frac{1}{|\mathcal{D}_{\text{aug}}|} \sum_{(\mathbf{z}_{\text{aug}}, y_{\text{aug}}) \in \mathcal{D}_{\text{aug}}} \mathcal{L}_{\text{ce}}(y_{\text{aug}}, f(\mathbf{z}_{\text{aug}})) \tag{15}$$

where $\mathcal{L}_{\text{aug}}$ denotes the augmentation loss, $\mathcal{D}_{\text{aug}}$ is the augmented dataset generated through diffusion path sampling strategy, $\mathbf{z}_{\text{aug}}$ is the augmented embedding generated by Eq. (11), y_{aug} is the corresponding truth label, and $f(\cdot)$ represents the classifier function.

3 Experiment

3.1 Experiment Design and Evaluation Metrics

The experiments were conducted on a 16.0 GB RAM, 3.60 GHz Intel (R) Core (TM) $i7-9700$K CPU. We adopt four evaluation metrics: Accuracy, Precision, Recall, and F1-Score to verify the performance of the DMVH-RL. Accuracy is applied to evaluate the overall performance of a classification model. Precision is used to measure the proportion of true positive predictions among all positive predictions made by the model. Recall represents the proportion of actual positive instances that the model correctly identifies out of all true positive samples. The F1-Score combines precision and recall through their harmonic mean, providing a more comprehensive evaluation of the model's performance for imbalanced datasets.

3.2 Dataset

We validated DMVH-RL on datasets from two clinical contexts: chronic atrophic gastritis (CAG) and reflux esophagitis (RE). Both datasets underwent the same preprocessing pipeline, including information extraction, cleaning, and standardiza- tion. Key entities were extracted referring to prescriptions, herbs, dosages, and syndromes. Terminology was standardized according to authoritative references, including Chinese Terms in Traditional Chinese Medicine and Pharmacy (2004)[1]. Herb attributes—namely properties, flavors, and meridian associations—were derived from the Dictionary of Chinese Materia Medica[2].

3.3 Model Comparisons and Analyses

To verify the performance of the DMVH-RL model, we compared it with three representative baselines, namely GCN, GAT, and GraphSAGE, on the CAG and RE datasets. As shown in Figs. 3, 4, we present the experimental results of the DMVH-RL and baselines on four evaluation metrics: Accuracy, Precision, Recall, and F1-Score.

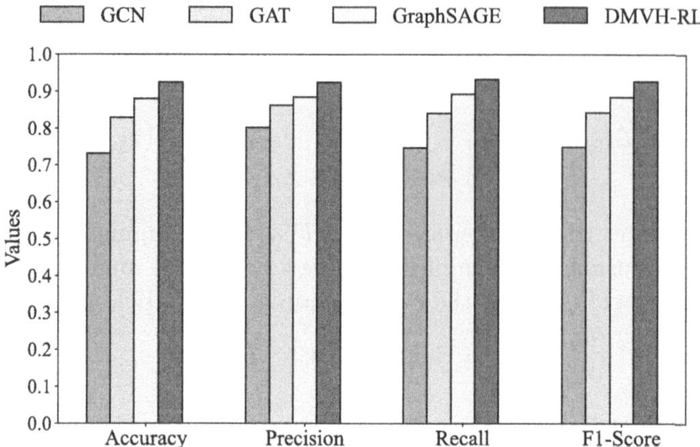

Fig. 3. Comparison of different models on four evaluation metrics using the CAG dataset.

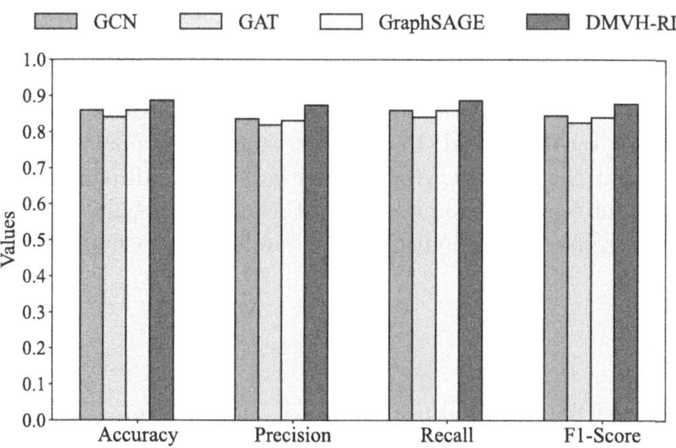

Fig. 4. Comparison of different models on four evaluation metrics using the RE dataset.

On the CAG dataset, DMVH-RL demonstrates superior performance across all evaluation metrics compared to the baseline methods. Specifically, DMVH-RL achieves an accuracy of 0.9244, which represents improvements of 19.33%, 9.53%, and 4.48% over GCN (0.7311), GAT (0.8291), and GraphSAGE (0.8796), respectively. For precision, DMVH-RL obtains 0.9247, outperforming GCN (0.8025), GAT (0.8627), and GraphSAGE (0.8846) by 12.22%, 6.20%, and 4.01%. The recall values show DMVH-RL at 0.9325, surpassing GCN (0.7476), GAT (0.8410), and GraphSAGE (0.8929) by 18.49%, 9.15%, and 3.96%. F1-Score results fur-

[1] Wu, J. (2004). Chinese Terms in Traditional Chinese Medicine and Pharmacy. Beijing: Science Press.

[2] Nanjing University of Chinese Medicine. (2006). Dictionary of Chinese Materia Medica. Shanghai Scientific Technical Publishers.

ther confirm DMVH-RL's effectiveness with a value of 0.9267, exceeding GCN (0.7490), GAT (0.8426), and GraphSAGE (0.8848) by 17.77%, 8.41%, and 4.19%. On the RE dataset, DMVH-RL achieves accuracy, precision, recall, and F1-Score values of 0.8864, 0.8736, 0.8864, and 0.8773, respectively, outperforming GCN (0.8598, 0.8359, 0.8598, 0.8447), GAT (0.8409, 0.8191, 0.8409, 0.8260), and GraphSAGE (0.8598, 0.8308, 0.8598, 0.8401) on all metrics.

3.4 Parameter Sensitivity Tests and Ablation Experiment

Furthermore, to explore the significance of various parameters, we conducted hyperparameter sensitivity tests for DMVH-RL on different learning rates and num_steps using the CAG dataset, and the results are shown in Figs. 5, 6 and Tables 1, 2. The learning rates are set from 0.01 to 0.00001; the numbers of diffusion steps are set from 1 to 7. The results demonstrate that DMVH-RL can achieve the best values of 0.9244, 0.9247, 0.9325, and 0.9267 on Accuracy, Precision, Recall, and F1-Score when the learning rate = 0.001 and the diffusion steps = 3. In addition, it is demonstrated that setting two parameters too large or too small may lead to worse results. Moreover, as shown in Table 3 and Fig. 7, we conducted the ablation experiment to verify the effectiveness of DMVH-RL. Specifically, A denotes the similarity-driven hypergraph reconstruction strategy, B represents the diffusion-aware strategy, and C refers to the hypergraph diffusion path sampling augmentation. Compared with A, DMVH-RL achieves at least a 24.14% improvement; compared with A+C, at least a 21.99% improvement; and compared with A+B, at least a 2.04% improvement. The best performance is achieved when integrating A, B, and C, with the effectiveness ranking being A+B+C, A+B, A+C, B, and C.

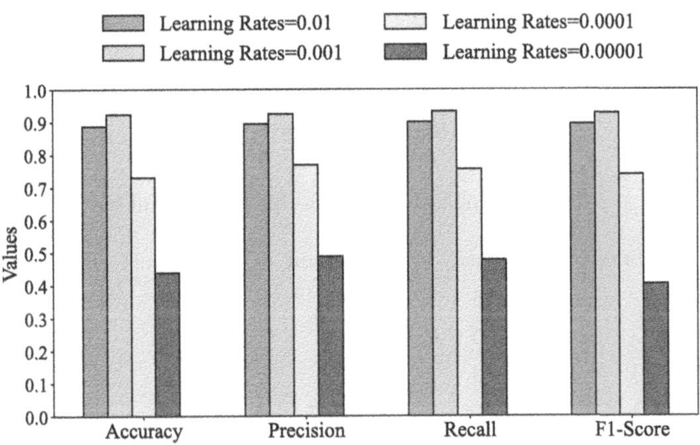

Fig. 5. The comparison plots of different learning rates on four evaluation metrics.

Table 1. Parameter sensitivity test on learning rates.

Learning Rates	Accuracy	Precision	Recall	F1-Score
0.01	0.8880	0.8946	0.9001	0.8943
0.001	**0.9244**	**0.9247**	**0.9325**	**0.9267**
0.0001	0.7311	0.7695	0.7550	0.7397
0.00001	0.4398	0.4887	0.4782	0.4040

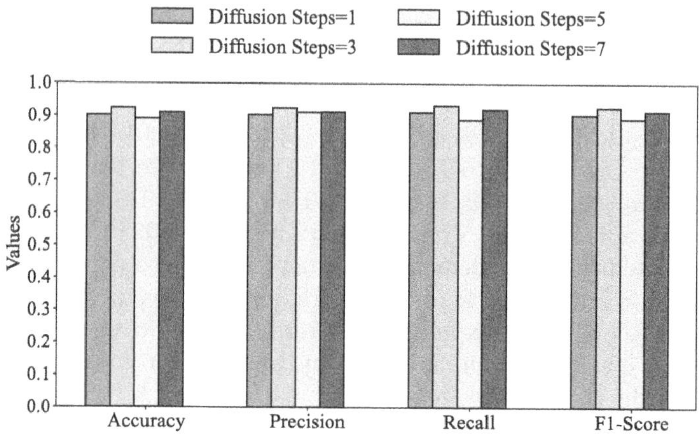

Fig. 6. The comparison plots of different diffusion steps on four evaluation metrics.

Table 2. Parameter sensitivity test on diffusion steps.

Diffusion Steps	Accuracy	Precision	Recall	F1-Score
1	0.9020	0.9030	0.9116	0.9037
3	**0.9244**	**0.9247**	**0.9325**	**0.9267**
5	0.8908	0.9118	0.8883	0.8914
7	0.9104	0.9128	0.9202	0.0.9143

Table 3. Ablation test on different modules.

Modules	Accuracy	Precision	Recall	F1-Score
A	0.6246	0.6833	0.6453	0.6249
A+C	0.6555	0.7048	0.6820	0.6566
A+B	0.9020	0.9037	0.9121	0.9031
A+B+C	**0.9244**	**0.9247**	**0.9325**	**0.9267**

A: similarity-driven hypergraph reconstruction; B: diffusion-aware strategy; C: diffusion path sampling augmentation.

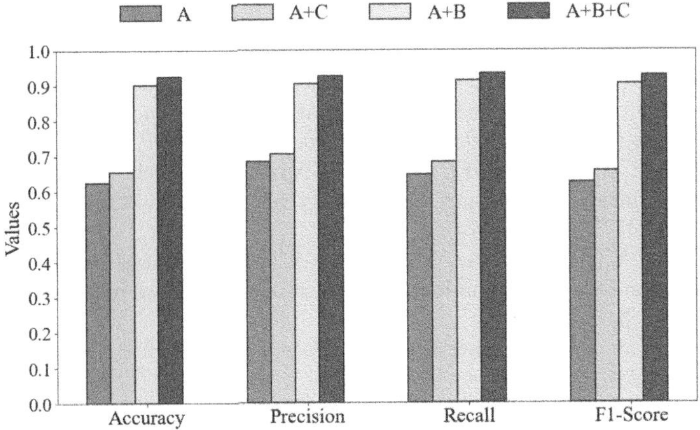

Fig. 7. The comparison plots of different modules on four evaluation metrics.

4 Conclusion

In this study, a diffusion-aware multi-view hypergraph representation learning model (DMVH-RL) is proposed to prompt the applications of intelligent medical robotics in TCM. The model develops a similarity-driven hypergraph reconstruction, hypergraph diffusion fusion network, and hypergraph diffusion path sampling augmentation to support intelligent medical robotics by enabling more accurate and reliable syndrome-based prescription recommendations. The DMVH-RL was verified on a real-world clinical dataset and evaluated on four representative metrics. Compared to baselines, including GCN, GAT, and GraphSAGE, the experimental results show that our model has superior performance. Furthermore, the hyperparameter sensitivity tests demonstrate that DMVH-RL achieves optimal performance when the learning rate = 0.001 and the number of diffusion steps = 3. Future work will focus on improving recommendation accuracy and generalization by exploring novel network architectures and integrating more comprehensive dimensions of TCM knowledge, such as molecular ingredients and their targets.

Acknowledgements. We acknowledge the funding support from the Hubei Provincial International Science and Technology Cooperation Project (2025EHA011) and Hubei Provincial Natural Science Foundation and TCM Innovation and Development Foundation of China (2024AFD267).

Disclosure of Interests. The authors have no competing interests to declare that are relevant to the content of this article.

References

1. Moghani, M., et al.: SuFIA: language-guided augmented dexterity for robotic surgical assistants. In: 2024 IEEE/RSJ International Conference on Intelligent Robots and Systems (IROS), pp. 6969–6976. IEEE (2024)
2. Bi, Y., Jiang, Z., Duelmer, F., Huang, D., Navab, N.: Machine learning in robotic ultrasound imaging: challenges and perspectives. Ann. Rev. Control Robot. Auton. Syst. **7** (2024)
3. Yu, F., Liu, Y., Wu, Z., Tan, M., Yu, J.: Adaptive gait training of a lower limb rehabilitation robot based on human-robot interaction force measurement. Cyborg Bionic Syst. **5**, 0115 (2024)
4. Yip, M., et al.: Artificial intelligence meets medical robotics. Science **381**(6654), 141–146 (2023)
5. Jin, Y., Ji, W., Shi, Y., Wang, X., Yang, X.: Meta-path guided graph attention network for explainable herb recommendation. Health Inf. Sci. Syst. **11**(1), 5 (2023)
6. Iqbal, T., et al.: Towards integration of artificial intelligence into medical devices as a real-time recommender system for personalised healthcare: state-of-the-art and future prospects. Health Sci. Rev. **10**, 100150 (2024)
7. Singh, M., Gupta, S., Bhardwaj, P., Tripathi, R., Mishra, J., Bhardwaj, R.: Integrating artificial intelligence and robotics for advancements in personalized medicine within life science. In: AIP Conference Proceedings. vol. 3254, p. 020009. AIP Publishing LLC (2025)
8. Sun, M., Niu, J., Yang, X., Gu, Y., Zhang, W.: CEHMR: curriculum learning enhanced hierarchical multi-label classification for medication recommendation. Artif. Intell. Med. **143**, 102613 (2023)
9. Huang, T.Y., et al.: Chinese intelligence prescription system improves prescription accuracy while decreasing labor and drug costs. BMC Health Serv. Res. **23**(1), 514 (2023)
10. Li, Y., Yu, D.: Research on intelligent prescription review system based on medical big data. In: Journal of Physics: Conference Series. vol. 1744, p. 042084. IOP Publishing (2021)
11. Wang, L., et al.: Artificial intelligence in clinical decision support systems for oncology. Int. J. Med. Sci. **20**(1), 79 (2023)
12. Nagi, F., Salih, R., Alzubaidi, M., Shah, H., Alam, T., Shah, Z., Househ, M.: Applications of artificial intelligence (AI) in medical education: a scoping review. Healthc. Transformation Inform. Artif. Intell. 648–651 (2023)
13. Sharma, K.: Personalized telemedicine utilizing artificial intelligence, robotics, and internet of medical things (IoMT). In: Handbook of Research on Artificial Intelligence and Soft Computing Techniques in Personalized Healthcare Services, pp. 301–323. Apple Academic Press (2024)
14. Chang, Y.H., et al.: Interactive healthcare robot using attention-based question-answer retrieval and medical entity extraction models. IEEE J. Biomed. Health Inform. **27**(12), 6039–6050 (2023)
15. Yang, Y., Rao, Y., Yu, M., Kang, Y.: Multi-layer information fusion based on graph convolutional network for knowledge-driven herb recommendation. Neural Netw. **146**, 1–10 (2022)
16. Dong, X., et al.: PresRecST: a novel herbal prescription recommendation algorithm for real-world patients with integration of syndrome differentiation and treatment planning. J. Am. Med. Inform. Assoc. **31**(6), 1268–1279 (2024)

17. Zhou, X., et al.: TCM-FTP: fine-tuning large language models for herbal prescription prediction. In: 2024 IEEE International Conference on Bioinformatics and Biomedicine (BIBM), pp. 4092–4097. IEEE (2024)
18. Zheng, X., Wu, H., Jin, H., Li, R.: FMCHS: Advancing traditional Chinese medicine herb recommendation with fusion of multiscale correlations of herbs and symptoms. arXiv preprint arXiv:2503.05167 (2025)
19. Liu, Z., et al.: TCM-KDIF: an information interaction framework driven by knowledge-data and its clinical application in traditional Chinese medicine. IEEE Internet Things J. **11**(11), 20002–20014 (2024)

Smart Insole Plantar Pressure Measurement Based on CNN-BiLSTM-Attention Network for Walking-Aid Robots

Silong Zhang[1,2,3], Hanchen Yao[2,3], Zetian Zhang[2,3], Yitao Li[2,3], Chengwei Huang[2,3], Houde Dai[2,3(✉)], and Gengfeng Zheng[4]

[1] College of Electrical Engineering and Automation, Fuzhou University, Fuzhou 350108, China
[2] Quanzhou Institute of Equipment Manufacturing, Fujian Institute of Research on the Structure of Matter, Chinese Academy of Sciences, Jinjiang 362216, China
dhd@fjirsm.ac.cn
[3] Fujian College, University of Chinese Academy of Sciences, Fuzhou 350002, China
[4] Fujian Key Laboratory of Special Intelligent Equipment Safety Measurement and Control, Fujian Special Equipment Inspection and Research Institute, Fuzhou 350008, China

Abstract. Accurate recognition of pedestrian movement intentions is crucial for walking-aid robots to achieve rapid and safe adaptation during gait rehabilitation. In this study, a hybrid CNN-BiLSTM-Attention network is proposed for predicting patients' multi-class motions with smart insole sensor data. To achieve this challenge, our proposed wearable system integrates 13 pressure sensors and a triaxial IMU within each insole, yielding a total of 48 synchronized channels comprising plantar pressure, acceleration, and angular velocity signals sampled at 50 Hz. This system captures four motion modes: stable walking, left turns, right turns, and emergency stops. Firstly, continuous signals are segmented into overlapping windows with a stride of 10 frames, which serve as input to two parallel 1D convolutional layers for extracting local temporal features. These features are processed into two stacked bidirectional LSTM layers to capture long-range dependencies in both time directions. Next, a multi-head self-attention module dynamically focuses on the most discriminative time steps. Finally, a global average pooling layer and a fully-connected classifier output the patients' intent predictions. Experimental results demonstrate that the proposed method achieved peak accuracy rates of 98.28% on the self-collected dataset and 97.58% in patient testing, significantly outperforming the SVM, 1D-CNN, and 2D-CNN baselines. Thus, it demonstrates robust early detection of turning and emergency stopping intentions. Furthermore, this lightweight and non-invasive method offers a reliable prediction solution for patients' movement intentions and holds significant promise for integration into next-generation rehabilitation robots.

Keywords: Smart insole · Human–robot interaction · Gait intention prediction · CNN–BiLSTM–Attention · Wearable sensors

This work was supported in part by the National Natural Science Foundation of China under Grant 61973293, the Major Science and Technology Project of Fujian Province under Grants 2024HZ025022, thethe Fujian Provincial Natural Science Foundation of China under Grant, under Grant 2025J08137.

Z. Hou et al. (Eds.): CIRAC 2025, CCIS 2885, pp. 188–197, 2026.
https://doi.org/10.1007/978-981-92-0045-0_13

1 Introduction

Assistive walking-aid robots have been developed to support individuals with gait impairments during rehabilitation [1]. A common cane-type robot follows the user at a fixed offset to provide lateral stabilization, a function especially valuable amid caregiver shortages and high supervision costs [2]. However, conventional human-following methods face challenges: vision-based approaches like RGB-D or LiDAR suffer from occlusion and lighting variations [3–5]; RF sensors such as radar and mmWave sensors, while more robust to occlusion, are prone to noise and multipath interference [6, 7]; all of which can impair reliable tracking in cluttered spaces [8].

To overcome this, researchers have turned to wearable sensors that avoid reliance on external line-of-sight. Various implementations have used foot force sensors [9], thigh-mounted IMUs [10], or IMU–laser fusion [11] to detect user movement under diverse conditions. Yet, these systems mostly provide reactive responses and cannot anticipate upcoming gait changes [12].

A promising yet underutilized modality for predictive gait intent is the smart insole. With embedded pressure arrays and IMUs, these devices capture real-time plantar pressure and foot dynamics. Clinically, such signals are key to detecting gait events and abnormalities [13], and recent models have used them to classify locomotion modes with high accuracy [14, 15]. Despite this potential, smart insoles are rarely integrated into robotic control systems.

In this work, we leverage dual-foot smart insole data to predict gait trends—such as turning or stopping—before execution, offering robots a more proactive understanding of user intent beyond camera-based sensing. Recent deep learning methods, especially hybrid CNN–LSTM networks with attention mechanisms, have shown strong performance on time-series sensor data [16]. CNN–BiLSTM–Attention models, in particular, have achieved superior results in various domains [17, 18], including gait phase and activity recognition using wearable sensors [19, 20].

Building on these insights, we propose FootTrendFormer, a CNN–BiLSTM–Attention framework that extracts spatial–temporal features from insole data and focuses on key moments via attention. It enables accurate early prediction of user movement direction, improving robotic responsiveness in rehabilitation contexts.

2 Methodology

2.1 Smart Insole System and Data Collection

In this study, we used a self-developed smart insole system to acquire pedestrian gait data (as shown in Fig. 1). Each insole contained multiple pressure sensors and an inertial measurement unit (IMU), enabling synchronous measurement of plantar pressure and foot motion. The pressure sensors were distributed across key load regions, such as the heel, metatarsal heads, and forefoot. The IMU, consisting of a tri-axial accelerometer and gyroscope, was embedded near the Achilles area to capture linear acceleration and angular velocity. The system offered a compact, flexible design that did not interfere with natural walking. Data from 48 channels (24 per foot) were transmitted wirelessly to a host PC at 50 Hz.

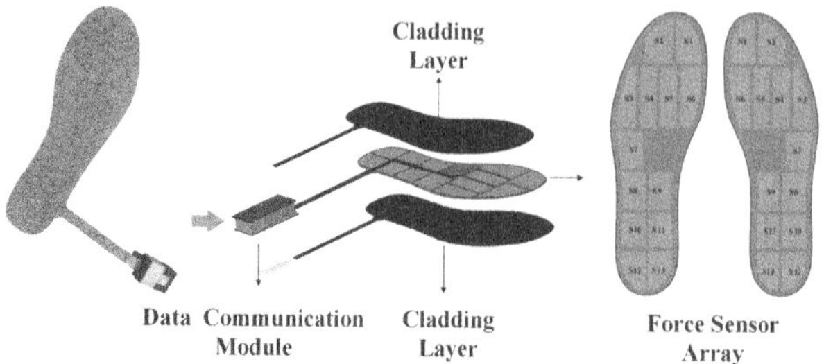

Fig. 1. Self-developed intelligent plantar pressure insole

Twenty healthy male subjects (mean age 25 ± 4 years, height 175 ± 8.4 cm, weight 70 ± 13.2 kg) participated in the experiment after providing informed consent. All tests were conducted on a level indoor walkway. Subjects wore the smart insoles inside their regular shoes and performed four types of movement—straight walking, left turn, right turn, and sudden stop—while using the assistive walking robot shown in Fig. 2. For the first three classes, subjects walked continuously for 10 s along a straight or curved path and repeated each trial 10 times. Sudden stops were randomly triggered by audio cues during normal walking to simulate abrupt halts. Consistent environmental conditions and rest intervals were maintained to minimize fatigue and experimental bias.

The raw multi-channel signals were preprocessed before training. A band-pass filter and moving-average smoothing were used to remove noise and artifacts. All channels were normalized to account for unit differences and inter-subject variability. The time-series data were then segmented into overlapping windows of length 20 frames with a stride of 10 frames, approximating the duration of a half to full step. Each window was labeled based on the movement occurring immediately afterward.

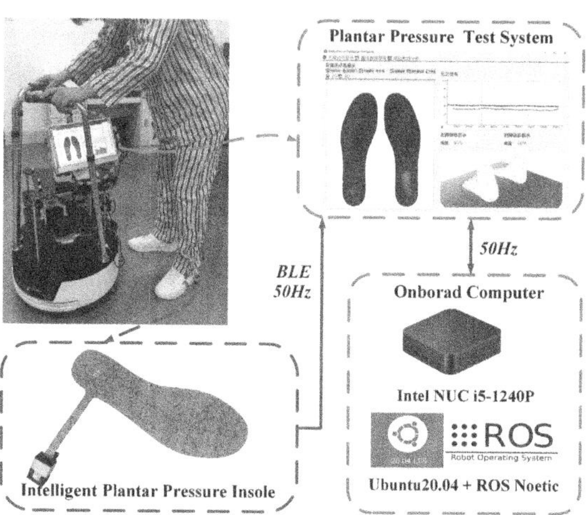

Fig. 2. Walking-assisting robot with intelligent plantar pressure insoles

2.2 Deep Model Architecture

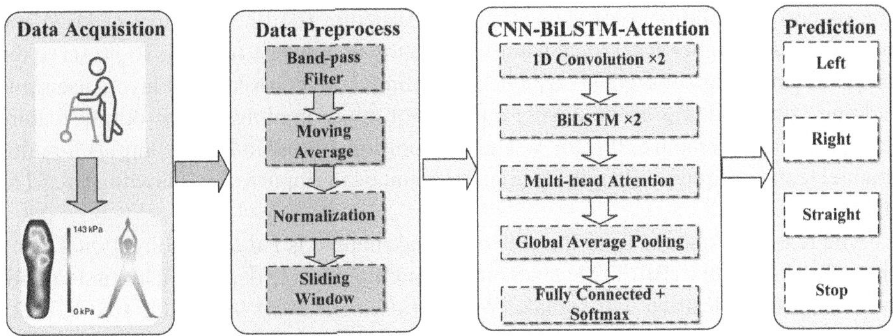

Fig. 3. Architecture of the proposed CNN–BiLSTM–Attention model

To achieve high-precision classification of pedestrian walking trends, we constructed a deep learning model based on a CNN-BiLSTM-Attention architecture. The model input is a multi-channel time-series signal of length 20 frames and dimension 48; the output is a probability distribution over the four movement classes (straight, left turn, right turn, or sudden stop). The overall architecture of the model is illustrated in Fig. 3. The network includes convolutional layers for extracting local temporal features, bidirectional long short-term memory (BiLSTM) layers for capturing long-term dependencies, a self-attention mechanism for focusing on key temporal segments, and a final fully connected layer for classification. Below we detail each component and provide the key mathematical expressions.

First, the multi-channel time-series input is passed through two layers of one-dimensional convolution to extract low-level features. Each convolutional layer comprises 64 one-dimensional filters with kernel size 3, meaning each filter's receptive field covers 3 consecutive time steps. Let the input to the l-th convolutional layer be the activation maps $\boldsymbol{a}^{(l-1)}$ with C_{l-1} channels. For the j-th filter in layer l, its linear convolution response $z_j^{(l)}(t)$ at time step t is computed as:

$$z_j^{(l)}(t) = \sum_{i=1}^{C_{l-1}} \sum_{k=1}^{K} W_{j,i}^{(l)}(k) a_i^{(l-1)}(t+k-1) + b_j^{(l)} \tag{1}$$

where K is the kernel size (here $K = 3$), $W_{j,i}^{(l)}(k)$ denotes the k-th weight of the j-th filter on input channel i, $b_j^{(l)}$ is the bias term, and $a_i^{(l-1)}(t+k-1)$ is the activation of channel i at time $t+k-1$ from the previous layer. This convolution operation performs a linear weighted sum over local windows of the input sequence, mining local pattern features. Then, a nonlinear activation is applied to the convolution output. In this model, each convolutional layer is followed by a Rectified Linear Unit (ReLU) activation:

$$a_j^{(l)}(t) = \max\{0, z_j^{(l)}(t)\} \tag{2}$$

where $\max\{0, z_j^{(l)}(t)\}$ denotes the element-wise ReLU that sets negative values to zero and retains positives unchanged. After convolution and ReLU, the model can extract key local gradient features within each time window and suppress non-salient patterns. The second convolutional layer has the same structure (64 filters of size $K = 3$) and further extracts higher-level local patterns from the first layer's outputs. To preserve the temporal length for subsequent sequence modeling, both convolutional layers use same padding (zero-padding at the edges) and do not apply pooling, so the output feature sequence length remains 20 frames. The convolutional module finally outputs a multi-channel feature sequence (length 20, channel count 64) as input to the following BiLSTM layers.

The feature sequence from the convolutional module is fed into Bidirectional Long Short-Term Memory (BiLSTM) layers to capture long-range dependencies and temporal context of pedestrian gait signals. We stack two BiLSTM layers: the first has 128 hidden units, and the second has 64 hidden units. Each BiLSTM consists of two LSTM sub-networks that process the sequence in forward and backward time directions, respectively, and then fuse their outputs at each time step. To explain, we first present the LSTM cell computations and then describe BiLSTM output fusion.

LSTM cell computations: An LSTM cell employs gating mechanisms to selectively remember or forget information over time, mitigating the vanishing gradient problem in vanilla RNNs. Given input x_t, previous hidden state $\boldsymbol{h}_{\mathbf{t-1}}$, and previous cell state $\boldsymbol{c}_{t-1}$, the LSTM updates at time t are:

$$\begin{cases} \mathrm{it} = \sigma(W_i\mathbf{x}_t + U_i\mathbf{h}_{t-1} + b_i) \\ ft = \sigma\left(W_f\mathbf{x}_t + U_f\mathbf{h}_{t-1} + b_f\right) \\ \mathrm{ot} = \sigma(W_o\mathbf{x}_t + U_o\mathbf{h}_{t-1} + b_o) \\ gt = \tanh\left(W_g\mathbf{x}_t + U_g\mathbf{h}_{t-1} + b_g\right) \\ \mathrm{C} = \mathbf{f}_t \odot \mathbf{c}_{t-1} + \mathbf{i}_t \odot \mathbf{g}_t \\ h_t = \mathbf{o}_t \odot \tanh(\mathbf{c}_t) \end{cases} \tag{3}$$

where $\sigma(\cdot)$ is the sigmoid activation, $\tanh(\cdot)$ is the hyperbolic tangent, W_* and U_* are weight matrices, b_* are biases, and $\odot$ denotes element-wise multiplication. These equations compute the input gate $\mathbf{i}_t$, forget gate$\boldsymbol{f}_t$, output gate $\boldsymbol{o}_t$, candidate cell $\boldsymbol{g}_t$, new cell state $\boldsymbol{c}_t$, and new hidden state $\boldsymbol{h}_t$.

BiLSTM output fusion: A BiLSTM processes the input sequence in both forward (from $t = 1$ to T) and backward (from $t = T$ to 1) directions, producing forward hidden states $\vec{\boldsymbol{h}}_1, \ldots \vec{\boldsymbol{h}}_T$ and backward hidden states $\overleftarrow{\boldsymbol{h}}_1, \ldots \overleftarrow{\boldsymbol{h}}_T$. At each time step t, these are fused into the BiLSTM output

$$\mathbf{h}_t^{(\mathrm{bi})} = \left[\vec{\mathbf{h}}_t \| \vec{\mathbf{h}}_t\right] \tag{4}$$

where $\|$ denotes vector concatenation. Since the first BiLSTM uses 128 units per direction, its output $\mathbf{h}_t^{(\mathrm{bi})}$ has dimension 256. The second BiLSTM layer takes the first layer's outputs as input and, with 64 units per direction, produces outputs of dimension 128 per time step. Both BiLSTM layers are configured with 'OutputMode = "sequence", so the full sequence of hidden states is retained for the attention mechanism.

Although BiLSTM extracts bidirectional features, different time steps may contribute unequally to the final prediction. To enable the model to attend automatically to key segments, we add a self-attention mechanism above the BiLSTM layers. We employ multi-head scaled dot-product self-attention to weight the BiLSTM output sequence. Let the second BiLSTM's output be $\mathbf{H} \in \mathbb{R}^{T\times d}$, with $T = 20$ and $d = 128$. We first project $\mathbf{H}$ into queries, keys, and values:

$$\mathbf{Q} = \mathbf{H}W^{Q}, \quad \mathbf{K} = \mathbf{H}W^{K}, \quad \mathbf{V} = \mathbf{H}W^{V} \tag{5}$$

where $W^{Q}, W^{K}, W^{V} \in \mathbb{R}^{d\times d}$. Single-head scaled dot-product attention is then

$$\mathrm{Attention}(\mathbf{Q}, \mathbf{K}, \mathbf{V}) = \mathrm{softmax}\left(\frac{\mathbf{Q}\mathbf{K}^{\top}}{\sqrt{d}}\right)\mathbf{V} \tag{6}$$

where softmax is applied row-wise. For multi-head attention with $h = 4$ heads:

$$\begin{cases} \mathrm{head}_i = \mathrm{Attention}(\mathbf{H}W_i^{Q}, \mathbf{H}W_i^{K}, \mathbf{H}W_i^{V}), \quad i = 1, \ldots, 4 \\ \mathbf{H}' = [\mathrm{head}_1 \| \mathrm{head}_2 \| \cdots \| \mathrm{head}_4]W^{O} \end{cases} \tag{7}$$

where $W^{O} \in \mathbb{R}^{(h,d)\times d}$. The output $\boldsymbol{H'} \in \mathbb{R}^{T\times d}$ is the attention-enhanced sequence.

The attention-enhanced sequence is globally pooled to produce a fixed-length feature vector. A fully connected layer with 4 outputs then computes:

$$\mathbf{z} = W^{(o)}\mathbf{u} + \mathbf{b}^{(o)}, \hat{y}_j = \frac{\exp(z_j)}{\sum_{k=1}^{4} \exp(z_k)}, \quad j = 1, \ldots, 4 \tag{8}$$

where $W^{(o)} \in \mathbb{R}^{4\times d}$ and $\boldsymbol{b}^{(o)} \in \mathbb{R}^{4}$. The class with highest is chosen.

3 Experiments and Analysis

We evaluated our CNN–BiLSTM–Attention model's ability to predict four movement intentions using two complementary validation schemes, reporting overall accuracy as our sole performance metric.

First, in the 10 fold cross validation (10 Fold CV) experiment, all 4,176 labeled sensor window samples were divided into 10 stratified folds—each fold preserving the relative proportions of Straight, Left, Right, and Stop movements as well as the distribution of subjects. In each of the 10 iterations, the model was trained on nine folds and tested on the remaining one, so that every window served exactly once as a held out sample. As summarized in Fig. 4, the confusion matrix exhibits a strong diagonal dominance: the model attained an overall accuracy of 98.3%. Notably, all Stop and Straight windows were correctly classified across all folds, while only 33 Left → Right and 39 Right → Left misclassifications occurred in total. This pattern highlights the architecture's exceptional capacity to distinguish sustained walking versus abrupt halts, with only minimal error in telling opposite turns apart.

Table 1. Performance comparison for the detection in four directions.

Model	**CNN–BiLSTM–Attention**	CNN–BiLSTM	CNN–LSTM	BiLSTM–Attention	BiLSTM	SVM	CNN (2-D)	CNN (1-D)
Accuracy(%)	**98.28**	97.13	96.02	97.24	95.71	90.92	91.98	91.79

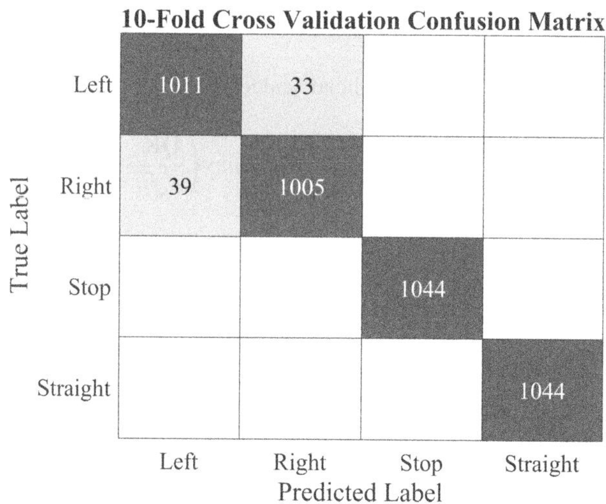

Fig. 4. Confusion matrix of the CNN-BiLSTM-Attention prediction model obtained through 10-fold cross validation

To compare the predictive performance of our model with seven other approaches, we implemented and evaluated: CNN–BiLSTM [21], combining convolution with bidirectional LSTM; CNN–LSTM [22], combining convolution with a unidirectional LSTM; BiLSTM–Attention [23], combining bidirectional LSTM with attention; pure BiLSTM [24]; support vector machine (SVM) [25], which relies on maximum-margin classification; 2-D CNN [26], treating channel–time data as grayscale images; and 1-D CNN [27], applying convolution along the temporal axis. The results (Table 1) show that our proposed CNN–BiLSTM–Attention model achieved the highest accuracy of 98.28%—here, the convolutional layers extract local temporal patterns in parallel via multiple filters, the BiLSTM captures forward and backward dependencies, and the attention module dynamically focuses on the most discriminative key frames, enhancing sensitivity to subtle motion changes. In comparison, CNN–BiLSTM, lacking the attention mechanism, still balances local and global features but drops to 97.13%; CNN–LSTM, with a unidirectional LSTM that only leverages past information, achieves 96.02%; BiLSTM–Attention, despite omitting convolutional extraction, reaches 97.24% by emphasizing key moments; pure BiLSTM, unable to fully mine local patterns, attains 95.71%; SVM, with limited linear separation in high-dimensional spaces, achieves only 90.92%; 2-D CNN, performing joint channel–time convolution, reaches 91.98%; and 1-D CNN, which efficiently extracts local temporal features but lacks cross-channel correlation, achieves 91.79%. This analysis demonstrates that the integrated CNN–BiLSTM–Attention model can more comprehensively extract and focus on both local and global features of temporal signals, thereby achieving optimal performance in multi-class gait recognition tasks.

To further probe generalization to completely unseen individuals, we conducted leave one subject out (LOSO) validation. Here, each participant's full set of windows was held out once as the test set, while the model was trained—and its hyperparameters tuned—exclusively on the data from the remaining subjects. Repeating this process for every subject yields a rigorous measure of how well the model can adapt to novel gait patterns. As shown in Table 2, the model achieved consistently high detection in four directions accuracy across all 20 participants, with most individual accuracies exceeding 95%, and an overall accuracy of 97.58%. This further underscores the model's ability to generalize across subjects with different gait characteristics.

Table 2. Result of leave one subject out experiment.

Detection Accuracy for Four Directions Across 20 Participants											Overall
Accuracy	100.00	98.09	99.52	100.00	92.82	92.82	98.09	97.61	99.04	96.65	**97.58**
(%)	98.56	91.39	93.78	99.52	99.04	99.52	100.00	95.67	100.00	99.52	

The aggregate confusion matrix for LOSO, shown in Fig. 5, again demonstrates a near perfect diagonal: the model achieved 97.58% accuracy. As in the 10 Fold CV, Stop and Straight classifications remained flawless, with only 44 Left → Right and 57 Right → Left errors observed.

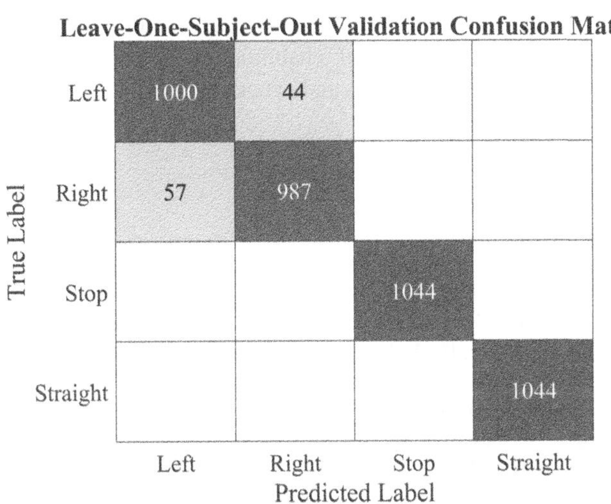

Fig. 5. Confusion matrix of the CNN-BiLSTM-Attention prediction model obtained through leave-one-subject-out experiment

Together, these two validation schemes confirm that our attention-enhanced hybrid CNN–BiLSTM architecture delivers both high overall accuracy and robust generalization. The near-zero confusion for Stop and Straight behaviors underlines the model's sensitivity to abrupt halts and steady walking, while the small number of left–right turn errors reflects only a modest overlap in their temporal signatures. These results suggest that our model offers a promising approach for real-time movement intention prediction, with strong generalization across both randomized folds and unseen individuals.

4 Conclusion

This paper proposes a CNN-BiLSTM-Attention plantar pressure measurement model for movement trend predictions by using wearable insole sensors. Moreover, the proposed CNN-BiLSTM-Attention architecture effectively extracts local sensor features, captures long-term temporal dependencies in gait sequences, and highlights critical moments through its attention mechanism. Consequently, experimental results show high classification accuracy and strong precision/recall for all four movement trends, including straight-line walking, left/right turning, and stopping actions. These results validate the effectiveness of the insole-based approach for early prediction of movement trend predictions.

The proposed prediction method holds particular relevance for rehabilitation robots. By integrating our method, the walking-aid robot can anticipate the patient's intended actions in advance. This enables the robot to adjust its path and dynamics proactively in harmony with the patient's movements. For instance, the robot could smoothly slow down when it detects that patients are going to stop, thereby preventing falls or collisions. In conclusion, the proposed method provides an effective and lightweight solution for enhancing human-robot interaction in gait rehabilitation. Future work focuses on evaluating the robot system with more patients and extending the model to predict additional gait patterns.

References

1. Tao, C., Yan, Q., Li, Y.: Hierarchical shared control of cane-type walking-aid robot. J. Healthc. Eng. **2017**(1), 8932938 (2017)
2. Yan, Q., Huang, J., Yang, Z., et al.: Human-following control of cane-type walking-aid robot within fixed relative posture. IEEE/ASME Trans. Mechatron. **27**(1), 537–548 (2021)
3. Liu, H., Wu, F., Zhong, B., et al.: Close-range human following control on a cane-type robot with multi-camera fusion. IEEE Rob. Autom. Lett. **8**(10), 6443–6450 (2023)
4. Islam, M.J., Hong, J., Sattar, J.: Person-following by autonomous robots: a categorical overview. Int. J. Rob. Res. **38**(14), 1581–1618 (2019)
5. Algabri, R., Choi, M.T.: Deep-learning-based indoor human following of mobile robot using color feature. Sensors **20**(9), 2699 (2020)
6. Cui, H., Dahnoun, N.: High precision human detection and tracking using millimeter-wave radars. IEEE Aerosp. Electron. Syst. Mag. **36**(1), 22–32 (2021)
7. Elsanhoury, M., Mäkelä, P., Koljonen, J., et al.: Precision positioning for smart logistics using ultra-wideband technology-based indoor navigation: a review. IEEE Access **10**, 44413–44445 (2022)

8. Conte, D., Furukawa, T.: Autonomous Bayesian escorting of a human integrating intention and obstacle avoidance. J. Field Rob. **39**(6), 679–693 (2022)
9. Wakita, K., Huang, J., Di, P., et al.: Human-walking-intention-based motion control of an omnidirectional-type cane robot. IEEE/ASME Trans. Mechatron. **18**(1), 285–296 (2011)
10. Trujillo-León, A., Ady, R., Reversat, D., et al.: Robotic cane controlled to adapt automatically to its user gait characteristics. Front. Rob. AI **7**, 105 (2020)
11. Cifuentes, C.A., Frizera, A., Carelli, R., et al.: Human–robot interaction based on wearable IMU sensor and laser range finder. Robot. Auton. Syst. **62**(10), 1425–1439 (2014)
12. Nikdel, P., Shrestha, R., Vaughan, R.: The hands-free push-cart: autonomous following in front by predicting user trajectory around obstacles. In: 2018 IEEE International Conference on Robotics and Automation (ICRA), pp. 4548–4554. IEEE (2018)
13. Chatzaki, C., Skaramagkas, V., Tachos, N., et al.: The smart-insole dataset: gait analysis using wearable sensors with a focus on elderly and Parkinson's patients. Sensors **21**(8), 2821 (2021)
14. Wang, Q., Guan, H., Wang, C., et al.: A wireless, self-powered smart insole for gait monitoring and recognition via nonlinear synergistic pressure sensing. Sci. Adv. **11**(16), eadu1598 (2025)
15. D'arco, L., Mccalmont, G., Wang, H., et al.: Application of smart insoles for recognition of activities of daily living: a systematic review. ACM Trans. Comput. Healthc. **5**(1), 1–34 (2024)
16. Liu, K., Liu, Y., Ji, S., et al.: A novel gait phase recognition method based on DPF-LSTM-CNN using wearable inertial sensors. Sensors **23**(13), 5905 (2023)
17. Ma, Z., Sun, Y., Ji, H., et al.: A CNN-BiLSTM-attention approach for EHA degradation prediction based on time-series generative adversarial network. Mech. Syst. Signal Process. **215**, 111443 (2024)
18. Wei, Z., Shaohua, J., Gang, B., et al.: A method for sound speed profile prediction based on CNN-BiLSTM-attention network. J. Mar. Sci. Eng. **12**(3), 414 (2024)
19. Deng, J., Zhang, S., Ma, J.: Self-attention-based deep convolution lstm framework for sensor-based badminton activity recognition. Sensors **23**(20), 8373 (2023)
20. Park, B., Kim, M., Jung, D., et al.: Smart insole-based abnormal gait identification: deep sequential networks and feature ablation study. Digit. Health **11**, 20552076251333000 (2025)
21. Wang, H., Wang, J., Cao, L., et al.: A stock closing price prediction model based on CNN-BiSLSTM. Complexity **2021**(1), 5360828 (2021)
22. Adefemi, K.O., Mutanga, M.B.: A robust hybrid CNN–LSTM model for predicting student academic performance. Digital **5**(2), 16 (2025)
23. Natha, S., Ahmed, F., Siraj, M., et al.: Deep BiLSTM attention model for spatial and temporal anomaly detection in video surveillance. Sensors **25**(1), 251 (2025)
24. Schuster, M., Paliwal, K.K.: Bidirectional recurrent neural networks. IEEE Trans. Signal Process. **45**(11), 2673–2681 (1997)
25. Cortes, C., Vapnik, V.: Support-vector networks. Mach. Learn. **20**, 273–297 (1995)
26. LeCun, Y., Bottou, L., Bengio, Y., et al.: Gradient-based learning applied to document recognition. Proc. IEEE **86**(11), 2278–2324 (2002)
27. Ince, T., Kiranyaz, S., Eren, L., et al.: Real-time motor fault detection by 1-D convolutional neural networks. IEEE Trans. Industr. Electron. **63**(11), 7067–7075 (2016)

Robotic Radar Perception

CFFANet: A Frequency-Enhanced and Context-Aware Network for Robust Robot Perception Using mmWave Radar

Xiao Han[1], Jiajia Shi[1](✉), Liu Chu[2], and Quan Shi[1]

[1] School of Transportation and Civil Engineering, Nantong University, Nantong 226019, China
shijj@ntu.edu.cn

[2] School of Physical Science and Technology, ShanghaiTech University, Shanghai 201210, China

Abstract. Robust perception under complex interference is vital for embodied intelligence and autonomous robotics. Millimeter-wave (mmWave) radar, with its strong penetration and all-weather capability, has emerged as a key sensor for robotic environmental awareness. However, incoherent interference and electromagnetic clutter severely degrade its time–frequency representations, impeding reliable target perception. To address this, we propose a Context-aware Frequency–Feature Attention Network (CFFANet), tailored for robot-centric radar interference suppression. First, a hybrid denoising pipeline combining sparse decomposition and multiscale wavelet fusion is developed to purify training labels and preserve signal structures. Second, a label-efficient training strategy is introduced, using clean target signals as supervision, thus enhancing generalization without interference annotations. Finally, we design CFFANet, a deep neural architecture integrating spatial–frequency joint modeling, frequency-aware attention, and dynamic residual reconstruction to achieve precise target recovery. Experiments on real millimeter-wave radar datasets validate that our method outperforms other algorithms in terms of interference mitigation and signal fidelity, providing a solid foundation for intelligent robot perception in real-world environments.

Keywords: Robot Perception · Millimeter-wave Radar · Interference Suppression · Deep Learning

1 Introduction

Driven by the rapid advancement of intelligent robotics, there is a growing demand for robots to achieve precise perception, comprehensive environmental understanding, and autonomous decision-making in complex and dynamic environments [1]. As a critical sensing component of embodied intelligent systems, millimeter-wave radar is increasingly replacing traditional sensors in mission-critical scenarios due to its all-weather capability, strong penetration, and robustness against occlusions [2]. At present, mmWave radar has been widely integrated into various robotic platforms, including autonomous driving systems, inspection robots, aerial and underwater mobile robots,

Z. Hou et al. (Eds.): CIRAC 2025, CCIS 2885, pp. 201–221, 2026.
https://doi.org/10.1007/978-981-92-0045-0_14

disaster rescue robots, and intelligent service robots. In these diverse task environments, visual and LiDAR-based perception systems often suffer from limitations caused by occlusion, lighting, and adverse weather conditions. In contrast, mmWave radar maintains stable performance in low-visibility scenarios such as rain, fog, and dust [3], continuously providing reliable distance and velocity measurements. This ensures consistent and robust environmental perception throughout the robot's operational cycle. Therefore, mmWave radar is not only a fundamental technology enabling multi-modal heterogeneous sensor fusion but also a core component that enhances robotic adaptability and intelligent decision-making in uncertain environments.

However, operating in open frequency bands, mmWave radar is particularly vulnerable to non-coherent interference from other radar systems or environmental reflections. This often leads to severe artifacts and noise in time–frequency representations [4], degrading performance in downstream tasks such as target detection, tracking, and recognition. Such interference severely compromises the clarity and structural integrity of the spectrograms, hindering the robot's ability to understand its surroundings, particularly in autonomous navigation and target identification. Therefore, for robotic applications, the development of highly robust, low-latency, and generalizable radar interference suppression techniques is essential to improving perceptual accuracy and system stability.

Although existing interference suppression and denoising methods have achieved promising results in specific contexts, they remain inadequate for the complex, dynamic environments faced by mobile robots. On one hand, traditional denoising algorithms lack flexibility when handling non-stationary radar signals, failing to adapt to local variations and multi-scale structures. On the other hand, most supervised learning methods rely heavily on interference-labeled samples, which are often scarce and unpredictable, limiting the effectiveness and generalization of trained models. Furthermore, many current approaches insufficiently model the frequency structure and interference characteristics of radar signals, leading to suboptimal target reconstruction accuracy.

To overcome these challenges, we propose a novel interference suppression framework tailored to robotic environmental perception, featuring the following innovations:

- We develop a denoising algorithm based on sparse decomposition and multi-scale wavelet fusion, leveraging the structural continuity of target signals and the sparsity of interference in the time–frequency domain. This enhances noise removal while preserving fine-grained details, significantly improving radar data quality and providing reliable supervision for model training.
- We introduce a supervision framework that uses clean target signals as learning labels, avoiding the need for explicit interference modeling or labeling. This approach alleviates the challenge of interference data scarcity and enhances model generalization and training feasibility.
- We propose a new network architecture—Context-aware Frequency–Feature Attention Network (CFFANet)—designed for robotic interference suppression. By combining spatial–frequency joint modeling, frequency-aware attention, and dynamic

residual reconstruction, the network effectively captures multi-scale signal features, achieves high-fidelity reconstruction of target reflections, and robustly suppresses non-stationary interference, thereby enhancing radar perception robustness in complex robotic environments.

2 Related Work

In recent years, with the growing application of millimeter-wave radar in complex environments, a variety of interference suppression techniques have been proposed to address its unique interference characteristics. Among them, signal-processing-based approaches have gained traction due to their ability to mitigate interference without increasing hardware complexity. These methods mainly include filtering, interference cancellation and reconstruction, signal separation, and deep learning techniques. Filtering-based methods are effective against stationary interference but often rely on reference signals that are difficult to obtain in real-world scenarios, leading to instability in suppression performance. Interference cancellation and reconstruction approaches can recover parts of the undistorted signal, but they heavily depend on accurate interference localization and risk mistakenly removing target components. Signal separation methods eliminate the need for explicit interference detection by exploiting differences in time- or frequency-domain characteristics between target and interference, but they tend to suffer from high computational cost and limited real-time capability. In contrast, deep learning–based methods learn to differentiate between target reflections and interference patterns directly from data by constructing training datasets and designing neural architectures. Without relying on predefined signal models, they offer greater adaptability to dynamic and multi-source interference scenarios.

Filtering methods remain a classical strategy for suppressing relatively stable or slowly varying interference by designing filters in time, frequency, or spatial domains. In the time domain, Jin et al. [5] introduced a half-spectrum separation method combined with least mean squares filtering, while Wang et al. [6] developed a dual recursive least squares architecture for better adaptation under dynamic interference. In the frequency domain, Wagner et al. [7] proposed nonlinear filtering to preserve signal phase while reducing dependence on thresholding. Spatial filtering, benefiting from MIMO radar's spatial diversity, enhances interference localization and suppression via beamforming and sparse reconstruction. For instance, Xia et al. [8] employed MUSIC-based bistatic localization, while Chen et al. [9] and Hu et al. [10] improved the reconstruction efficiency of beat signals and their multi-domain sparse recovery. Bechter et al. [11], Yang et al. [12], and Nnamani et al. [13] expanded multi-angle interference handling through digital beamforming, compressive sensing, and cooperative beam control, while Wu et al. [14] and Liu et al. [15] integrated subspace projection and adaptive main-lobe optimization to enhance robustness in complex scenarios. Although efficient and easy to implement, filtering methods struggle to adapt to non-stationary or fast-changing interference due to reliance on static thresholds and fixed models.

Interference cancellation and reconstruction techniques aim to detect interference regions, isolate interference components, and reconstruct complete signals, offering effective suppression of short-term or localized burst interference. For noise detection, Jin et al. [5] utilized spectral symmetry, Lee et al. [16] applied wavelet-based threshold decomposition, and Rock et al. [17] employed convolutional neural networks to automatically detect intermediate frequency noise. In interference detection, Okuda et al. [18] and Umehira et al. [19] proposed iterative suppression strategies based on adaptive thresholding, Dubey et al. [20] used autoencoders for end-to-end detection, Wang et al. [6] employed histogram analysis for rapid localization, and Yang et al. [12] introduced iterative target removal to enhance weak interference visibility. For signal reconstruction, Lee et al. [16] applied wavelet techniques, while Rameez et al. [21] and Li et al. [22] combined AR prediction with mode decomposition. Wang et al. [23] applied atomic norm minimization, Torres et al. [24] adopted phase compensation strategies, and Zhang et al. [25] proposed dual-domain sparse optimization. These methods offer high reconstruction accuracy and work well when interference is sparse and well-characterized, but are sensitive to interference detection accuracy and computational overhead, making them less suitable for large-scale deployment in complex environments.

Signal separation methods leverage sparsity differences between interference and targets across domains to avoid pulse-wise detection, often using transform-based decomposition and sparse optimization. Representative techniques include EMD [15], IMT-EMD [26], and variational mode decomposition (VMD) methods [22, 27], which effectively extract modal characteristics. Doppler and beat-frequency-based separation was explored by Lee et al. [28] and López-Valcárcel et al. [29]. Morphological component analysis (MCA) combined with tunable Q-factor wavelet transforms (TQWT) was adopted by Uysal et al. [30] and Xu et al. [31] to decompose signal components. Further improvements include double-layer L_1 optimization [32] and row-sparse regularization frameworks [33]. These methods are effective in separating non-stationary interference but are generally computation-intensive and sensitive to off-grid mismatches, limiting their real-time applicability in robotic systems.

Deep learning approaches have shown superior capacity in modeling high-dimensional nonlinear features, breaking through the limitations of traditional signal models and enabling automatic extraction of interference–target differences through end-to-end training. Liu et al. [34] employed LSTM to optimize spectrum allocation based on past observations, facilitating dynamic interference avoidance. Wang et al. [35] proposed complex-valued CNNs (CV-CNNs) to preserve phase relationships and improve post-processing performance. Dubey et al. [20] integrated interference mitigation and target detection in a single-stage pipeline to enhance robustness. For model optimization, Rock et al. [17] analyzed quantization strategies in small CNNs; Chen et al. [36] introduced a detect–reconstruct dual-network to repair corrupted samples and reduce annotation costs; Flandermeyer et al. [37] developed a recurrent attention mechanism for adaptive waveform selection in cognitive radar; Zhang et al. [38] proposed an unsupervised adaptive suppression network optimized via frequency-domain priors; and Chen et al. [39] and Wang et al. [40] employed multi-channel and dilated convolutional structures to enhance feature discrimination. Despite excellent generalization and adaptability, these methods often require large datasets and complex training pipelines, posing challenges in data acquisition, real-time processing, and lightweight deployment.

3 Data Preprocessing

In the training of millimeter-wave radar interference suppression models, high-quality training labels play a crucial role in determining model performance. However, real-world radar measurements inevitably contain noise and weak interference components. Directly using the original time–frequency maps as labels can mislead the model to learn incorrect signal features. Therefore, this section designs a comprehensive data preprocessing pipeline based on the physical and noise characteristics of mmWave radar signals, aiming to extract the true structure of target signals through principled denoising algorithms and generate clean, high-confidence supervision data.

3.1 Time–Frequency Representation Generation

Millimeter-wave radar typically adopts Frequency-Modulated Continuous Wave (FMCW) modulation, and its demodulated and sampled echo signals exhibit instantaneous frequency variations that reflect target motion. To extract both temporal and frequency domain behaviors of targets, Short-Time Fourier Transform (STFT) is commonly applied for time–frequency analysis.

Given the 1D radar signal $S(t)$, it is segmented into multiple windows, and the STFT on each window is computed as:

$$S(t,f) = \int_{-\infty}^{+\infty} s(\tau) \cdot \omega(\tau - t) \cdot e^{-j2\pi f\tau} d\tau \tag{1}$$

where $\omega(\tau - t)$ is the analysis window function, balancing time–frequency resolution; f denotes the instantaneous frequency capturing Doppler effects; and $S(t,f)$ is the complex-valued time–frequency matrix, with $|S(t,f)|$ representing the signal energy distribution over time and frequency.

The resulting spectrogram reflects the energy concentration patterns of target echoes in both time and frequency. Target reflections typically appear as continuous, high-intensity streaks, while background noise is more scattered and diffuse.

3.2 Global Noise Suppression via Sparse Decomposition

Target signals in mmWave radar exhibit spatially localized, sparse structures in the time–frequency domain, while noise tends to be broadly distributed, low in energy, and unstructured. Based on sparse modeling theory, global denoising is achieved by decomposing the signal into a sparse representation.

Assuming the spectrogram $S(t,f)$ can be represented on a sparse dictionary Φ, we have:

$$S(t,f) = \Phi \cdot \alpha + N(t,f) \tag{2}$$

where $\Phi \epsilon R^{M \times N}$ is a predefined or learned dictionary, α is the sparse coefficient vector, and $N(t,f)$ is the additive noise.

The sparse decomposition is formulated as the following optimization problem:

$$\min_{\alpha}\|\alpha\|_1 + \frac{\lambda}{2}\|S(t,f) - \Phi \cdot \alpha\|_2^2 \tag{3}$$

where $\|\alpha\|_1$ enforces sparsity to suppress redundant basis elements; the reconstruction error $\|S(t,f) - \Phi \cdot \alpha\|_2^2$ ensures fidelity to the original spectrogram. The weight λ balances sparsity and reconstruction quality, and can be adaptively estimated from signal energy statistics.

This step effectively eliminates noise components not represented in the dictionary and retains the dominant structural patterns of target signals. However, its local high-frequency noise suppression capability is limited, requiring further refinement via wavelet denoising.

3.3 Local Detail Denoising Via Multi-Scale Wavelet Transform

Target signatures manifest at different time–frequency scales: far-range targets are typically weak and localized, while near-range targets exhibit strong, broadband reflections. Wavelet analysis enables precise local smoothing, effectively suppressing high-frequency noise while preserving structural edges and multi-scale detail, thus enhancing the signal-to-noise ratio of training labels.

The sparsely reconstructed signal $S_{sparse}(t,f)$ is subjected to a 2D discrete wavelet transform (DWT) to obtain multi-scale components:

$$S_{sparse}(t,f) \longrightarrow \{A_J(t,f), D_j(t,f), \cdots, D_1(t,f)\} \tag{4}$$

where $A_J(t,f)$ denotes the approximation (low-frequency) coefficients at scale J, preserving the main target structure, while $D_j(t,f)$ are the detail (high-frequency) coefficients at scale j, containing noise and edge information.

Soft-thresholding is applied to each $D_j(t,f)$:

$$\hat{D}_j(t,f) = \text{sign}(D_j(t,f)) \cdot \max(|D_j(t,f)| - T_j, 0) \tag{5}$$

where the threshold T_j is adaptively estimated based on Gaussian noise statistics:

$$T_j = \sigma_j\sqrt{2\log(N)} \tag{6}$$

where σ_j is the estimated noise standard deviation at scale j, computed via median absolute deviation from high-frequency components, and N denotes the total number of spectrogram pixels.

In summary, the proposed hierarchical denoising strategy integrates sparse decomposition and wavelet-based denoising to address both global and local noise components. Sparse modeling removes low-amplitude, widespread background noise, while multi-scale wavelet analysis suppresses local high-frequency interference and preserves structural signal features. This combination significantly enhances the clarity and fidelity of target signal representations, avoids overfitting or signal distortion typical in traditional denoising methods, and yields high-quality training labels for robust model learning in radar interference suppression tasks.

4 Network Architecture

In dynamic and complex environments, the autonomous perception capabilities of robotic systems rely heavily on high-quality environmental sensing. Millimeter-wave radar, with its all-weather operability, strong penetration, and occlusion resistance, has emerged as a critical sensing modality in robotic perception systems. However, in real-world deployments, radar echoes are often corrupted by external factors such as other radar devices, communication interference sources, and cluttered electromagnetic environments. These interferences typically manifest as non-cooperative, non-Gaussian, and non-stationary signals, often characterized by short bursts, high intensity, and significant frequency drift. When superimposed onto the radar returns, they can obscure or distort the target's time–frequency signatures, severely degrading the robot's perception accuracy and task-level decision-making.

From a mathematical perspective, the suppression of incoherent interference can be formulated as a nonlinear, non-stationary signal separation problem. Let the observed radar time–frequency signal be:

$$X(t,f) = S(t,f) + I(t,f) + N(t,f) \tag{7}$$

where $X(t,f)$ denotes the complex-valued intensity distribution of the received signal at time-frequency coordinates (t,f); $S(t,f)$ represents the desired target echo; $I(t,f)$ denotes the incoherent interference, typically exhibiting high energy, frequency discontinuity, and spatial irregularity; and $N(t,f)$ is additive system noise, assumed to follow Gaussian or approximately Gaussian distribution.

Under strong interference, the frequency structure of the target signal and the interference often overlaps significantly, rendering traditional thresholding, filtering, or template-based techniques ineffective. To accurately recover the target component $S(t,f)$, we formalize the task as a structured signal recovery problem, which seeks to learn a deep nonlinear mapping function: $F_0 : R^{T \times F} \rightarrow R^{T \times F}$ parameterized by θ, such that the reconstructed signal $\hat{S}(t,f) = F_0(X(t,f))$ satisfies the following optimization objective:

$$\theta^* = \underset{\theta}{\operatorname{argmin}} L(F_0(X), S) + \lambda \cdot \Omega(\theta) \tag{8}$$

where $L(\bullet)$ denotes a reconstruction loss function, $\Omega(\theta)$ is a regularization term to control model complexity and prevent overfitting, and λ is a hyperparameter that balances the two terms. This optimization framework reflects the dual objective of accurate signal reconstruction and effective discriminative feature learning.

This formulation highlights the underlying challenge of structured signal recovery in the presence of strong interference. The interference is often localized in space and highly discontinuous in frequency, while the target signal exhibits spectral smoothness and structural regularity. Therefore, designing a neural network with joint spatial–frequency modeling capability, adaptability to non-stationary distributions, and dynamic feature selection is essential for addressing this problem.

Motivated by these insights, we propose the Context-aware Frequency–Feature Attention Network, as shown in Fig. 1. This network is tailored to the physical and statistical properties of mmWave radar signals and is designed to suppress unstructured interference through coordinated spatial context modeling and frequency-aware enhancement mechanisms. A residual reconstruction strategy is further introduced to improve the expressive capacity for target signals. As an end-to-end interference suppression framework, CFFANet eliminates the need for hand-crafted thresholds or fixed filtering rules. Instead, it leverages deep learning to autonomously learn discriminative features across multiple scales and modalities, thereby enhancing the robustness and accuracy of radar perception in complex environments.

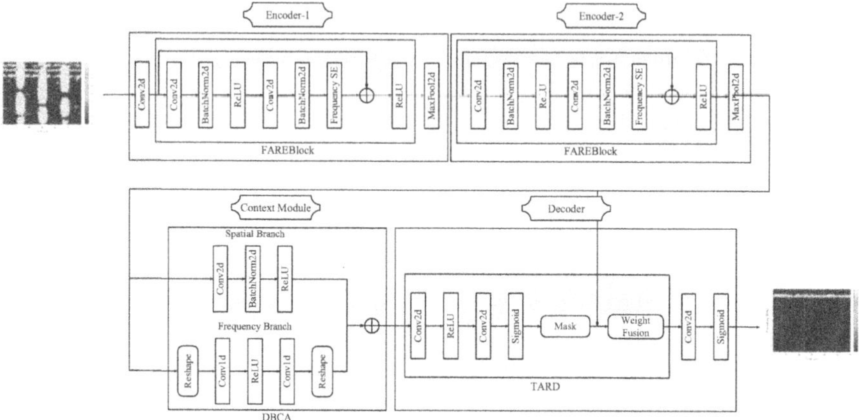

Fig. 1. CFFANet Network Architecture

4.1 Frequency-Aware Residual Extraction Block

The Frequency-Aware Residual Extraction Block is designed to address the challenge of feature extraction in environments with strong interference and weak radar signals. Traditional convolutional neural networks primarily rely on spatial convolutions to capture local patterns. While effective at modeling spatial structures, these approaches often neglect the frequency-domain characteristics of radar targets. In mmWave radar perception, target signals typically exhibit stable, structured spectral patterns, whereas interference tends to manifest as irregular or bursty spectral components. As such, relying solely on spatial convolution is insufficient to robustly distinguish between targets and interference.

To overcome this limitation, the Frequency-Aware Residual Extraction Block (FAREBlock) augments standard spatial convolution with a global frequency-aware attention mechanism. This enables the network to adaptively emphasize frequency regions with meaningful physical characteristics. Furthermore, a residual connection is incorporated to fuse the input with the enhanced features, mitigating gradient vanishing and preserving feature integrity. Through the joint modeling of spatial and frequency features, FAREBlock enables more precise interference suppression and target enhancement.

Spatial Convolutional Feature Extraction. The first component of FAREBlock performs spatial convolution to capture local correlations within the two-dimensional time–frequency input. This module consists of two convolutional layers, each followed by Batch Normalization and ReLU activation, enhancing nonlinearity and training convergence. Given an input feature map $X \in R^{B \times C \times H \times W}$, the output feature map F is computed as:

$$F = ConvBNReLU(ConvBNReLU(X)) \tag{9}$$

where B is the batch size, C is the number of channels, and H, W are the spatial dimensions. The first convolution expands the receptive field, capturing broader spatial context, while the second refines local spatial patterns, improving the description of the target's spatial continuity and shape. This spatial encoding provides the foundation for subsequent frequency modeling and residual integration.

Frequency Squeeze-and-Excitation Mechanism. Given that interference often exhibits distinct patterns in the frequency domain, FAREBlock introduces a frequency attention mechanism to adaptively weight frequency bands based on global statistics. This mechanism highlights the frequency regions corresponding to target signals while suppressing irrelevant or noisy bands.

For the spatial features $F \in R^{B \times C \times H \times W}$, global average pooling is first applied across spatial dimensions to extract per-channel frequency statistics:

$$s_c = \frac{1}{H \times W} \sum_{i=1}^{H} \sum_{j=1}^{W} F_{c,i,j} \tag{10}$$

where s_c reflects the average response of channel c, representing its contribution across the frequency dimension.

Next, a two-layer fully connected (FC) attention subnetwork models the inter-channel frequency dependencies. The first FC layer reduces dimensionality followed by ReLU activation:

$$z_c = ReLU(W_1 \cdot s_c + b_1) \tag{11}$$

where $W_1 \in R^{\frac{C}{r} \times C}$ and $b_1 \in R^{\frac{C}{r}}$ are the weight and bias of the first FC layer, and r is the channel reduction ratio.

Then, the second FC layer projects the result back to the original dimension and applies a sigmoid function to obtain the frequency attention weight:

$$a_c = \sigma(W_2 \cdot z_c + b_2) \tag{12}$$

where $W_2 \in R^{\frac{C}{r} \times C}$ and $b_2 \in R^{C}$ are the weight matrix and bias term of the second fully connected layer, respectively, and $\sigma(\bullet)$ denotes the Sigmoid function, which is used to normalize the frequency weight range.

Finally, the frequency weight a_c of each channel is multiplied channel by channel with the original feature map to realize the adaptive adjustment of the importance of each frequency interval:

$$\tilde{F}_{c,i,j} = a_c \times F_{c,i,j} \tag{13}$$

where $\widetilde{F}_{c,i,j}$ denotes the frequency-enhanced $c - th$ channel in the $i - th$ row and $j - th$ column of the eigenvalue.

Residual Connection and Nonlinear Enhancement. To retain both original spatial features and enhanced frequency information, FAREBlock employs a residual connection:

$$O = ReLU\left(X + \widetilde{F}\right) \tag{14}$$

where O denotes the output feature map. This residual design facilitates effective information flow across layers, alleviates gradient vanishing, and supports flexible feature fusion—allowing the network to balance raw and enhanced representations for better generalization.

In summary, FAREBlock integrates spatial convolution and frequency-aware modeling into a unified feature extraction framework tailored for interference suppression. In the spatial domain, convolutional layers extract localized structures crucial for modeling the physical and temporal evolution of radar targets. In the frequency domain, the attention mechanism adapts channel-wise responses based on spectral statistics, allowing the network to focus on reliable frequency bands while suppressing anomalous components. The residual pathway preserves original information and reinforces model expressiveness through nonlinear activation.

Compared to traditional spatial convolution modules, FAREBlock achieves dual-domain optimization, extending beyond local spatial descriptors to jointly encode frequency characteristics. This enables robust target enhancement under non-stationary interference. Furthermore, the lightweight frequency attention mechanism imposes minimal computational overhead, making FAREBlock well-suited for real-time deployment on edge robotic platforms. Overall, FAREBlock significantly strengthens the stability and robustness of robotic perception in multi-source interference scenarios, offering a more reliable sensing foundation for downstream autonomous tasks.

4.2 Dual-Branch Contextual Attention Module

In robotic autonomous perception tasks, environmental interference signals not only exhibit local anomalies but also spread across spatial and frequency domains at various scales. For instance, certain types of interference may appear as spatially diffused patterns, while others may concentrate within specific frequency bands, forming band-shaped contamination. As a result, conventional convolutional models that rely on single-domain processing often fail to fully capture such multiscale interference patterns, leading to insufficient feature extraction and reduced perception accuracy.

To address this challenge, we propose the Dual-Branch Contextual Attention (DBCA) module, which models global contextual dependencies in both the spatial and frequency domains through two separate branches: a Spatial Branch and a Frequency Branch. By jointly capturing local-to-global relationships in both dimensions, DBCA enables a more comprehensive understanding of complex interference backgrounds and enhances the network's ability to isolate targets in cluttered environments.

Spatial Context Modeling. The spatial branch aims to capture local structural patterns and the spatial diffusion characteristics of noise and interference. Given an input feature map $\in R^{B \times C \times H \times W}$, a 3×3 convolution kernel W_s, followed by Batch Normalization and ReLU, is applied to extract spatial context features:

$$S = ReLU(BN(W_s * X)) \tag{15}$$

where $*$ denotes 2D convolution, and $W_s \epsilon R^{C \times C \times 3 \times 3}$ is the convolution kernel. The output S captures local dependencies between the target and background in the spatial domain, effectively enhancing the model's ability to learn the distribution of spatially diffuse interference.

Frequency Context Modeling. The frequency branch is motivated by the observation that mmWave radar signals often suffer from band-like interference concentrated along the frequency axis. To capture long-range dependencies between frequency subbands, we apply a series of 1D convolutions along the channel (frequency) dimension.

First, the input feature X is reshaped along its spatial dimensions to obtain:

$$X_f = reshape(X, (B, C, H \times W)) \tag{16}$$

Then, two successive 1D convolutions with non-linear activation are applied:

$$F' = ReLU\left(W_f^{(1)} * X_f\right) \tag{17}$$

$$F = W_f^{(2)} * F' \tag{18}$$

where $*$ denotes 1D convolution, $W_f^{(1)} \in R^{C \times C \times k}$, $W_f^{(2)} \in R^{C \times C \times k}$ are the 1D convolution kernels, and k is the kernel size, which balances contextual range and computational complexity. The output $F \in R^{B \times C \times (H \times W)}$ models the global frequency-domain dependencies across subbands.

Finally, the reshaped output is returned to its original spatial form:

$$F_{reshape} = reshape(F, (B, C, H \times W)) \tag{19}$$

Dual-Branch Fusion and Output. The spatial context feature S and frequency context feature $F_{reshape}$ are element-wise summed to obtain the fused contextual representation:

$$O = S + F_{reshape} \tag{20}$$

This fusion strategy combines complementary spatial and frequency information, enabling the model to detect both localized and distributed interference patterns, thereby achieving global suppression of multi-source interference.

In summary, the DBCA module provides a dual-domain contextual modeling mechanism that significantly enhances the network's ability to perceive and suppress complex interference. In the spatial domain, convolutional operations effectively extract localized structures, improving sensitivity to target contours, background textures, and spatially diffused anomalies—essential for robots to recognize subtle environmental changes.

In the frequency domain, 1D convolutions build long-range dependencies across subbands, enabling the model to adaptively emphasize target frequency regions and suppress periodic or band-shaped interference commonly observed in radar signals.

This joint spatial–frequency optimization enables DBCA to move beyond single-perspective modeling, achieving robust representation of interference patterns across domains and scales. Additionally, DBCA employs lightweight convolutional operations and local attention mechanisms, maintaining low computational overhead suitable for real-time deployment on edge robotics platforms.

Compared to conventional convolution or attention modules, DBCA significantly enhances the network's interference suppression capacity and robustness, while offering a stable and reliable feature basis for downstream robotic perception tasks. The integration of DBCA empowers the overall system to retain high target extraction accuracy even under severe multi-scale, multi-frequency interference, supporting accurate environmental understanding and autonomous decision-making.

4.3 Target-Aware Residual Decoding

To further enhance the reconstruction of target signals under strong interference conditions, we design a Target-Aware Residual Decoding (TARD) module. This module aims to improve signal fidelity in target regions while suppressing residual background interference through an adaptive reconstruction mechanism. Built upon residual learning and adaptive masking, TARD enables selective enhancement of informative regions and prevents the erroneous amplification of interference during reconstruction.

TARD not only performs fine-grained decoding of contextual features obtained from the previous DBCA module but also adaptively integrates spatial information from earlier stages, ensuring a robust fusion of signal structure and context.

Residual Reconstruction Mechanism. TARD first applies a residual connection to combine the original input x with its nonlinearly transformed counterpart $f(x)$, yielding an enhanced representation:

$$R = \phi(x) + F(x; \Theta) \tag{21}$$

where R denotes the output after residual reconstruction, $\phi(x)$ represents an identity mapping or a simple linear projection preserving the original features, and $F(x; \Theta)$ is a convolutional network with learnable parameters Θ that extracts nonlinear residual components. This residual learning design helps preserve spatial fidelity while amplifying subtle yet critical target information, mitigating risks of overfitting or feature degradation introduced by deeper layers.

Specifically, $F(x; \Theta)$ consists of two sequential 3×3 convolutional layers, which strike a balance between modeling local structures and maintaining a reasonable receptive field—satisfying robotic systems' requirements for both accuracy and efficiency.

Adaptive Masking Mechanism. To distinguish between target and background regions, TARD introduces an adaptive mask mechanism. A learnable attention mask

M is computed to regulate the flow of reconstruction information:

$$M = \sigma(W_2 \cdot \delta(W_1 * R)) \tag{22}$$

where W_1 and W_2 are learnable 1×1 convolutional kernels, $*$ denotes the convolution operation, $\delta(\bullet)$ is the ReLU activation function, and $\sigma(\bullet)$ is the Sigmoid function. This mask identifies salient regions by emphasizing discriminative features between target and interference areas and constrains the activation range within [0, 1], allowing the network to assign varying reconstruction weights across different regions.

The final output of TARD is a weighted fusion of the reconstructed residuals and the original DBCA features, defined as:

$$Y = M \odot R + (1 - M) \odot X \tag{23}$$

where Y is the reconstructed output, $\odot$ denotes element-wise multiplication, and X is the output of the DBCA module. This expression shows that the model tends to retain the reconstructed feature R when the mask M tends to 1, and the model tends to retain the original feature X when M tends to 0, realizing the balanced optimization of region adaptation.

In summary, TARD effectively addresses the limitations of conventional convolutional decoding by introducing residual learning to preserve original feature integrity while enhancing critical target structures. The adaptive masking mechanism ensures selective enhancement of salient regions and suppresses noise amplification in irrelevant areas. Compared with direct convolution-based reconstruction, TARD offers a more targeted and context-aware decoding strategy-especially suited for robotic perception tasks in dynamic, interference-rich environments.

By refining both target reconstruction and interference suppression, TARD contributes significantly to the overall robustness of the perception system. It lowers false reconstruction rates and provides a more accurate and reliable feature foundation for downstream tasks such as target detection, path planning, and environmental understanding.

5 Experiment

This section describes the radar data acquisition setup and parameters, compares the proposed method with state-of-the-art interference suppression approaches, and demonstrates the superior performance of our framework.

5.1 Experimental Setup

To evaluate the effectiveness of our proposed method under real-world conditions, we utilized two Texas Instruments AWR1642 radars in combination with a DCA1000 data acquisition system. One radar was designated as the ego radar to capture echo signals from moving targets, while the other functioned as the interference radar, as shown in Fig. 2, actively emitting interfering signals. The experiments were conducted under the following two scenarios:

(a) Interference-Free Scenario: The interference radar was deactivated, and the ego radar collected only the echo signals reflected from moving targets. These clean recordings were used to generate ground-truth supervision labels for network training, ensuring the accuracy and integrity of the target signal.
(b) Interference Scenario: The interference radar was activated to emit disruptive signals, while the ego radar simultaneously captured mixed echo signals containing both target reflections and interference. These contaminated signals were used as network inputs to train the model for robust interference suppression.

The specific parameter settings for the two radars are shown in the Table 1:

Table 1. Radar parameter settings for the experimental scenarios

Radar Parameter	Parameter values	
	Victim radar	Aggressor Radar
Bandwidth(MHz)	2401.44	1619.28
Sweep time(μs)	60	60
Chirp rate(MHz/μs)	40.024	26.988
Sampling rate(Ksps)	10000	10000

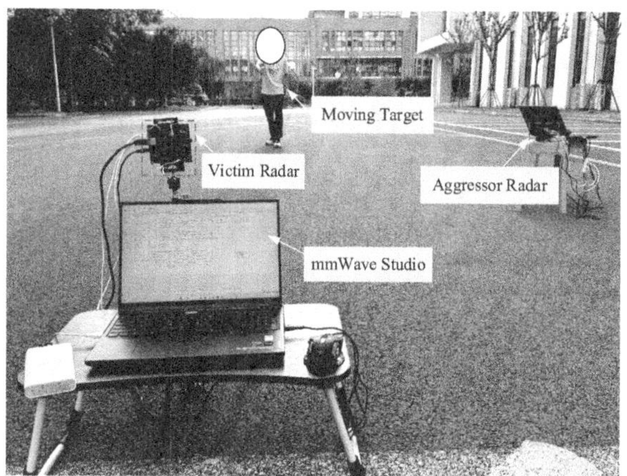

Fig. 2. Experimental Setup

5.2 Experimental Results

We constructed a dataset comprising 4,300 time-frequency map for training and 700 for testing. The proposed method was compared against several baseline techniques, including Fully Convolutional Networks (FCN) [41], traditional Convolutional Neural Networks (CNN) [42], Residual Networks (ResNet) [43], classical wavelet thresholding methods [16] and Generative Adversarial Network (GAN) [44]. Evaluation was conducted across two key dimensions: interference suppression capability and signal reconstruction quality.

Quantitative Metric Comparison. To comprehensively assess the performance of our method in suppressing interference within millimeter-wave radar TF spectrograms, we employed three widely adopted evaluation metrics: Signal-to-Interference-plus-Noise Ratio (SINR), Root Mean Square Error (RMSE), and Peak Signal-to-Noise Ratio (PSNR). These metrics collectively measure signal enhancement effectiveness, reconstruction error, and overall image fidelity, respectively, providing a multi-perspective evaluation of the interference suppression and signal recovery capabilities of each approach.

SINR quantifies the ratio of target signal power to residual interference and noise power, indicating the effectiveness of the suppression algorithm. A higher SINR gain suggests stronger interference mitigation. It is defined as:

$$SINR = 10\log_{10}\frac{P_{signal}}{P_{\text{int}erface} + P_{noise}} \tag{24}$$

where P_{signal}, $P_{interference}$ and P_{noise} denote the power of the target signal, interference, and noise, respectively.

RMSE measures the discrepancy between the reconstructed signal and the ground truth. It is computed as:

$$RMSE = \sqrt{\frac{1}{N}\sum\nolimits_{t=1}^{n}[x(t) - \hat{x}(t)]^2} \tag{25}$$

where $x(t)$ is the original target signal and $\hat{x}(t)$ is the estimated signal. Lower RMSE values indicate a closer match between the denoised output and the reference signal.

PSNR assesses the perceptual quality of the restored TF spectrograms, defined as:

$$PSNR = 10 \cdot \log_{10}\left(\frac{{}^{\text{I}}\text{m}ax^2}{MSE}\right) \tag{26}$$

$$MSE = \frac{1}{N}\sum\nolimits_{t=1}^{n}[x(t) - \hat{x}(t)]^2 \tag{27}$$

where I_{max} denotes the maximum possible pixel value. Higher PSNR values suggest better preservation of energy and structural integrity in the TF domain.

As shown in Fig. 3, the |ΔSINR| comparison demonstrates that the proposed CFFANet significantly outperforms FCN, CNN, ResNet, wavelet-based denoising, and GAN. GANs, as generative adversarial models, can achieve partial interference suppression by learning the distributions of target and interference signals. However, their outputs often exhibit instability in complex environments, leading to fluctuating suppression performance. In contrast, CFFANet is specifically designed for the non-stationary characteristics of mmWave radar interference, where the DBCA module captures inconsistent interference patterns through dual-branch space–frequency modeling, and the

FAREBlock strengthens the spectral stability of target reflections. Together, they provide a much higher SINR gain by effectively separating structured target signals from anomalous spectral components.

The RMSE comparison in Fig. 4 further validates CFFANet's superior signal reconstruction accuracy. Traditional CNNs rely on shallow pixel-wise modeling, FCNs only apply coarse context fusion, and wavelet denoising is constrained by static thresholds. GANs, while capable of generating smoother outputs, often produce features that deviate from the true distribution, introducing spurious artifacts or over-smoothing effects, which leads to higher reconstruction errors. By contrast, CFFANet employs hierarchical feature extraction combined with the TARD module's adaptive residual fusion, which dynamically adjusts denoising intensity according to local signal structures. This, along with frequency-aware attention, ensures the preservation of key spectral components, resulting in the lowest RMSE among all methods.

The PSNR comparison in Fig. 5 shows that CFFANet also achieves the best performance in terms of image quality. Wavelet thresholding smooths noise but sacrifices edge details; FCNs and CNNs suffer from shallow architectures or insufficient TF modeling, and ResNet, although alleviating training difficulties with residual connections, lacks explicit frequency-domain awareness. GAN reconstructions, while visually smooth, fail to preserve high-frequency details, limiting overall energy fidelity. In contrast, CFFANet integrates spatial convolution, frequency-domain modeling, and dynamic residual reconstruction to preserve both the continuity and energy concentration of target signals. Consequently, the reconstructed spectrograms closely resemble interference-free references in both structural and energetic aspects, which is reflected in the superior PSNR scores.

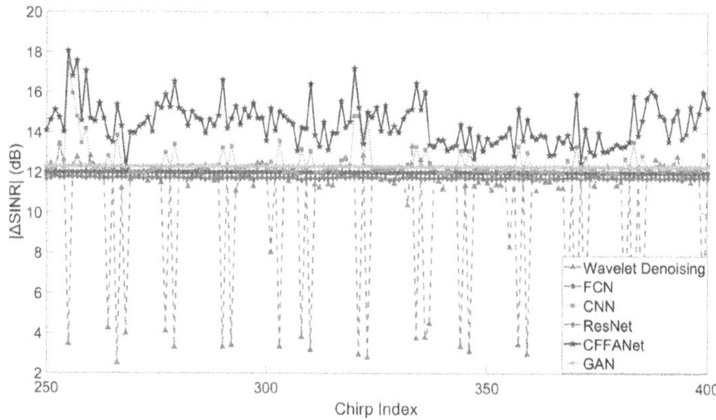

Fig. 3. Comparison of |ΔSINR| of the method proposed in this paper with other methods

Visualization of Results. The visualization results of the proposed interference suppression method are shown in Fig. 6. After processing by our approach, the TF spectrograms exhibit significantly enhanced clarity of target features, while interference and noise in the background are effectively suppressed. The resulting spectrograms display desirable characteristics, including concentrated energy distribution, structural continuity, and a smooth background. These superior results demonstrate the effectiveness of our

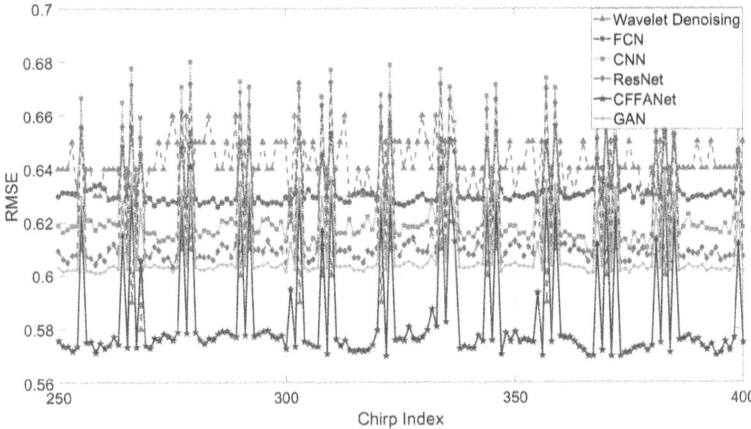

Fig. 4. Comparison of RMSE of the method proposed in this paper with other methods

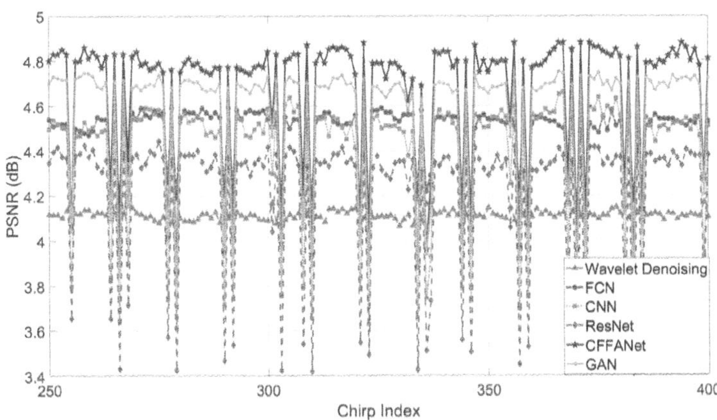

Fig. 5. Comparison of PSNR of the method proposed in this paper with other methods

combined innovations in both data preprocessing and network architecture design, substantially enhancing the mmWave radar system's target perception and anti-interference capabilities in complex environments.

In the preprocessing stage, we employ a hybrid denoising strategy that integrates sparse decomposition with multiscale wavelet denoising to fully exploit the radar signal's sparsity and multiscale TF characteristics. The sparse decomposition separates the radar signal into sparse bases and noise/interference components, enabling effective decoupling and reducing the impact of background noise on training data quality. Meanwhile, the multiscale wavelet denoising hierarchically suppresses interference at different frequency bands, ensuring the preservation of essential TF structures in target signals. This joint denoising framework significantly improves the signal-to-noise ratio of training samples, allowing the network to accurately learn the intrinsic characteristics of target signals during training—laying a solid foundation for interference suppression from the source.

Furthermore, the proposed CFFANet architecture enhances the network's modeling capacity for interference suppression via spatial–frequency joint representation, frequency-enhanced residual learning, and dynamic reconstruction mechanisms. Specifically, the DBCA module jointly leverages spatial and frequency convolutions to precisely capture differences in the spatial-frequency distributions between target and interference signals, thus improving the network's capacity to identify and suppress interference. The FAREBlock applies a frequency-aware attention mechanism that adaptively emphasizes key frequency components of the target signal, making the reflected energy more salient in the spectrogram. The TARD module utilizes dynamic masking and residual learning to adaptively balance between target preservation and interference removal, ensuring robust signal reconstruction under nonstationary interference. These multi-level and multi-perspective enhancements enable CFFANet to suppress non-target components effectively while accurately reconstructing the TF structure of target signals under complex and high-interference scenarios.

In conclusion, through a combination of innovative denoising strategies and advanced deep network architecture, the proposed method significantly improves both the discernibility of target signals and the suppression of background interference in radar spectrograms. The final TF outputs exhibit strong energy concentration and structural integrity, while effectively reducing the negative impact of noise and interference on target detection. These results validate the proposed method's efficacy and practicality in mmWave radar interference suppression and target perception tasks.

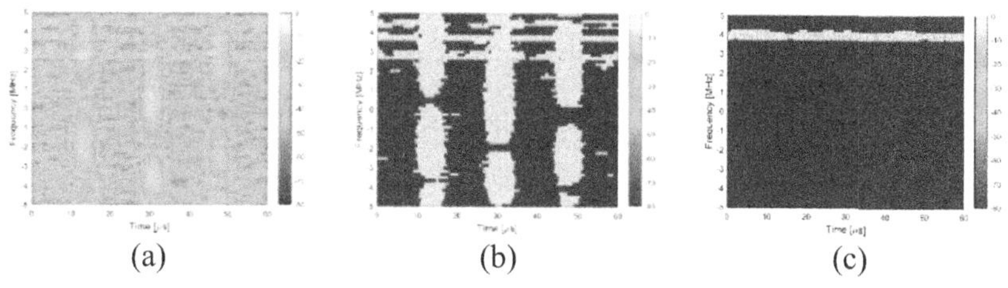

Fig. 6. (a) Raw radar with interference time-frequency map (b) Time-frequency map before interference suppression (c) Time-frequency map after interference suppression

6 Conclusion

This paper addresses the challenge of millimeter-wave radar interference suppression for robotic perception in complex environments by proposing a comprehensive framework that integrates data preprocessing with deep modeling. To mitigate background noise contamination in raw radar echoes, a denoising algorithm based on sparse decomposition and multiscale wavelet fusion is designed. This approach effectively enhances the label quality of training samples while preserving the structural integrity of target signals.

To overcome the difficulty of acquiring interference-labeled samples and address the instability of interference distributions, we innovatively adopt the target signal as the supervision label. This reformulates the training paradigm into a more generalizable framework, breaking the reliance on interference priors commonly seen in traditional methods.

Building on this foundation, we further propose a novel deep interference suppression network CFFANet. CFFANet extracts multi-scale interference features through spatial–frequency joint modeling, enhances target dominant frequency components via frequency-aware attention mechanisms, and leverages a dynamic residual reconstruction strategy to improve the network's robustness against nonstationary interference. Experimental results demonstrate that the proposed method outperforms state-of-the-art baselines in terms of SINR, RMSE, and PSNR, achieving superior performance in both target reconstruction and interference suppression.

In summary, this work presents a systematic interference suppression solution for mmWave radar-based robotic perception, covering both signal preprocessing and deep network design. It offers strong generalization and practical deployment potential while ensuring high-fidelity target perception. Future research will explore collaborative interference modeling across heterogeneous sensors and the extension of unsupervised learning under weak-labeling conditions, aiming to further enhance the system's real-time performance and robustness in dynamic, cluttered environments.

References

1. Harlow, K., Jang, H., Barfoot, T.D., Kim, A., Heckman, C.: A new wave in robotics: survey on recent MmWave radar applications in robotics. IEEE Trans. Robot. **40**, 4544–4560 (2024)
2. Chen, H., Liu, Y., Cheng, Y.: A robust robot perception framework for complex environments using multiple mmWave radars. IEEE J. Sel. Top. Sig. Proces. **18**, 380–395 (2024)
3. Patole, S.M., Torlak, M., Wang, D., Ali, M.: Automotive radars: a review of signal processing techniques. IEEE Signal Process. Mag. **34**, 22–35 (2017)
4. Xu, Z., Xue, S., Wang, Y.: Incoherent interference detection and mitigation for millimeter-wave FMCW radars. Remote Sens. **14**, 4817 (2022)
5. Jin, F., Cao, S.: Automotive radar interference mitigation using adaptive noise canceller. IEEE Trans. Veh. Technol. **68**, 3747–3754 (2019)
6. Wang, P., Yin, X., Rodríguez-Piñeiro, J., Chen, Z., Zhu, P., Li, G.: A dual-recursive-least-squares algorithm for automotive radar interference suppression. IEEE Trans. Intell. Transp. Syst. **24**, 10603–10617 (2023)
7. Wagner, M., Sulejmani, F., Melzer, A., Meissner, P., Huemer, M.: Threshold-free interference cancellation method for automotive FMCW radar systems. In: 2018 IEEE International Symposium on Circuits and Systems (ISCAS), pp. 1–4. IEEE, Florence (2018)
8. Xia, D.-P., Zhang, L., Wu, T., Meng, X.-D.: A Mainlobe interference suppression algorithm based on Bistatic airborne radar cooperation. In: 2019 IEEE Radar Conference (RadarConf), pp. 1–6. IEEE, Boston, MA, USA (2019)
9. Chen, S., Stockel, P., Taghia, J., Kuhnau, U., Martin, R.: Iterative 2D sparse signal reconstruction with masked residual updates for automotive radar interference mitigation. EURASIP J. Adv. Sig. Proces. **2022** (2022)
10. Hu, X., Li, Y., Lu, M., Wang, Y., Yang, X.: A multi-carrier-frequency random-transmission chirp sequence for TDM MIMO automotive radar. IEEE Trans. Veh. Technol. **68**, 3672–3685 (2019)

11. Bechter, J., Rameez, M., Waldschmidt, C.: Analytical and experimental investigations on mitigation of interference in a DBF MIMO radar. IEEE Trans. Microw. Theor. Techn. **65**, 1727–1734 (2017)
12. Yang, S., Shang, X., Zhang, D., Sun, Q., Chen, Y.: IMIA: interference mitigation via iterative approaches for automotive radar. IEEE Trans. Radar Syst. **1**, 753–766 (2023)
13. Nnamani, C.O., Sellathurai, M.: Interference and noise cancellation for joint communication radar (JCR) system based on contextual information. IEEE Open J. Commun. Soc. **4**, 1855–1865 (2023)
14. Wu, Z., Zhu, S., Xu, J., Lan, L., Zhang, M.: Interference suppression method with MR-FDA-MIMO radar. IEEE Trans. Aerosp. Electron. Syst. **59**, 6250–6264 (2023)
15. Liu, Z., Wu, J., Yang, S., Lu, W.: DOA estimation method based on EMD and MUSIC for mutual interference in FMCW automotive radars. IEEE Geosci. Remote Sens. Lett. **19**, 1–5 (2022)
16. Lee, S., Lee, J.-Y., Kim, S.-C.: Mutual interference suppression using wavelet Denoising in automotive FMCW radar systems. IEEE Trans. Intell. Transport. Syst. **22**, 887–897 (2021)
17. Rock, J., Roth, W., Toth, M., Meissner, P., Pernkopf, F.: Resource-efficient deep neural networks for automotive radar interference mitigation. IEEE J. Sel. Top. Signal Process. **15**, 927–940 (2021)
18. Okuda, T., Makino, Y., Umehira, M., Wang, X., Takeda, S., Kuroda, H.: Prototype development and experimental performance evaluation of FMCW radar using iterative interference suppression technique. In: 2019 International Radar Conference (RADAR), pp. 1–6 (2019)
19. Umehira, M., Okuda, T., Wang, X., Takeda, S., Kuroda, H.: An adaptive interference detection and suppression scheme using iterative processing for automotive FMCW radars. In: 2020 IEEE Radar Conference (RadarConf20), pp. 1–5 (2020)
20. Dubey, A., Fuchs, J., Madhavan, V., Lubke, M., Weigel, R., Lurz, F.: Region based single-stage interference mitigation and target detection. In: In: 2020 IEEE Radar Conference (RadarConf20), pp. 1–5. IEEE, Florence, Italy (2020)
21. Rameez, M., Pettersson, M., Dahl, M.: Interference compression and mitigation for automotive FMCW radar systems. IEEE Sensors J. **22**, 19739–19749 (2022)
22. Li, Y., Feng, B., Zhang, W.: Mutual interference mitigation of millimeter-wave radar based on Variational mode decomposition and signal reconstruction. Remote Sens. **15**, 557 (2023)
23. Wang, C., Tong, J., Cui, G., Zhao, X., Wang, W.: Robust interference cancellation for vehicular communication and radar coexistence. IEEE Commun. Lett. **24**, 2367–2370 (2020)
24. Torres, L.L.T., Grebner, T., Werbunat, D., Waldschmidt, C.: Automotive radar interference mitigation by subtraction of the interference component. IEEE Microw. Wirel. Technol. Lett. **33**, 1397–1400 (2023)
25. Zhang, H., et al.: Dual-domain feature-oriented interference suppression for FMCW automotive radar. IEEE Sensors J. 1–1 (2024)
26. Wu, J., Yang, S., Lu, W., Liu, Z.: Iterative modified threshold method based on EMD for interference suppression in FMCW radars. IET Radar, Sonar Navig. **14**, 1219–1228 (2020)
27. Li, J., et al.: Multidomain separation for human vital signs detection with FMCW radar in interference environment. IEEE Trans. Microw. Theor. Tech., 1–16 (2023)
28. Lee, W.-H., Lee, S.: Geometric sequence decomposition-based interference cancellation in automotive radar systems. IEEE Access. **10**, 4318–4327 (2022)
29. López-Valcárcel, L.A., García Sánchez, M., Fioranelli, F., Krasnov, O.A.: An MTI-like approach for interference mitigation in FMCW radar systems. IEEE Trans. Aerosp. Electron. Syst. 1–16 (2023)
30. Uysal, F.: Synchronous and asynchronous radar interference mitigation. IEEE Access. **7**, 5846–5852 (2019)

31. Xu, Z., Yuan, M.: An interference mitigation technique for automotive millimeter wave radars in the tunable Q-factor wavelet transform domain. IEEE Trans. Microw. Theor. Tech. **69**, 5270–5283 (2021)
32. Xu, Z.: Bi-level l1 optimization-based interference reduction for millimeter wave radars. IEEE Trans. Intell. Transp. Syst. **24**, 728–738 (2023)
33. Wang, Y., Huang, Y., Wen, C., Zhou, X., Liu, J., Hong, W.: Mutual interference mitigation for automotive FMCW radar with time and frequency domain decomposition. IEEE Trans. Microw. Theor. Tech. **71**, 5028–5044 (2023)
34. Liu, P., Liu, Y., Huang, T., Lu, Y., Wang, X.: Decentralized automotive radar Spectrum allocation to avoid mutual interference using reinforcement learning. IEEE Trans. Aerosp. Electron. Syst. **57**, 190–205 (2021)
35. Wang, J., Li, R., He, Y., Yang, Y.: Prior-guided deep interference mitigation for FMCW radars. IEEE Trans. Geosci. Remote Sens. **60**, 1–16 (2022)
36. Chen, S., Taghia, J., Kühnau, U., Pohl, N., Martin, R.: A two-stage DNN model with mask-gated convolution for automotive radar interference detection and mitigation. IEEE Sensors J. **22**, 12017–12027 (2022)
37. Flandermeyer, S.A., Mattingly, R.G., Metcalf, J.G.: Deep reinforcement learning for cognitive radar Spectrum sharing: a continuous control approach. IEEE Trans. Radar Syst. **2**, 125–137 (2024)
38. Zhang, H., Wei, S., Wang, M., Hu, Y., Shi, J., Cui, G.: FUAS-net: feature-oriented unsupervised network for FMCW radar interference suppression. IEEE Trans. Microw. Theor. Tech. **1–18** (2023)
39. Chen, S., Klemp, M., Taghia, J., Kühnau, U., Pohl, N., Martin, R.: Improved target detection through DNN-based Multi-Channel interference mitigation in automotive radar. IEEE Trans. Radar Syst. **1**, 75–89 (2023)
40. Wang, J., Ding, M., Yarovoy, A.: Interference mitigation for FMCW radar with sparse and low-rank Hankel matrix decomposition. IEEE Trans. Signal Process. **70**, 822–834 (2022)
41. Ristea, N.-C., Anghel, A., Ionescu, R.T.: Fully convolutional neural networks for automotive radar interference mitigation. In: 2020 IEEE 92nd Vehicular Technology Conference(VTC2020-Fall), pp. 1–5. IEEE, Victoria, BC, Canada (2020)
42. Rock, J., Toth, M., Messner, E., Meissner, P., Pernkopf, F.: Complex signal Denoising and interference mitigation for automotive radar using convolutional neural networks. In: 2019 22th International Conference on Information Fusion (FUSION), pp. 1–8 (2019)
43. Fan, W., et al.: Interference Mitigation for Synthetic Aperture Radar Based on Deep Residual Network
44. Cui, X., Li, D., Li, Z., Ou, J.: A GAN noise modeling based blind denoising method for guided waves. Measurement. **188**, 110596 (2022)

GAU-Net: A Feature Enhancement Network for Hand Gesture Recognition Using Millimeter-Wave Radar Point Clouds

Qingbo Xia[1], Jiajia Shi[1(✉)], Liu Chu[2], and Quan Shi[1]

[1] School of Transportation and Civil Engineering, Nantong University, Nantong 226019, Jiangsu, China
shijj@ntu.edu.cn

[2] School of Physical Science and Technology, Shanghai Tech University, Shanghai 201210, China

Abstract. With the development of embodied intelligence and robot interaction technologies, constructing intelligent perception and natural human-robot interaction systems that adapt to complex environments has become a research focus. In scenarios such as intelligent transportation and emergency command, reliable gesture recognition is crucial for achieving natural human-robot interaction. Vision-based methods often perform poorly in situations with occlusion or poor lighting, while millimeter-wave radar can provide robust and privacy-protecting perception. However, its point cloud data is sparse and noisy, which poses challenges for feature modeling. To improve the perception performance of models under such sparse point cloud conditions, this paper proposes a lightweight point cloud recognition network GAU-Net that integrates local geometric modeling and context enhancement mechanisms. The network incorporates the GeoConv module and the AUG-Unit module. The GeoConv module captures the direction-sensitive geometric relationships of the point cloud, enhancing the robot's spatial perception ability to small structural changes; the AUG-Unit module, through perturbation encoding and global attention mechanisms, improves the feature continuity and semantic consistency during the point cloud upsampling process, thereby significantly enhancing the system's discriminative performance and robustness under sparse input conditions.

Keywords: Millimeter-Wave Radar · Point Cloud Gesture Recognition · Self-Attention Mechanism · Lightweight Network

1 Introduction

As urban transportation systems expand rapidly, the contradiction between the sharp increase in the number of motor vehicles and limited road resources is becoming increasingly acute. Traditional methods that rely on static control facilities such as traffic lights are slow to respond in special situations such as rush hour or inclement weather [1], and are unable to meet the urgent demand for real-time, efficient dispatching in modern

Z. Hou et al. (Eds.): CIRAC 2025, CCIS 2885, pp. 222–240, 2026.
https://doi.org/10.1007/978-981-92-0045-0_15

intelligent transportation systems. While human traffic police can temporarily alleviate localized congestion, their dispatch methods primarily rely on visual communication and hand gestures, which are difficult for autonomous driving systems or intelligent robot platforms to accurately recognize and respond to [2], making this a key bottleneck in human-vehicle-road collaborative control. Therefore, achieving automatic recognition of traffic police hand gestures, particularly enabling service or traffic patrol robots to understand and respond to human hand gestures, has become a prerequisite for building natural human-machine interaction systems [3].

Compared to traditional visual or wearable devices, millimeter-wave radar offers advantages such as non-contact operation, robustness to obstructions, all-weather sensing, and privacy-friendly capabilities, making it an increasingly important sensing method for robot systems to perceive human movements [4]. By analyzing the time-frequency information and micro-motion changes in echo signals, millimeter-wave radar can stably capture human dynamics in complex environments, demonstrating significant engineering application potential [5]. However, the point cloud data it outputs is often sparse, unstructured, and susceptible to noise interference, posing significant challenges to the expressive capability and generalization performance of point cloud-based motion recognition algorithms [6]. Traditional geometric feature methods struggle to effectively model the spatio-temporal semantic associations and higher-order structural changes in complex traffic gestures [7].

To enhance the interactive understanding capabilities of robotic systems, this paper proposes a traffic gesture recognition network called GAU-Net for sparse millimeter-wave point clouds. By employing local geometric modeling and feature enhancement mechanisms, GAU-Net effectively improves a robot's ability to understand and respond to gesture semantics during natural interactions. Specifically, the network introduces a Geo Convolution module to perform direction-sensitive modeling of local geometric structures, enhancing the robot's perception of subtle structural differences in point clouds. Additionally, an Attention Upsampling with Guidance Unit(AUG-Unit) module is designed to integrate perturbation encoding and self-attention mechanisms during the point cloud sampling stage, thereby improving interpolation accuracy and global semantic consistency. Experimental results demonstrate that this method achieves outstanding performance in millimeter-wave point cloud gesture recognition tasks, exhibiting good robustness and deployment efficiency, and showcasing its application potential in achieving natural human-robot interaction in intelligent robot systems. Our contributions can be summarized as follows:

- We propose a lightweight point cloud recognition framework, GAU-Net, tailored for dynamic gesture recognition in sparse and noisy millimeter-wave radar data, enabling robust human-robot interaction.
- A local structure modeling method integrating GeoConv is proposed, which enhances the point cloud's perception of geometric changes in gestures through direction-sensitive feature extraction, and is applicable to sparse and unstructured millimeter-wave data.

- The AUG-Unit module is proposed to improve feature expression and interpolation performance, introducing perturbation guidance and self-attention mechanism, effectively enhancing geometric consistency and context expression during the upsampling process of point clouds.

2 Related Work

In recent years, millimeter-wave radar has made remarkable technological progress in the field of gesture recognition, especially with the introduction and application of deep learning technology, which has continuously optimized and innovated related recognition methods [8]. The extensive application of deep learning, particularly convolutional neural networks and recurrent neural networks, has significantly improved the accuracy and robustness of gesture recognition, promoting the wide application and practical deployment of millimeter-wave radar technology in complex scenarios [9].

Multiple studies have demonstrated that the integration of millimeter-wave radar and deep learning technology has achieved remarkable results in the field of gesture recognition. Kim et al. [10] proposed a micro-Doppler gesture classification method based on an optimized deep convolutional neural network (DCNN), which achieved a classification accuracy of 87.12% on a 77GHz Doppler radar dataset by adjusting hyperparameters such as the number of convolutional layers, filter quantity, and size. Zhao et al. [11] designed a gesture separation network (GSN) and a convolutional neural network—long short-term memory (CNN-LSTM) fusion model, which separated the features of dual-target gestures through dynamic range-angle images (DRAI) and achieved an average separation accuracy of 93% in an interleaved interference scenario, with a cross-environment recognition rate of 81.6%. Xia et al. [12] proposed a gesture recognition method based on the moving scattering center model and a multi-channel CNN, combined with a three-dimensional feature representation of distance-Doppler-angle, which increased the palm gesture recognition rate to 93% in the case of target interleaving and to 75.6% in the case of parallel targets in a random dynamic interference environment, an improvement of approximately 16% compared to traditional single-dimensional feature methods. Zhao et al. [13] designed a gesture separation network based on the CNN-LSTM architecture, which could effectively extract dual-target features and achieved a recognition rate of 93% in interleaved interference. Jin et al. [14] further proposed a dual-branch architecture of CNN-Transformer, introducing a multi-head self-attention mechanism to suppress dynamic noise and achieving an accuracy rate of 96% in complex scenarios.

Although existing methods based on 2D images have made certain progress in terms of accuracy and robustness, their ability to model 3D geometric features in sparse point clouds remains insufficient. Meanwhile, mainstream point cloud processing methods generally neglect local structure modeling and the issue of semantic consistency during the upsampling process. In response to the characteristics of sparse and low-density point clouds generated by millimeter-wave radar, this paper proposes a point cloud recognition network, GAU-Net, which integrates direction-aware local modeling and perturbation-guided attention upsampling mechanisms. The aim is to enhance the geometric modeling capability and consistency of feature representation, thereby significantly improving the recognition accuracy and robustness in gesture recognition tasks.

3 Methodology

3.1 Point Cloud Generation

Although existing methods based on two-dimensional images have made certain progress in terms of accuracy and robustness, their ability to model three-dimensional geometric features in sparse point clouds remains insufficient. Meanwhile, the point cloud generation system proposed in this study (see Fig. 1), achieves joint perception of distance and velocity based on the 2D-FFT algorithm, effectively extracting the distance and velocity information of targets [15]. To enhance the system's detection capability for weak targets, we combined incoherent accumulation technology, thereby improving the sensitivity of target detection [16]. Additionally, the 2D-CFAR algorithm was employed to construct an adaptive detection window, further enhancing the performance of target detection. To achieve more accurate multi-dimensional angle estimation, the system generates point cloud data that integrates spatial and intensity features based on the MUSIC algorithm.

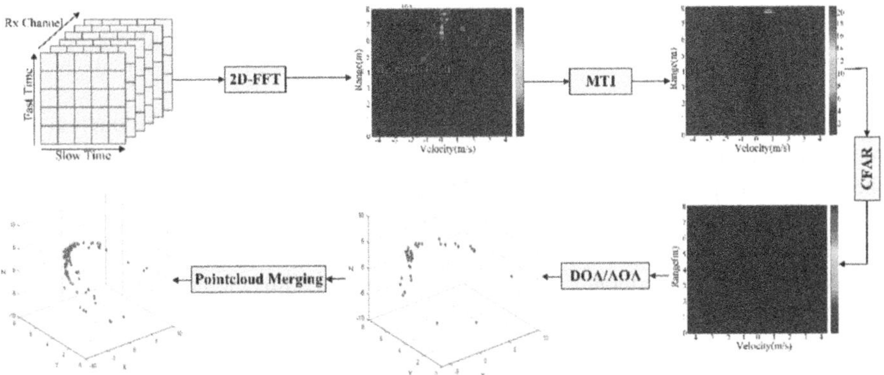

Fig. 1. Point cloud generation

Incoherent Doppler Detection. In the traffic gesture recognition task, in order to extract key dynamic features such as motion speed, action frequency and displacement range, short-time Fourier transform (STFT) is usually employed to conduct time-frequency feature analysis on radar signals, and the Doppler information in the radar echoes is integrated to construct a multi-dimensional feature space [17]. Firstly, one-dimensional Fourier transform (1D-FFT) is performed on each chirp signal in the fast time direction to obtain the spectral distribution of the target in the distance dimension, which is specifically expressed as follows:

$$X_{\text{range}}(k) = \sum_{n=0}^{N_{\text{fast}}-1} x(n) \cdot e^{-\frac{j2\pi kn}{N_{\text{fast}}}}, 0 \leq k < N_{\text{fast}} \tag{1}$$

in the process, $X_{\text{range}}(k)$ represents the frequency component of the k distance unit, $x(n)$ is the time-domain sampling value of the Chirp signal, N_{fast} is the number of sampling points in the fast time dimension, k represents the specific unit index, corresponding to different distances. Subsequently, an FFT is performed in the slow time direction to extract the distribution position of the target on the velocity unit, which is specifically expressed as:

$$X_{\text{velocity}}(m) = \sum_{k=0}^{M_{\text{slow}}-1} X_{\text{range}}(k) \cdot e^{-\frac{j2\pi mk}{M_{\text{slow}}}}, 0 \leq m < M_{\text{slow}} \quad (2)$$

in the process, $X_{\text{velocity}}(m)$ represents the frequency component of the m velocity unit after the FFT in the slow time dimension, M_{slow} represents the number of Chirp in the slow time dimension, m represents the velocity index, corresponding to different velocities. Through the above processing, the joint spectral information of the target in the distance and velocity dimensions can be obtained. To further enhance the detectability of weak targets, the system introduces the non-coherent accumulation strategy. During this process, by averaging the power spectra of multiple frames of signals, the signal-to-noise ratio is effectively improved, which is expressed as:

$$P_{\text{accum}}(k, m) = \frac{1}{L} \sum_{l=1}^{L} \left| X_{\text{velocity}}^{(l)}(k, m) \right|^2 \quad (3)$$

among them, $P_{\text{accum}}(k, m)$ represents the power spectrum value after non-coherent accumulation, L indicates the number of accumulated frames, and $X_{\text{velocity}}^{(l)}(k, m)$ represents the complex amplitude at (k, m) in the 2D-FFT result of the L frame.

Non-coherent accumulation does not require phase correction for different frames, so it has stronger robustness compared to the coherent accumulation method. In the presence of Doppler frequency shift and phase instability, this method shows significant advantages in the detection accuracy of low signal-to-noise ratio targets in complex backgrounds.

Static Noise Suppression Based on MTI. Among them, in order to further enhance the detection capability of moving targets, this paper introduces the Moving Target Indication (MTI) method [18] after constructing the distance-velocity spectrum. This method effectively suppresses the clutter interference caused by static background objects by performing differential processing on the echo data of consecutive frames in the slow time dimension, thereby enhancing the response ability to dynamic traffic gesture signals. Specifically, it is expressed as:

$$X^{(l)}(k, m) = X_{\text{velocity}}^{(l)}(k, m) - X_{\text{velocity}}^{(l-1)}(k, m) \quad (4)$$

this differential operation is equivalent to introducing a high-pass filter in the frequency domain, whose transfer function is:

$$H(f) = 1 - e^{-j2\pi fT} \quad (5)$$

where, T represents the inter-frame sampling period. This high-pass filter can effectively suppress low-frequency static noise components while retaining the Doppler frequency shift information of moving targets. The enhanced Doppler echo $X^{(l)}(k, m)$ after MTI filtering is input to the two-dimensional constant false alarm rate (CFAR) detection module to extract candidate target points.

Target Detection Based on CFAR. Building upon the framework of the original 1D-CFAR, the 2D-CFAR introduces a two-dimensional background window to enhance the spatial robustness of target detection [19]. In contrast to the 1D-CFAR method, which constructs detection thresholds solely in the range or velocity dimension, the 2D-CFAR performs detections in the joint range-velocity spectrum, effectively improving the detection accuracy. The specific representation is as follows:

$$\begin{cases} \mathcal{H}_1 : X(i,j) \geq \alpha \cdot \mu_{bg} \\ \mathcal{H}_0 : X(i,j) < \alpha \cdot \mu_{bg} \end{cases} \tag{6}$$

where, $X(i, j)$ represents the target echo energy of the detection unit at the i row and j column in the two-dimensional spectrum matrix, μ_{bg} represents the statistical mean of the background noise of the reference unit, and α is the adaptive threshold factor, which is specifically expressed as:

$$\alpha = \left(P_{fa}^{-\frac{1}{N_{Win}-1}} - 1 \right)^{-1} \tag{7}$$

where, P_{fa} represents the preset constant false alarm probability, and N_{Win} indicates the total number of reference units, which is determined by the window geometry. The specific detection window is expressed as:

$$N_{Win} = (2L_{ref} + 1)^2 - \left(2L_{guard} + 1\right)^2 \tag{8}$$

where, L_{ref} denotes the reference unit layer count, which specifies the number of concentric rectangular layers centered around the protection unit, while L_{guard} represents the guard unit layer count, which serves to isolate the detection unit from the reference unit, thereby preventing the leakage of target energy into the reference region.

DOA and AOA Estimates. To enhance the accuracy of direction estimation, this paper introduces the Multiple Signal Classification (MUSIC) algorithm to achieve joint high-resolution estimation of AOA (Angle of Arrival) and DOA (Direction of Arrival) without presetting the number of targets [20]. Specifically, after completing the range detection, the snapshot data of the distance unit where the target is located is input into the MUSIC algorithm to precisely estimate the incident directions in azimuth and elevation angles, based on the following standard signal model:

$$X(t) = AS(t) + N(t) \tag{9}$$

where, $X(t)$ represents the snapshot data matrix, $A = [a_1, a_2, \ldots, a_N]$ is the steering matrix, and $S(t)$ and $N(t)$ correspond to the signal vector and noise vector respectively. The relationship between the output power spectrum of the MUSIC algorithm and the signal power in each direction is specifically expressed as:

$$P_{MUSIC}(\theta, \phi) = \frac{1}{a^H(\theta, \phi)R^{-1}a(\theta, \phi)} \tag{10}$$

where, $R = E\{X(t)X^H(t)\}$ is the covariance matrix, and $a(\theta, \phi)$ represents the two-dimensional steering vector, which is specifically expressed as:

$$a(\theta, \phi) = \left[1, \cdots, a_{ij}(\theta, \phi)\right]^T \tag{11}$$

among them, the elements $a_{ij}(\theta, \phi)$ of the guiding vector are expressed as:

$$a_{ij}(\theta, \phi) = e^{-\frac{j2\pi}{\lambda}(x_i \cos\theta \cos\phi + z_i \sin\phi)} \tag{12}$$

where, x_i and z_i are the indices of the array elements in the horizontal and vertical directions, respectively. By conducting a two-dimensional search on the spatial spectrum function $P_{\text{MUSIC}}(\theta, \phi)$, high-resolution estimation of the AOA/DOA of any incident signal can be achieved. Subsequently, by combining the distance information, the estimated polar coordinate parameters are converted into three-dimensional Cartesian coordinates to generate spatial point cloud data. Ultimately, each point can be represented as a three-dimensional vector:

$$p_i = (x_i, y_i, z_i) \tag{13}$$

3.2 NETWORKCONSTRUCTION

In the point cloud recognition network constructed in this study, the local structure modeling and global semantic enhancement mechanisms are fully integrated to enhance the feature representation ability of the sparse point cloud from millimeter-wave radar (see Fig. 2). The network first introduces the GeoConv module, and through the dense connection of multiple GeoConv modules, the explicit modeling of local geometric relationships is achieved. On this basis, the AUGUnit is further designed. Through the self-attention mechanism, it models the global context information, effectively alleviating the distribution mismatch problem in the feature reconstruction process, and improving the discriminability and consistency of the final point cloud representation. The overall network architecture realizes deep semantic modeling from local to global while maintaining the integrity of the point cloud geometry.

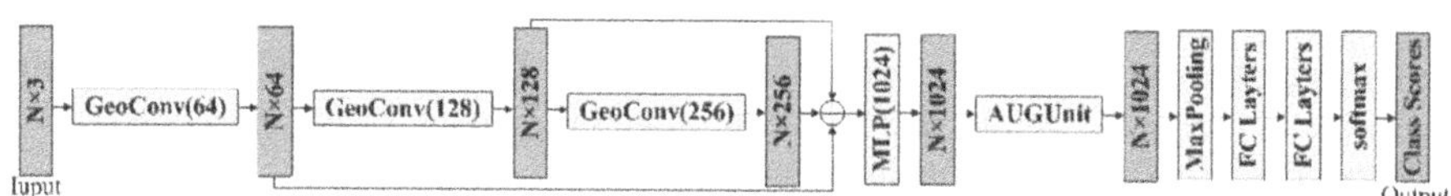

Fig. 2. Overall network structure diagram

Geo Convolution. This study proposes a point cloud feature extraction module named GeoConv based on geometric relationship modeling, aiming to effectively explore the correlation between local geometric structures and edge features in point cloud data (see Fig. 3). Traditional point cloud feature extraction methods often neglect the geometric relative relationships among points when constructing local context modeling, making it difficult to capture spatial structure details. However, this module can effectively enhance the model's perception of local geometric shapes, topological relationships, and semantic regions by constructing a local adjacency graph and explicitly modeling edge features, especially suitable for 3D point cloud scenes with complex boundaries or local deformations. Specifically, the input of the GeoConv module is point cloud data of size N × 3, which is specifically represented as:

$$P = \{p_i\}_{i=1}^{N}, p_i \in R^3 \tag{14}$$

where, N represents the number of points, and p_i denotes the three-dimensional coordinate vector of the i point. First, for each point p_i, the KNN method is used to find its k nearest neighbor points in the Euclidean space, which is specifically expressed as:

$$N_{(i)} = argmin^{(k)}\{ \|p_j - p_i\|_2 | j = 1, \cdots, Nj \neq \text{i}\} \tag{15}$$

where, $N_{(i)}$ represents the neighbor index set of point p_i, and $\|\bullet\|_2$ denotes the Euclidean norm. Subsequently, to capture the relative geometric relationship between a point and its neighborhood, a feature embedding is constructed for each point i with its neighboring points $j \in N_{(i)}$, which is specifically expressed as:

$$g_{ij} = \varnothing(p_j - p_i) \tag{16}$$

where, Ø(•) denotes the shared multilayer perceptron (MLP) employed for non-linear dimensionality elevation of the three-dimensional relative position $p_j - p_i \in R^3$. Subsequently, the maximum pooling operation is utilized to aggregate all embedded features within the neighborhood, thereby obtaining the local contextual features of point i, which can be formally expressed as:

$$h_i = \max(g_{ij}) \tag{17}$$

where, $h_i \in R^C$ denotes the feature representation of point i, while $g_{ij} \in R^C$ represents the feature embedding between point i and its neighboring point j.

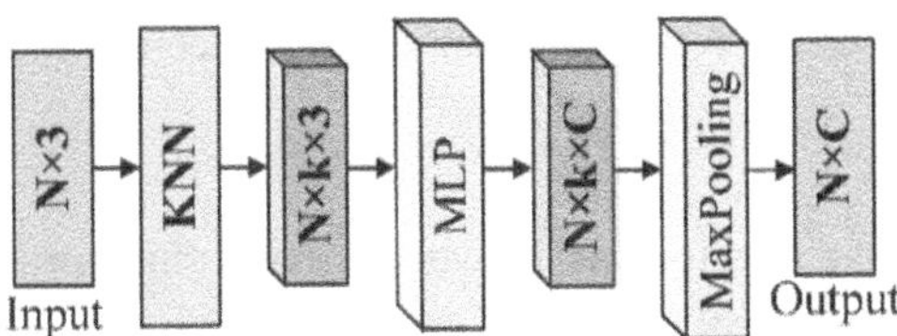

Fig. 3. GeoConv

Attention Upsampling with Guidance Unit. To enhance the feature representation ability and geometric structure modeling effect during the point cloud upsampling process, we designed the AUGUnit (see Fig. 4 Fig. 3). This module integrates perturbation encoding and self-attention mechanism, which can expand the number of points while dynamically learning the global dependency relationship among points. It also enhances the semantic expression of features while preserving local geometric details, thereby achieving more robust feature interpolation and refinement. The module takes the original point cloud feature of $N \times C$ as input. Firstly, the number of points is expanded to $rN \times C$ through replication operation, and the perturbation encoding $e \in R^{rN \times 1}$ is concatenated to form the enhanced feature:

$$F_{aug} \in R^{rN \times (C+1)} \tag{18}$$

then, it is normalized, which is specifically expressed as:

$$F' = LayerNorm(F_{aug}) \tag{19}$$

to capture the context dependency, a standard self-attention module is constructed. The normalized features F' are projected respectively into queries (Q), keys (K), and values (V), and then normalized. Specifically, it is expressed as:

$$\begin{cases} Q = F'W_Q \\ K = F'W_k \\ v = F'W_v \end{cases} \tag{20}$$

where, W_Q, W_k, and W_v are learnable projection matrices. Then, the scaled dot-product attention matrix is calculated, which is specifically expressed as:

$$A = softmax\left(\frac{QK^T}{\sqrt{d}}\right) \tag{21}$$

where, $A \in R^{rN \times rN}$ is the attention weight matrix. The global context feature is obtained by weighted aggregation of the value vector based on the attention matrix, which is specifically expressed as:

$$F_{att} = AV \tag{22}$$

then, residual connections and normalization operations are introduced to stabilize training and enhance feature representation, which is specifically expressed as:

$$F_1 = LayerNorm(F' + F_{att}) \tag{23}$$

then, F_1 is input into the feed forward network to extract high-order nonlinear features, which is specifically expressed as:

$$F_2 = LayerNorm(F' + FFN(F_1)) \tag{24}$$

finally, the dimension is compressed back to $rN \times C$ through a linear mapping MLP, which is specifically represented as:

$$F_{out} = MLP(F_2) \tag{25}$$

In summary, the AUG-Unit effectively mitigates issues of feature redundancy and geometric distortion in point cloud upsampling through its dual mechanism of explicit perturbation guidance and attention fusion, thereby providing more discriminative feature support for subsequent point cloud reconstruction or recognition tasks.

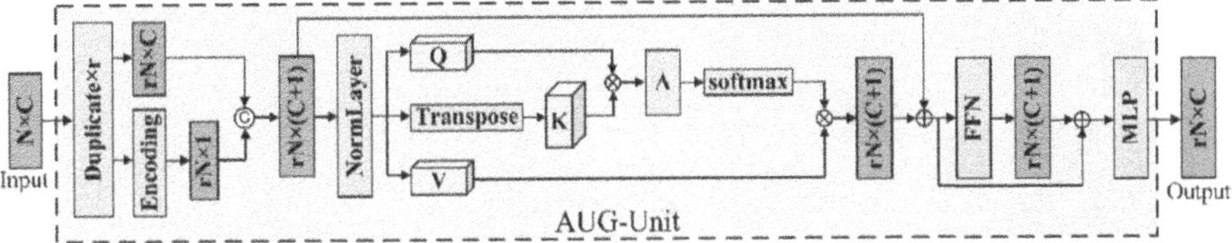

Fig. 4. AUG-Unit

4 Experiment

4.1 Data Collection

This study established an experimental platform for traffic gesture perception based on the IWR6843ISK millimeter-wave radar module and the DCA1000EVM data acquisition card (see Fig. 5 Fig. 3). It systematically analyzed the spatio-temporal characteristics of dynamic traffic gestures and the point cloud modeling methods. The specific radar parameter settings are shown in the Table 1. Fig. 5 (a) presents the complete radar perception system set up in an outdoor scene. The IWR6843ISK serves as the core sensor, operating in the 60–64 GHz frequency band, equipped with a 3-transmit 4-receive antenna array, featuring a 120° horizontal field of view and a 30° vertical field of view, and supporting millimeter-level resolution and low-power real-time perception capabilities. The accompanying DCA1000EVM data acquisition module supports a data transmission rate of up to 1 Gbps, meeting the real-time processing requirements of high-density point cloud streams. Fig. 5 (b) and Fig. 5 (c) respectively show the moving interference targets and gesture performers in the experimental scene, simulating the background dynamic targets existing in real traffic environments and enhancing the robustness of recognition. Fig. 5 (d) presents the data acquisition and visualization processing platform, which captures and replays the millimeter-wave raw data through TI mmWave Studio. The right side of the Fig. 5 (e)-(l) shows the three-dimensional point cloud visualization results of eight typical traffic gestures after data preprocessing, corresponding to: lane change, go straight, left turn wait, left turn, pull over, stop, slow down, and right turn.

During the data collection process, some samples introduced background interference targets moving at a constant speed of 0.8 m/s, with an appearance probability of approximately 20%, to enhance scene complexity and the generalization ability of the data. Ultimately, we constructed a point cloud gesture dataset containing 9,600 samples, covering the above eight types of traffic command actions. Additionally, to clarify the radar parameter configuration, this paper's appendix provides a detailed parameter setting table for the IWR6843ISK, including frame rate, bandwidth, chirp count, sampling frequency, and transmission power, among other key items, providing a reference for subsequent reproduction and expansion research.

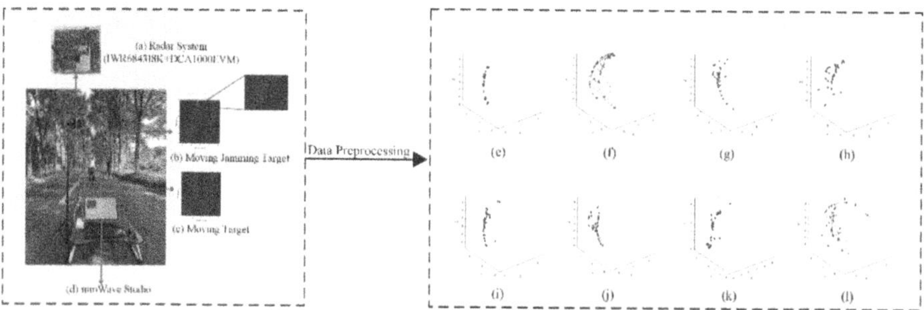

Fig. 5. The left picture shows the gesture sensing experimental platform and the experimental environment, while the right one presents the point cloud data of different gestures after data preprocessing, including (e) lane changing, (f) going straight, (g) waiting to turn left, (h) turning left, (i) pulling over, (j) stopping, (k) decelerating, and (l) turning right.

Table 1. Millimeter-wave radar parameter settings

Parameter	Value
Number of transmit antennas	3
Number of receive antennas	4
Number of frames	256
Frame time	100 ms
Total bandwidth	1798.92 MHz
Number of Chirps	96
Number of ADC samples	96
Sampling Frequency	10 MHz

4.2 Network Traning Strategies and Optimization Methods

To effectively train and optimize the proposed GAU-Net model, this paper first introduces a certain degree of interference into the original point cloud data to better fit the actual application scenarios, thereby enhancing the model's robustness and generalization ability. Subsequently, the dataset is divided into training, validation, and test sets in a 5:3:2 ratio: the training set is used for learning and optimizing the model parameters, the validation set is used to evaluate the model's generalization performance and adjust the hyperparameters to improve its adaptability to different data distributions, and the test set is used for final performance evaluation to verify the model's reliability and practicality in real-world environments, thereby enhancing the credibility of the research results and their engineering application value.

To prevent GAU-Net from getting stuck in local optima during training, this paper set four initial learning rates of 0.001, 0.003, 0.009, and 0.03 for training and testing. The experimental results show that when the initial learning rate is 0.003, the loss and accuracy curves are the most stable and the convergence speed is the fastest (see Fig. 6 Fig. 7 Fig. 3). Therefore, all subsequent experiments adopt this learning rate.

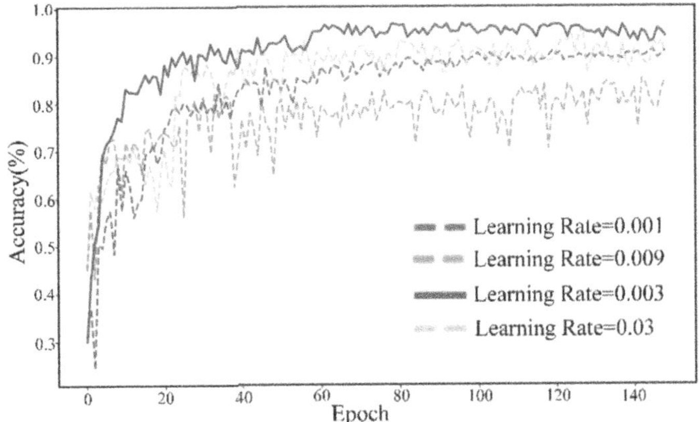

Fig. 6. Verify accuracy curve.

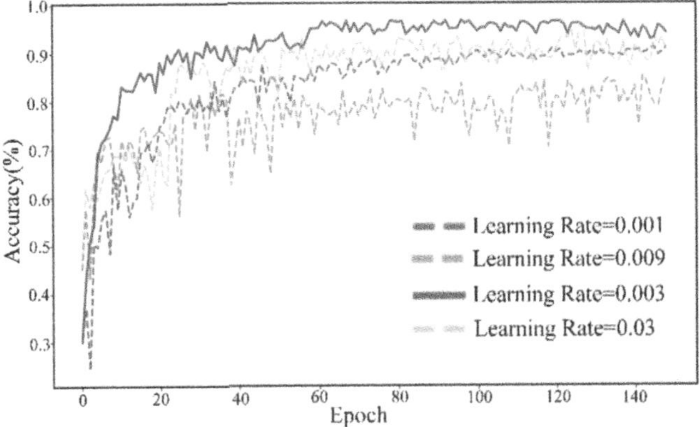

Fig. 7. Training loss curve.

4.3 Accuracy Comparison

The confusion matrix is a key tool for evaluating the performance of classification models. It quantitatively reflects the correspondence between the true categories and the predicted results in a matrix form, intuitively presenting the distribution of correctly classified and misclassified samples, providing an important basis for subsequent model optimization and performance analysis. The experimental results show the confusion matrices of four different network models in the point cloud eight-classification task, facilitating the comparison of their classification performance.

From Fig. 8 (a), it can be seen that the overall classification accuracy of PointCNN is 74%, and there are obvious confusion phenomena in multiple categories. For example, there are high misclassification rates between category 0 and category 7, and between category 3 and category 5, indicating that this model still has certain limitations in local structure modeling. In contrast, the overall accuracy of the PointNet model shown in Fig. 8 (b) has increased to 84%, showing a more concentrated diagonal distribution in most categories, but there are still confusions in fine-grained category distinctions. Further, the PointNet++ model in Fig. 8 (c) achieves an overall accuracy of 86%, with enhanced discrimination ability between category boundaries, and a clearer diagonal in the confusion matrix, demonstrating its advantages in hierarchical feature extraction and local structure perception. The GAU-Net model shown in Fig. 8 (d) performs the best, with an accuracy of 92%, showing extremely low misclassification rates in all categories, especially maintaining high recognition accuracy between easily confused categories (such as category 5 and 6), reflecting its strong capabilities in feature enhancement and context modeling.

As shown in the Fig. 8 (a), PointCNN achieves an overall accuracy of 74%, with category-specific accuracy distributed discretely. High-frequency confusion exists between lane-change gestures and deceleration gestures, right-turn gestures, and several transitional actions. As shown in the Fig. 8 (b), PointNet improves the overall accuracy to 84% with enhanced overall convergence. However, significant misclassifications between lane change gestures and left turn waiting gestures, as well as left turn gestures, remain unresolved. As shown in the Fig. 8 (c), PointNet++ further mitigates some confusions through multi-scale local feature aggregation, raising the overall accuracy to 86%. However, minor mutual misclassifications between lane change gestures and pull-over/stop gestures or deceleration gestures remain. Simultaneously, the recognition rates for stop gestures and right-turn gestures show notable improvement. As shown in the Fig. 8 (d), DGCNN achieves an overall accuracy of 88%. By leveraging an iterative update mechanism based on dynamic image neighborhoods to enhance local topology and semantic relationship modeling, it further reduces residual cross-action confusion. This significantly decreases misclassifications between lane change and deceleration gestures, as well as between left turn waiting and left turn gestures, while also lowering occasional confusion between pull-over and stop gestures. As shown in the Fig. 8 (e), KPConv maintains stable recognition rates across all gesture categories within the range of approximately 0.88–0.92, with overall cross-category confusion not exceeding 0.03, demonstrating high category discrimination and recognition stability. As shown in the Fig. 8 (f), the proposed GAU-Net elevates overall accuracy to 92%. Its global-local coordination, feature enhancement, and context interaction mechanisms effectively suppress common misclassifications, further concentrating recognition rates for primary action categories within the 0.88–0.95 range.

Based on the above results, it can be seen that as the model structure progresses from basic to enhanced, point cloud deep learning methods demonstrate significant performance improvements in complex spatial structure modeling and fine-grained category discrimination. Particularly, the outstanding performance of GAU-Net further confirms the effectiveness and necessity of introducing enhanced units in improving the accuracy of point cloud classification.

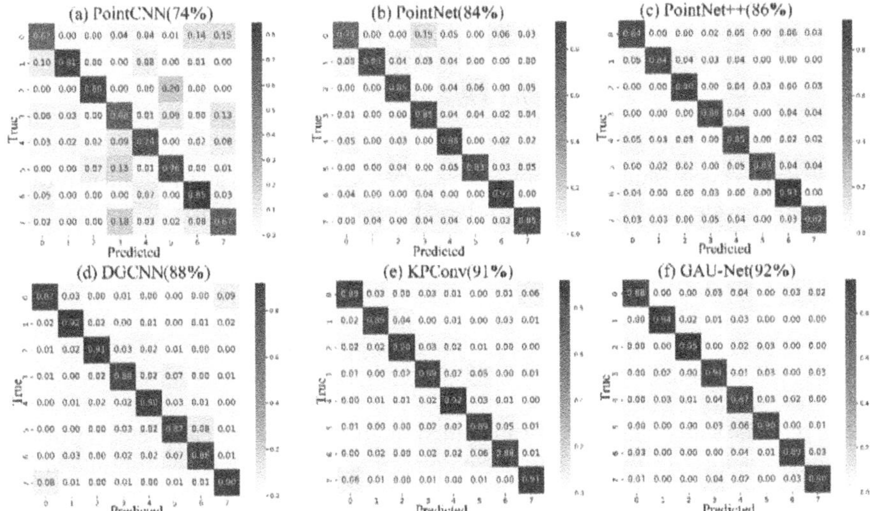

Fig. 8. Confusion matrix diagrams for different networks, where (a)-(e) are confusion matrix diagrams for other networks, and (f) is confusion matrix diagrams for the network proposed in this paper. class indices 0–7 correspond respectively to: 0 lane changing, 1 going straight, 2 waiting to turn left, 3 turning left, 4 pulling over, 5 stopping, 6 decelerating, 7 turning right.

4.4 Comparison of Different Performance Indicators

Based on the above research, the classification performance of different models is evaluated by comparing the accuracy, precision, recall, F1 value, Kappa coefficient and other classification performance indicators of the data confusion matrix [21]. Accuracy is the proportion of correct classifications, which is specifically expressed as:

$$Accuracy = \frac{TP + TN}{TP + FN + FP + TN} \tag{26}$$

where, true positive (TP) is the number of samples that belong to the category and are correctly predicted; false positive (FP) is the number of non-category samples that are wrongly predicted as belonging to the category; false negative (FN) is the number of samples that belong to the category but are predicted as belonging to other categories; true negative (TN) is the number of samples that are correctly predicted as belonging to other categories.

Precision measures the proportion of samples predicted as positive examples by the model that are truly positive examples. Specifically, it is expressed as:

$$Precision = \frac{TP}{TP + FP} \tag{27}$$

Recall measures the proportion of true positive cases predicted by the model, it is expressed as:

$$Recall = \frac{TP}{TP + FN} \tag{28}$$

The F1 value is the harmonic mean of precision and recall, used to comprehensively evaluate the classification performance of a model, it is expressed as:

$$F1 = \frac{2 * Precision * Recall}{Precision + Recall} = \frac{2 * TP}{2 * TP + FN + FP} \tag{29}$$

The Kappa coefficient is used for consistency testing and can also be used to measure classification accuracy. Its calculation is based on the confusion matrix, which represents the error reduction ratio between classification and completely random classification. The mean, used to comprehensively measure the classification performance of the model, it is expressed as:

$$Kappa = \frac{P_0 - P_e}{1 - P_e} \tag{30}$$

where, p_0 is the sum of the correctly classified sample numbers of each category divided by samples, that is, the overall classification accuracy. The calculation formula of p_e is as follows:

$$P_e = \frac{a1 * *b1 + a2 * b2 + \cdots + ac * bc}{n * n} \tag{31}$$

As shown in the figure(see Fig. 9), the performance of six typical point cloud classification models was compared and analyzed from four dimensions: Average Precision, Average Recall, Average F1, and Kappa coefficient. The results indicated that GAU-Net achieved the best performance in all evaluation metrics, specifically with an average precision of 0.9167, an average recall of 0.9158, an average F1 score of 0.9098, and a Kappa coefficient of 0.9089, outperforms the other five models. Particularly in terms of the Kappa coefficient, GAU-Net demonstrated stronger consistency and robustness, verifying its superior discriminative ability and generalization performance in complex point cloud classification tasks.

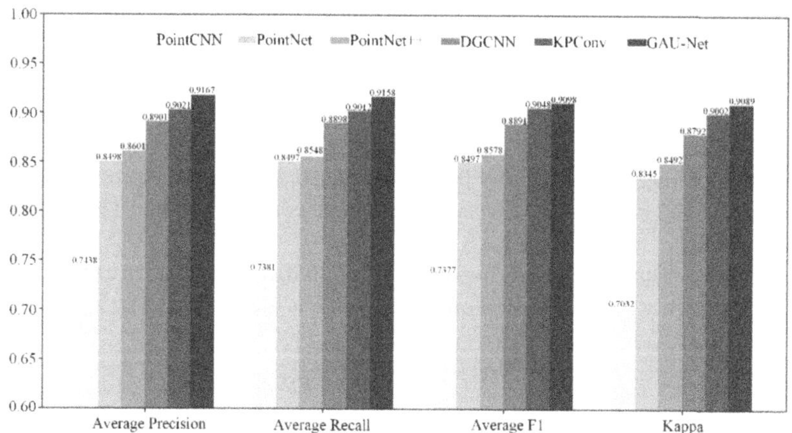

Fig. 9. Results chart of different classification indicators.

4.5 Comparison of Computing Resources and Inference Efficiency

In this section, a comparative analysis of the GAU-Net model and other mainstream point cloud classification models in terms of computational resource requirements is conducted. The comparison results are presented in Table 1. The table lists the total number of trainable parameters (Total Params), parameter memory size (Params Size), total model size (Total Size), and inference time (Inference Time) for each model, providing a comprehensive assessment of their performance in terms of resource consumption and inference efficiency.

From the Table 2, there are significant differences among the models in terms of parameter scale and inference efficiency. PointCNN has 2.10×10^6 parameters, with a parameter memory usage of 21 MB, a total model size of 27.2 MB, and an inference time of 19.7 ms. PointNet has the largest number of parameters, reaching 4.00×10^7; its parameter and total model sizes are 25.3 MB and 33.3 MB respectively, with an inference time of 25.3 ms. PointNet++ contains 1.20×10^7 parameters, occupying 12 MB of parameter memory and 18 MB total model size, but its inference time is as high as 163.2 ms, showing a clear disadvantage in real-time performance for complex point cloud processing. DGCNN also has 1.20×10^7 parameters, but through architectural design its parameter and total model sizes are only 6 MB and 7 MB, with an inference time of 22 ms, achieving good inference efficiency while maintaining moderate representational capacity. KPConv has 1.50×10^7 parameters, with parameter and total model sizes of 18 MB and 25 MB, and an inference time of 75 ms; its more refined kernel representation introduces higher computational overhead. In contrast, GAU-Net contains only 1.27×10^6 parameters, with both parameter and total model sizes of 4.9 MB, and an inference time of just 9.78 ms. It achieves the fastest inference speed under very low resource usage, demonstrating outstanding efficiency and deployment friendliness, making it especially suitable for point cloud classification scenarios that are sensitive to real-time performance and computational resources.

Table 2. Comparison of Model Memory Consumption and Parameter Size.

Model	Total Params	Params Size(MB)	Total Size(MB)	Inference Time(ms)
PointCNN	2.10e6	21	27.2	19.7
PointNet	4.00e7	25.3	33.3	25.3
PointNet++	1.20e7	12	18	163.2
DGCNN	1.20e7	6	7	22
KPConv	1.50e7	18	25	75
GAU-Net	1.27e6	4.9	4.9	9.78

4.6 Ablation Experiments

In GAU-Net, we conducted ablation experiments around the two key modules, GeoConv and AUG-Unit, to verify the impact of each module on the model's performance. The experimental parameters were set consistently with the previous experiments. The specific ablation models included: (a) the basic model without GeoConv and AUG-Unit; (b) the model with only the GeoConv module; (c) the model with only the AUG-Unit module; (d) the complete model with both GeoConv and AUG-Unit. The classification accuracy of each model is shown in the Table 3. The results indicate that both GeoConv and AUG-Unit modules can significantly improve the model's performance, and the combination of the two performs the best. Specifically, GeoConv can effectively model the local geometric structure of point clouds, while AUG-Unit enhances the feature expression ability through perturbation encoding and attention mechanism. Both play important roles in the point cloud classification task.

Table 3. Model component ablation study.

Model	GeoConv	AUG-Unit	Accuracy
a	No	No	73.012%
b	Yes	No	81.617%
c	No	Yes	86.361%
d	Yes	Yes	91.882%

5 Conclusion and Future Work

In GAU-Net, we conducted ablation experiments around the two key modules, GeoConv and AUG-Unit, to verify the impact of each module on the model's performance. The experimental parameters were set consistently with the previous experiments. Specifically, in this paper, we address the challenges of sparsity, structural deficiency, and noise interference in millimeter-wave radar point clouds for traffic gesture recognition by proposing a point cloud recognition framework that integrates local geometric modeling and global feature enhancement. This method enhances local structure modeling by introducing the GeoConv module, and uses the AUG-Unit module to introduce perturbation coding and self-attention mechanism during upsampling to enhance feature representation. At the same time, it combines the Global Refinement Unit to achieve multi-scale global semantic fusion and context consistency optimization. Experimental results show that our method achieves significant performance improvements in multiple millimeter-wave point cloud gesture recognition tasks, demonstrating stronger expressive power, discriminative ability, and robustness, outperforming existing mainstream point cloud recognition models and showing promising application prospects.

In the future, we will further explore multi-modal fusion to enhance cross-environment perception capabilities, introduce few-shot learning and self-supervised mechanisms to alleviate label dependency, and achieve efficient deployment on edge computing devices through model compression and lightweight design. Additionally, for the temporal characteristics in dynamic gestures, we can combine time modeling techniques in the future to enhance the model's understanding of complex motion patterns, providing technical support for reliable gesture interaction in intelligent transportation.

References

1. Zhou, S., Zhang, W., Peng, D., Liu, Y., Liao, X., Jiang, H.: Adversarial WiFi sensing for privacy preservation of human behaviors. IEEE Commun. Lett. **24**, 259–263 (2020). https://doi.org/10.1109/LCOMM.2019.2952844
2. Liang X., Bu X., Qin F., Dang X.: A Robust Perception Algorithm Based on a Radar and LiDAR for Intelligent Driving (2021)
3. Savoie, P., Cameron, J.A.D., Kaye, M.E., Scheme, E.J.: Automation of the timed-up-and-go test using a conventional video camera. IEEE J. Biomed. Health Inform. **24**, 1196–1205 (2020). https://doi.org/10.1109/JBHI.2019.2934342
4. Hazra, S., Santra, A.: Robust gesture recognition using Millimetric-wave radar system. IEEE Sens. Lett. **2**, 1–4 (2018). https://doi.org/10.1109/LSENS.2018.2882642
5. Cui, W., et al.: BackSwipe: Back-of-device word-gesture interaction on smartphones. In: Proceedings of the 2021 CHI Conference on Human Factors in Computing Systems, pp. 1–12. ACM, Yokohama Japan (2021). https://doi.org/10.1145/3411764.3445081
6. Dang, X., Ke, W., Hao, Z., Jin, P., Deng, H., Sheng, Y.: Mm-TPG: traffic policemen gesture recognition based on millimeter wave radar point cloud. Sensors. **23**, 6816 (2023). https://doi.org/10.3390/s23156816
7. Wang, Z., Li, G., Yang, L.: Dynamic hand gesture recognition based on micro-Doppler radar signatures using hidden gauss–Markov models. IEEE Geosci. Remote Sens. Lett. **18**, 291–295 (2021). https://doi.org/10.1109/LGRS.2020.2974821
8. Zhu, P., Zhou, H., Cao, S., Yang, P., Xue, S.: Control with gestures: a hand gesture recognition system using off-the-shelf smartwatch. In: 2018 4th International Conference on Big Data Computing and Communications (BIGCOM), pp. 72–77. IEEE, Chicago, IL (2018). https://doi.org/10.1109/BIGCOM.2018.00018
9. Wang, Z., Yu, Z., Lou, X., Guo, B., Chen, L.: Gesture-radar: a dual Doppler radar based system for robust recognition and quantitative profiling of human gestures. IEEE Trans. Hum. Mach. Syst. **51**, 32–43 (2021). https://doi.org/10.1109/THMS.2020.3036637
10. Kim, Y., Toomajian, B.: Application of Doppler radar for the recognition of hand gestures using optimized deep convolutional neural networks. In: 2017 11th European Conference on Antennas and Propagation (EUCAP), pp. 1258–1260. IEEE, Paris, France (2017) https://doi.org/10.23919/EuCAP.2017.7928465
11. Huang, R., Li, Z., Wang, S., Wang, R., Li, J., Xu, Z.: A RD-T network for hand gesture recognition based on millimeter-wave sensor. In: 2020 IEEE 5th International Conference on Signal and Image Processing (ICSIP), pp. 308–312. IEEE, Nanjing, China (2020). https://doi.org/10.1109/ICSIP49896.2020.9339325
12. Xia, Z., Luomei, Y., Zhou, C., Xu, F.: Multidimensional feature representation and learning for robust hand-gesture recognition on commercial millimeter-wave radar. IEEE Trans. Geosci. Remote Sens. **59**, 4749–4764 (2021). https://doi.org/10.1109/TGRS.2020.3010880
13. Zhao, H., Ma, Y., Lu, Y., Liu, K.: DGSCR:double-target gesture separation and classification recognition based on deep learning and millimeter-wave radar. IEEE Sensors J. **23**, 26701–26711 (2023). https://doi.org/10.1109/JSEN.2023.3319339
14. Jin, B., Ma, X., Hu, B., Zhang, Z., Lian, Z., Wang, B.: Gesture-mmWAVE: compact and accurate millimeter-WAVE radar-based dynamic gesture recognition for embedded devices. IEEE Trans. Hum. Mach. Syst. **54**, 337–347 (2024). https://doi.org/10.1109/THMS.2024.3385124
15. Lang, Y., Wang, Q., Yang, Y., Hou, C., He, Y., Xu, J.: Person identification with limited training data using radar micro-Doppler signatures. Micro Opt. Tech. Lett. **62**, 1060–1068 (2020). https://doi.org/10.1002/mop.32125

16. Kim, Y., Alnujaim, I., Oh, D.: Human activity classification based on point clouds measured by millimeter wave MIMO radar with deep recurrent neural networks. IEEE Sensors J. **21**, 13522–13529 (2021). https://doi.org/10.1109/JSEN.2021.3068388
17. Islam, S.M.M., Borić-Lubecke, O., Zheng, Y., Lubecke, V.M.: Radar-based non-contact continuous identity authentication. Remote Sens. **12**, 2279 (2020). https://doi.org/10.3390/rs12142279
18. Chen, Z., Li, G., Fioranelli, F., Griffiths, H.: Personnel recognition and gait classification based on multistatic micro-Doppler signatures using deep convolutional neural networks. IEEE Geosci. Remote Sens. Lett. **15**, 669–673 (2018). https://doi.org/10.1109/LGRS.2018.2806940
19. Wang, J.: CFAR-based interference mitigation for FMCW automotive radar systems. IEEE Trans. Intell. Transport. Syst. **23**, 12229–12238 (2022). https://doi.org/10.1109/TITS.2021.3111514
20. Belfiori, F., van Rossum, W., Hoogeboom, P.: Application of 2D MUSIC algorithm to range-azimuth FMCW radar data
21. Li, Y., Li, Q., Gao, C., Gao, S., Wu, H., Liu, R.: PFENet: towards precise feature extraction from sparse point cloud for 3D object detection. Neural Netw. **185**, 107144 (2025). https://doi.org/10.1016/j.neunet.2025.107144

Author Index

Z. Hou et al. (Eds.): CIRAC 2025, CCIS 2885, pp. 241–242, 2026.
https://doi.org/10.1007/978-981-92-0045-0

Z

The manufacturer's authorised representative in the EU is Springer Nature Customer Service Centre GmbH, Europaplatz 3, 69115 Heidelberg, Germany. If you have any concerns regarding our products, please contact ProductSafety@springernature.com

Printed and bound by CPI Group (UK) Ltd, Croydon, CR0 4YY
21/07/2026
02173377-0001